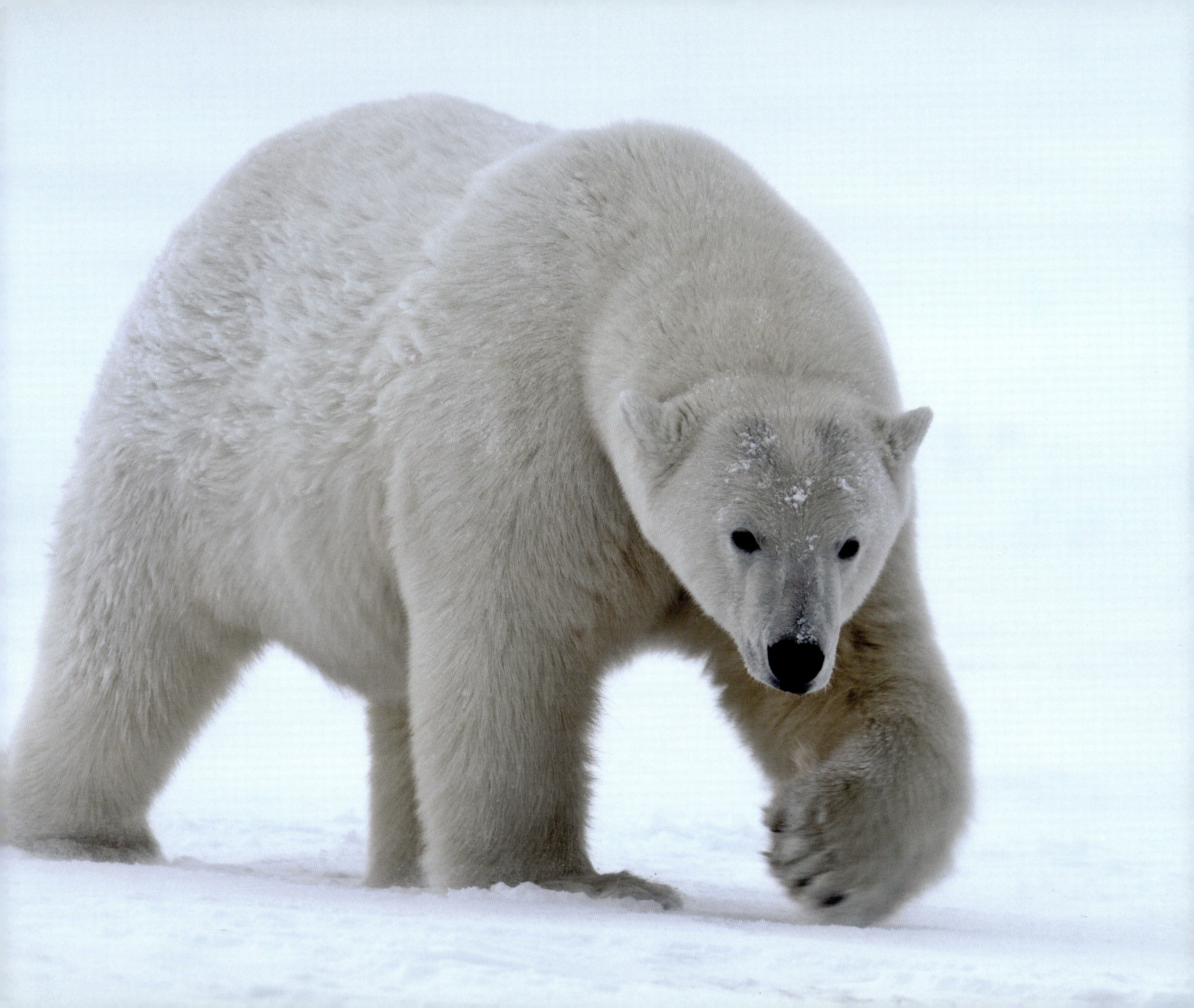

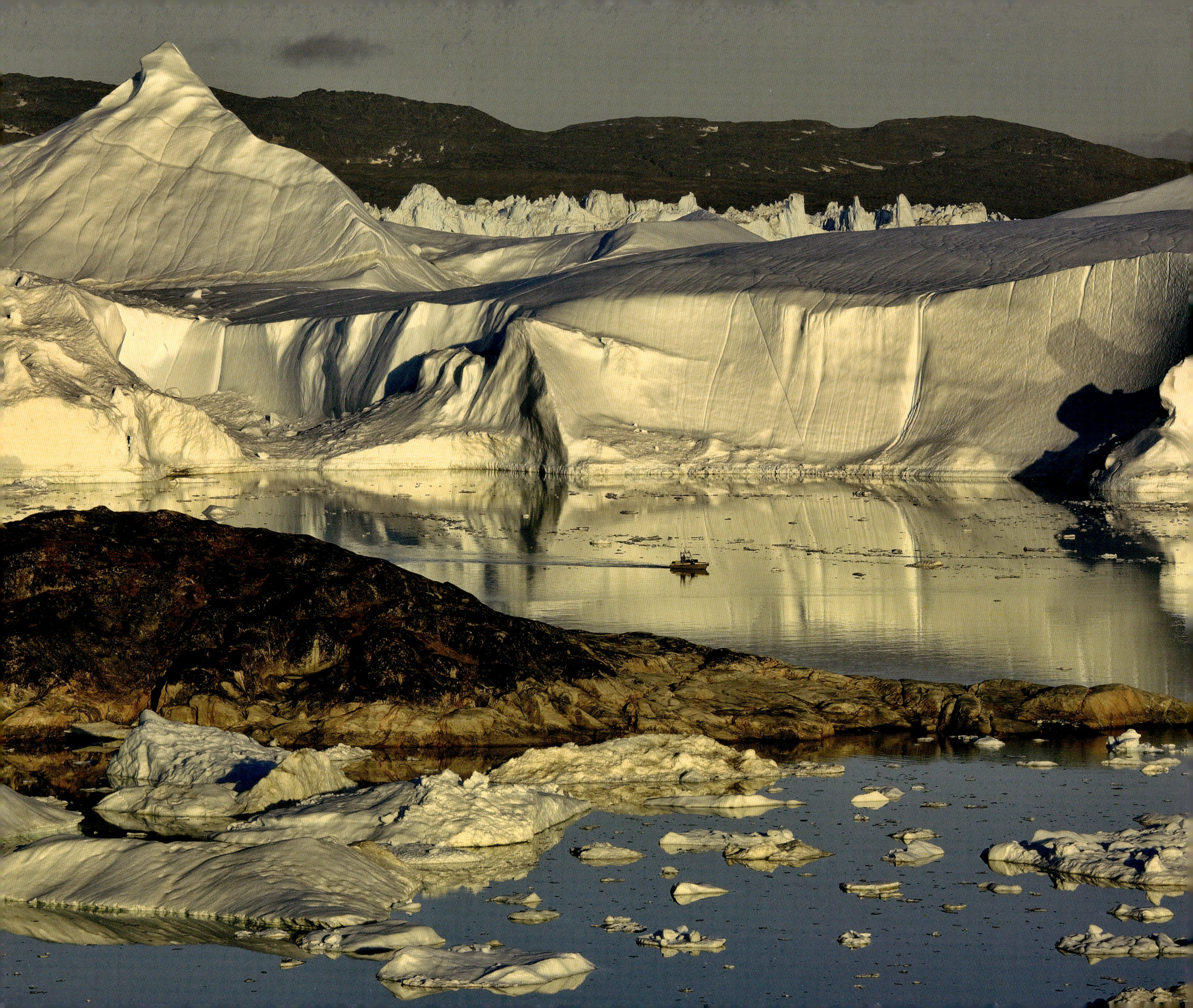

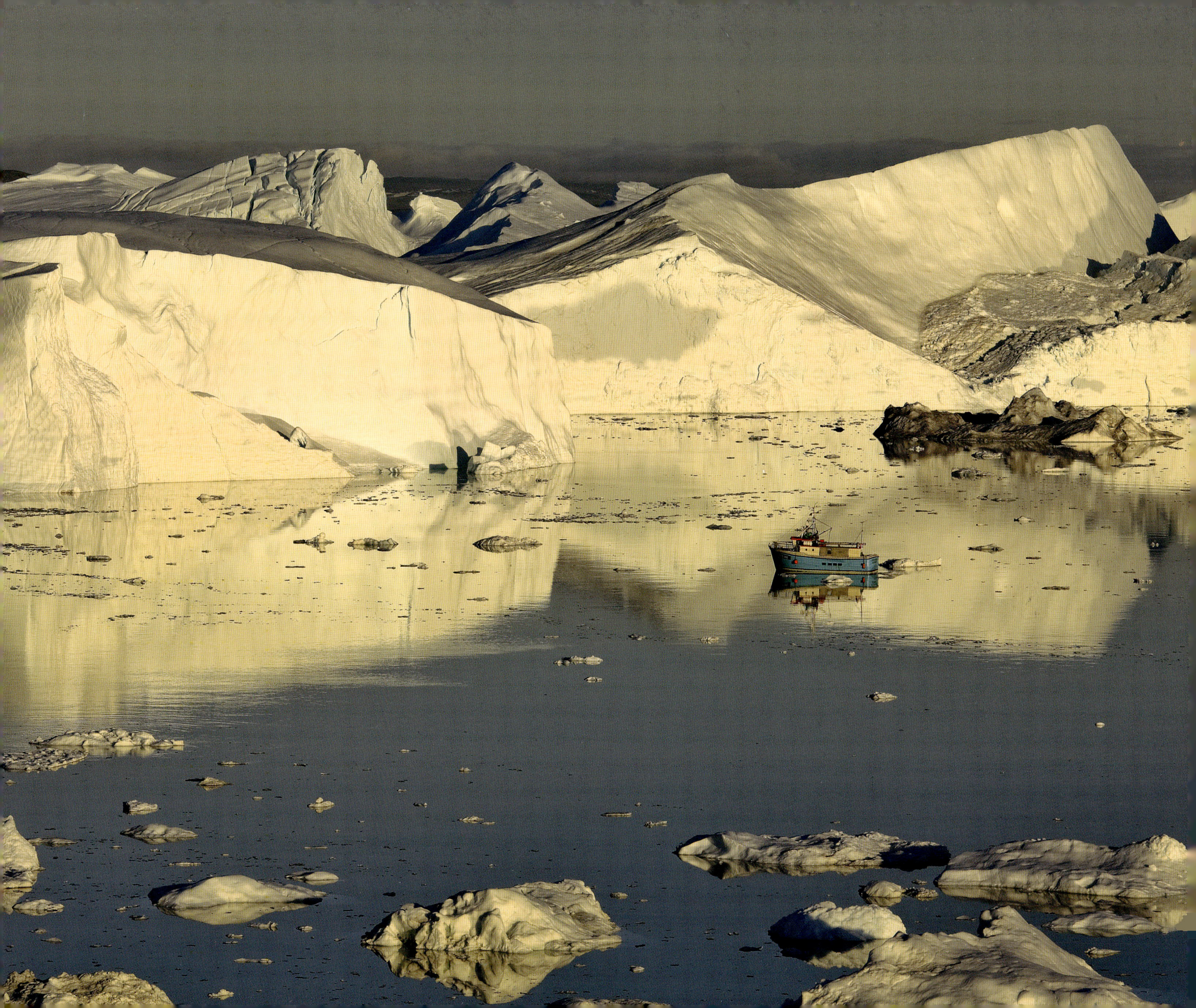

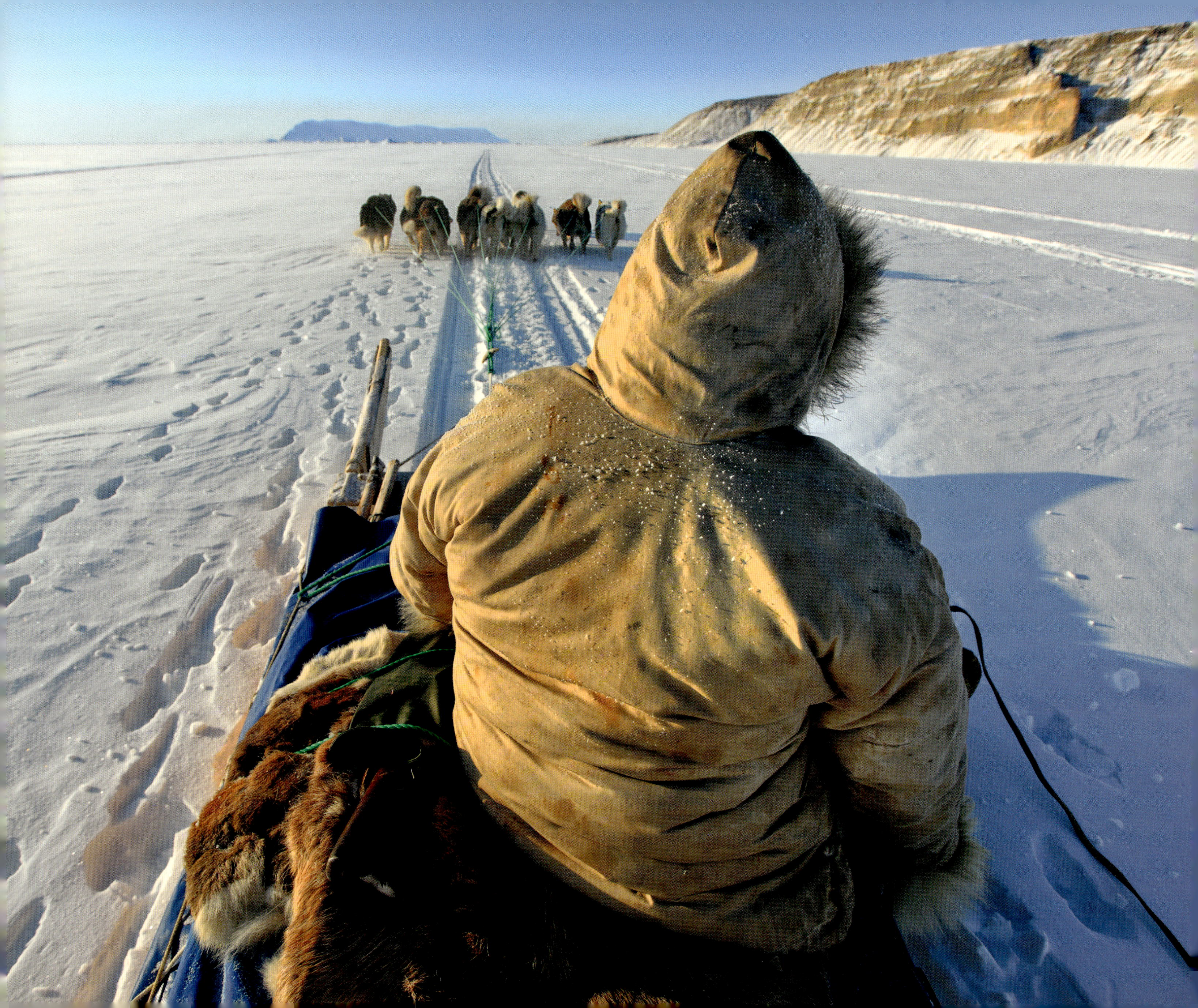

Thomas Henningsen (Text)
Bernd Römmelt (Photography)

The Arctic

Treasure of the North

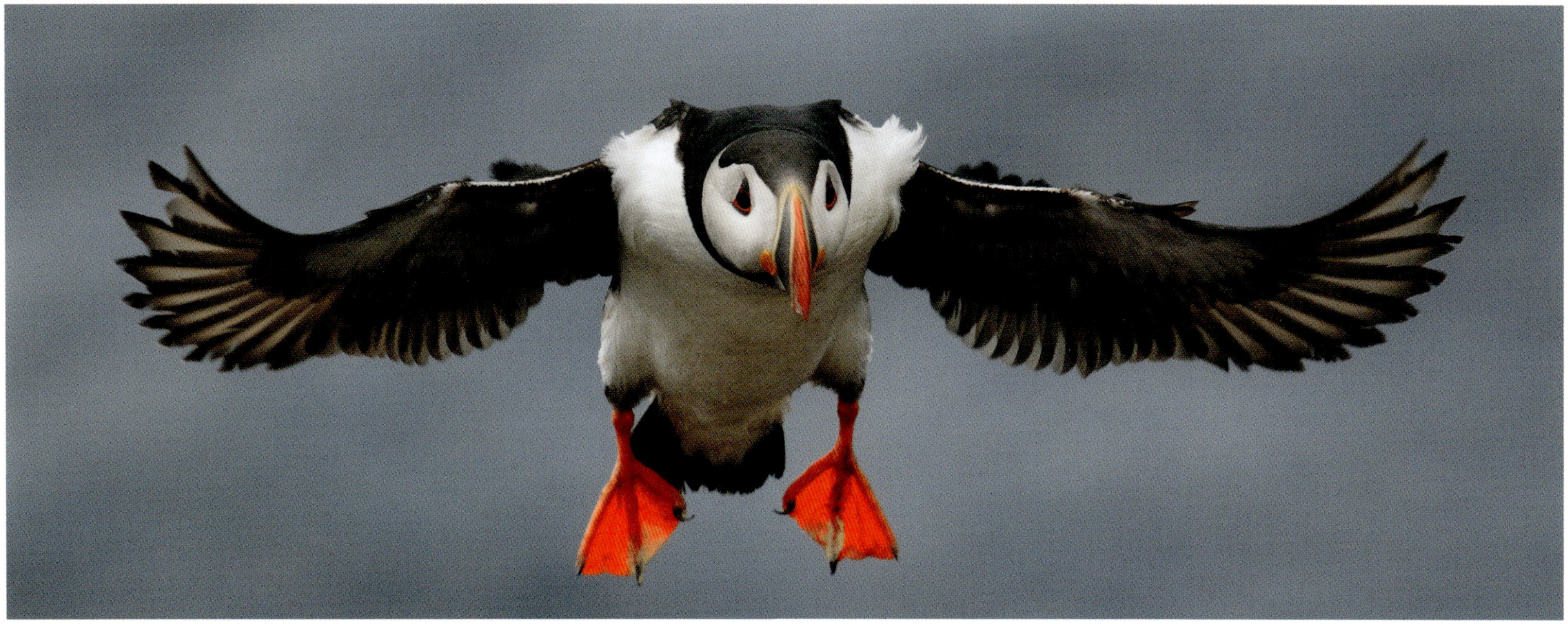

WHITE STAR PUBLISHERS

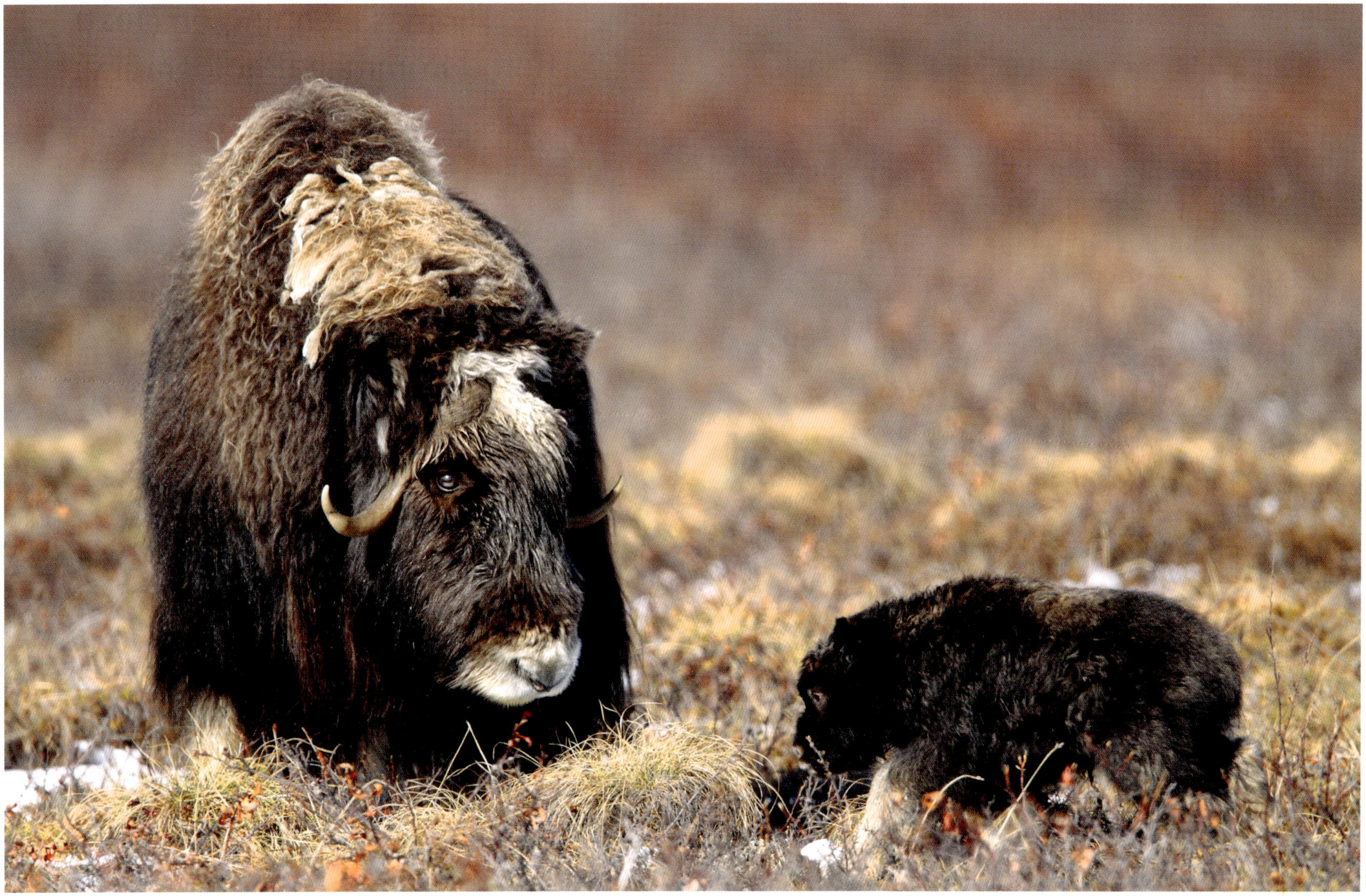

"For all inhabitants of the Arctic
and all who love the Far North
as much as I do."

Bernd Römmelt

"For Naila, Bosse, Kester and Lukas and all children
and 'youngsters' who can experience the Arctic
themselves, or are interested in it or dream about it."

Thomas Henningsen

CONTENTS

Foreword	8
Map	10
The Arctic – Treasure of the North	12
The Arctic of North America – a Treasure of the Animal Kingdom	16
Greenland's Arctic – a Treasure Trove of Snow and Ice	76
Europe's Arctic – the Continent's Wilderness	124
Russia's Arcitc – Treasure Chest of Many Arctic Peoples	178
Climate Change – the White Paradise is Melting	196
Greenpeace in the Arctic	206
Imprint	208

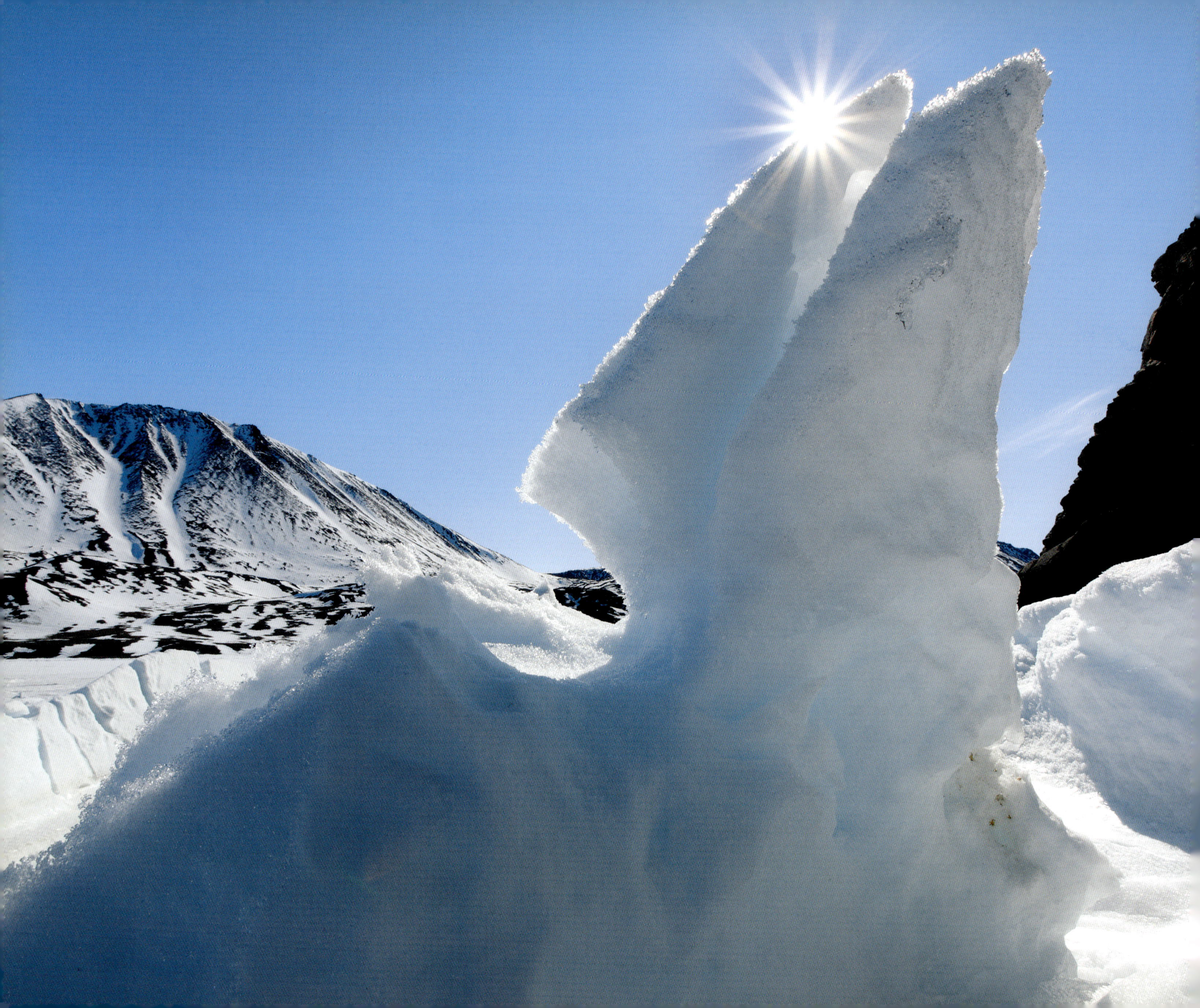

FOREWORD

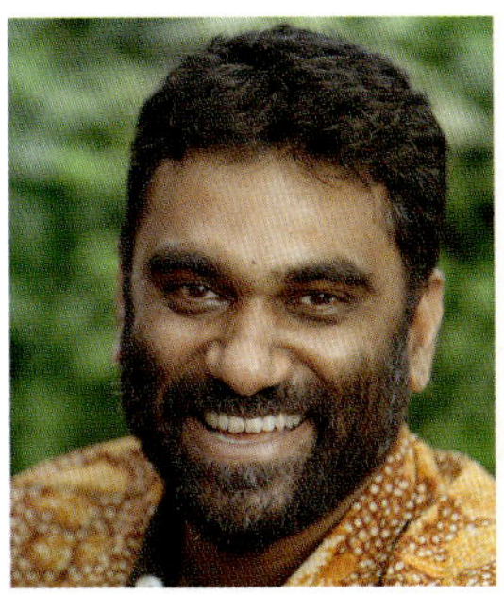

Kumi Naidoo

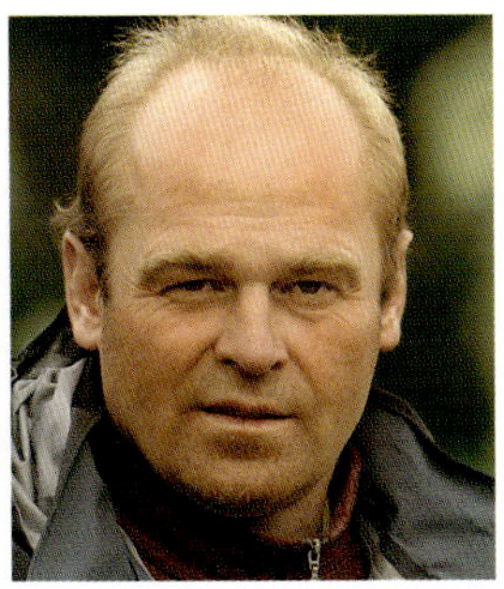

Thomas Henningsen

As an African, for me – Kumi – the Arctic is geographically the furthest place on the planet. As an environmentalist, it is one of the closest places to my heart.

The Arctic is one of the last places of pristine wilderness, a treasure for bio-diversity, human culture and a main driver of global climate [change].

However, as things stand today, the Arctic is under great threat from extractive industries, particularly oil, gas, mining and fishing – as are many other areas on our planet that are rich in natural resources.

The ecosystem in the Arctic is infinitely more sensitive and vulnerable due to the slower "metabolism" of polar areas, which means that pollution has a much stronger impact on all life forms. While in many delicate areas there is the possibility of nature recovering from the assaults of mankind, it is unlikely to be the case in the Arctic.

The fact that oil companies are allowed to drill without disclosing plans for how they would prevent or clean up after a catastrophic spill such as the disaster in the Gulf of Mexico in 2010 illustrates the true horror of the current situation.

The Arctic is in a league of its own. If we lose this awesome place, the predicted impacts would be extreme and would be felt all over the Earth due to a dramatic and drastic rise in sea level – scores of islands and coastal regions would be devastated by flooding.

We have had the honour of meeting with people in Greenland, Canada, Alaska, Russia and Lapland whose very lives and survival depend on a healthy and intact polar environment. These proud polar peoples are aware of the precarious state of their ancestral lands and care very deeply about the preservation of their environment and the lands in which they live.

With this book, we are aiming to provide the public and responsible decision makers with further insight on what we will lose should we choose to continue to feed our fossil fuel addiction by exploiting oil reserves in the Arctic.

A protected Arctic could be the needed turning point of that trend.

We will fight for the future of the Arctic, because we need to win, if we do not want to risk all.

The Arctic is a true treasure of our planet and it needs to be protected because in the end it also protects us.

Kumi Naidoo and Thomas Henningsen
Greenpeace

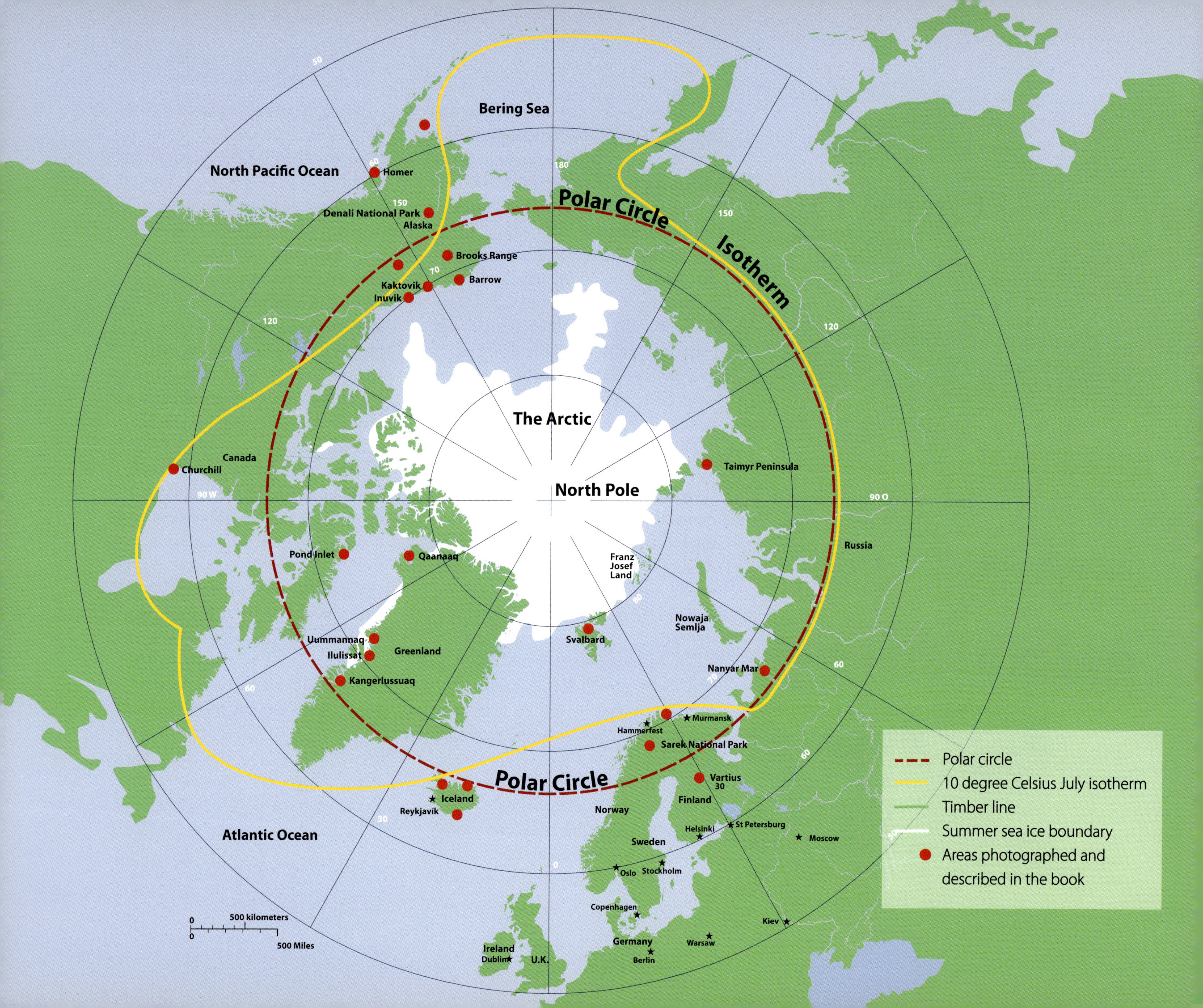
Bering Sea
North Pacific Ocean
Homer
Denali National Park
Alaska
Brooks Range
Barrow
Kaktovik
Inuvik
Polar Circle
Isotherm
The Arctic
North Pole
Canada
Churchill
Taimyr Peninsula
Russia
Pond Inlet
Qaanaaq
Franz Josef Land
Svalbard
Nowaja Semlja
Uummannaq
Ilulissat
Greenland
Kangerlussuaq
Nanyar Mar
Hammerfest
Murmansk
Sarek National Park
Polar Circle
Iceland
Reykjavík
Vartius
Finland
Norway
Sweden
Helsinki
St Petersburg
Moscow
Oslo
Stockholm
Atlantic Ocean
Copenhagen
Germany
Berlin
Warsaw
Kiev
Ireland
Dublin
U.K.
0 500 kilometers
500 Miles
Polar circle
10 degree Celsius July isotherm
Timber line
Summer sea ice boundary
Areas photographed and described in the book

MAP

The Arctic – the world's ice cap – is an enormous region in the north, covering approximately five percent of the world's surface, four percent of the world's ocean surface and eight percent of the world's land mass. What constitutes the Arctic region is not universally agreed: there are various definitions of where and how the boundaries should be drawn.

According to one definition, the Arctic comprises all areas north of the polar circle, the longitude at which the sun no longer rises, or sets, on the two solstices.

A second definition describes the Arctic as all areas north of the timber line, the boundary beyond which trees can no longer grow because of the low temperatures.

A third definition states that the Arctic encompasses all regions north of the ten degree Celsius July isotherm, in other words those regions that do not exceed an average temperature of ten degrees Celsius during the warmest month (usually July).

These last two definitions do not posit permanently defined boundaries, as they change over time. They therefore primarily describe the living conditions of the area rather than a geographically or astronomically determined line.

According to all definitions, however, the Arctic consists of both land and sea: the Arctic Ocean and parts of Alaska, northern Canada, Scandinavia and Russia, as well as many islands, including Greenland and Svalbard. The Arctic Ocean alone has a surface area larger than that of Europe, and is more than 5,000 metres deep in some places. During the winter, it is almost entirely covered with pack ice. This is ice that is formed at very low temperatures out of freezing seawater, the salt in which does not freeze but sinks to the bottom. This swimming ice, between one and a maximum of three metres thick, does not lie stably in one position in the ocean, but is almost completely subject to a drift because of sea currents. As a result of climate change, the melting of this ice that occurs during the summer is increasing dramatically from one year to the next. In just a few years or, at most, a few decades, the entire Arctic could therefore be free of sea ice during the summer months. The map shows the expansion of the summer sea ice in the year 2010.

As a result of the winter snowfall over hundreds of thousands of years, the vast majority of Arctic ice is onshore, however: in the north of Canada, for example, or on Spitsbergen and the other islands of Svalbard, but mainly on Greenland (which by itself contains ten percent of the global ice deposit). The onshore glaciers calve into the sea, so that floating icebergs, some of which are of gigantic proportions, are formed.

THE ARCTIC – TREASURE OF THE NORTH

There are many fascinating natural environments and regions on Earth. Some of them are spectacular. A handful of them are almost beyond our imagination. The Great Barrier Reef off the coast of Australia is such a place, as are the forests of giant Sequoia trees on the west coast of North America, the Serengeti in Africa with its herds of animals, the majestic mountains of the Himalayas and also the polar regions of the Antarctic and the Arctic.

The Arctic is much more than just a region around the North Pole. Covering some 26 million square kilometres, it is bigger than the entire North American continent and about two and a half times bigger than Europe. Some two-thirds of this vast area is sea, known as the Arctic Ocean, much of which is covered by ice. The sea ice is mostly only a few metres, or sometimes as little as just one metre or less thick. The layer of ice covering Greenland, however, has grown over the course of millions of years to a thickness of up to 3,400 metres. The remaining one-third is land – the northern parts of Alaska, Canada, Scandinavia and Siberia as well as numerous islands including Svalbard, Novaya Semlya and the world's largest island, Greenland. The Arctic has eight direct littoral states: Canada, Denmark (Greenland), Iceland, Norway, Sweden, Finland, Russia and the United States (Alaska).

The Arctic may appear to be a harsh region which is hostile to life, but it is full of wonders and secrets and unique treasures. It contains some of the largest wildernesses and last unspoiled areas left on Earth. A natural paradise inhabited by distinctive animal species which are only found here like the polar bear, the musk ox, the snowy owl and the narwhal.

The Arctic Ocean remains the last undeveloped habitat on this planet.

Unlike the Antarctic, humans have lived north of the Arctic Circle for thousands of years – some four million of them today, including a few hundred thousand of the Arctic's original inhabitants: the Inuit, Eskimo, Sami, Nenets, Dolgan and Yakut, to name just a few. These peoples still live in a world torn between ancient traditions and modernity.

The northern polar region plays a very special role in the framework of global cycles on Earth. It is a vast reservoir of fresh water and it's huge ice sheet acts like a giant air conditioner keeping the rest of the globe cool. It thus helps to create conditions which make life possible as we know it. The huge masses of sea ice which are formed every year in the Arctic Ocean make heavier salt water sink to the bottom of the sea and thus prompt the circulation of the ocean currents, which again are responsible for the relatively pleasant climatic conditions we enjoy here on Earth.

In a recently published report *Arctic Treasure: Global Assets Melting Away* by the highly respected Pew Trust Foundation in the United States, the climatic benefit which the Arctic provides for our planet has just been estimated at an incredible economic value of US$ 24 trillion in the next forty years alone – this is some US$ 500 billion per year.

Here, a serious problem arises. Human activity is warming the planet through thousands of coal-fired power stations, vast fleets of cars, aircrafts and ships that burn petrol, diesel and kerosene, and a deforestation industry that operates on a global scale. They all have already caused a global warming effect that is making the sea ice retreat and become much thinner. By 2007, half of the Arctic sea ice that usually remains in summer had disappeared. Now the melting of the ice cap in Greenland is happening more slowly but will surely be a main contributor to a rise in the sea level, which will flood vast areas and cause not millions but billions of people to flee from their homes. And as if that were not enough, drilling for oil all over the Arctic has already begun, so that it can be used as fuel to cause still more damage to the climate – a vicious circle with fatal results.

But there is another Arctic too – a fascinating world of snow and ice. The aim is to preserve it, to protect it from direct exploitation and global warming caused by human action. That means that an important part of the future of life on Earth will be decided specifically in the far north. In fact, it should be clear to everyone that the survival of the Arctic is not just a "nice to have", it is a question of our own survival. "The Arctic must not die", to rephrase the words of the famous zoologist Bernhard Grzimek, which were once applied to the Serengeti.

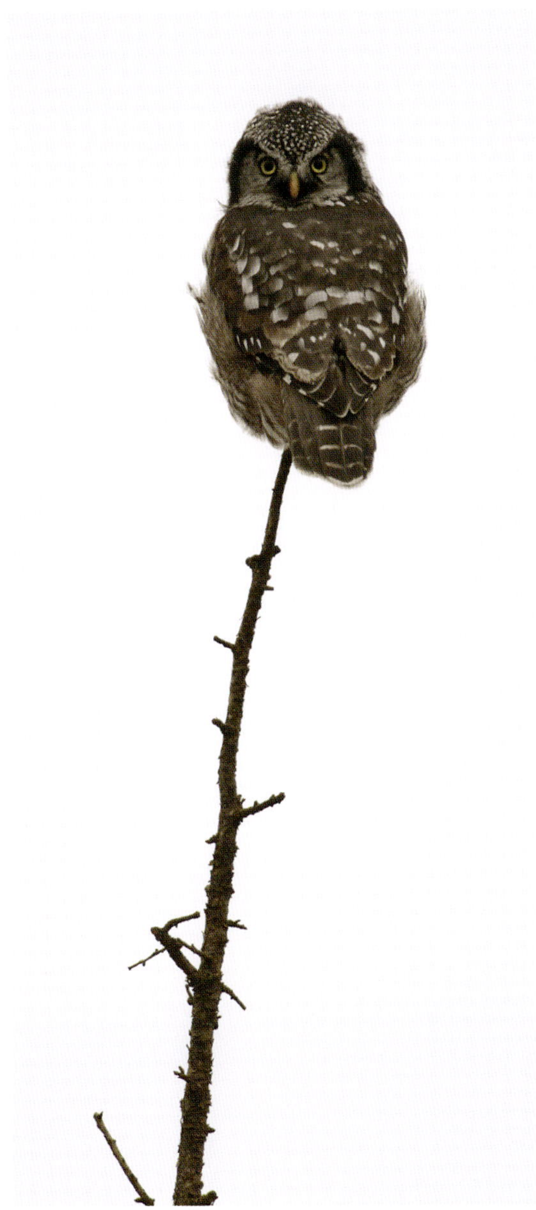

During the past twelve years, the photographer Bernd Römmelt has travelled the Arctic more or less continuously and has attempted with his remarkable feeling for light and subject to capture these wonders in his pictures. No effort was too great, no faraway region too remote. During his long expeditions, he succeeded in creating portraits of the rich animal life in the far north of America; the celestial phenomena such as the Polar lights; the unique world of snow and ice on Greenland; Europe's last wilderness in Lapland; the unique bird life of Iceland; and the impressive life of the first inhabitants, the Inuit, the Eskimo, the Sami, the Yakut and others, in such a way that they will arouse in many readers the wish and the determination to defend this treasure of the north.

Northern hawk owl near Inuvik, Northwest Territories, northern Canada.

Pages 14/15: Morning mist over the wintery Richardson Mountains, Northwest Territories, northern Canada.

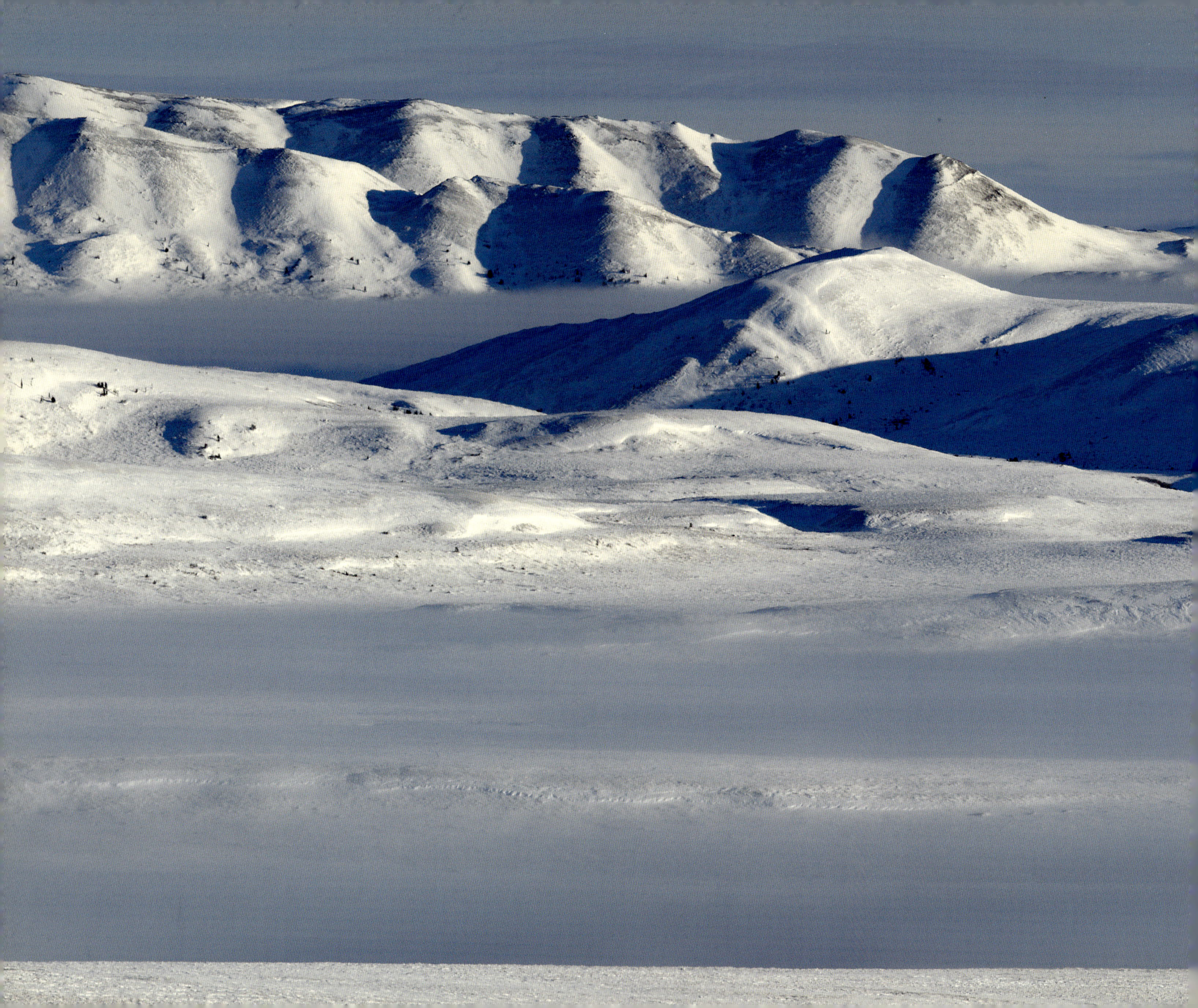

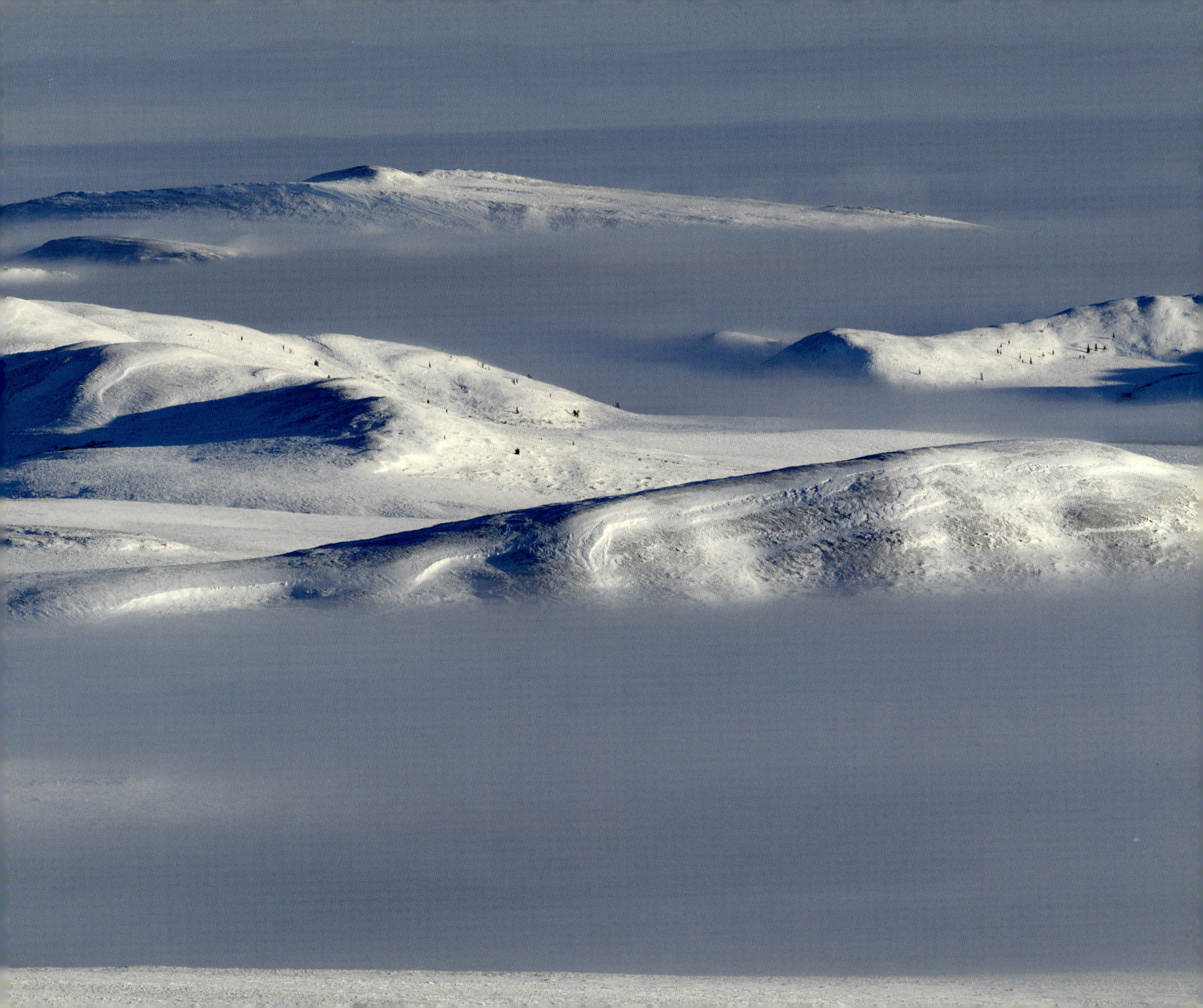

THE ARCTIC OF NORTH AMERICA – A TREASURE OF THE ANIMAL KINGDOM

Approximately 5,000 years ago, hunter-nomads travelled, probably in small groups, from the high plains of what is now Mongolia to the narrow land bridge that existed between present-day Russia and Alaska. From here, they continued to head ever further eastwards and finally reached the region where their descendants live to this day – the coast of North America. It is very hard to imagine how they could have survived the long, arduous journey; the cold, the storms and the months of darkness.

Edible plants were available, but the huge energy requirements of the nomads during such a migration could only really be satisfied with food from the large number of indigenous animals. The hunters must have encountered a wide variety of animal species, and indeed this was perhaps even the main reason for their long search for a new place to live. The descendants of these hunter-nomads, the Inuit, the Eskimos and other Arctic peoples, eventually settled almost exclusively along the coast. To this day, their diet is provided by the animals there: fish, seals, walrus and whales.

Of course it is possible to tell countless tales of the animal world of the Arctic and the adjoining sub-arctic regions. Take, for example, the male narwhal that has a 2–3 metre-long, horn-like, twisted tusk protruding from its jaw – thus fuelling the tales of the mythical unicorn. Or even the Pacific salmon, which migrates in large numbers to the rivers to spawn. Having provided food for grizzly bears and bald eagles, the salmon also serve as valuable fertiliser for many plants and even trees. Or the musk ox, with the longest and warmest coat in the entire animal kingdom. Standing close together, with the young animals safe and protected in the middle, the musk ox herd acts as a

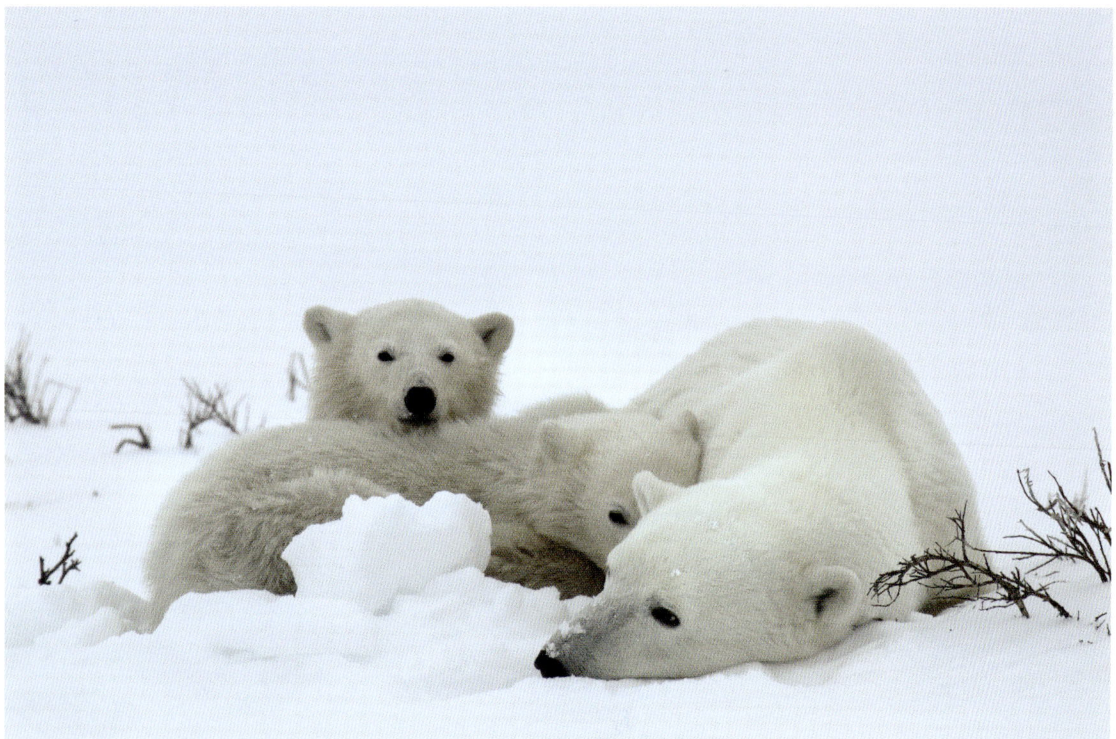

Polar bear mother with her two six-month-old cubs. Cape Churchill, Hudson Bay, Canada.

living shield which protects their young from being attacked by wolves.

There are two animal species that make their mark on life in the Arctic and serve as symbols for life and survival in the rapidly changing world in the high north. They could not be more different from each other: The polar bear, the king of the Arctic regions, and the gnat, the curse of the north.

The gnats swarm in unbelievable numbers in the few brief summer weeks, making the lives of all warm-blooded creatures almost unbearable. The vast herds of caribou flee before them, abandoning for weeks on end the lush pastures where they should really be feeding to gain weight in order to survive the next winter. Instead, they take refuge in higher regions where food is less plentiful in order to escape the gnats. Caribou can lose over a litre of blood in a single week when the gnats appear in such numbers.

And here, too, it is the changing climate which gives the gnats this advantage. Gnats need fresh water so that their larvae can develop. Even a small puddle is sufficient for them to lay their eggs which, a few days later, will develop into a new generation.

The continued thawing of the permafrost layer, the increased frequency of rain, the ever-earlier melting of snow and ice now increases the number of small ponds that are so advantageous for the gnats of the Arctic. For some, however, like the countless insect-eating birds that flock to the Arctic in summer, this curse is also a blessing. Yet, in general, the proliferation of gnats is a negative one.

Things are very different for the polar bear, the so-called undisputed king of this icy realm. In its evolution, the polar bear has adapted to the harsh conditions better than virtually any other animal species, thanks to its incredibly thick coat of fur. The air trapped in its hollow hairs provides additional insulation. Its black skin absorbs even the smallest amount of warmth from the sun. Its swimming prowess explains its classification as a marine mammal alongside whales, seals, sea otters and manatees. Its strength and endurance enables the polar bear to hunt and kill large walruses, beluga whales and narwhals, alongside its standard fare of seals. And yet it seems as if the polar bear's skilled adaptation and strength will be to no avail in the face of the massive effects of climate change. In many regions, the patches of sea ice on which they hunt seals are disappearing with alarming rapidity. The stretches of water they have to cross by swimming are increasing in size and often sap their strength, with fatal effects. Today, emaciated and even dead polar bears are found along the coasts with increasing frequency.

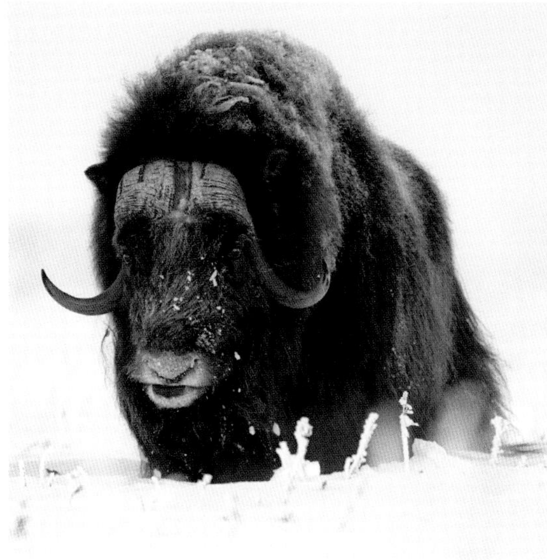

The 25,000 or so polar bears still in existence must not be allowed to suffer the fate of the "Little Polar Bear" Lars, whose story is still read at night in countless children's bedrooms. He set out in search of a new place to live; in reality, however, there would be no prospect of return. And it must not be allowed to come to pass that one day we gaze at polar bears in zoos (like Knut, the polar bear cub in Berlin) because their habitat has been destroyed and it is no longer possible for them to survive and live in freedom in the wild. The habitat of this remarkable creature, which has become the symbol of the melting Arctic ice, must be preserved and protected to the last.

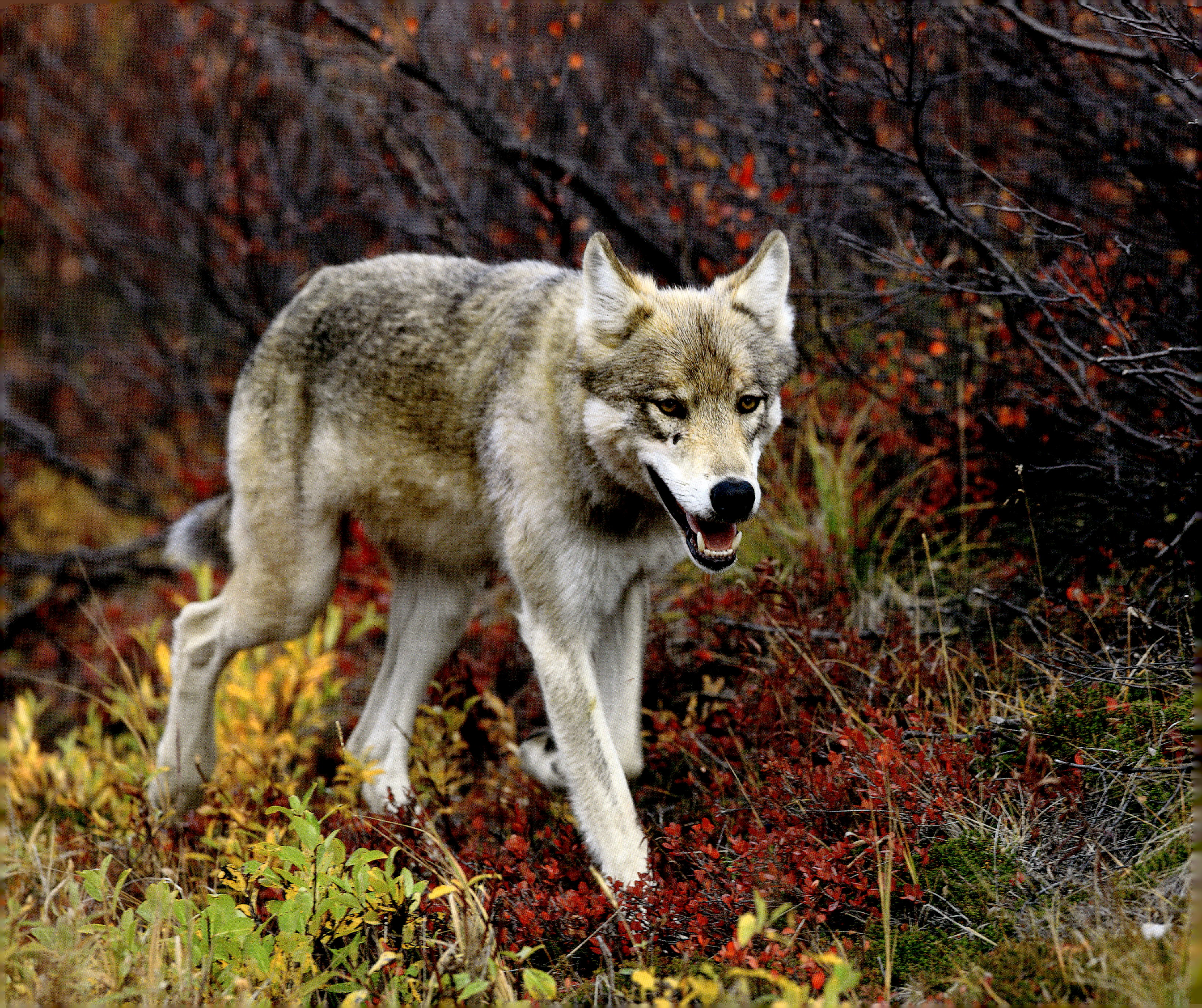

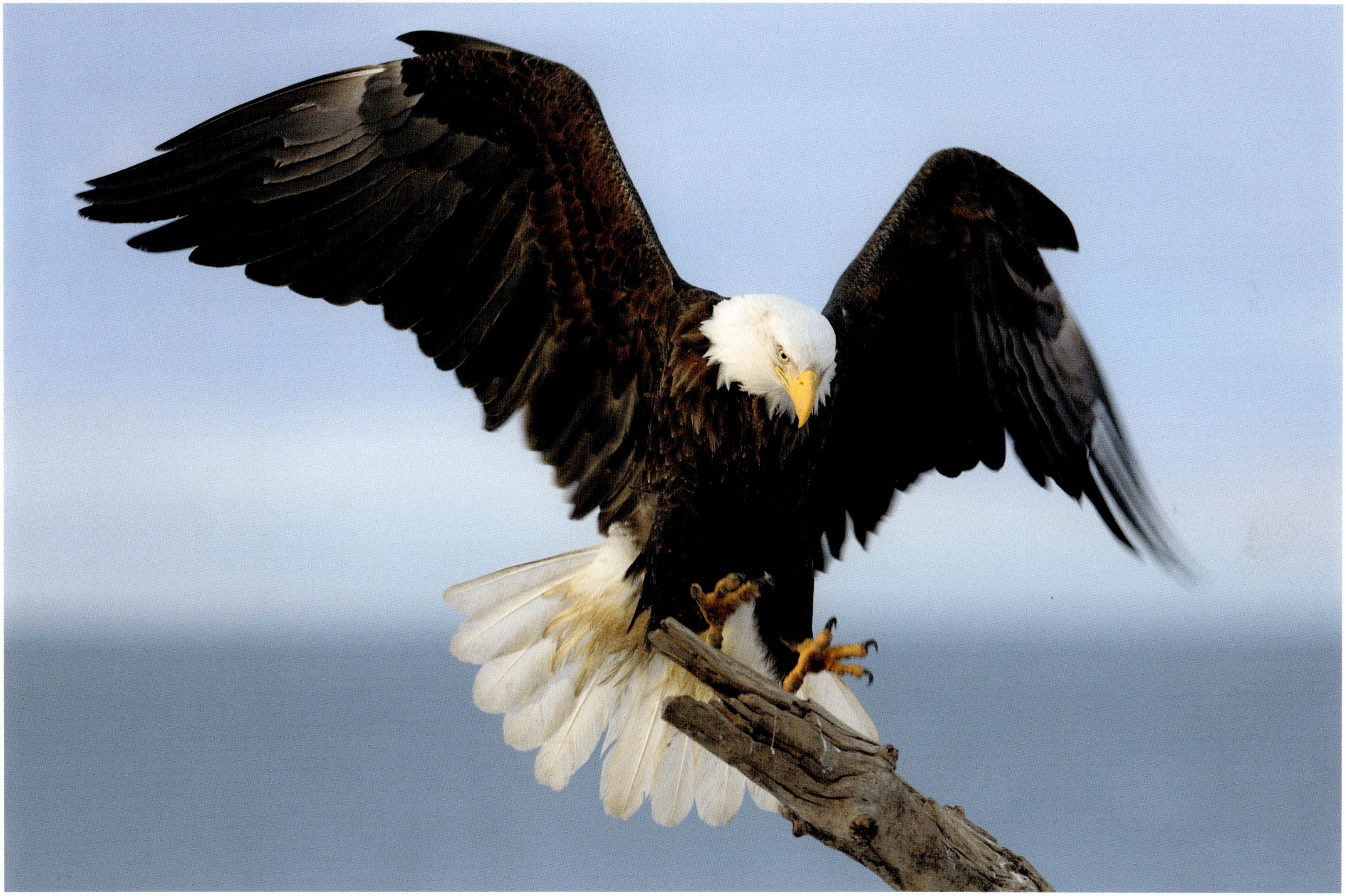

Even in the far north of Alaska, one rarely comes across wolves. These animals are very wary as a result of having been hunted by humans. Denali National Park, Alaska.

The bald eagle is the second-largest North American bird of prey, after the Californian condor. It is still common on Alaska's coasts. Almost extinct, these impressive birds have at least partially recovered, reaching a population of more than 100,000 birds today. Most of them live in Alaska. Southern Alaska.

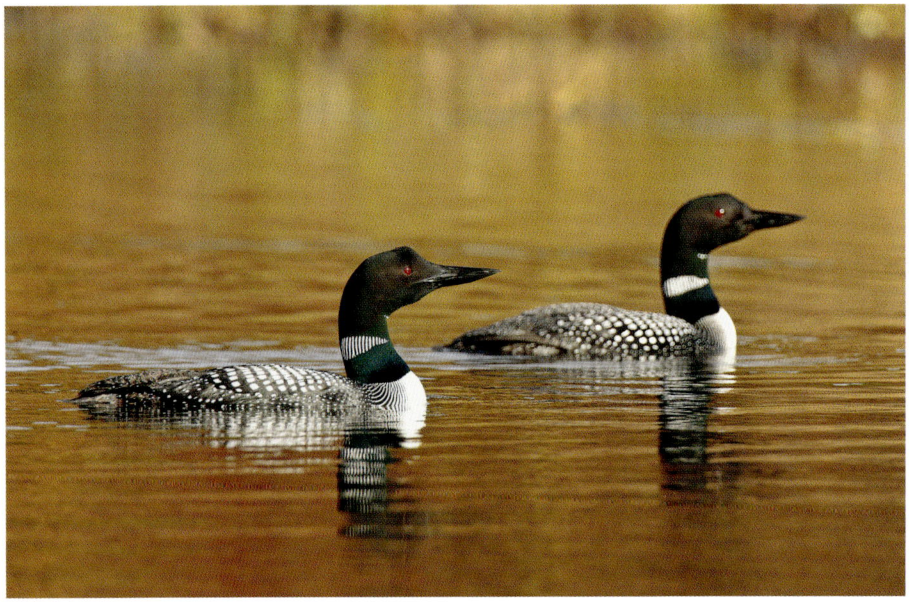
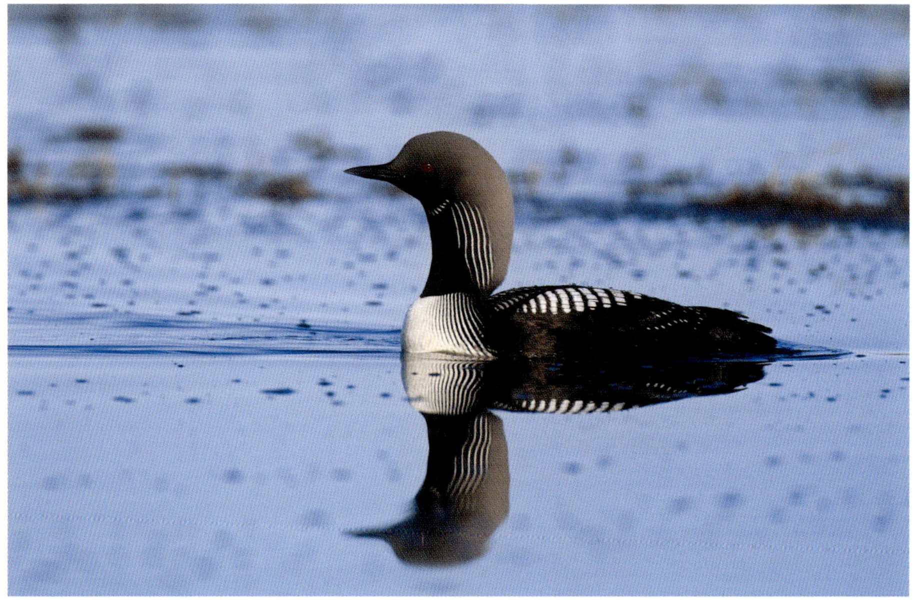
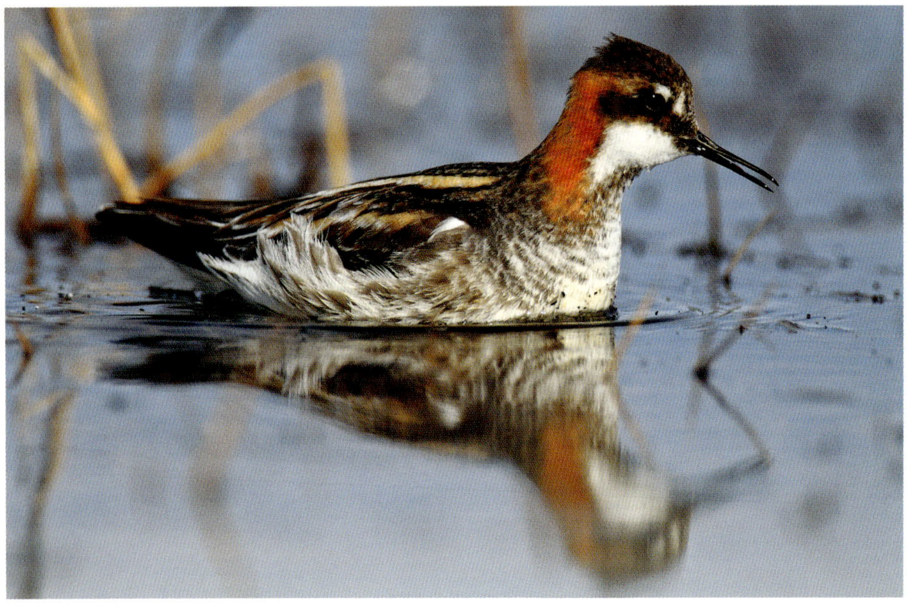
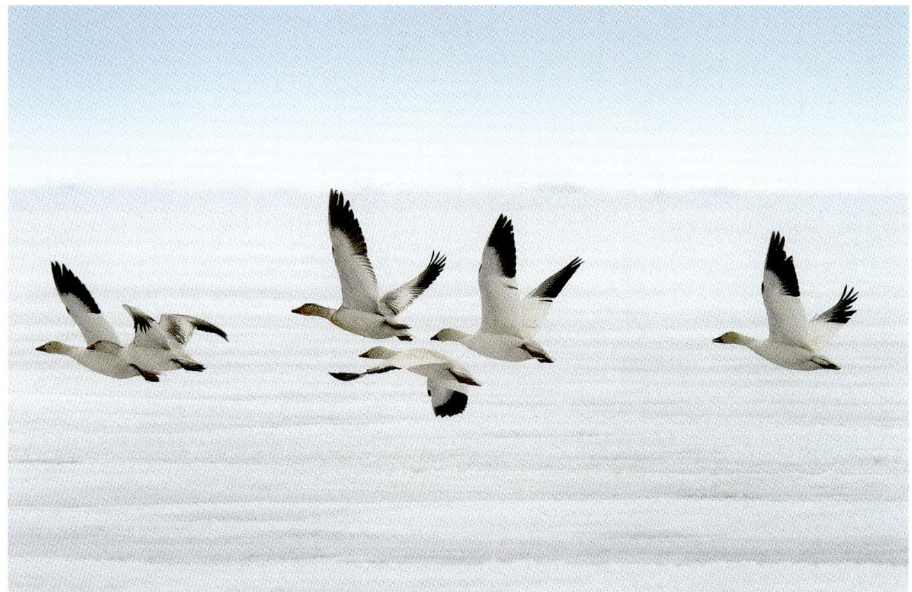

Attracted by the rich food supply, millions of birds migrate to the coasts of Alaska and Canada every spring to breed and raise their young. Clockwise from top left: Great northern loon, Denali National Park, central Alaska; Pacific loon, Barrow, northern Alaska; Snow goose, Baffin Bay, Nunavut, northern Canada; Red-necked phalarope, Barrow, northern Alaska.

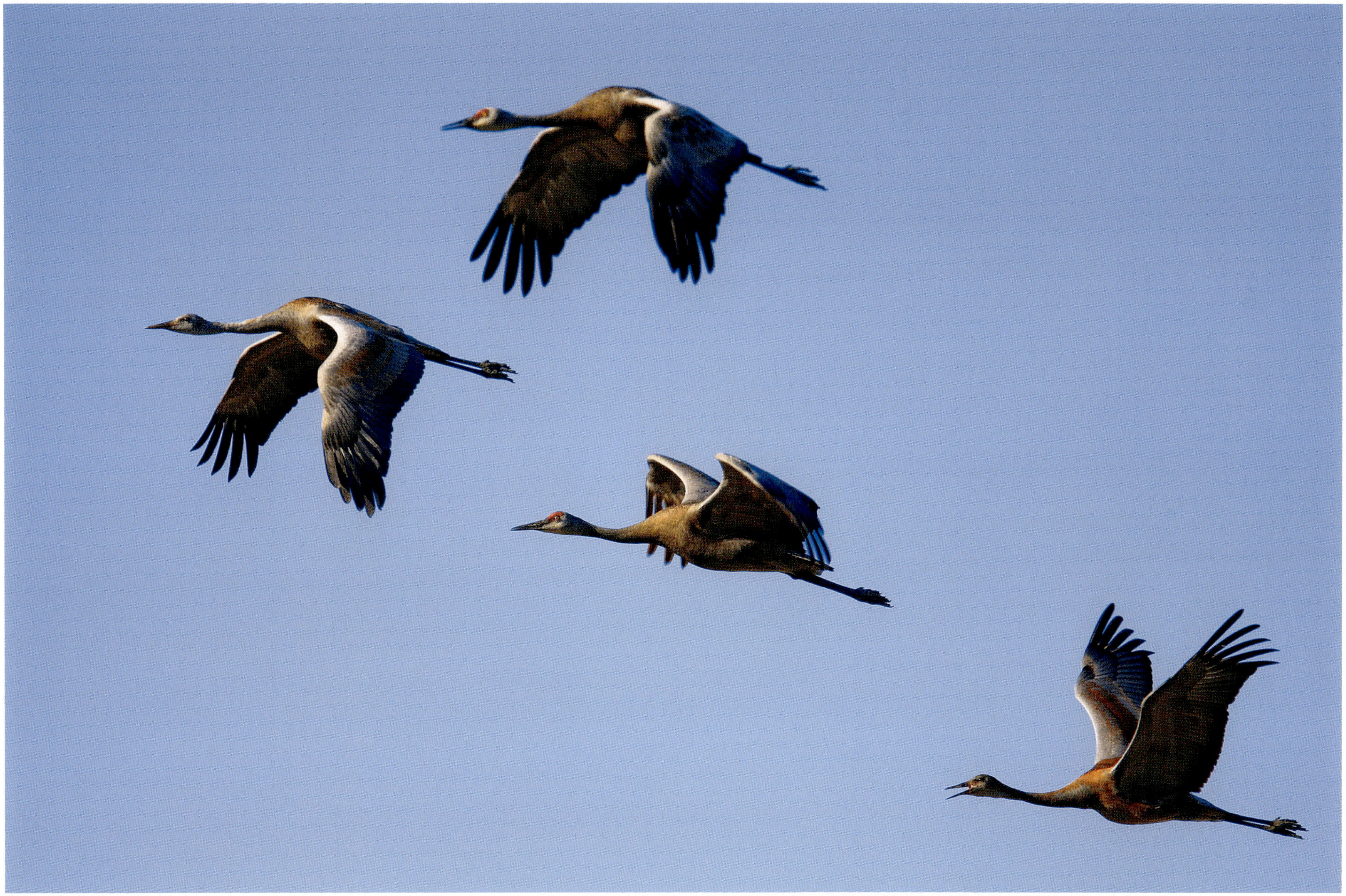

Of all the different types of crane, sandhill cranes migrate the furthest: up to 8,000 kilometres from Mexico or the south of the USA to the far north. Yukon Flats, central Alaska.

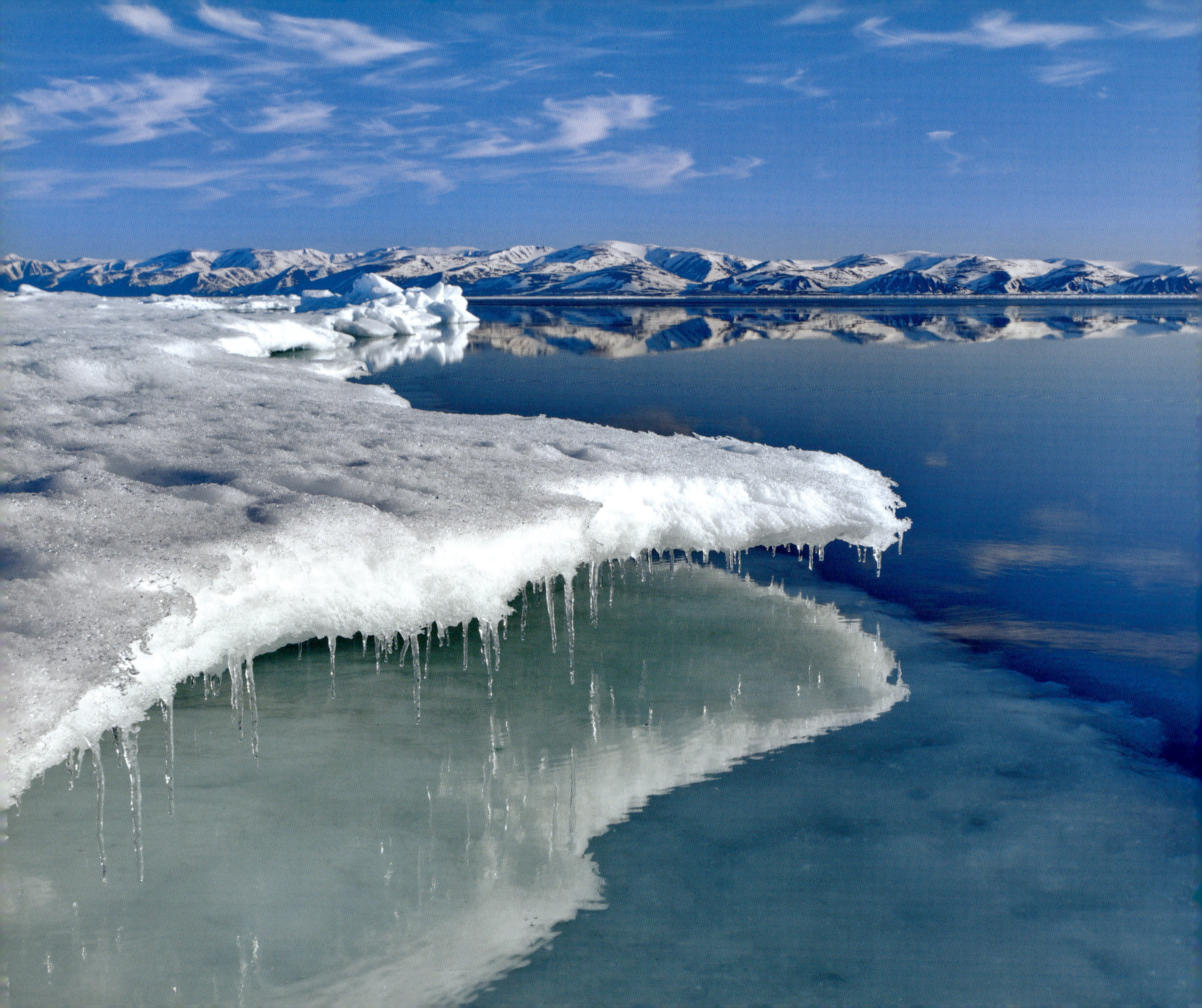

The pack ice breaks up in June in the far north of Canada. Waterways are formed along the edges of the ice, and these are used by many animals to reach their feeding grounds.

Groups of narwhals, too, congregate along the edges of the pack ice, searching for fish, squid and crabs underneath. The males, which are up to four metres in length, have a two to three-metre-long helical tooth that juts out of the upper jaw. During the Middle Ages, this precious ivory was bought and sold in Europe. In the stories about these creatures, their teeth became horns, giving rise to the legends about the mythical unicorn. Baffin Bay, Nunavut, northern Canada.

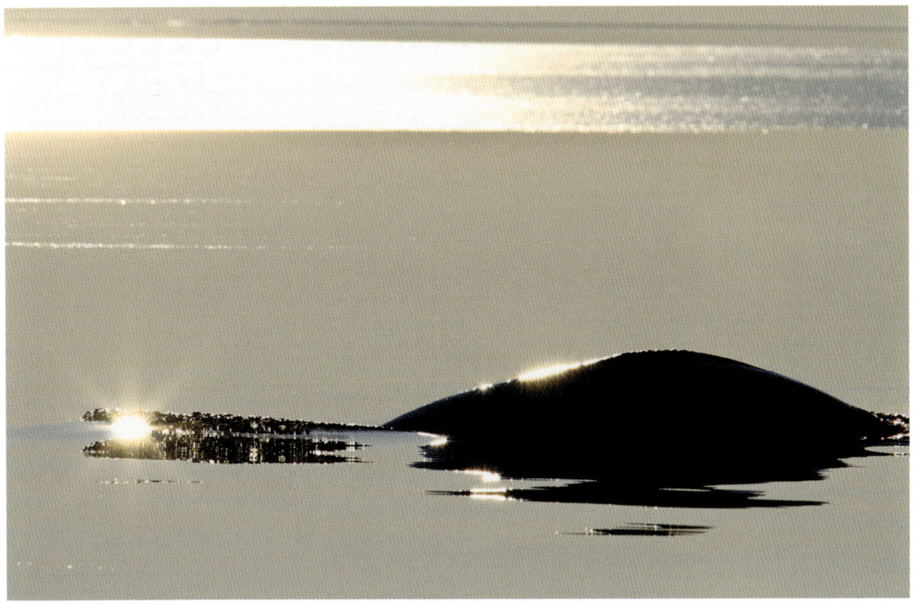

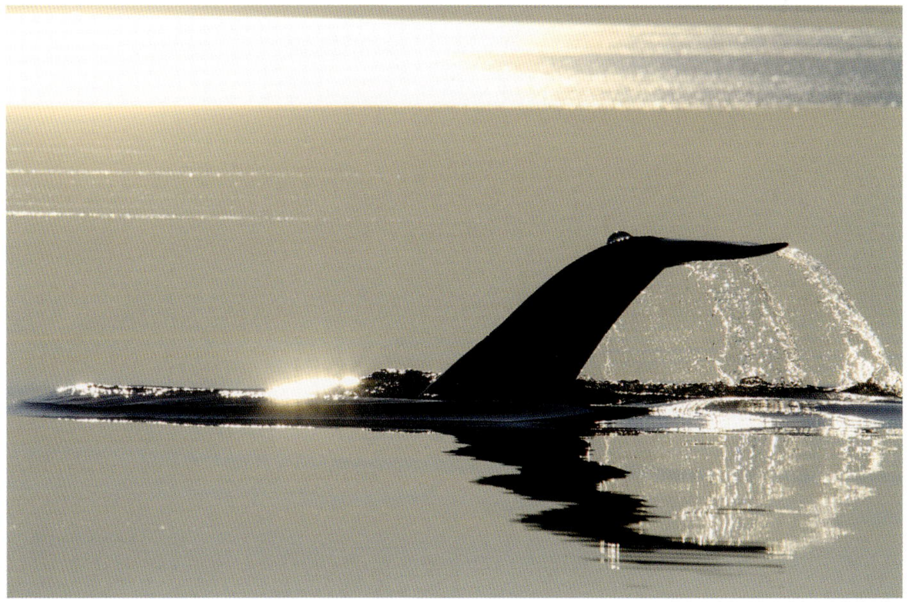

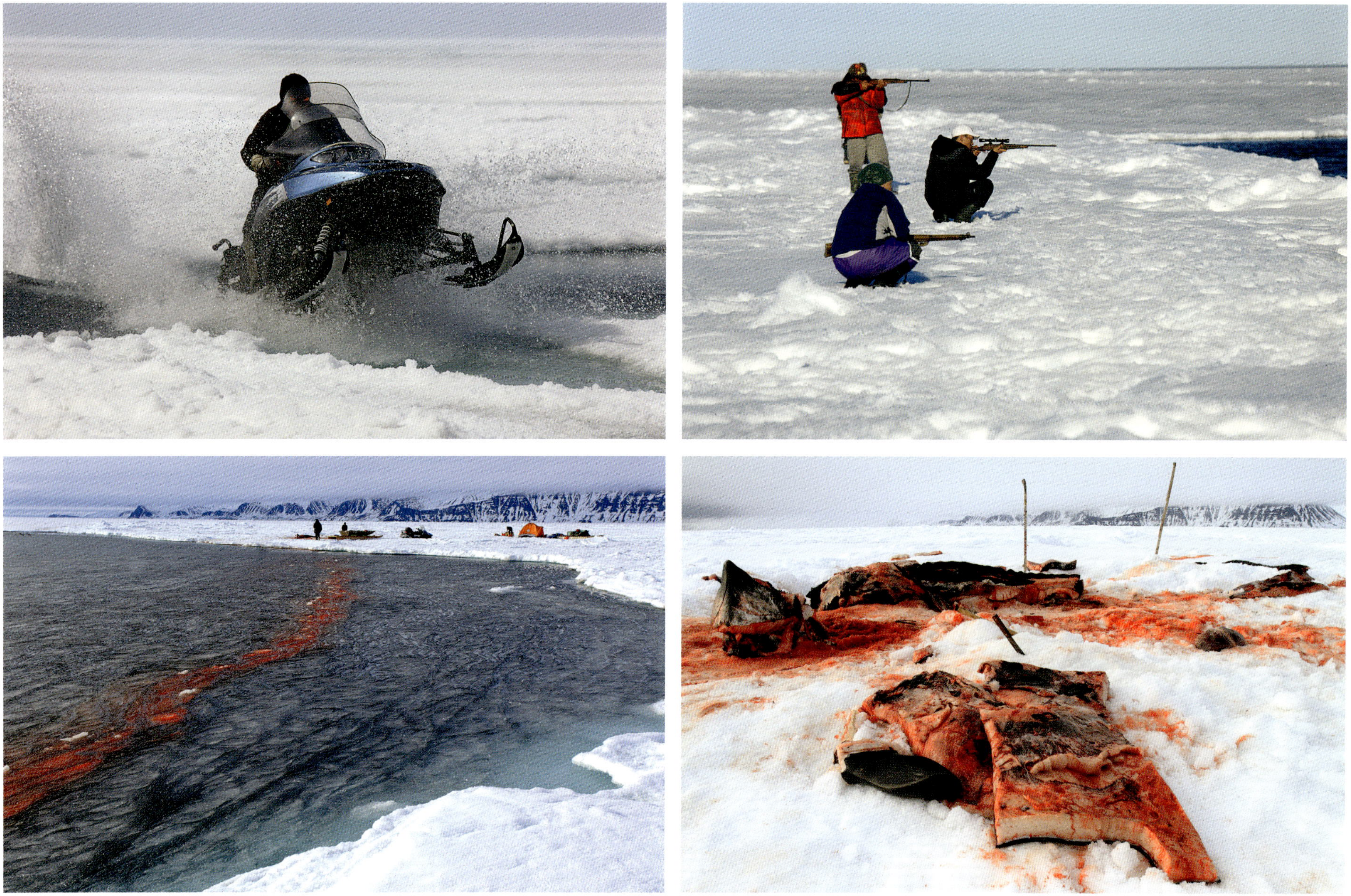

In the spring, the Inuit hunt whales, particularly along the edges formed by the breaking up of the pack ice. The meat serves as an important source of nutrition rich in fat. The original inhabitants of the Arctic have hunted whales for thousands of years. In contrast to "white" peoples, the Inuit have never practised commercial whaling.

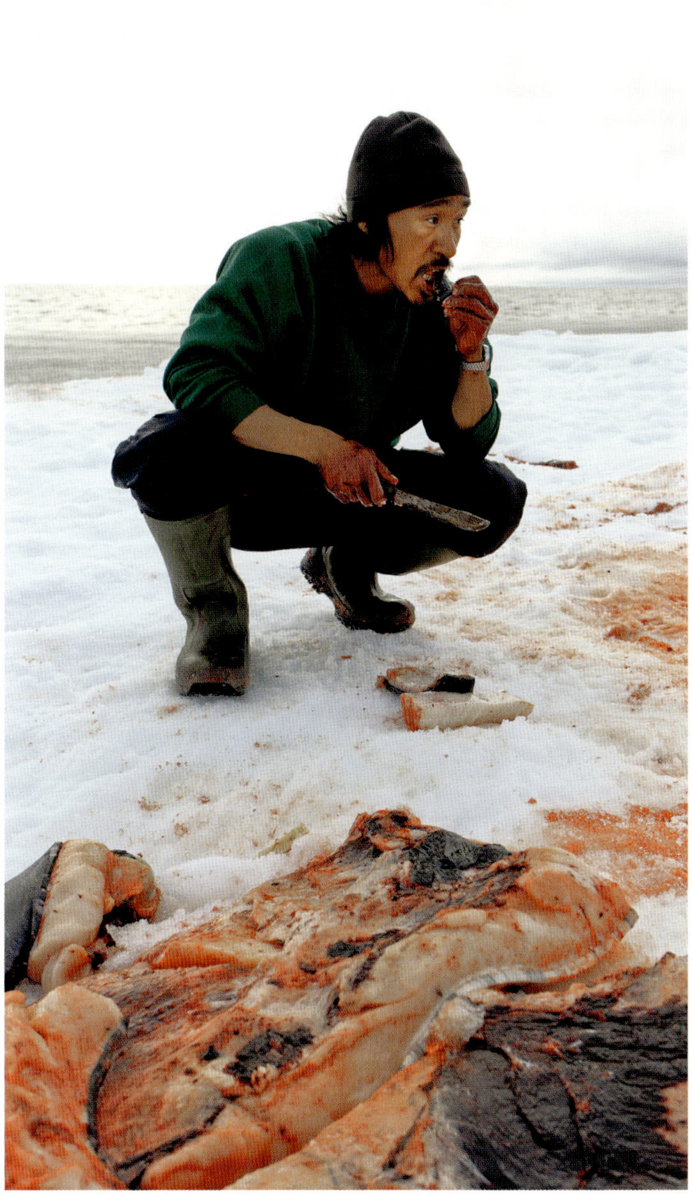

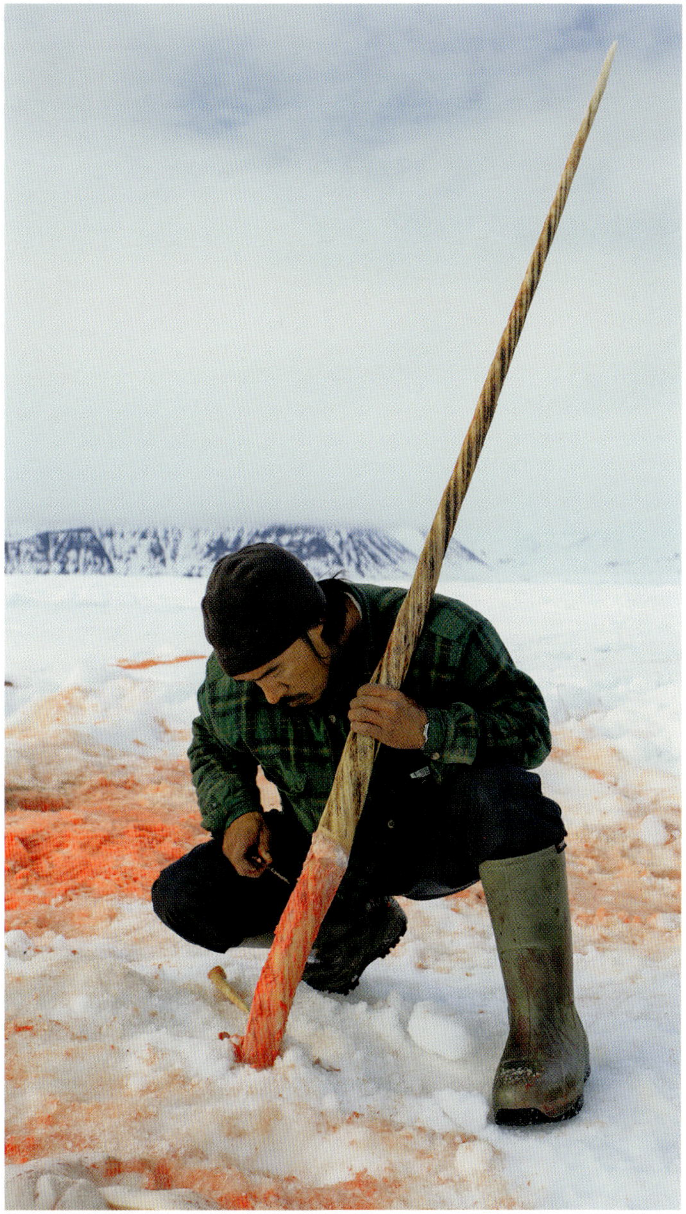

Hunting with guns nowadays is considered to be problematic, however, as a large number of whales are injured or killed and then lost. This means that more animals than necessary are killed. Now, the worldwide population of 23,000 narwhals has been classified as endangered.

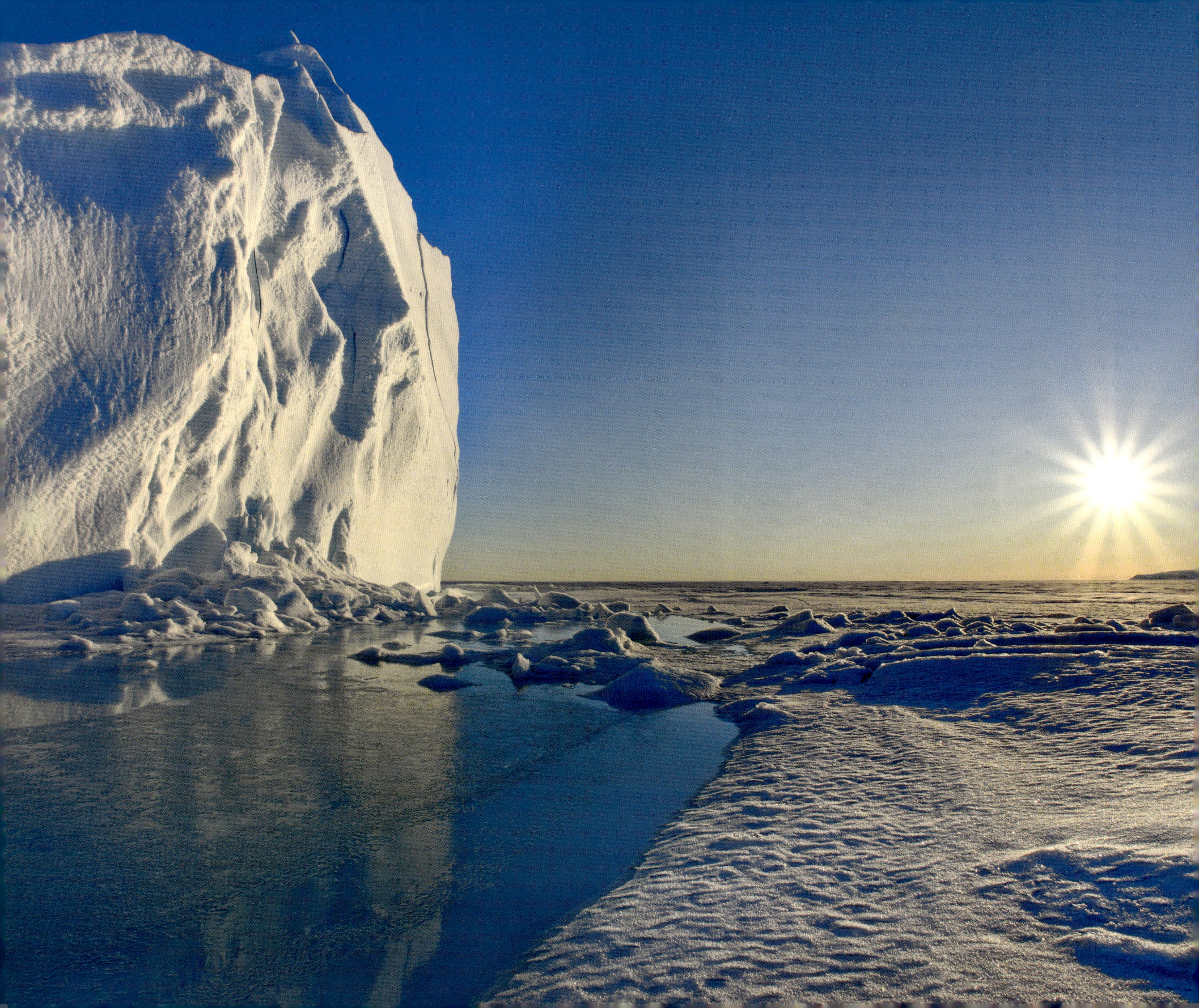

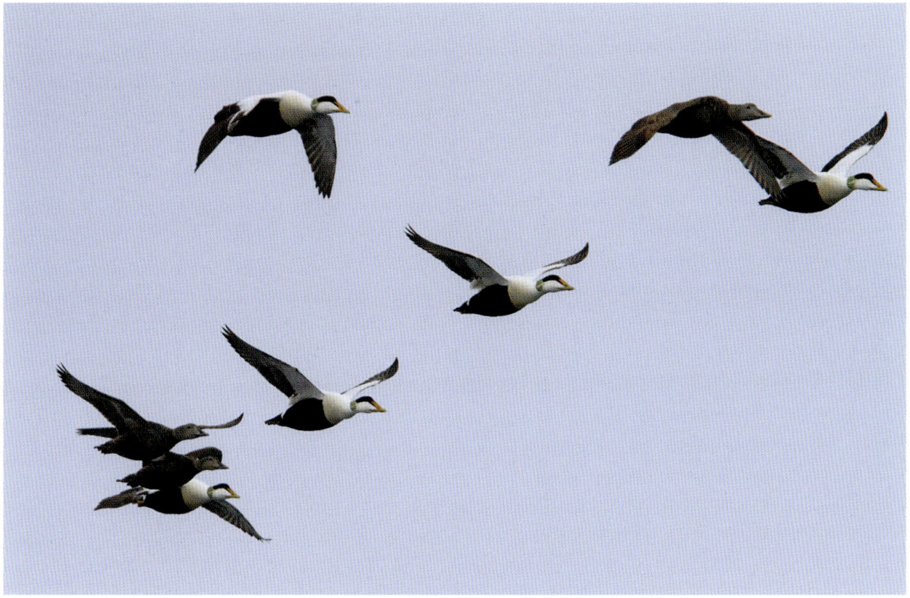

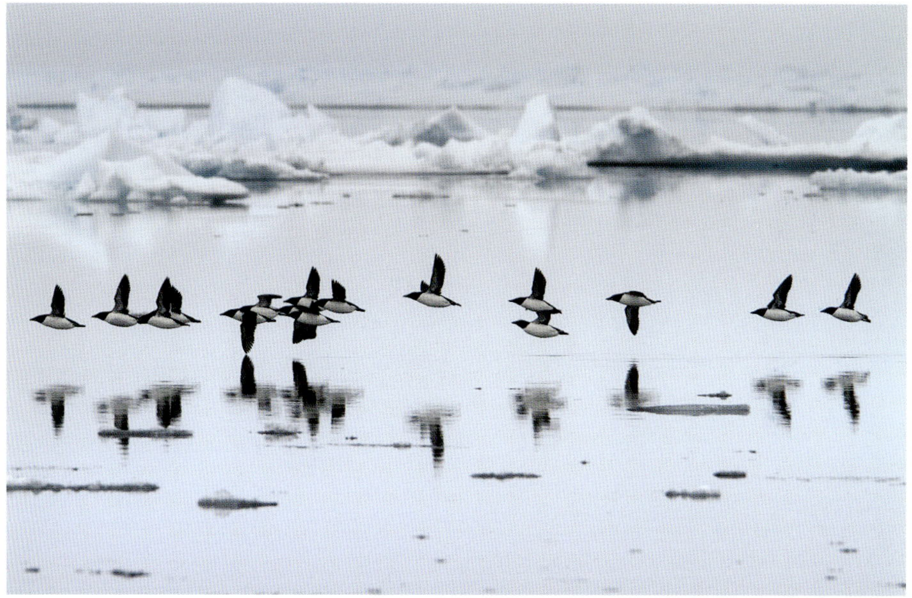

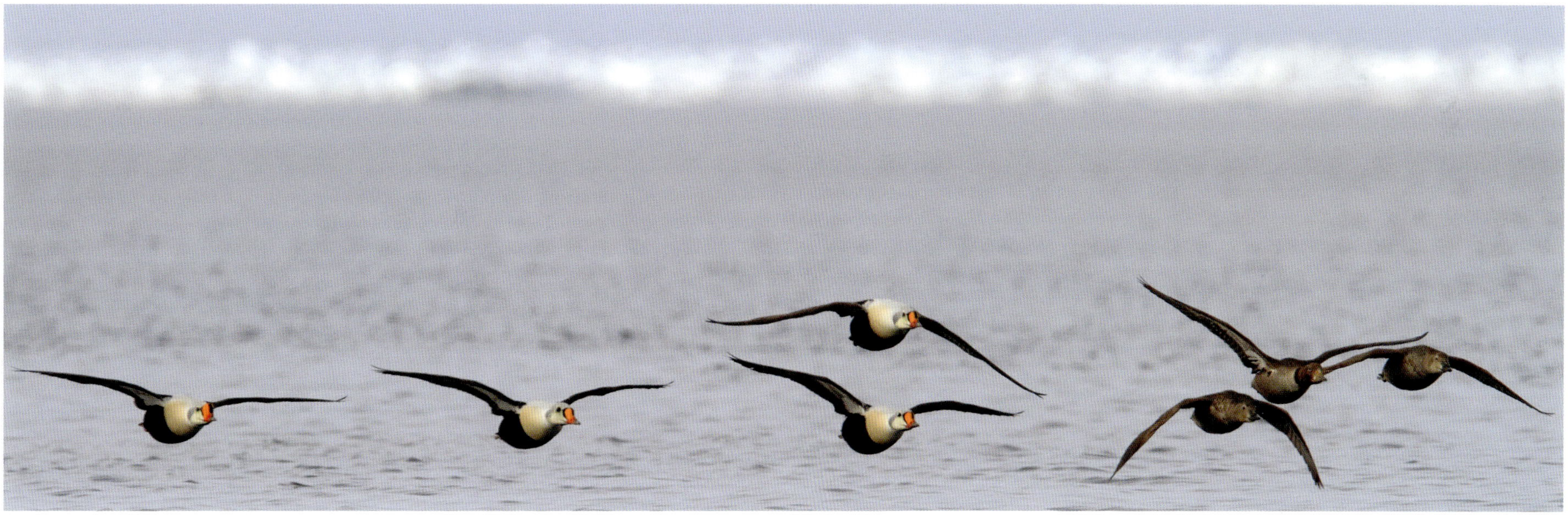

Left: It is June and the midnight sun has reached its highest point. In the high Arctic, the sun will not disappear from the horizon again until August. Baffin Bay, Nunavut, northern Canada.

Innumerable water birds gather at the edge of the pack ice each summer: flocks of common eider, thick-billed murres and king eiders search for food here. The thick-billed murre and common eider even hunt for fish.

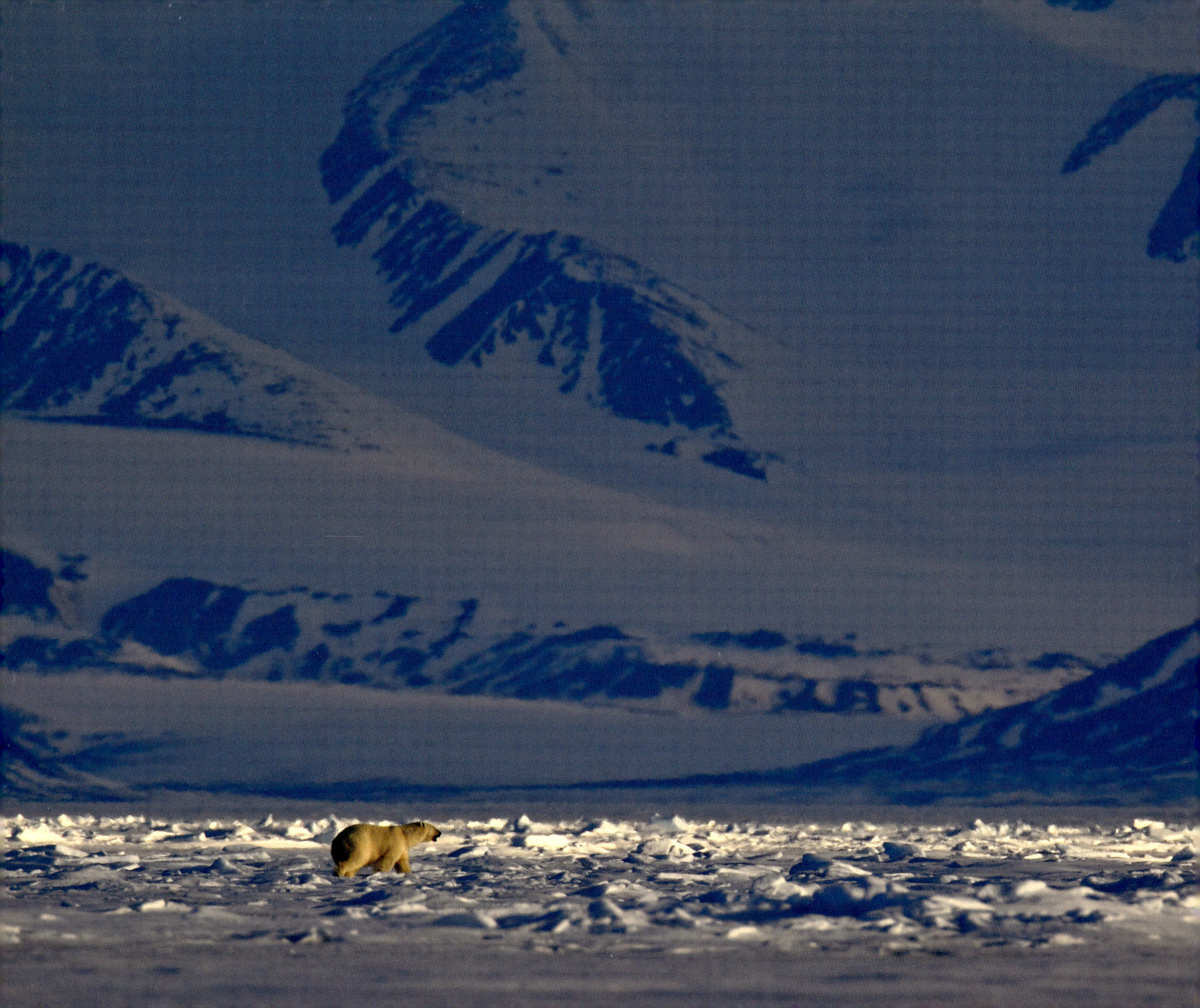

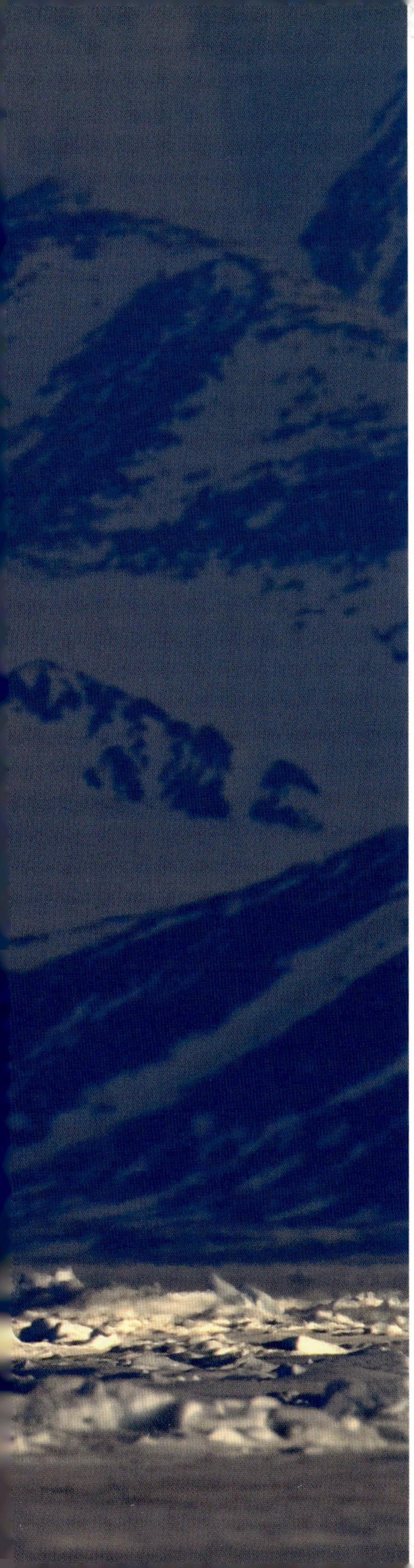

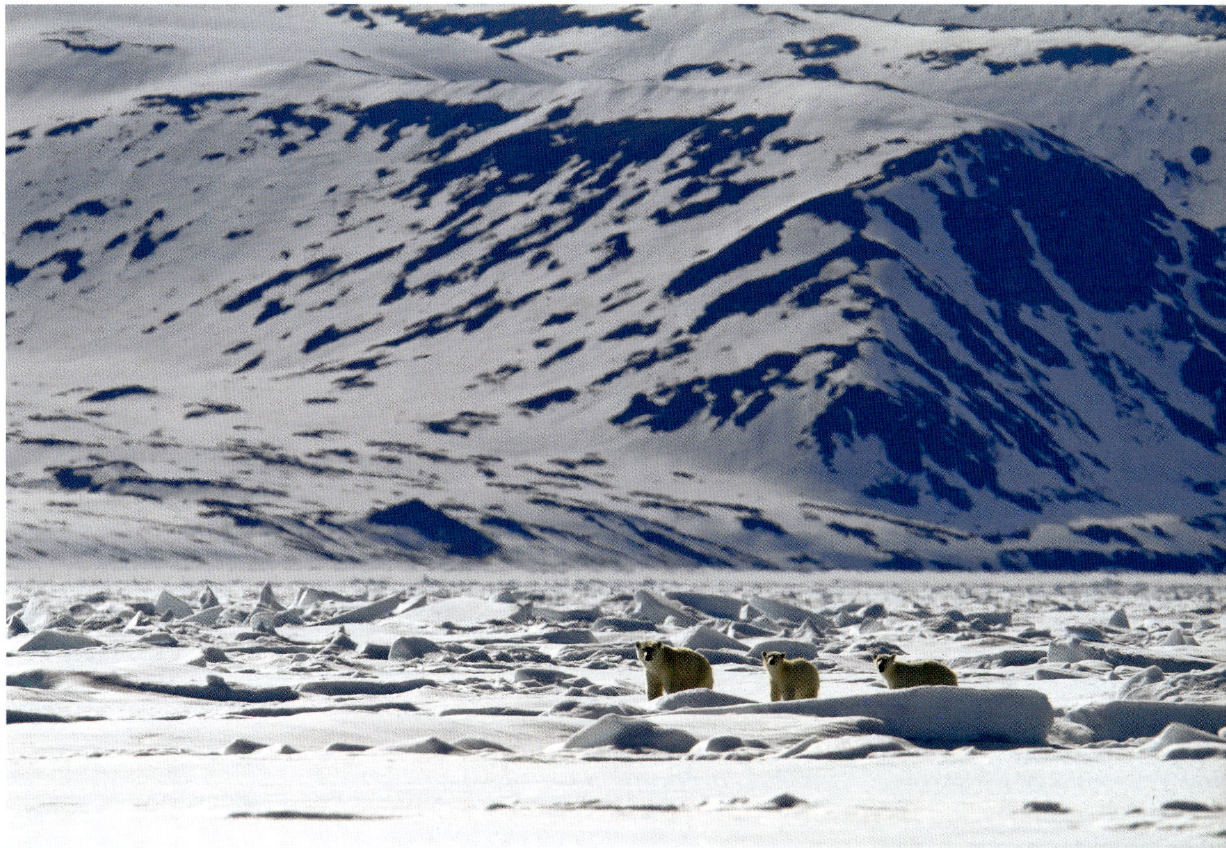

A polar bear mother with her two cubs on the pack ice. The cubs stay with their mother for the first few years before fending for themselves. Baffin Bay, Nunavut, northern Canada.

The "King of the Arctic", the polar bear, is also indefatigable in its search for food. Baffin Bay, Nunavut, northern Canada.

Pack ice is the polar bear's habitat. This is where their most important prey is to be found: seals. The polar bear is a highly specialised hunter, perfectly adapted to the tough conditions of the Arctic. Underneath the thick, white, water-repellent fur is black skin, covering a 10 to 15-centimetre-thick layer of fat, which keeps the bear warm. Furthermore, the outer hairs of the polar bear's fur are hollow, yet another excellent form of heat insulation. Its small head and small ears also prevent too much loss of heat.

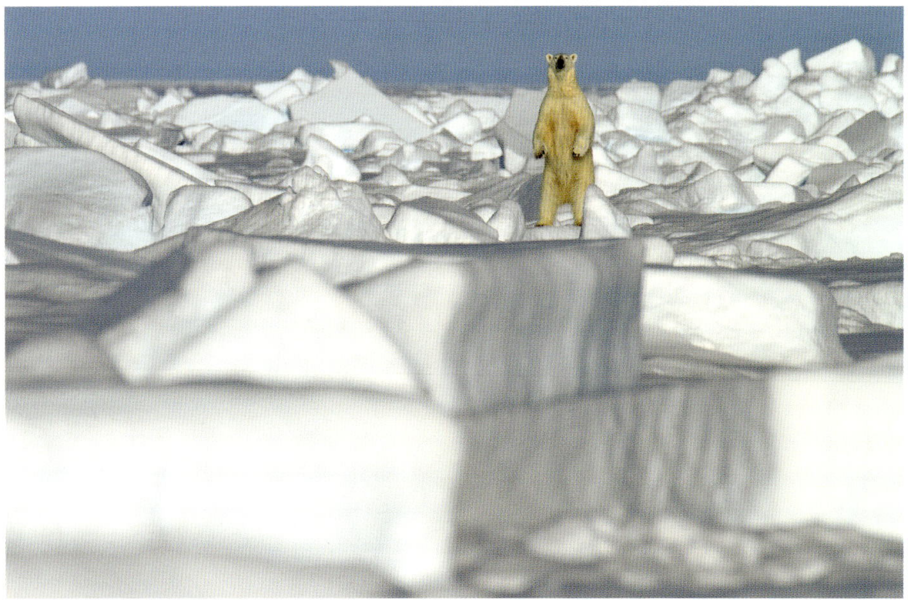

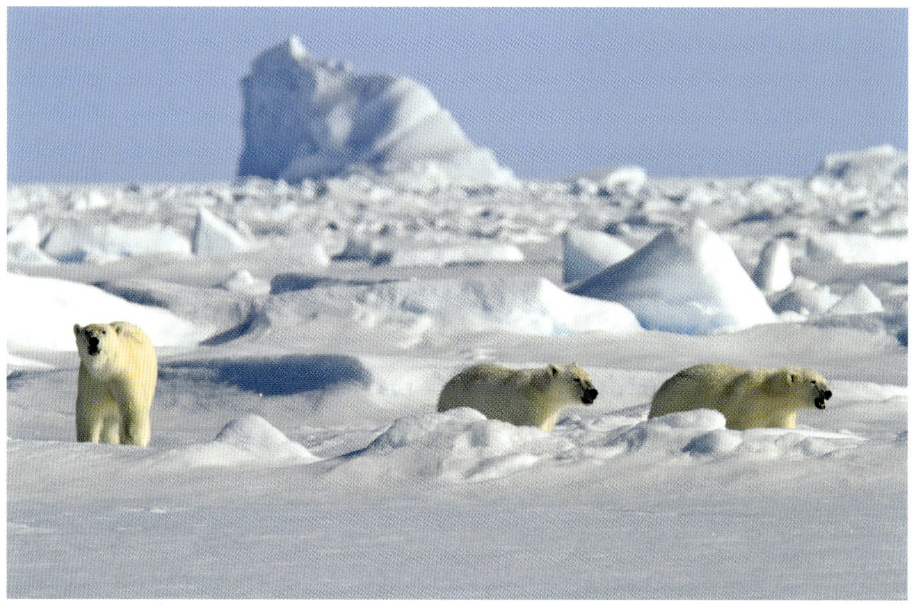

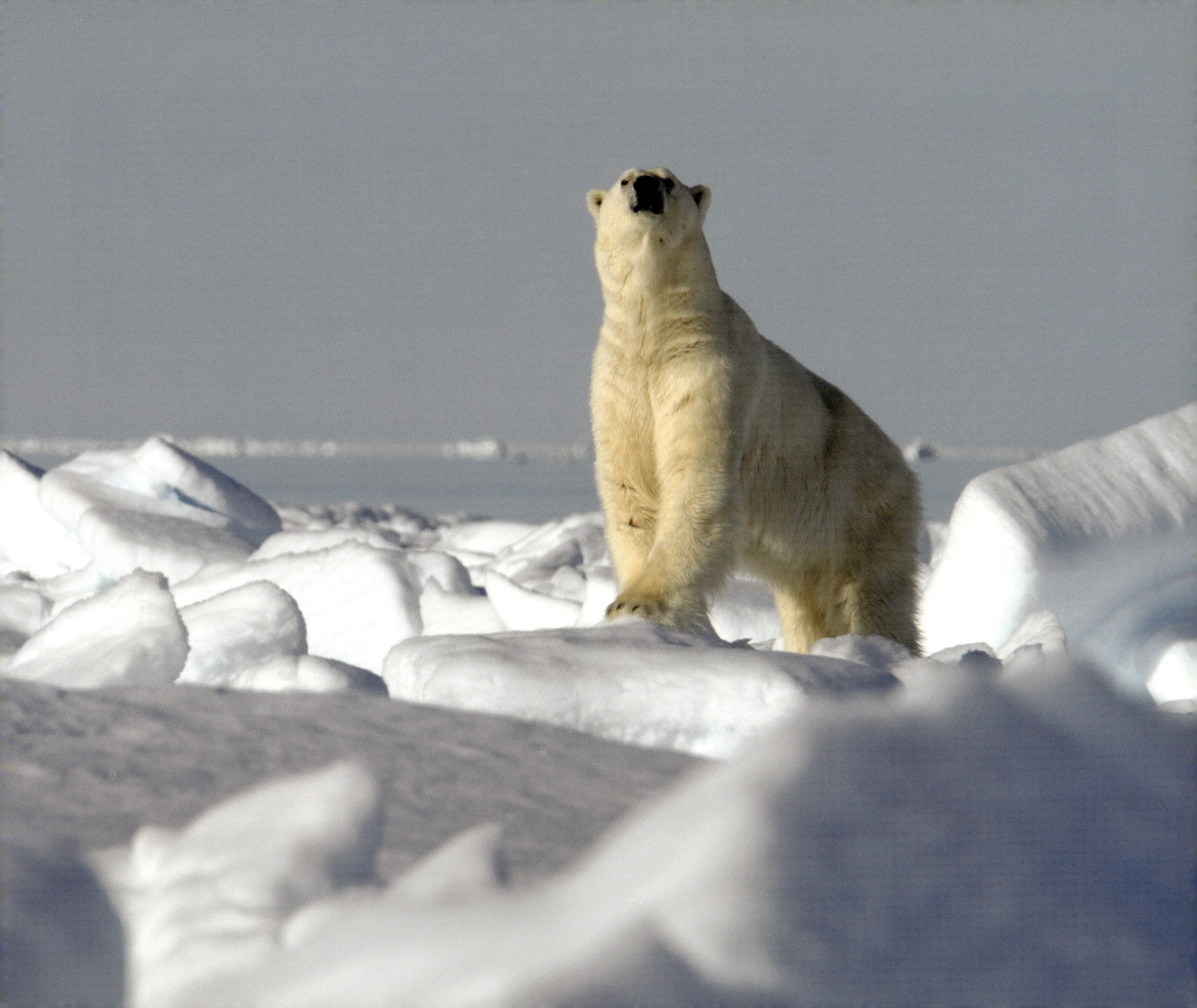

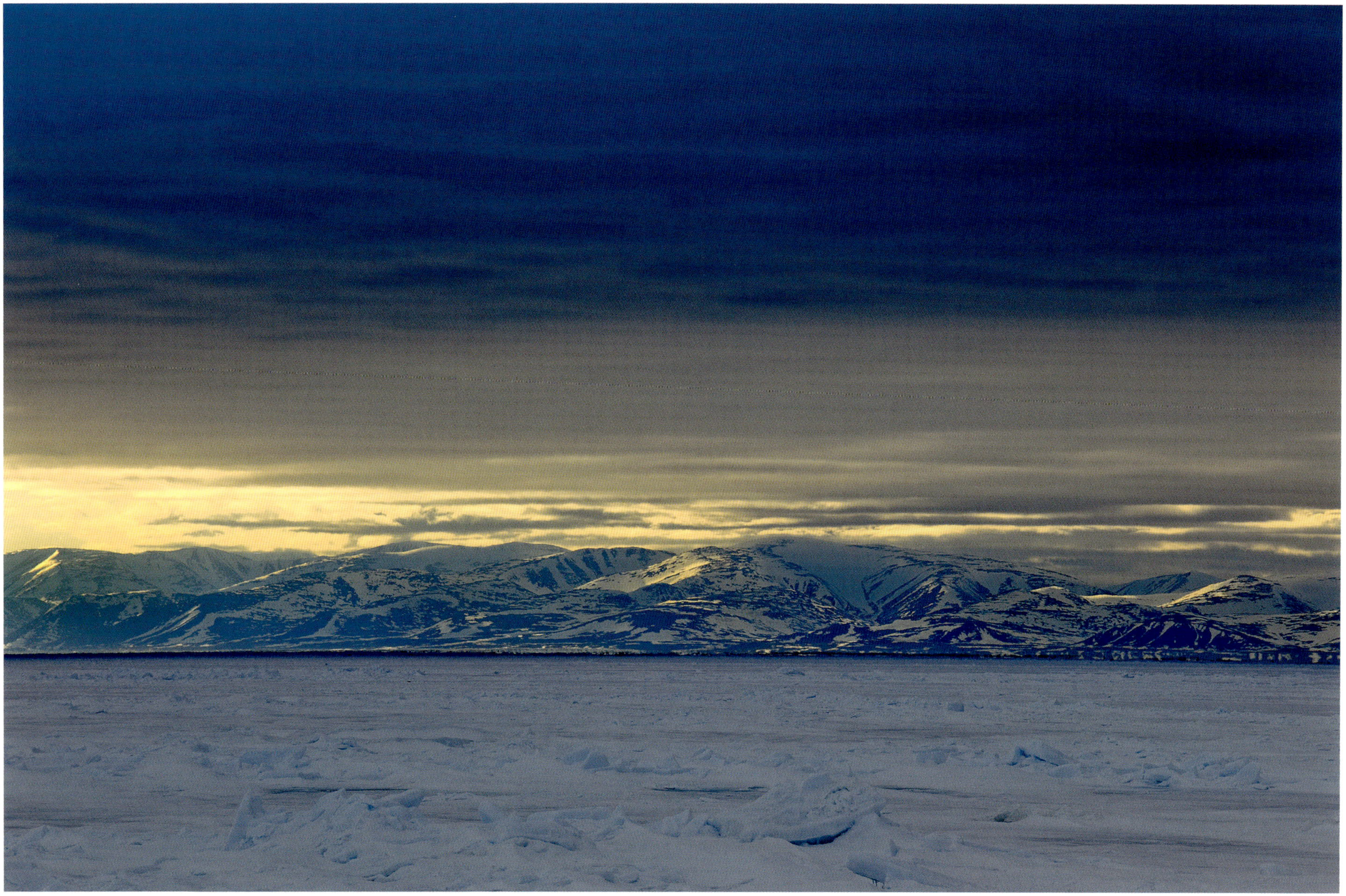

The weather looks as though it is about to change. This can happen within a very short time in the high Arctic. One must be prepared year-round for strong snow storms, known as blizzards, which regularly reach speeds of over 60 kilometres an hour.

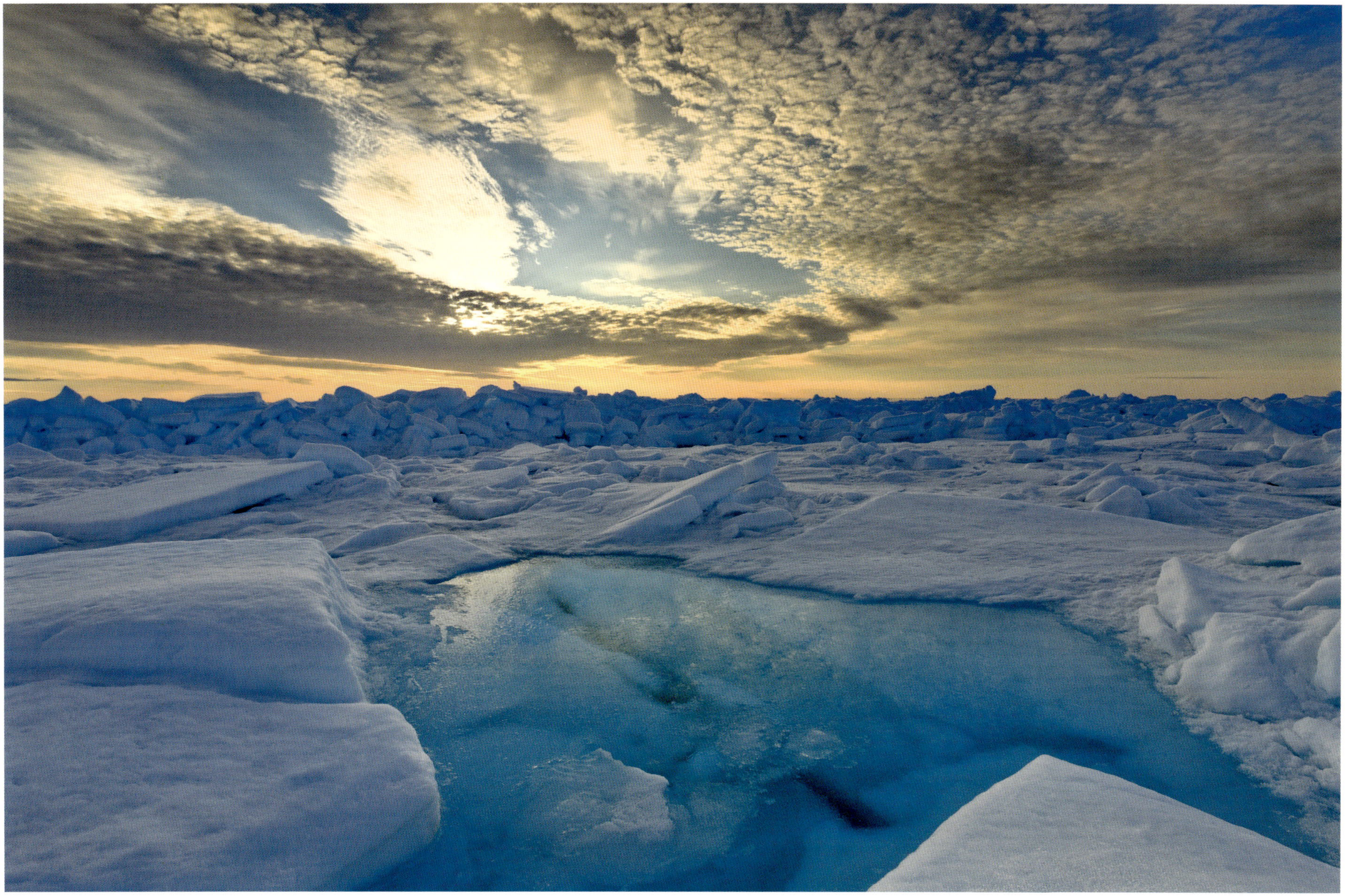

The pack ice, up to three and a half metres thick, begins to melt in mid June in the high Arctic. The big meltwater pools are an unmistakable sign that the Arctic's short summer is just around the corner.

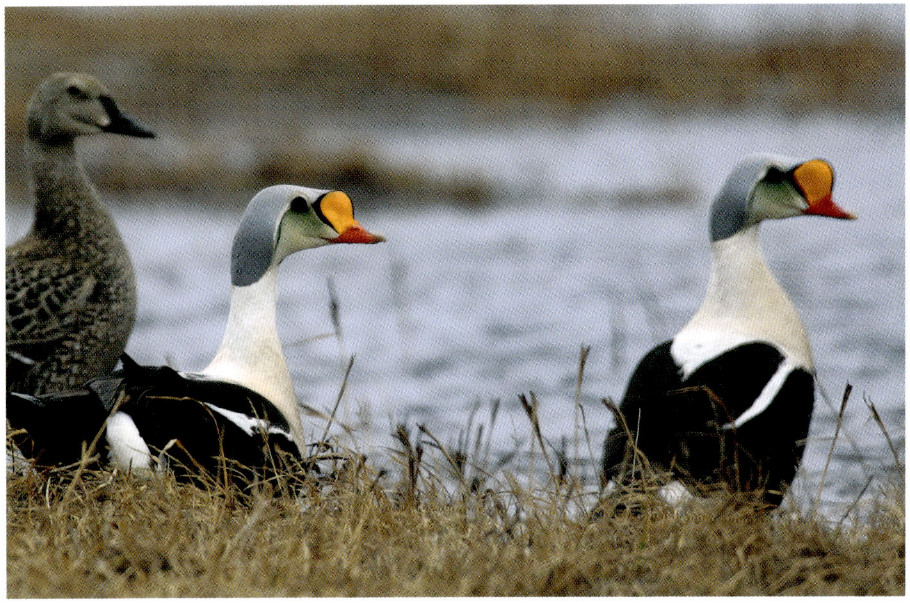

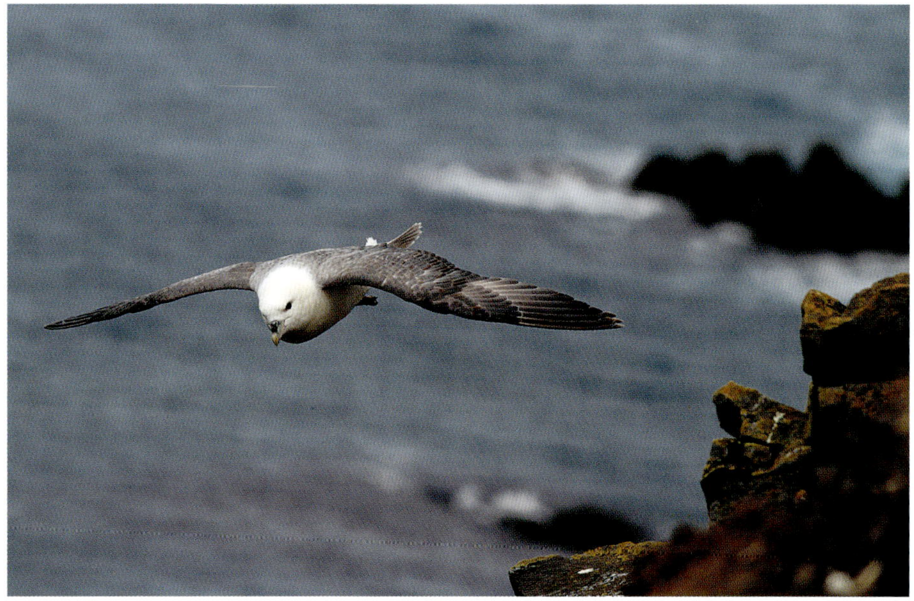

The king eider (left) is considered by many to be among the most beautiful duck species. The birds spend up to ten months a year at sea. They can dive for up to two minutes and plummet to depths of 15 metres in search of crabs and insect larvae in the Arctic Ocean. Barrow, northern Alaska.
The northern fulmar (right) is to be found in the north of the Atlantic and Pacific oceans. It nests on rock islands and along cliff lines. Southwestern Alaska.

Pages 36/37: autumn is the most colourful season in the far north. In late August, the tundra becomes a sea of many hues of yellow, golden and reddish colours. Ogilvie Mountains, Yukon Territory, northern Canada.

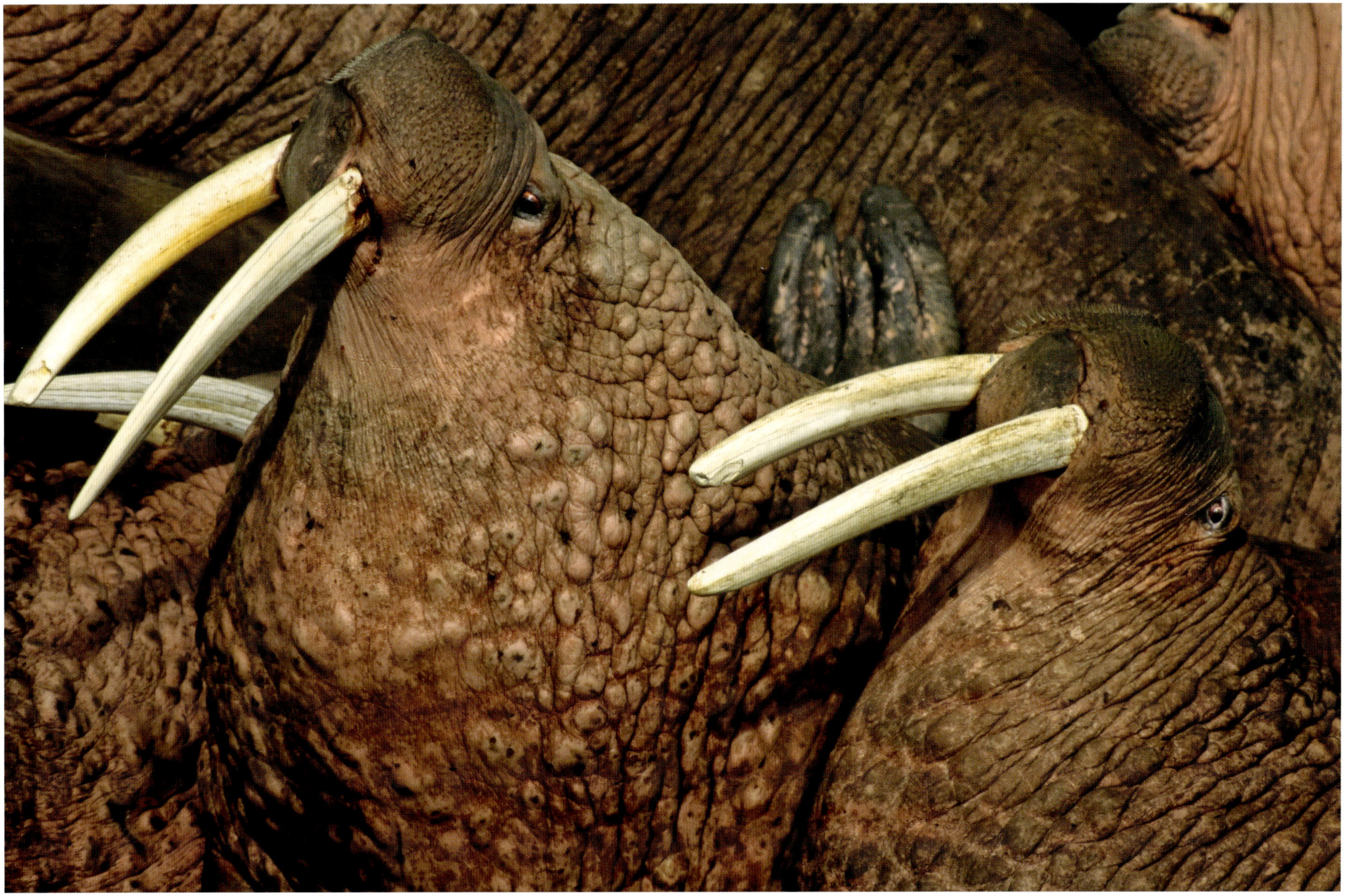

Walruses are the largest seal species. A fully grown male can be up to four metres long and weigh as much as 1,200 kilograms. They are elegant swimmers all the same, and exceptional divers. Their tusks have a variety of functions: they help the walrus to climb out of the water; to pull itself forward on land; to make breathing holes; defend itself against polar bears; they also serve as a status symbol and even as a head rest.

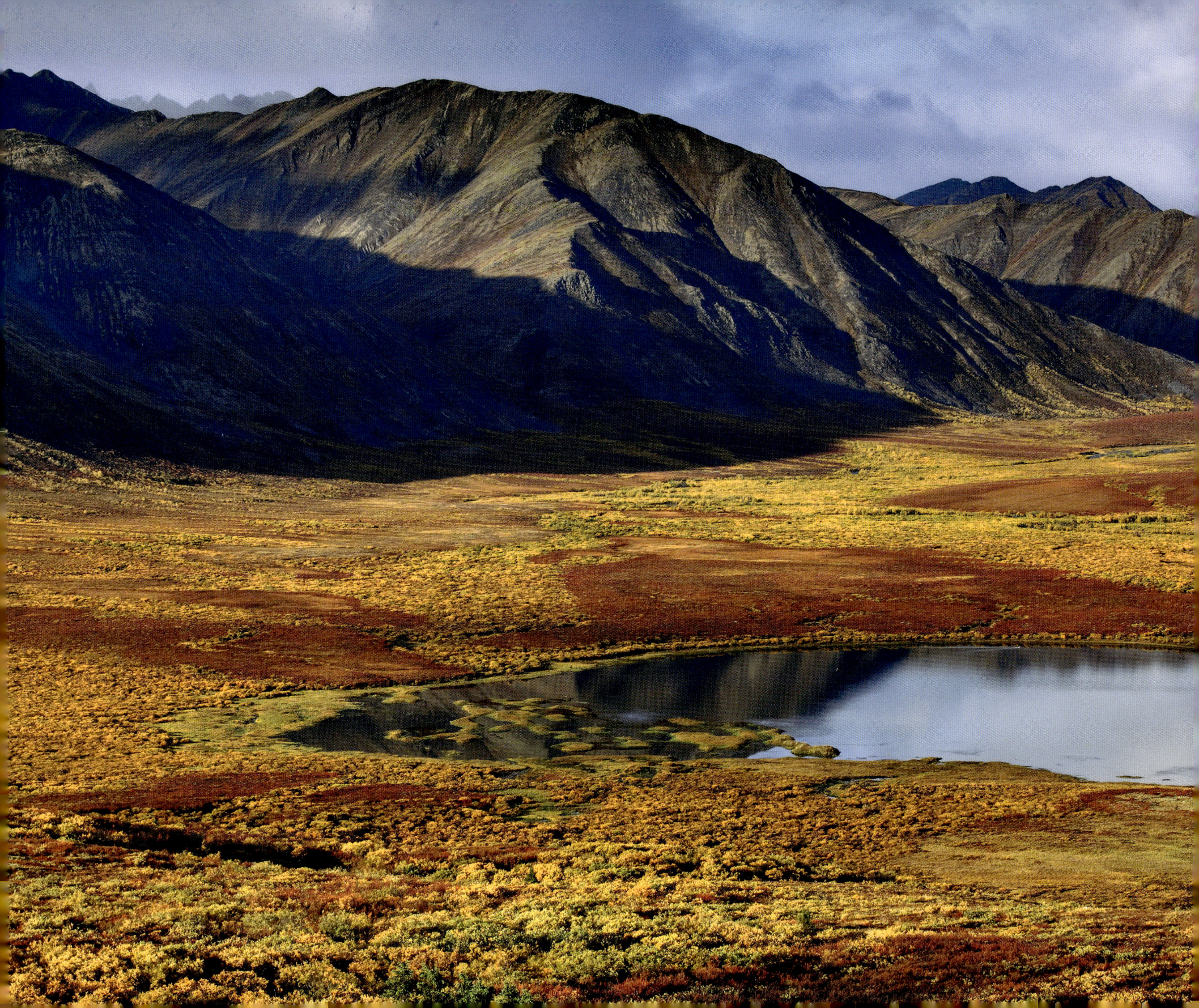

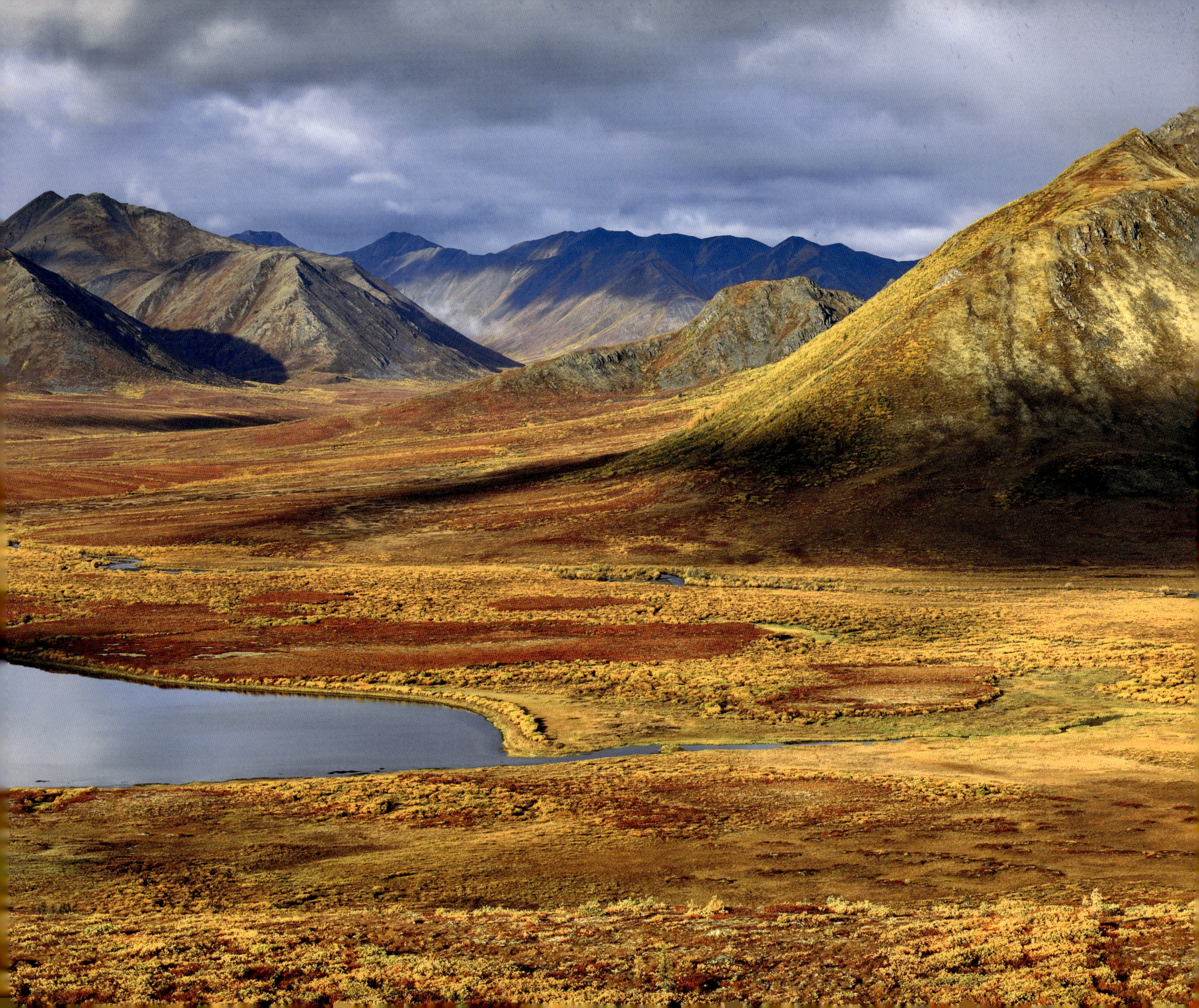

Caribous belonging to the famous Porcupine caribou herd. Caribous belong to the deer family. In contrast to most other deer species, however, both the male and the female have antlers. Their European relatives, reindeer, are considerably smaller. The Porcupine herd consists of more than 120,000 animals and is named after the Porcupine River. This river is more than 700 kilometres long and snakes through the Canadian Yukon Territory before flowing into the Yukon River at Fort Yukon (Alaska). The members of the Porcupine herd migrate an incredible 2,500 kilometres between their winter range in the Canadian Yukon Territory and their summer grazing areas by the Arctic Ocean in northern Alaska. This is one of the longest migration routes on earth performed by land mammals.

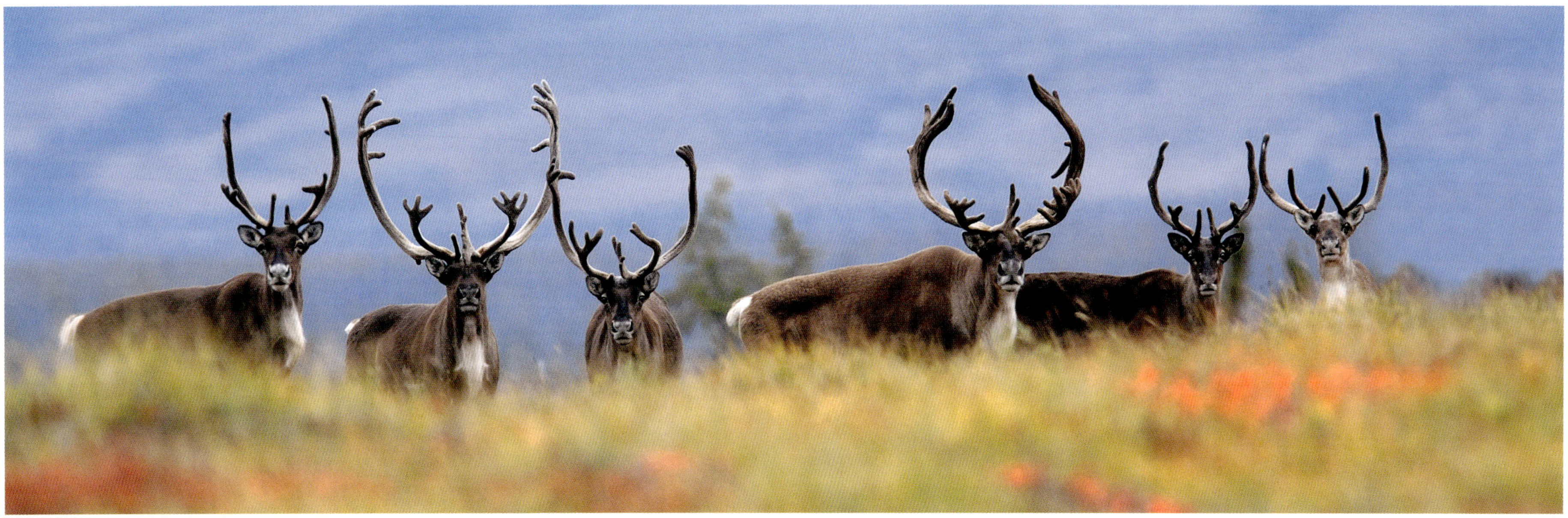

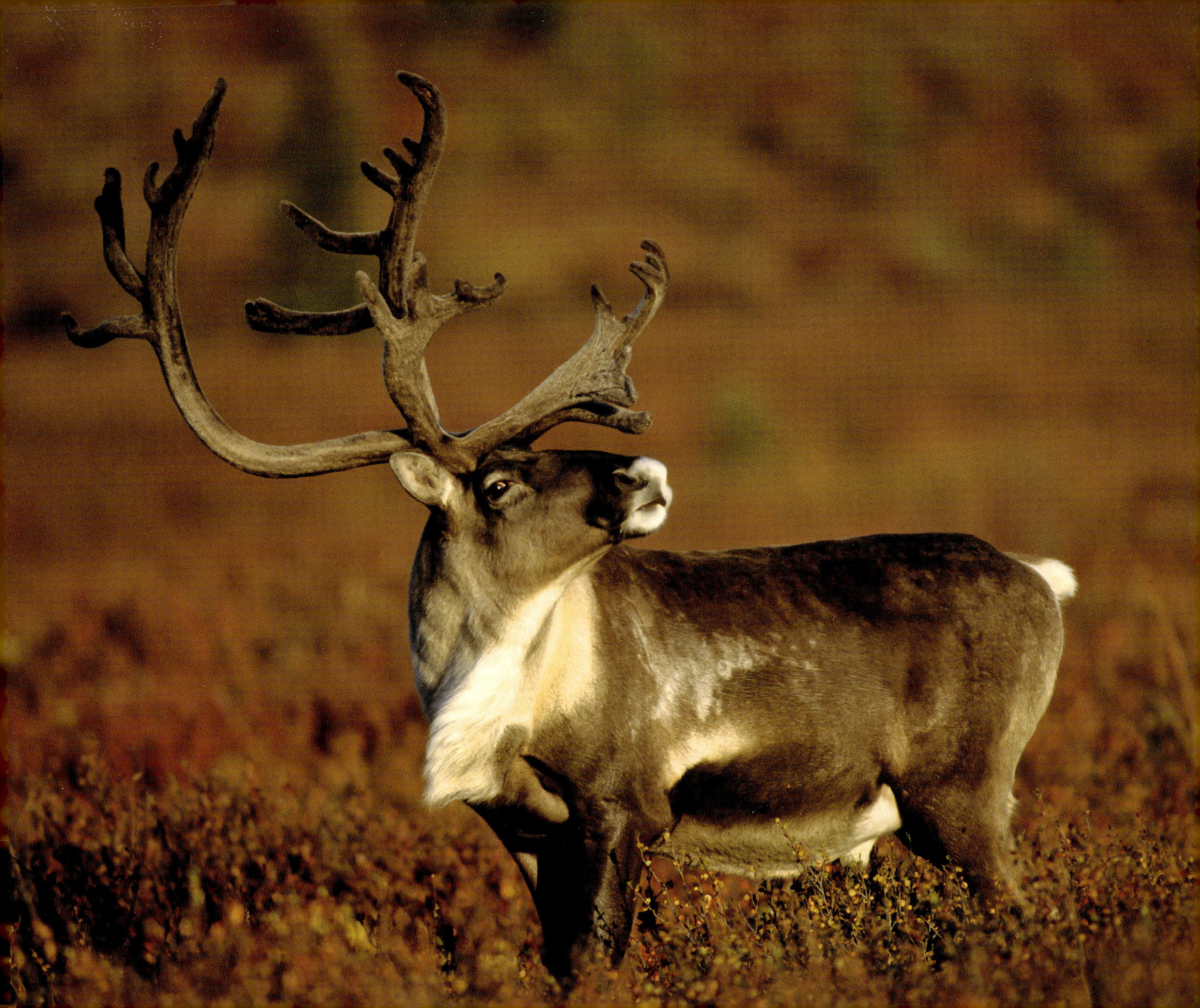

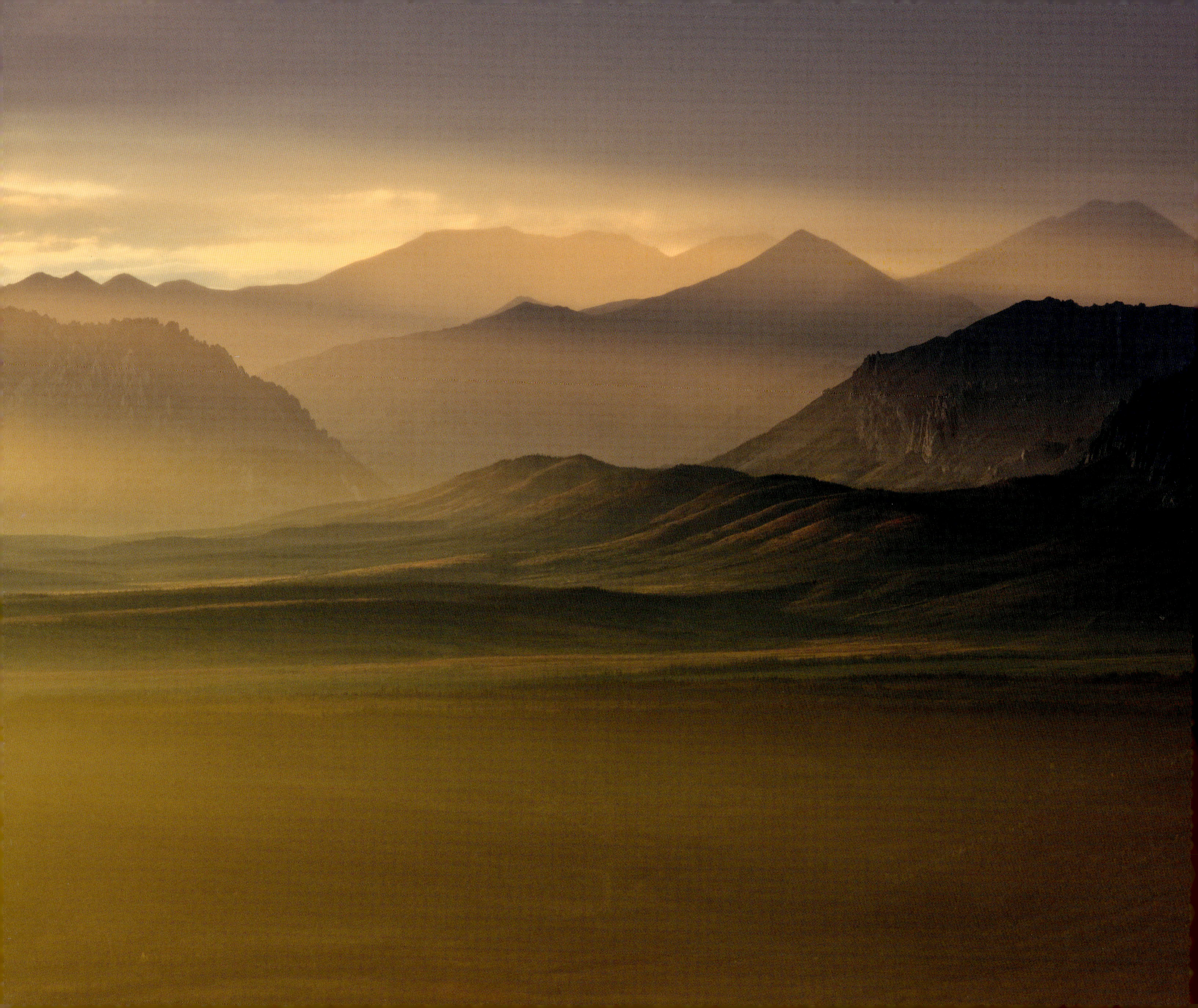

Following a cold September night, swathes of fog waft across the valleys of the Ogilvie Mountains in the Canadian Yukon Territory.

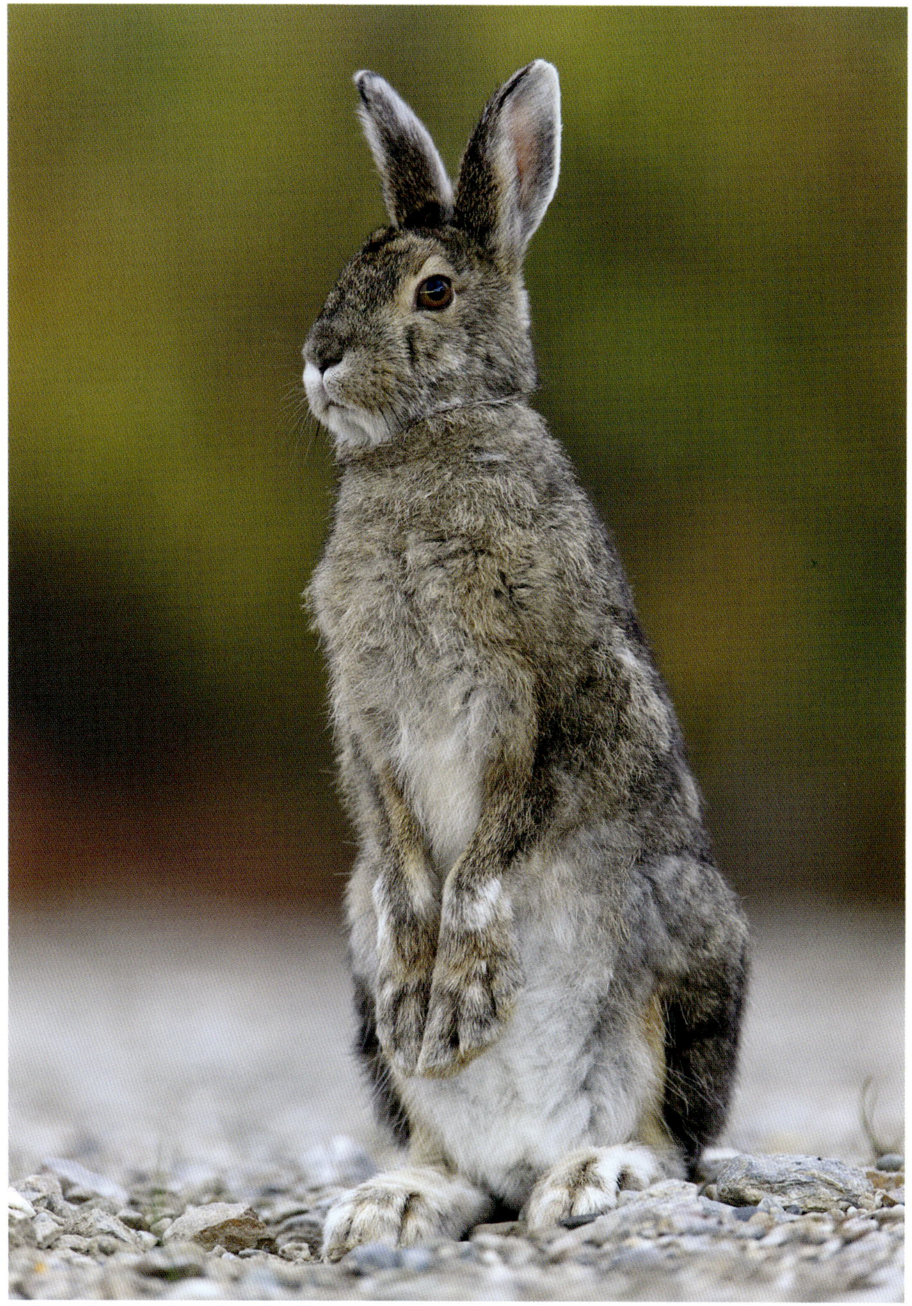

The snowshoe hare has a brown-grey coat during the summer months. It changes colour in the winter (in order to be well camouflaged) to become as white as snow. Brooks Range, northern Alaska.

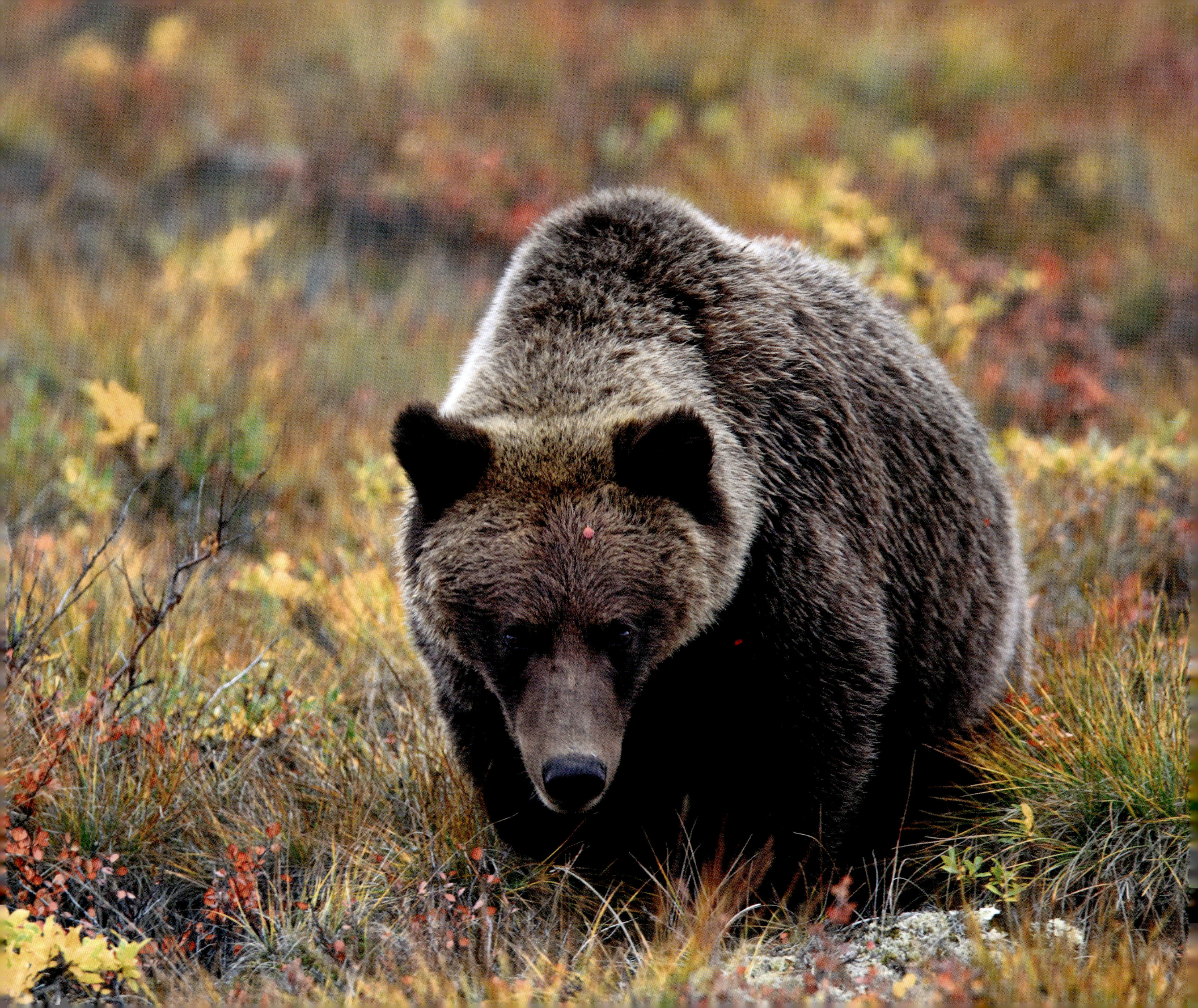

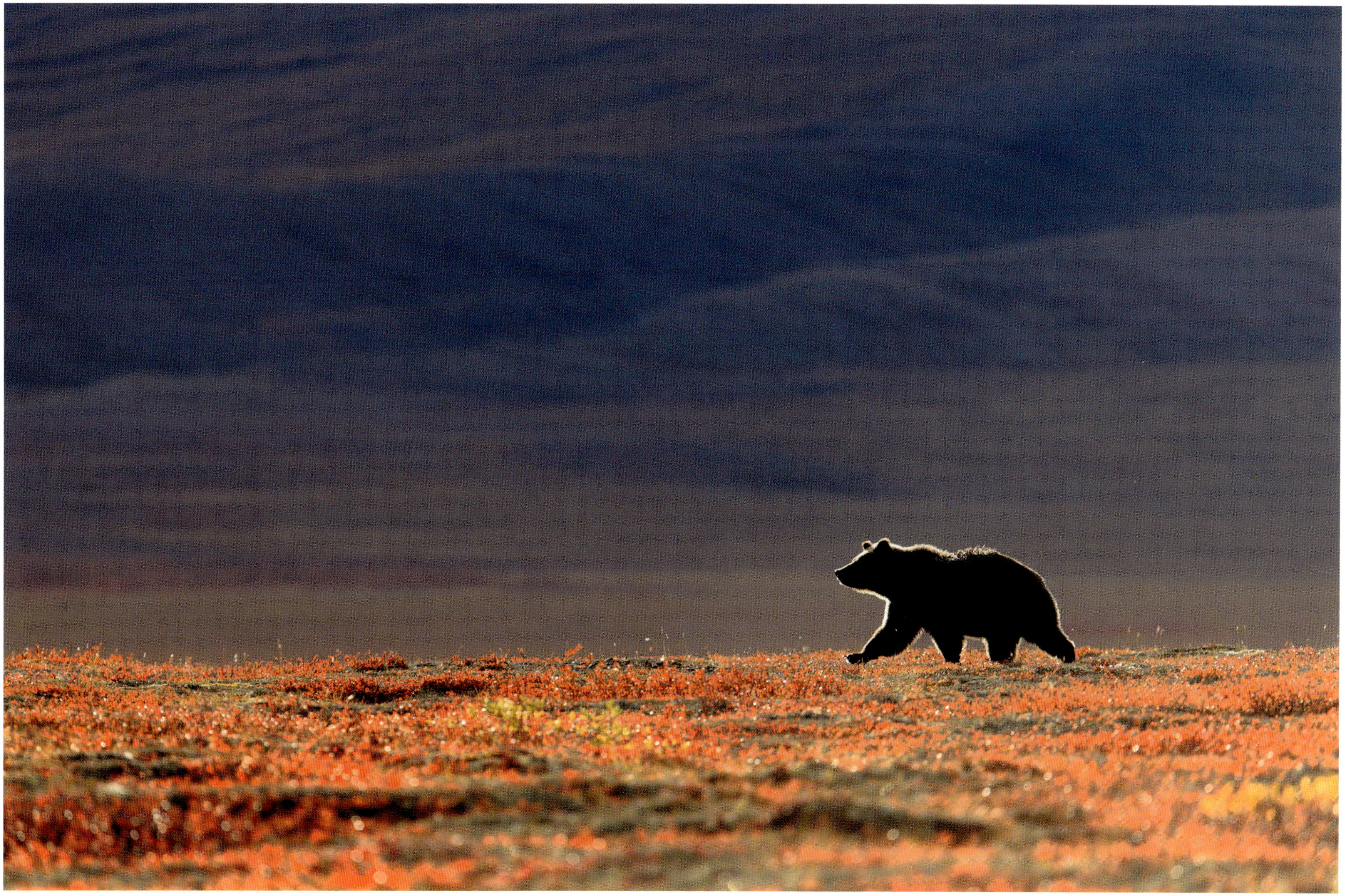

A grizzly bear in the Richardson Mountains, Northwest Territories, northern Canada. The habitat of the North American brown bear extends far beyond the polar circle. During the summer months, meetings between the roughly equal-sized grizzly and polar bears in the treeless tundra areas are therefore not unusual, and tend to be harmless.

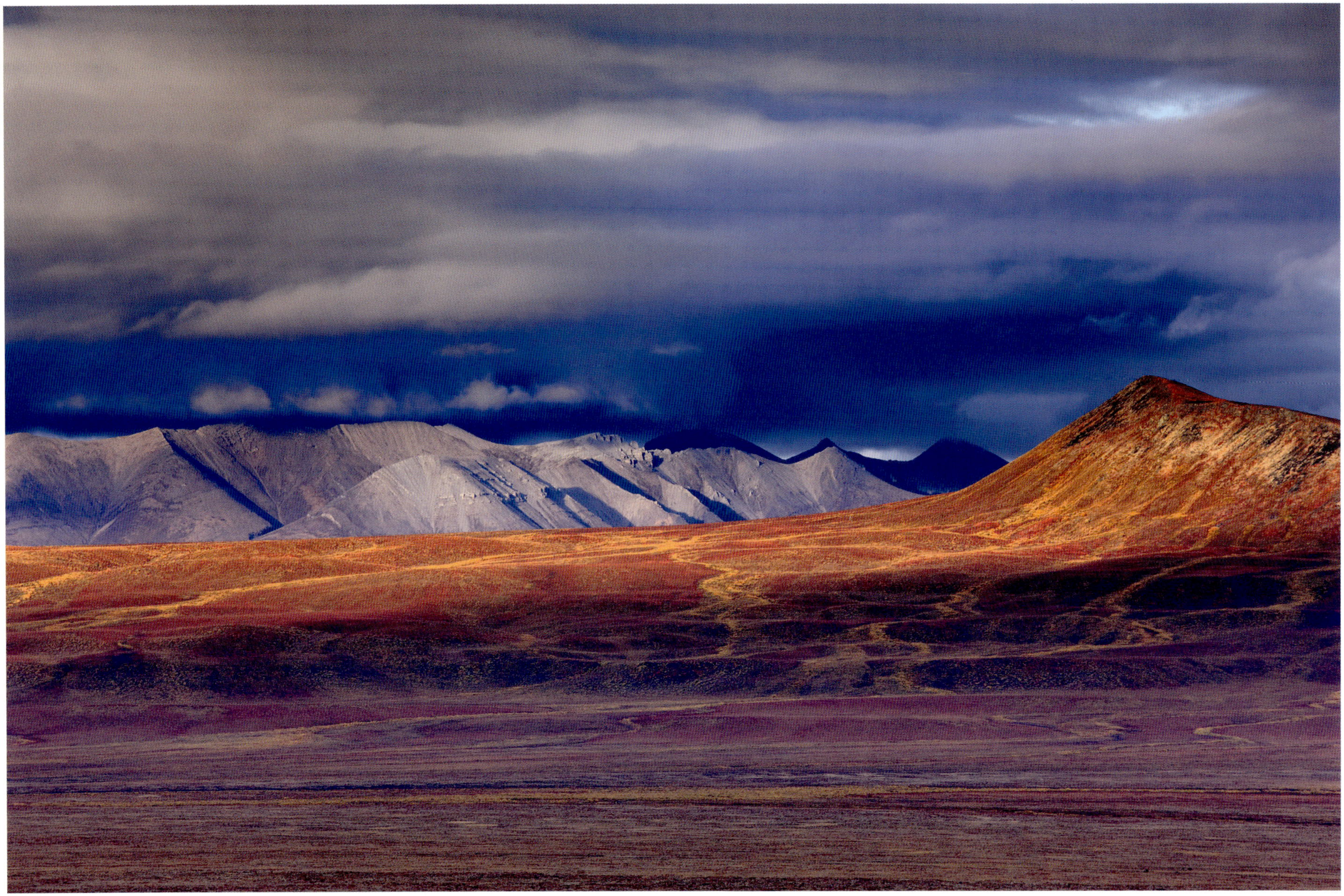

The autumn in the far north often lasts just two weeks. Nature puts on a fantastic display of colours one last time before the arrival of winter in the Richardson Mountains, Northwest Territories and in the Ogilvie Mountains, Yukon Territory, northern Canada.

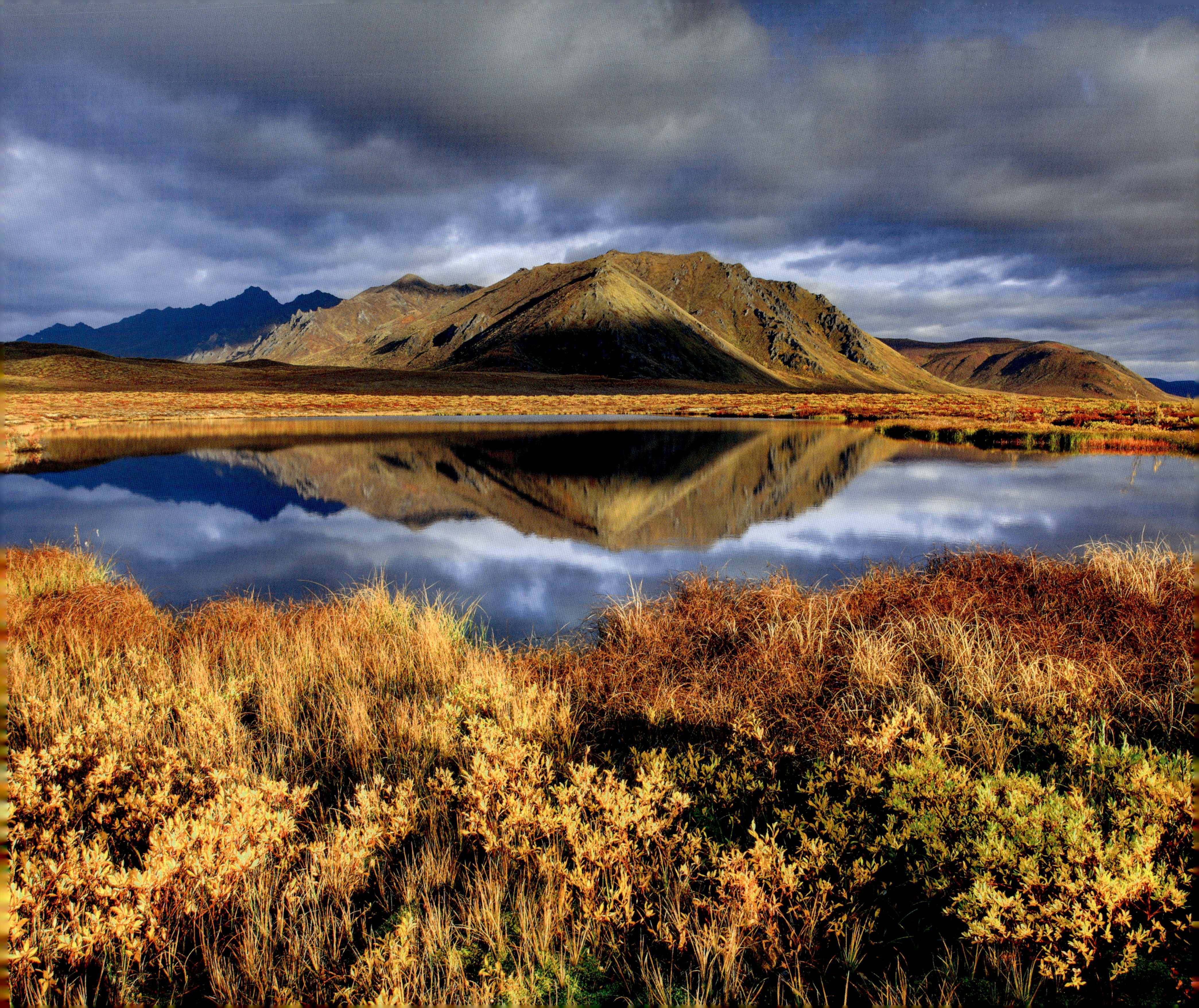

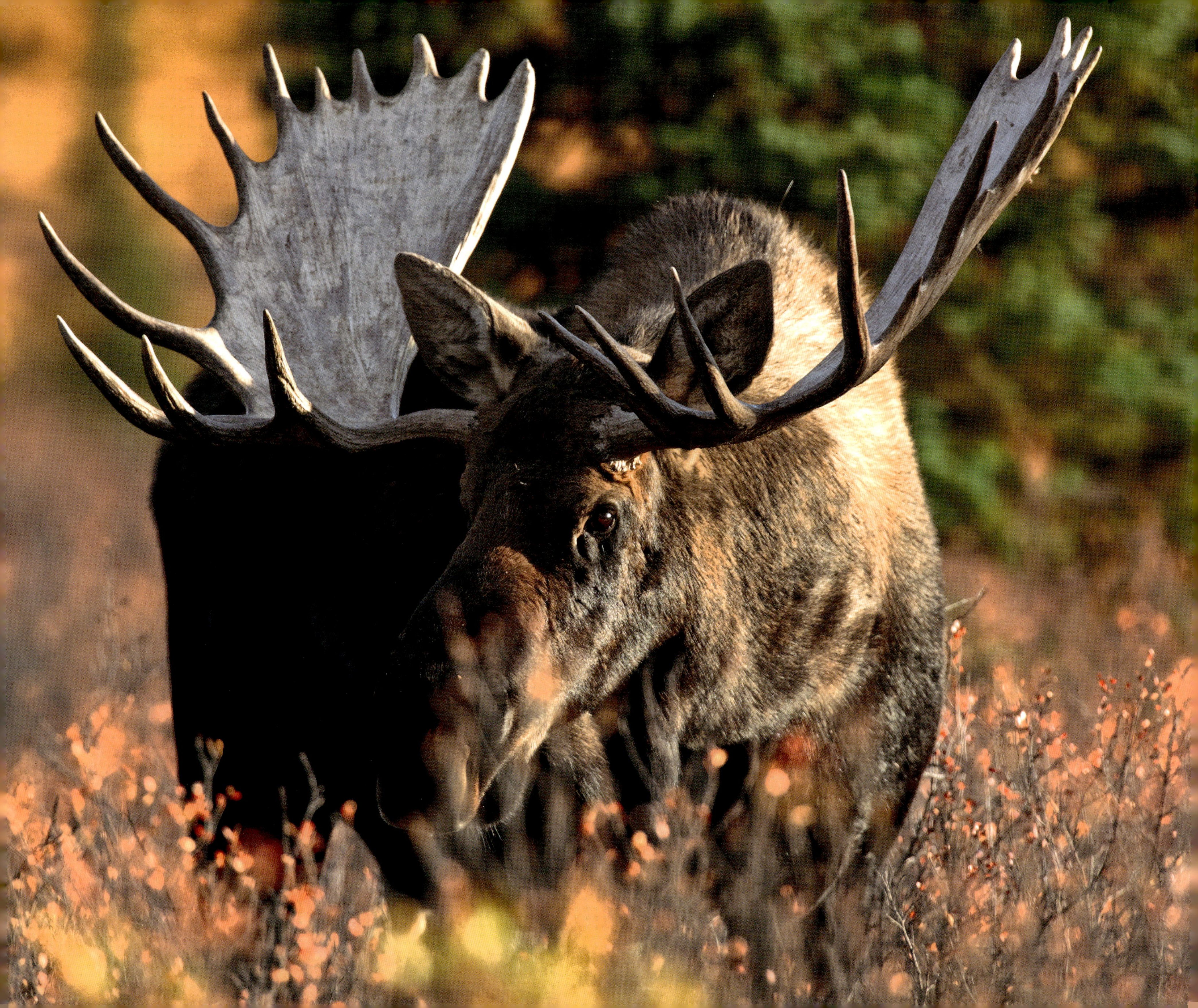

The largest elks in the world live in Alaska. They are also North America's largest wild animals. These giants' antlers can have a span of almost two metres and they can weigh well over 20 kilograms. The animals themselves can weigh as much as 1,000 kilograms. Denali National Park, Alaska.

The Arctic ground squirrel (left) brings together large supplies of seeds, grains, nuts and roots, which are stored underground for its eight-month-long hibernation. Richardson Mountains, Northwest Territories, northern Canada.
Dall Sheep (right), such as this one in the Brooks Range in northern Alaska, live only in the mountainous regions of Alaska and of northwestern Canada.

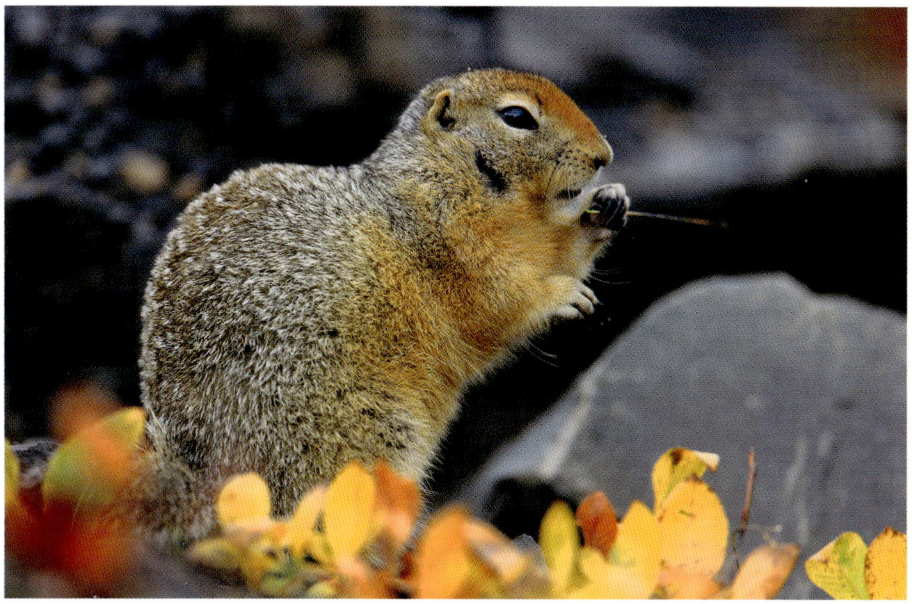

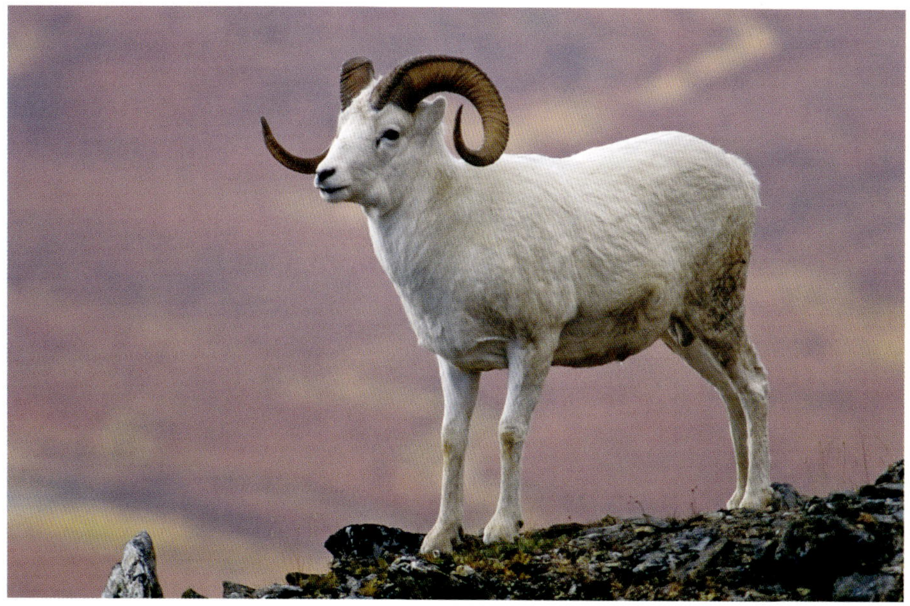

Left: Arctic fox with its winter fur. Cape Churchill, Hudson Bay, Canada. Centre: Although the red fox tends to live in more moderate climes, it is also to be found in the Arctic regions. Richardson Mountains, Northwest Territories, northern Canada. Right: A variant of the red fox, the so-called cross fox, has a cross-shaped dark marking on its back. Northwest Territories, northern Canada.

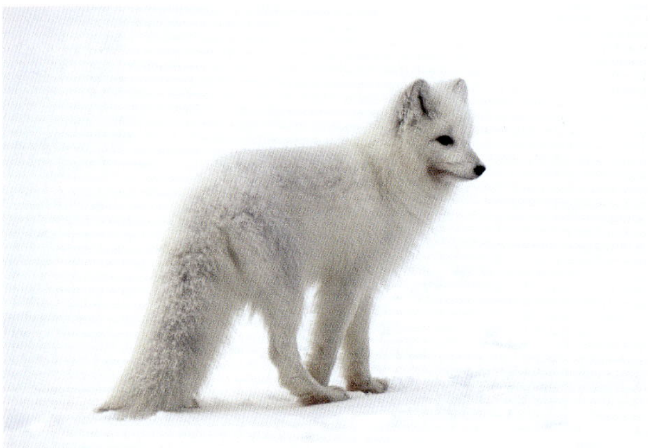

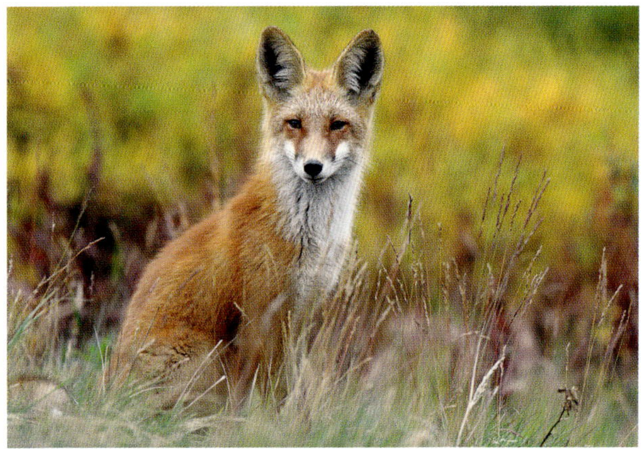

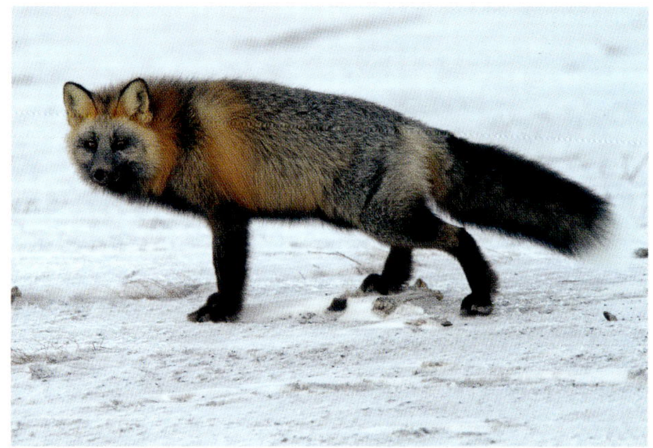

In contrast to the red fox, the considerably smaller Arctic fox changes colour in the winter. Its fur is greyish during the summer, and becomes as white as snow in the winter. The scientific name means "rabbit-footed fox" because the Arctic fox's paws are covered with dense fur, as are those of the Arctic hare. Kaktovik, Arctic National Wildlife Refuge, northern Alaska.

Pages 50/51: A polar bear mother with her approximately six-month-old cub. Kaktovik, Arctic National Wildlife Refuge, northern Alaska.

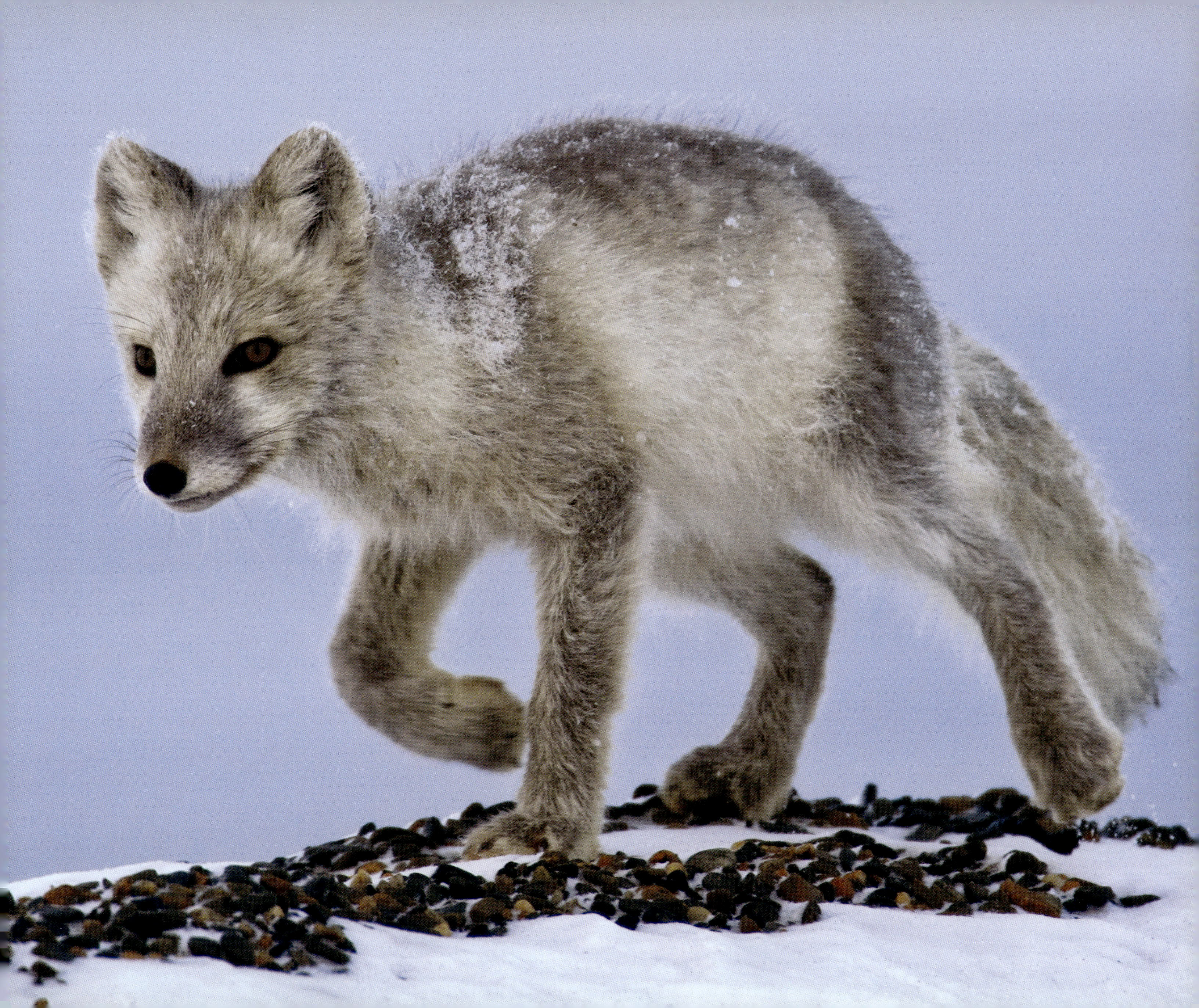

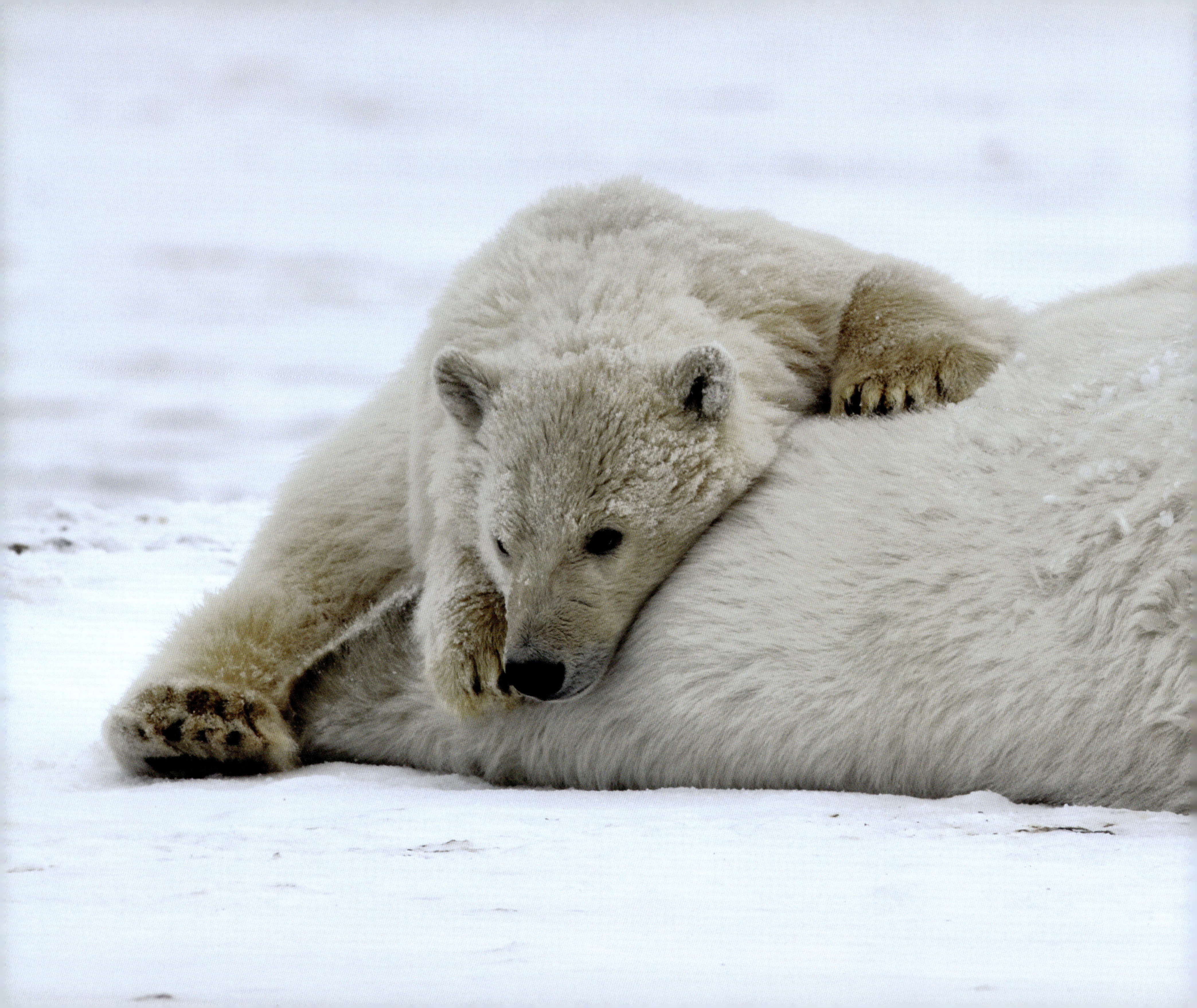

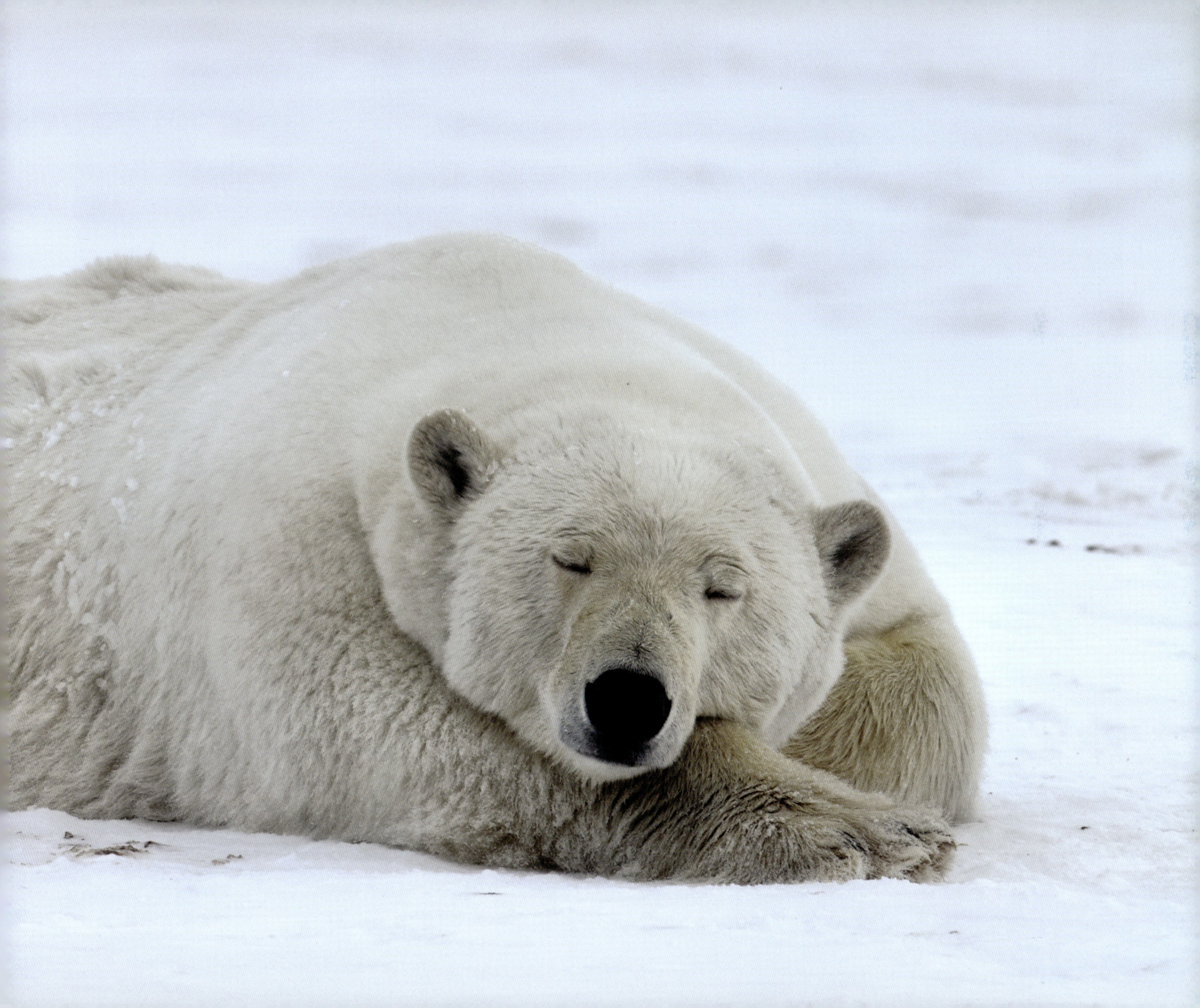

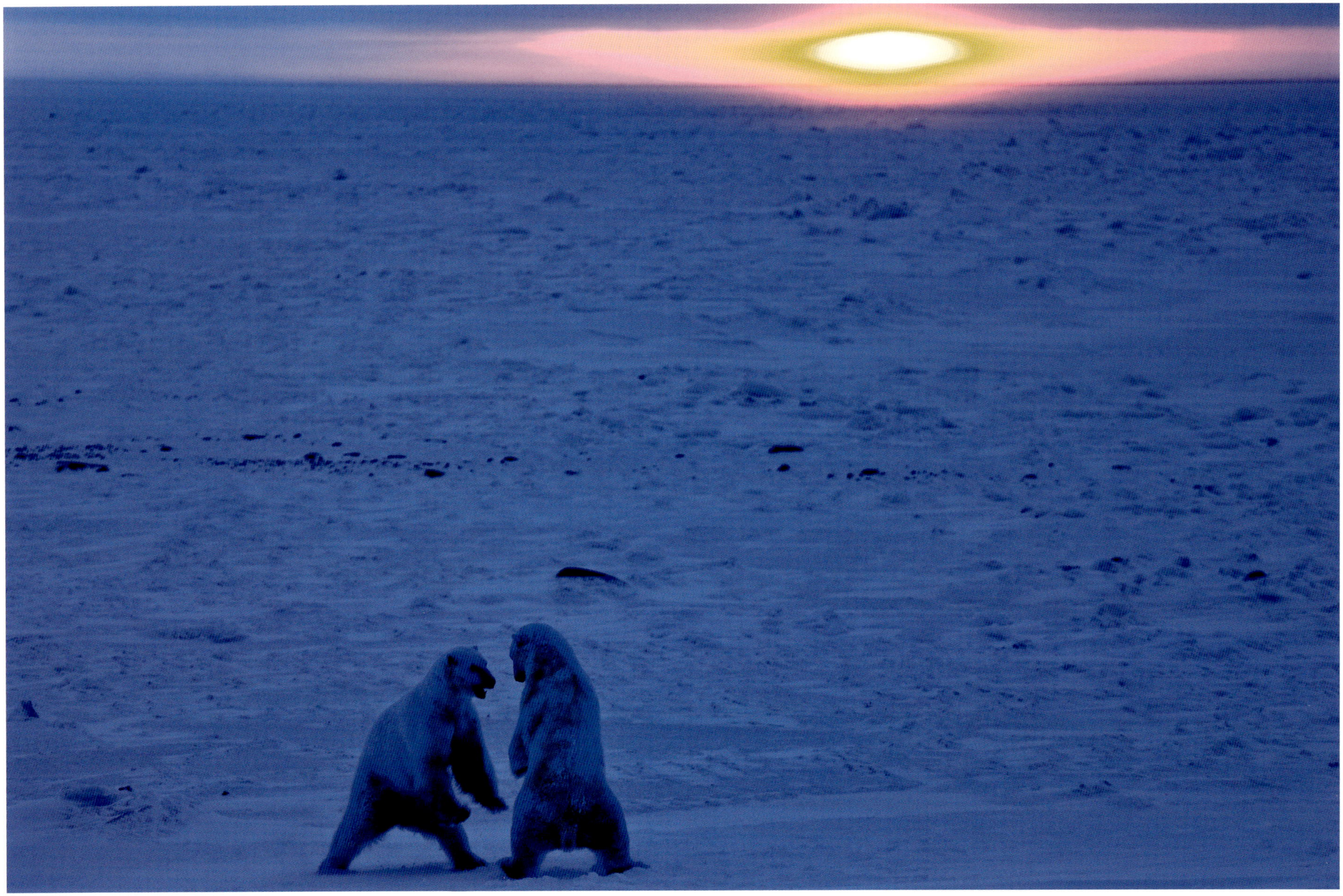

The famished bears wait longingly for pack ice to form on Hudson Bay. They have gone hungry for several months and now want to get out onto the pack ice to hunt their favourite prey: seals. The bears while away the wait with largely harmless competitive fights, which often last just a few seconds. Cape Churchill, Hudson Bay, Canada.

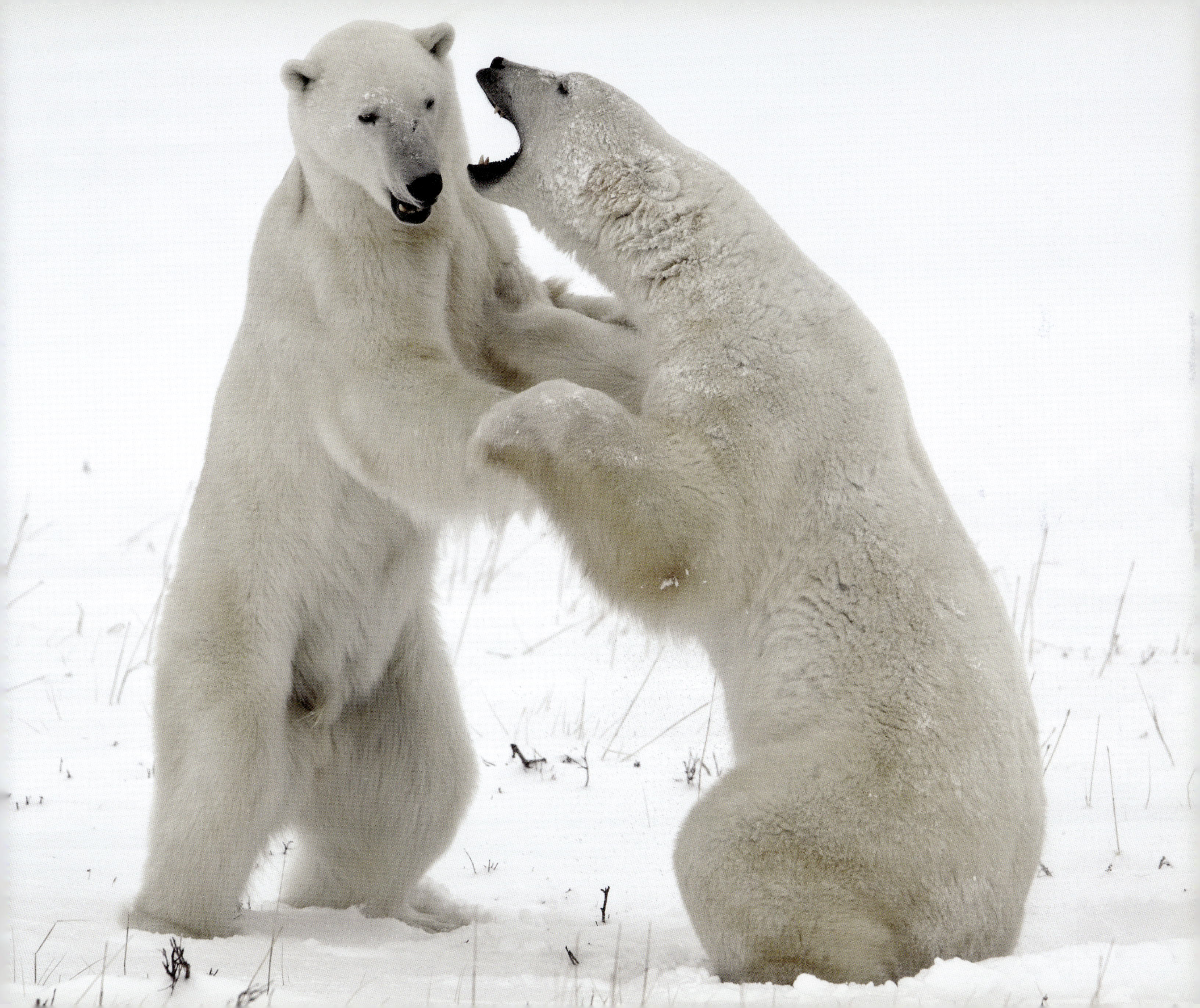

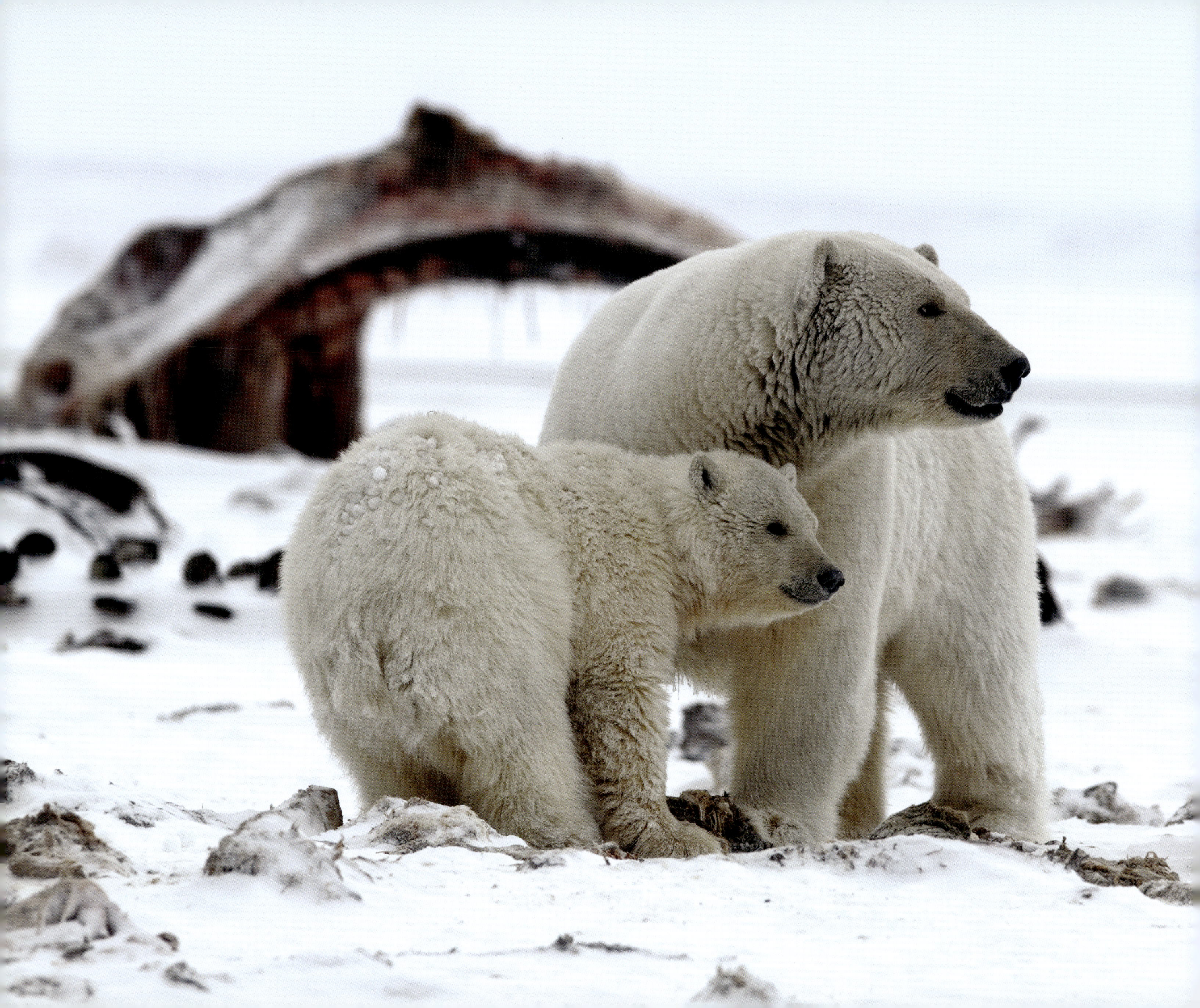

"I'm sitting in the car with my guide Robert Thompson. We are right by the Arctic Ocean, not far from the small Inuit village of Kaktovik in northern Alaska. A large polar bear mother lies about 15 metres away. She is completely relaxed as she watches her two cubs play around the remains of a bowhead whale killed by the Inuit. Robert tells me this polar bear mother's interesting story. She broke her foot last autumn and was visibly suffering a great deal. The Inuit began to wonder whether it would be better to shoot the animal, but didn't do it. Half a year later, in the spring, the polar bear mother reappeared with two perfectly healthy, exceedingly lively cubs. She had not only recovered quite well from the injury, but had even managed to give birth to two young polar bears, and to shepherd them through the first difficult months of life. I was fortunate enough to be able to observe the mother with her two cubs up close for ten days. The little family came to the whale bones every day to eat their fill."

Bernd Römmelt

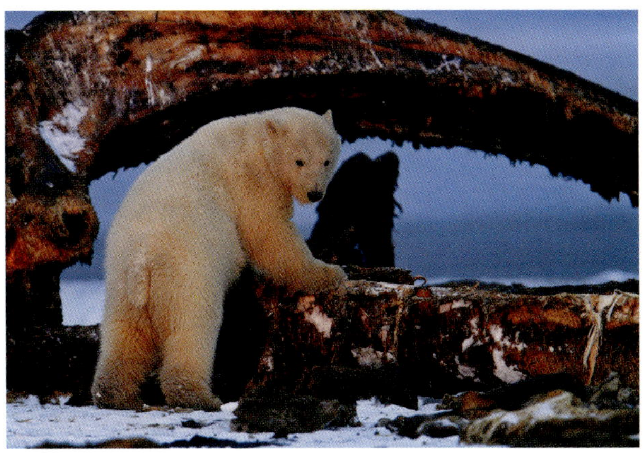

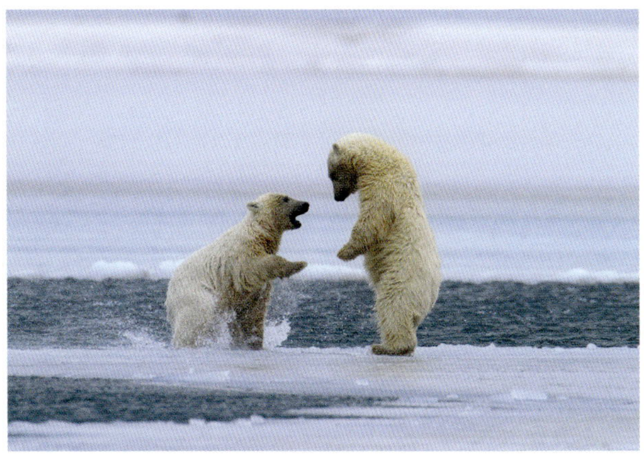

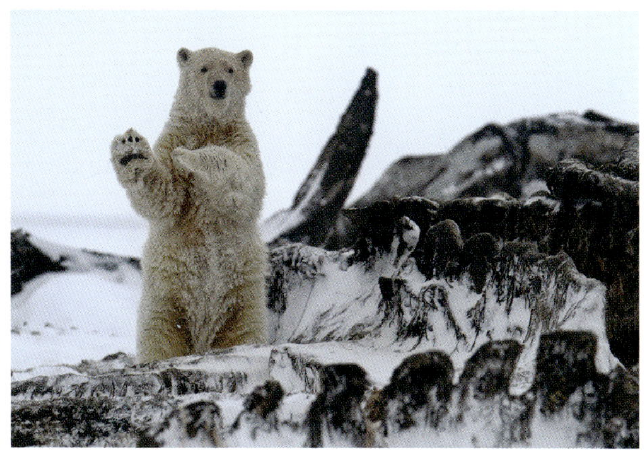

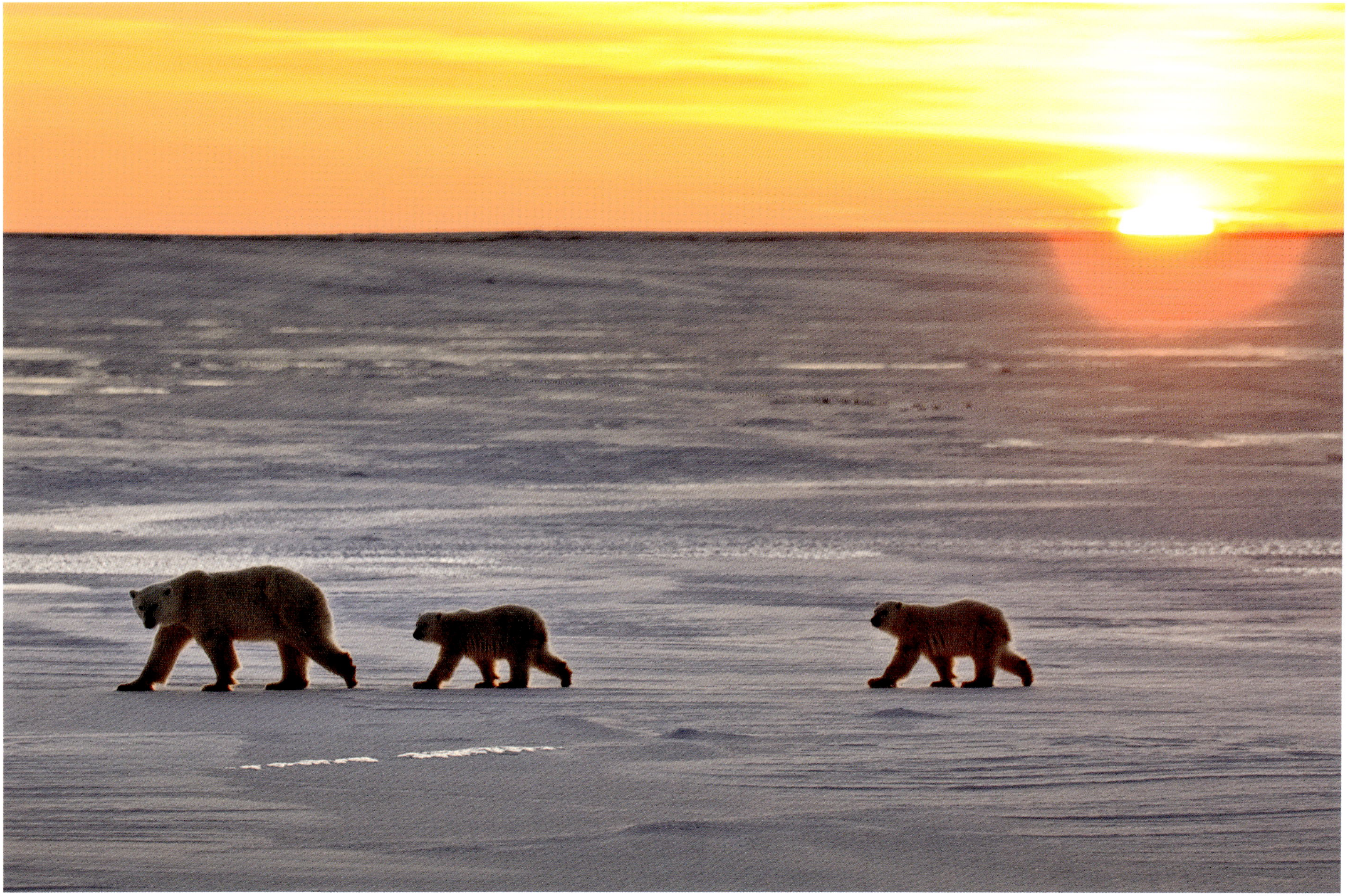

Polar bears are plantigrades. Neither ice nor deep snow poses a problem. The large, furry soles of their feet mean that they hardly slip, even on icy surfaces. Polar bears are excellent swimmers and are sea mammals, like whales, seals, sea otters and sea cows. Cape Churchill, Hudson Bay, northern Canada.

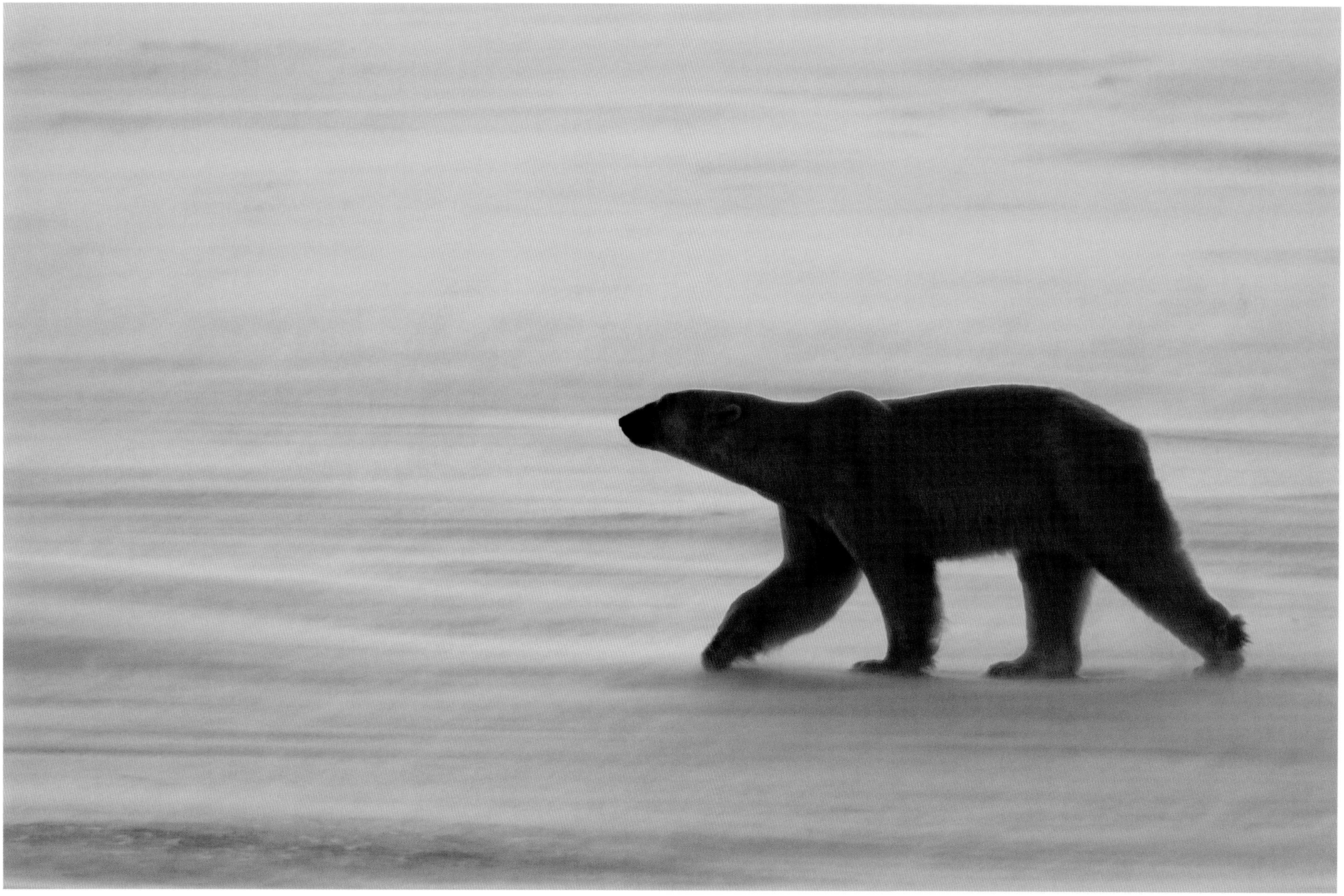

These animals are not just perfectly adapted to life on ice: with their dense, water-repellent fur and paddle-shaped, webbed front paws, they are fast swimmers. This allows them to cover distances far in excess of 100 kilometres by swimming. Cape Churchill, Hudson Bay, northern Canada.

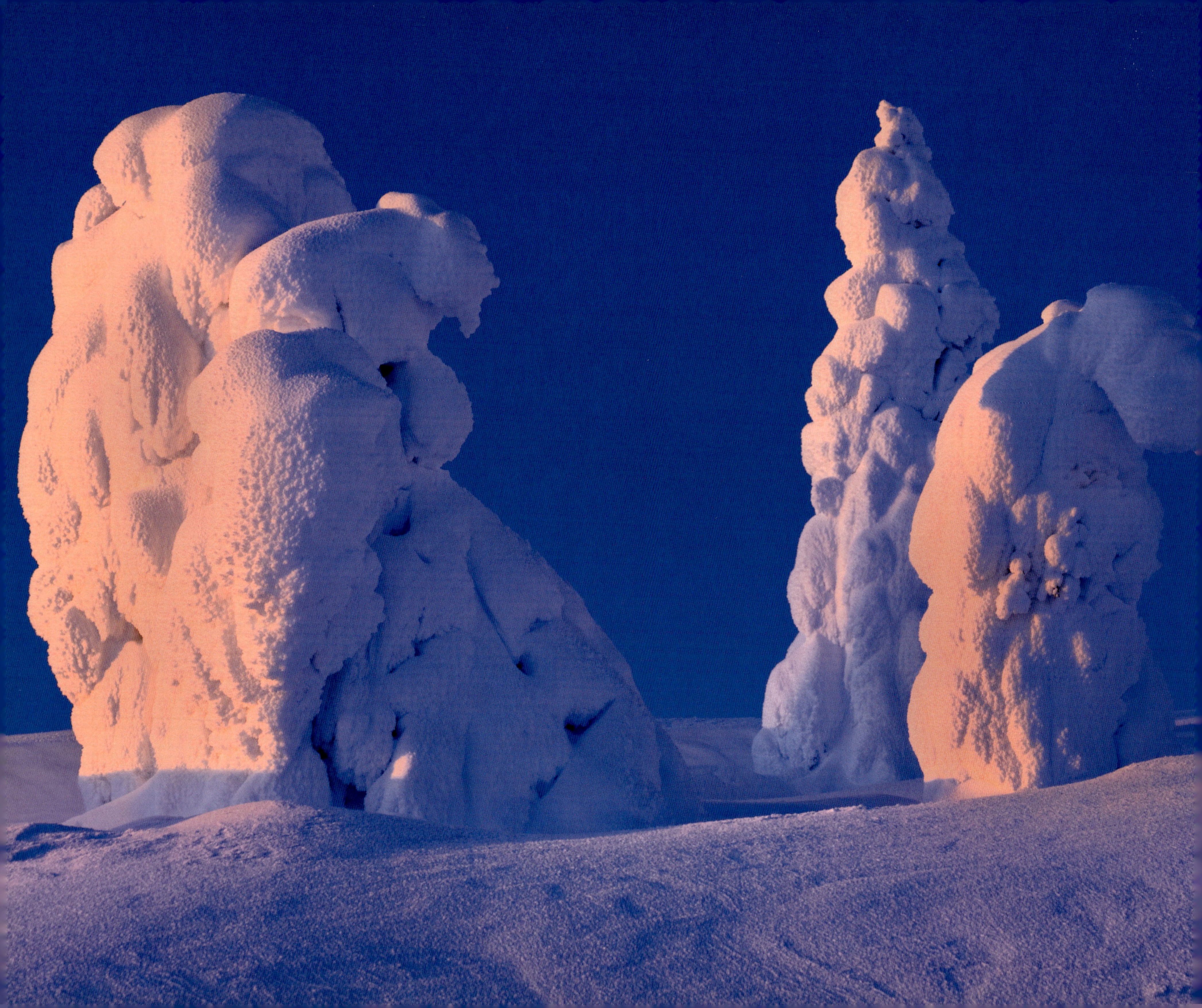

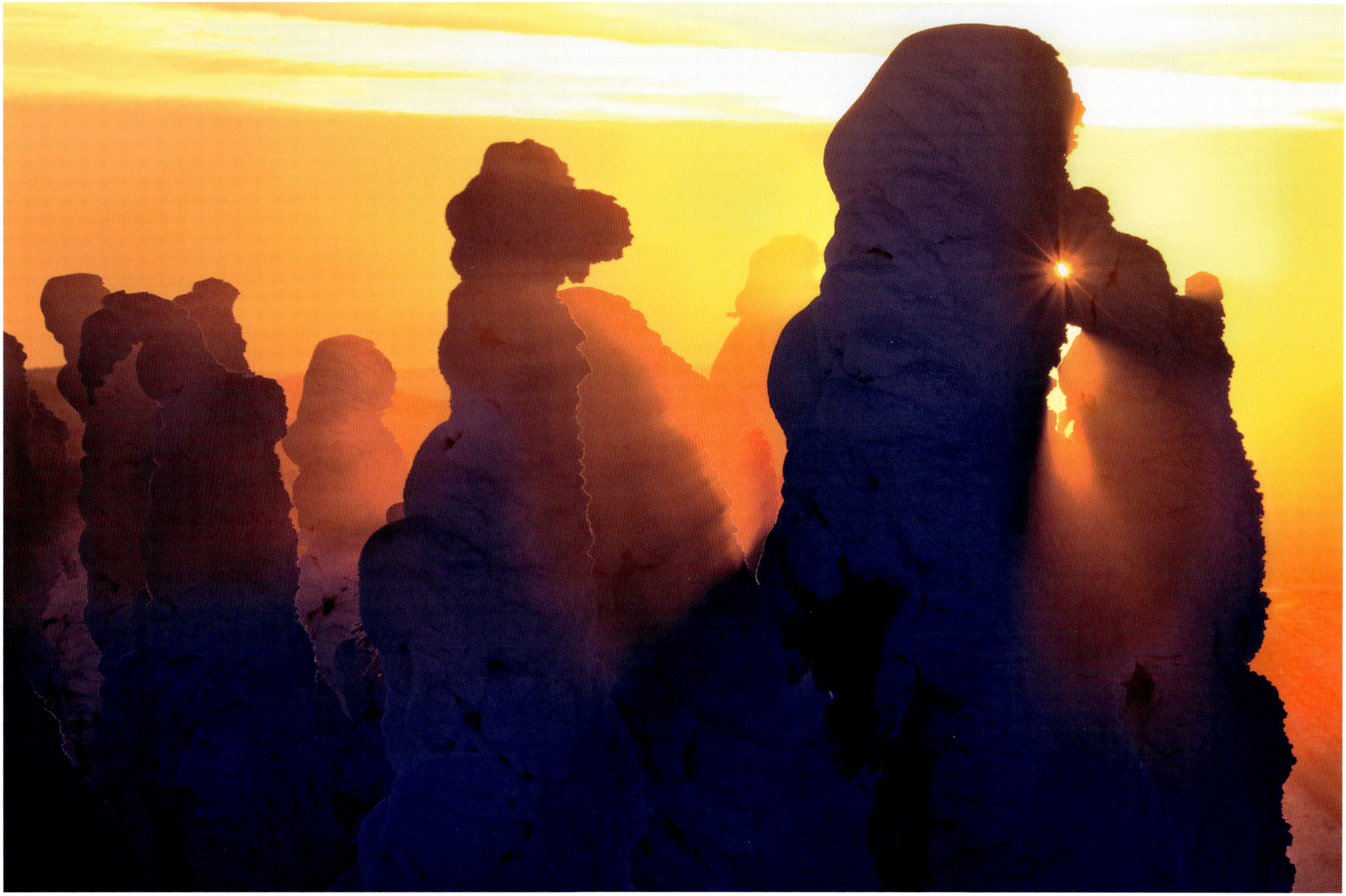

Damp air, strong winds and heavy snowfall have covered the trees in a thick coat of ice and snow, so that they resemble sculptures dipped in icing. Yukon River, northern Alaska.

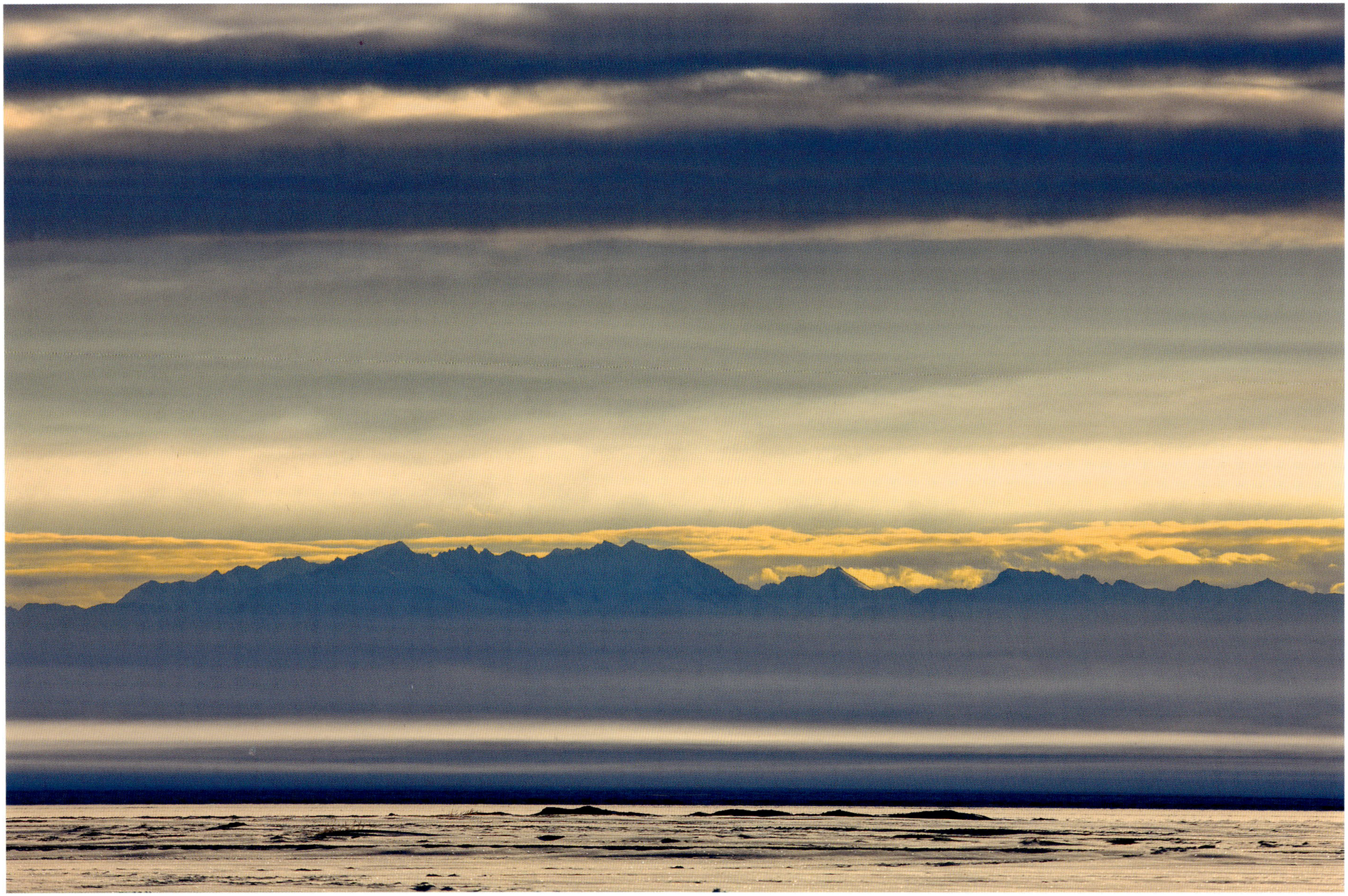

The Brooks Range in northern Alaska is among the wildest mountain ranges in North America. The 1,300-kilometre-long mountain range is located north of the polar circle. In the winter, the temperature can drop to minus 50 degrees.

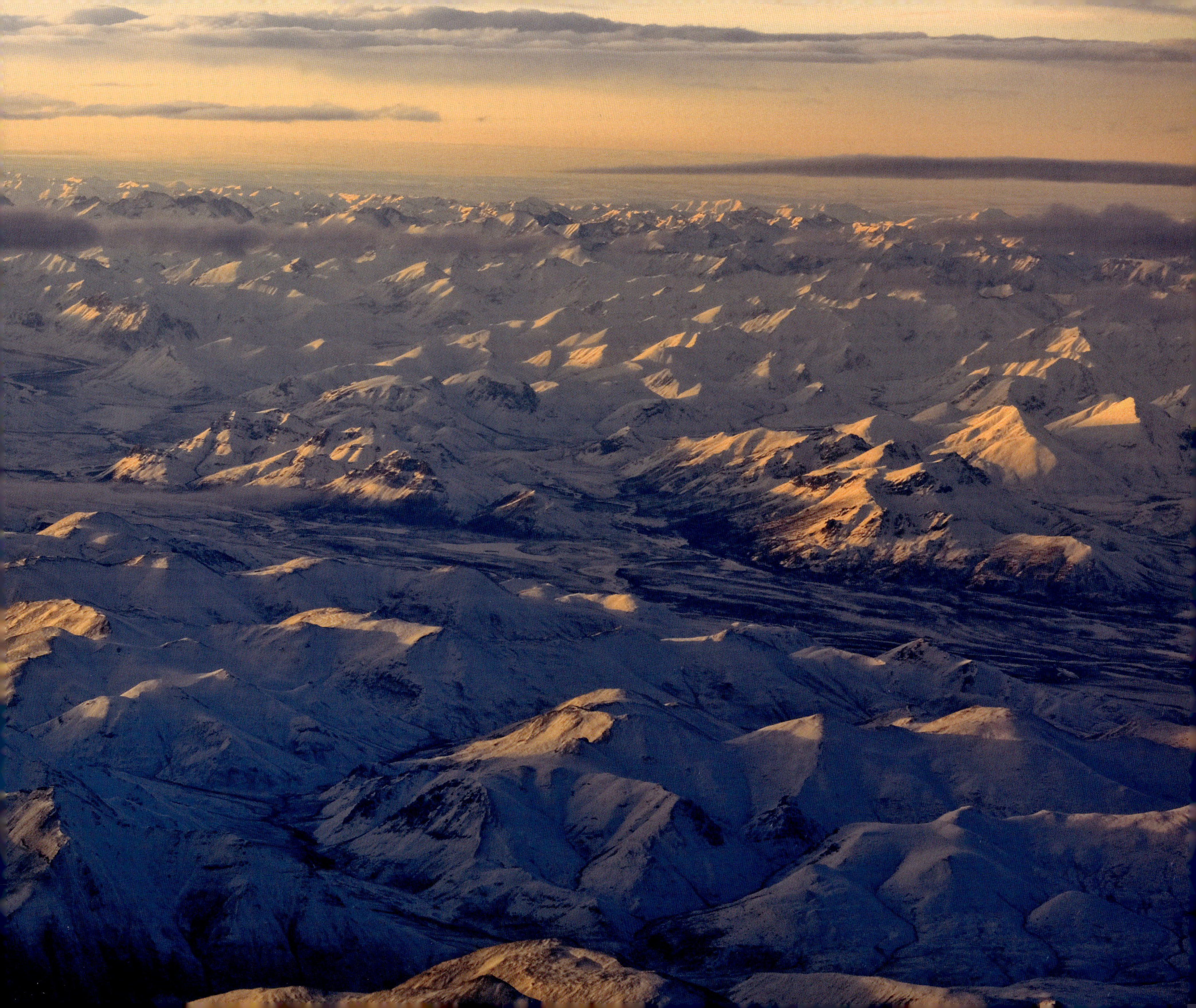

The Inuit call the musk ox "umimmaq": the animal with fur like a beard. That is a good description of these scraggy ungulates, who belong to the goat family despite their large size. It is precisely because of this fur that they are able to survive in the Arctic. Their coat is composed of several layers. Under-neath the scraggy guard hairs, which reach down almost to their hoofs, lies an approximately five-centimetre-thick, very dense layer of wool. These wool hairs are among the finest of natural fibres and are, allowing for their weight, eight times as warm as sheep's wool. This virtually wind and waterproof fur, in combination with a thick layer of fat, allows the musk ox to survive even the lowest temperatures.

Their behaviour when faced with the threat posed by wolves and bears is noteworthy: the older and larger animals form a sort of circular phalanx, facing outwards with their forward-twisted horns. The calves and younger animals are kept in the middle, thereby protected from any attack. In order to see during the long polar night, musk oxen have large pupils and highly sensitive retinas. When the sun appears above the horizon again, they can narrow their pupils to horizontal slits or even close them entirely to prevent snow blindness. North Slope, northern Alaska.

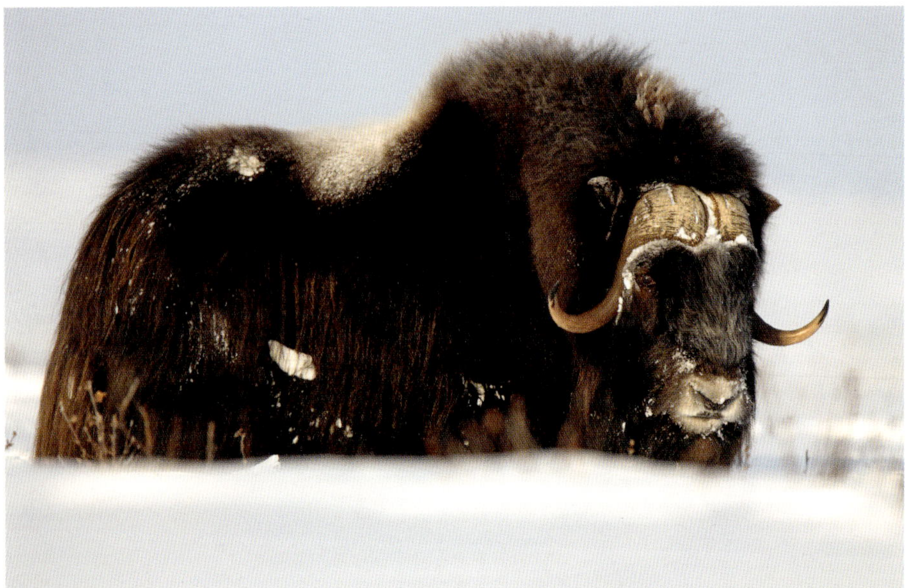

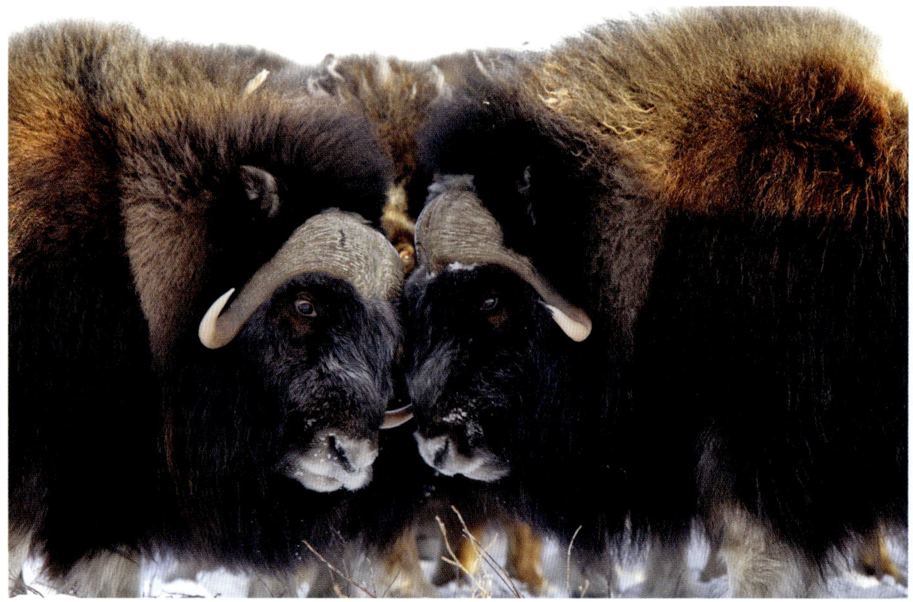

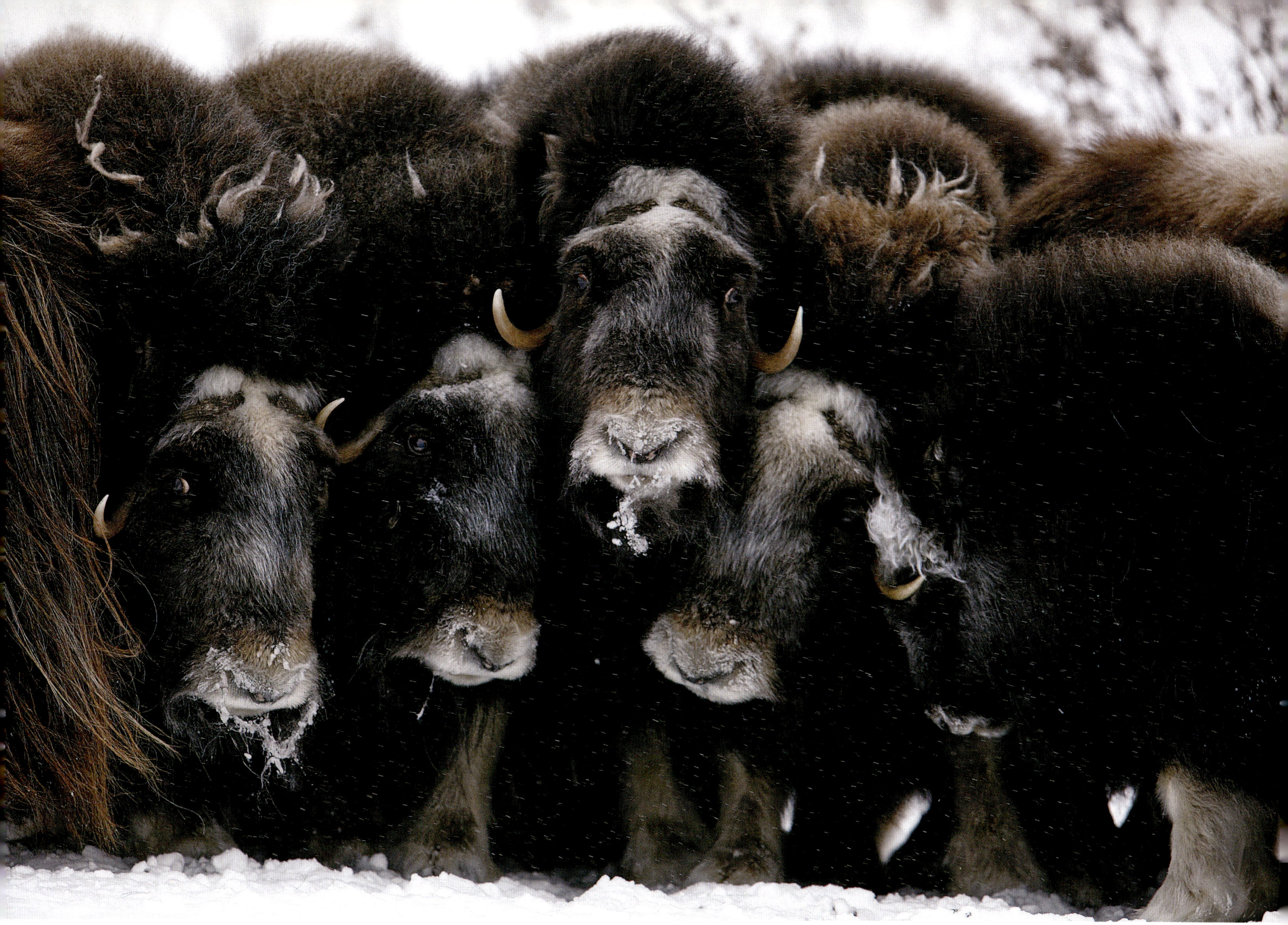

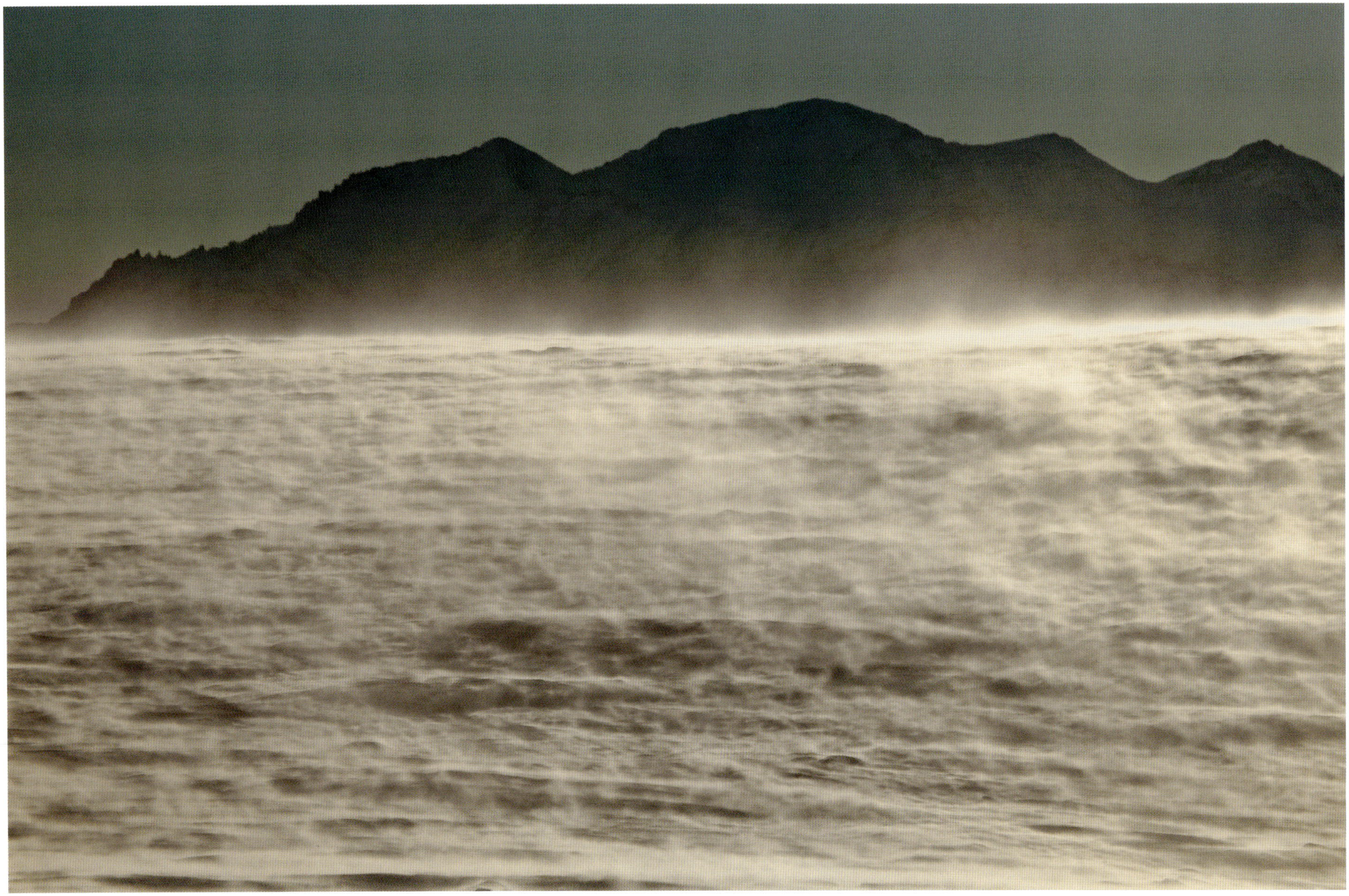

The wind is a constant companion in the treeless north. The difference between the measured temperature and the felt temperature when the wind blows (the so-called wind-chill factor) is often considerable. Left: A blizzard sweeps across the tundra in northern Alaska. Right: A storm over the Richardson Mountains, Northwest Territories, northern Canada.

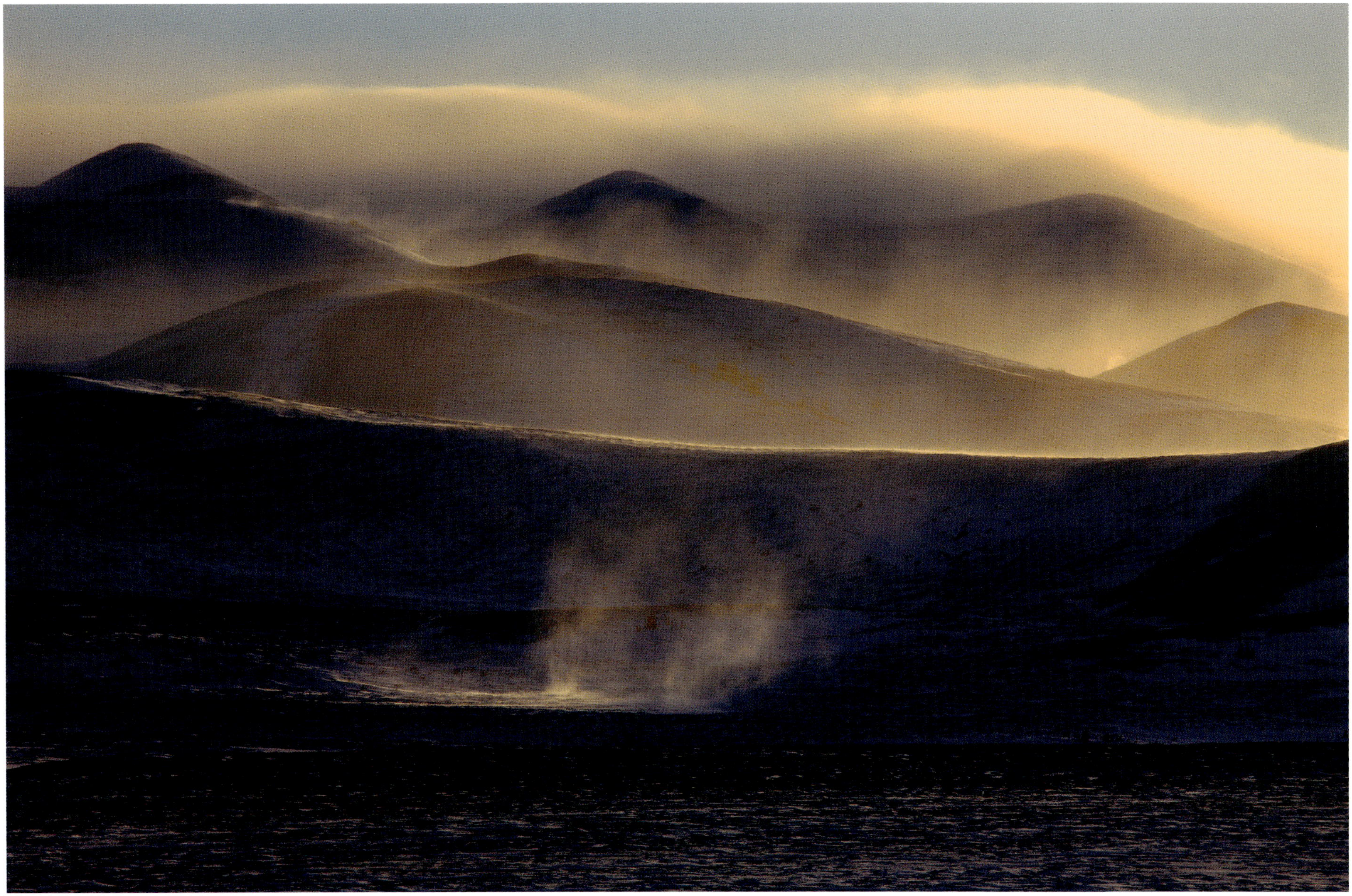

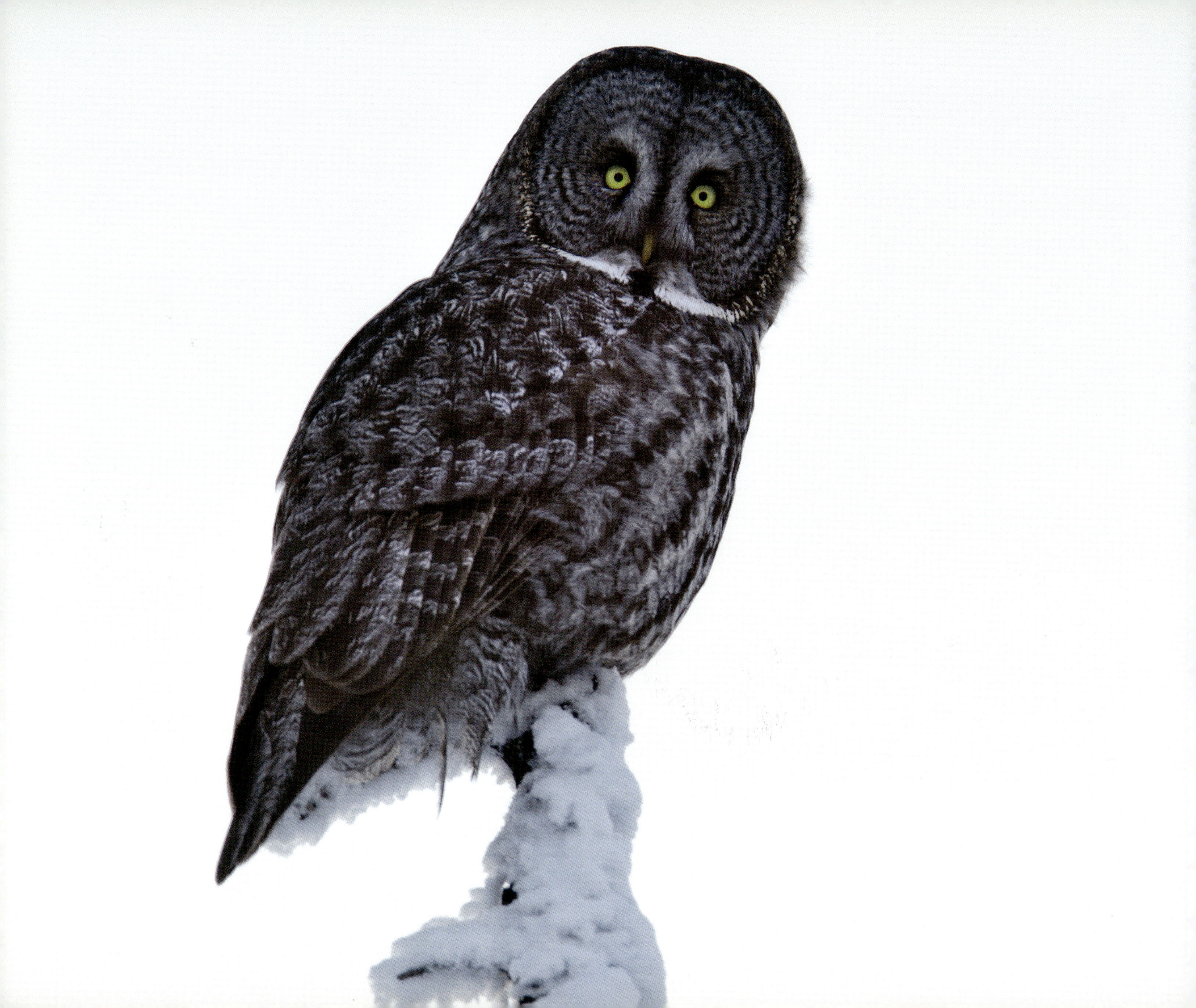

"I am robert thompson, I am inupiat, also known as eskimo. The pack ice, that which remains through the summer, would always be in sight of land. Now it is from 3 to 7 hundred miles from the shore. The animals we have depended on for thousands of years are being seriously affected; our culture, which has been in existence for thousands of years, is in serious peril. Climate change is happening so fast that the animals cannot adapt. Some will become extinct. It is sad to see this happening before my eyes. We must do what we can to stop the effects of climate change. We must do this so future generations of inupiat will know we cared. Human beings caused the climate change. Clean alternative energy is the answer. We must stop the use of fossil fuel. The debate is over."

Robert Thompson, resident of Kaktovik, Alaska

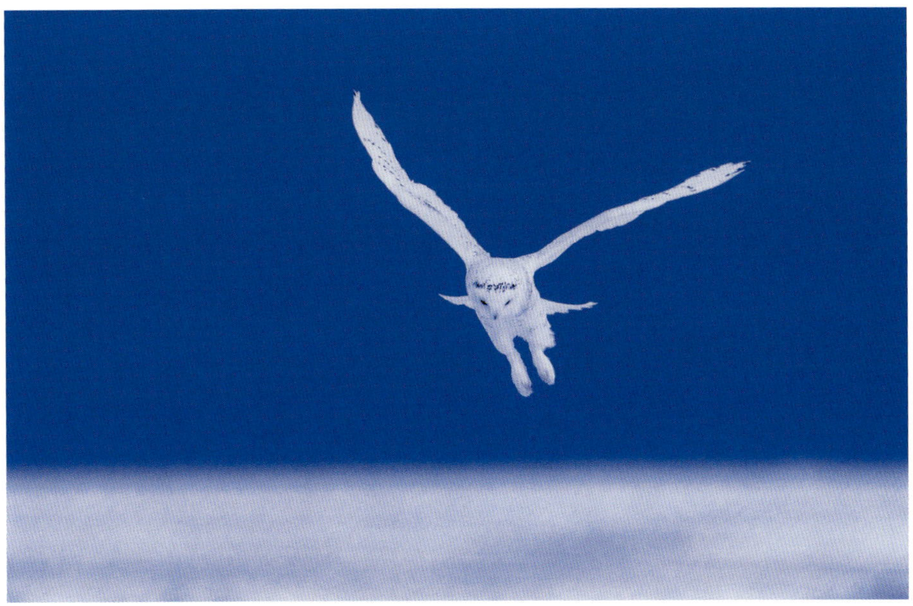

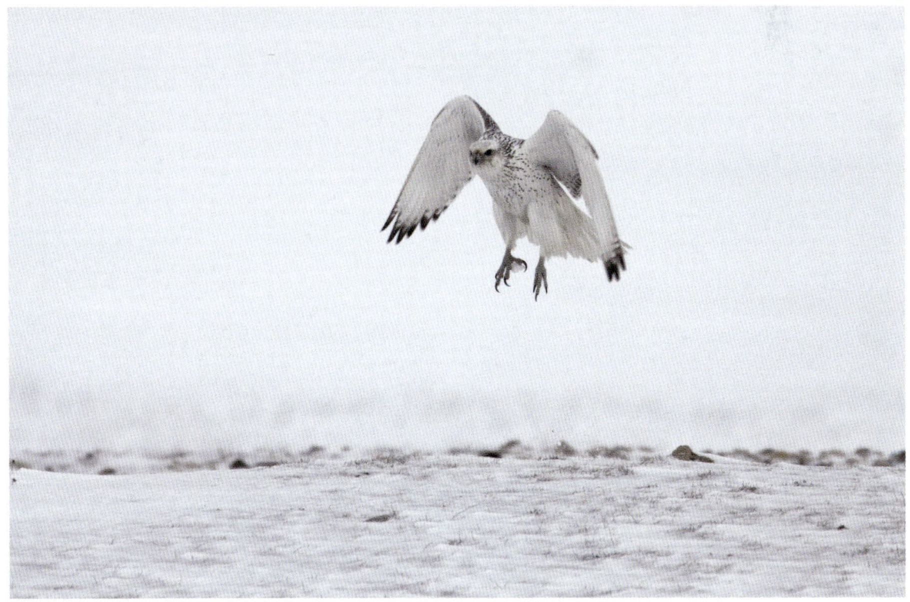

These are three of the rarest birds of the far north. The great grey owl lives in the endless taiga woods of the far north. The snowy owl nests straight on the ground during the summer in the flat tundra. The gyrfalcon is to be found throughout the Arctic. Cape Churchill, Hudson Bay, Canada.

The willow grouse (left) is one of a small number of bird species that spends the entire year in the Arctic. Both females and males have red-brown plumage in the summer, although the underside remains white during that period. The male's bright-red eyebrows (right) are characteristic. In the winter; the remaining plumage turns white. Brooks Range, northern Alaska.

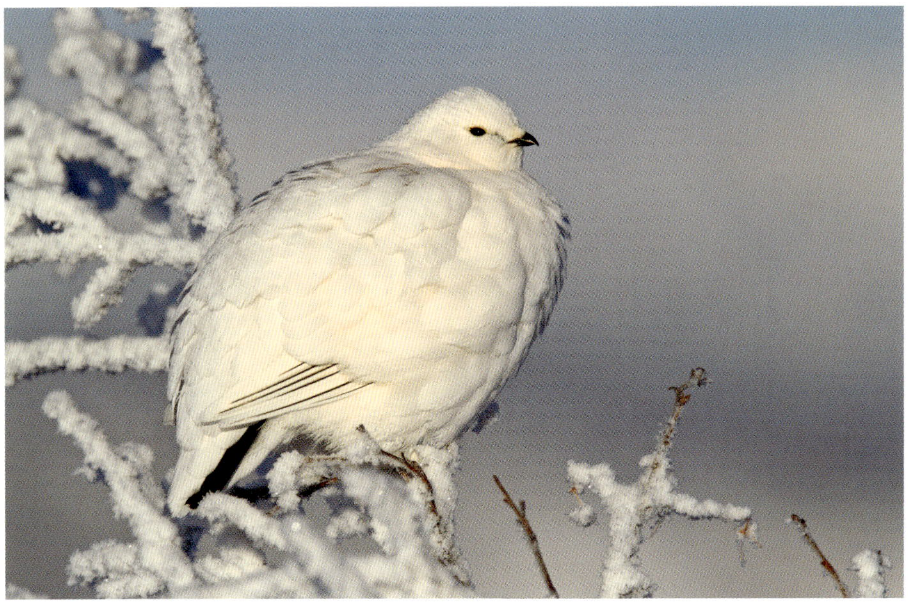

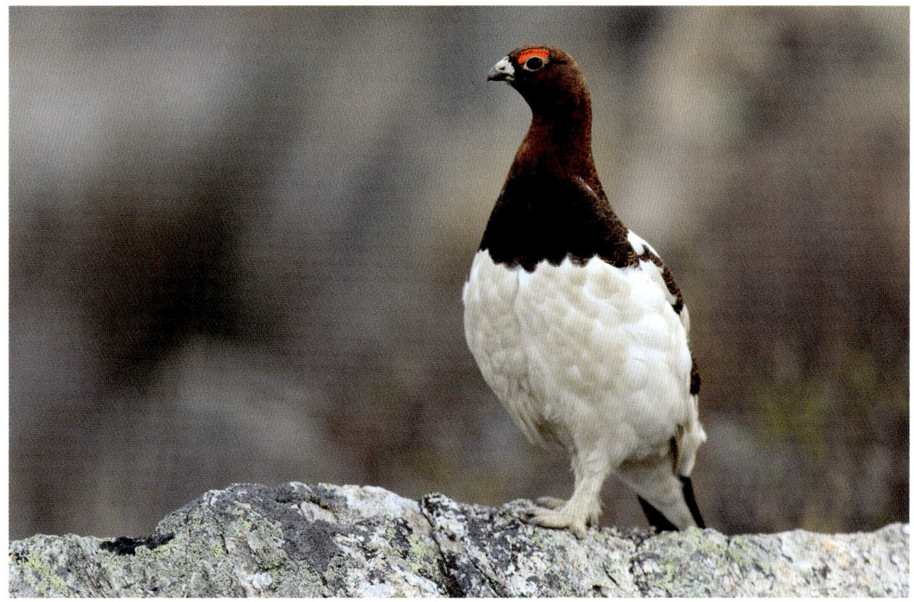

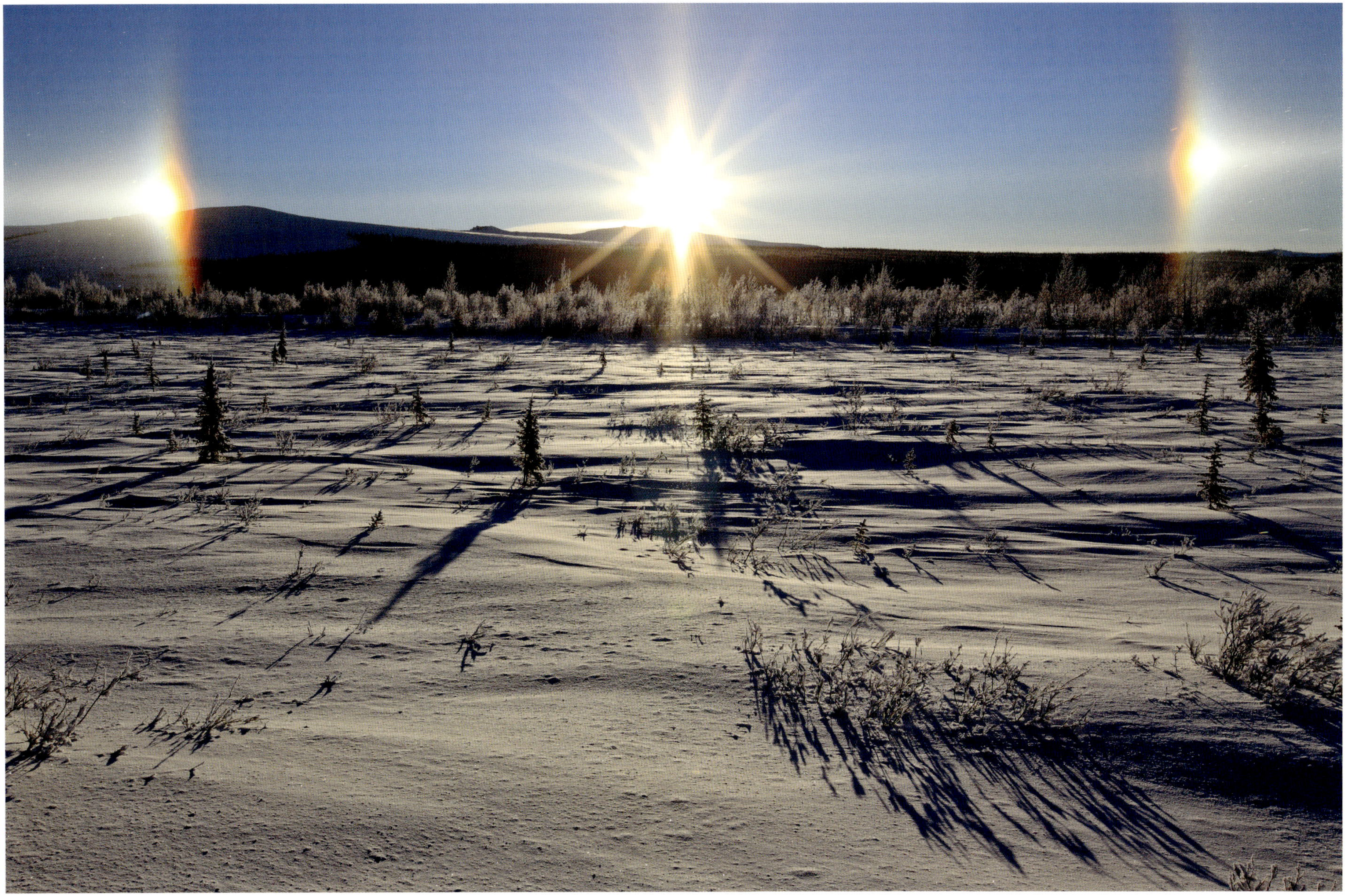

So-called sundogs appear in low temperatures, when billions of ice crystals float through the air.
The sun's light is bent in the tiny ice crystals, conjuring these unusual apparitions onto the Arctic sky.
Brooks Range, northern Alaska.

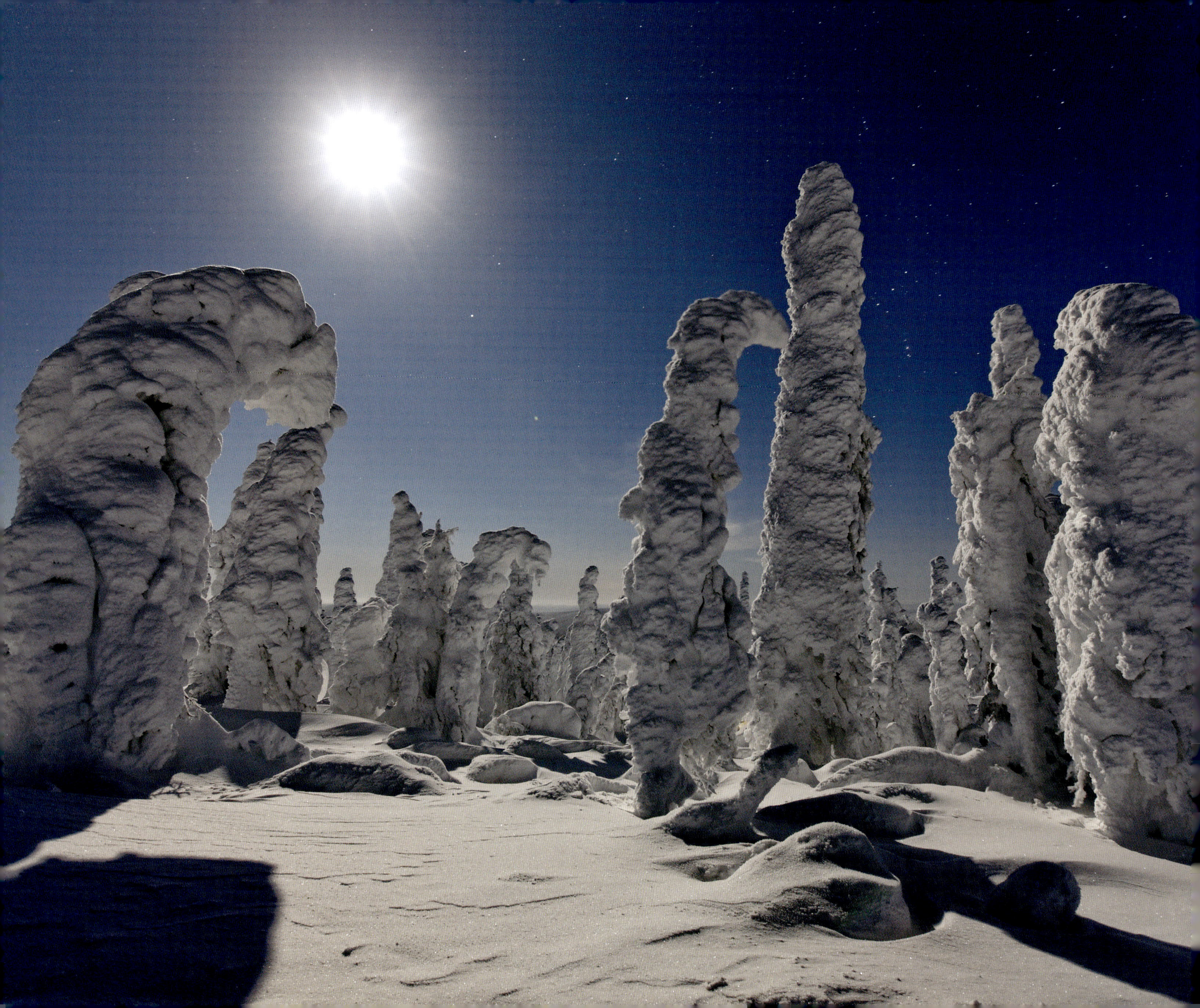

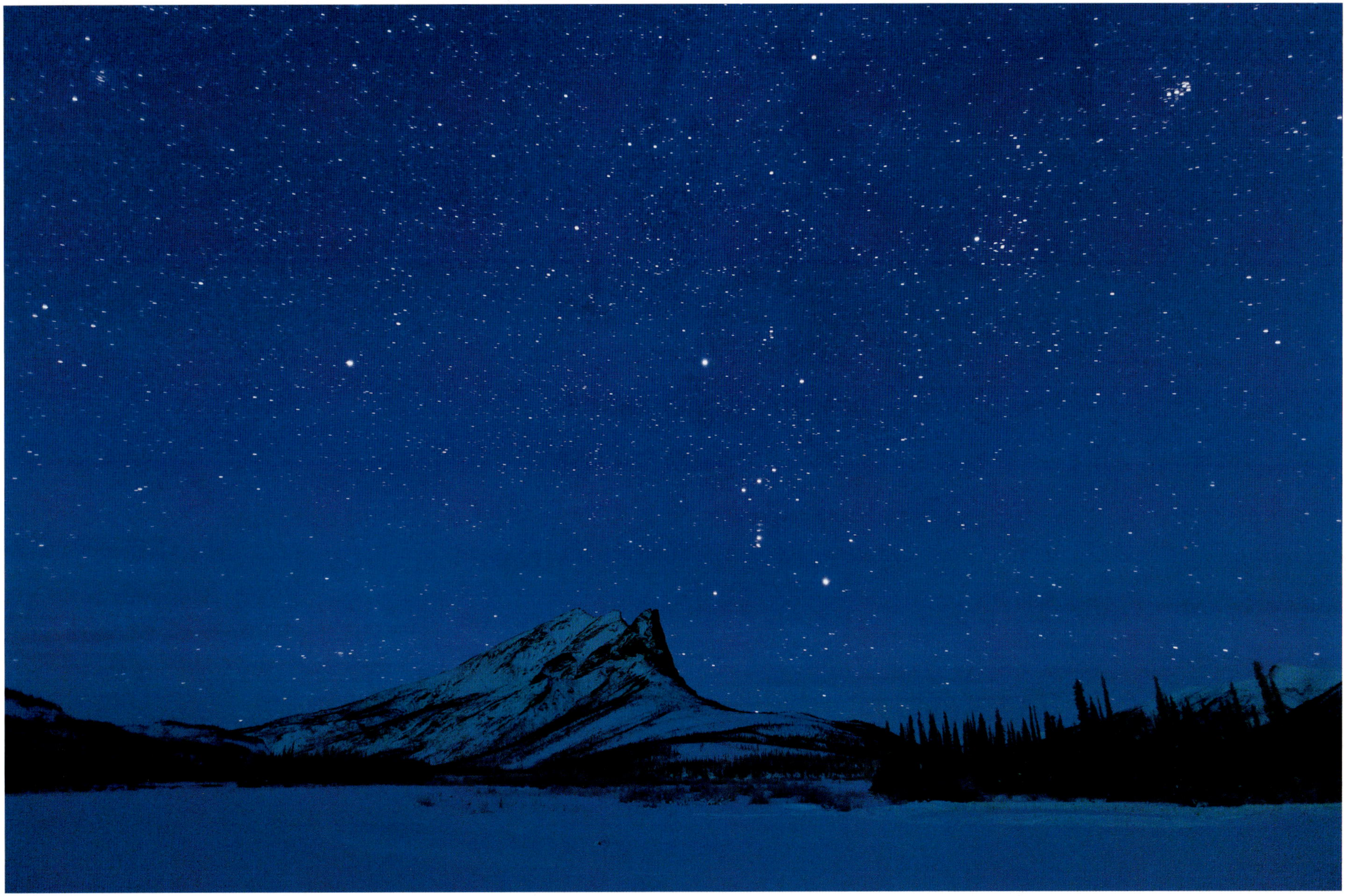

The polar night is not always pitch black, as is commonly assumed. Moonlight in particular is reflected in the white snow, making the polar night as bright as day, such as here in northern Alaska (left). Even the light emitted by the stars suffices to bring a little bit of light into the dark polar night, as can be seen here, at Sukakpak Mountain in the Brooks Range, northern Alaska.

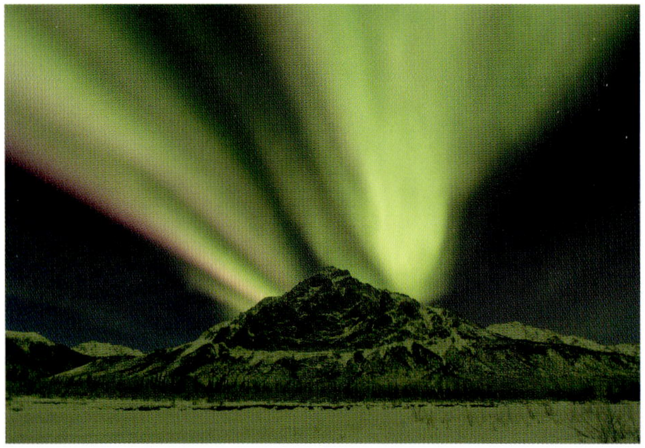 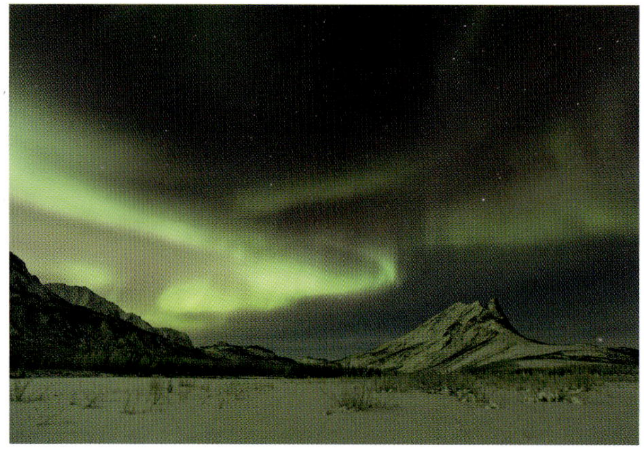

"Half past midnight, minus 42 degrees Celsius. I am standing in the unique mountain landscape of the Brooks Range in north Alaska, and waiting. Nothing happens for hours, although the sky is clear and the stars are visible. Just as I am about to quit, a faintly glowing, greenish-white arc appears in the sky. Without having to think about it, I know what that means: northern lights. At last! Gradually, the arc becomes stronger and the green becomes deeper. I begin to expose the film. The northern lights become more and more intense. Now, they begin to flicker, and to move swiftly across the sky. It is a veritable eruption of northern lights. Yellow, green, red: I can distinguish all the colours. The entire night sky is covered in polar lights. It is incredible. I have never experienced anything like it. After just 20 minutes or so, it is all over. In my opinion, the night-time spectacle of the aurora borealis is one of the most impressive phenomena that can be seen on this earth."

Bernd Römmelt

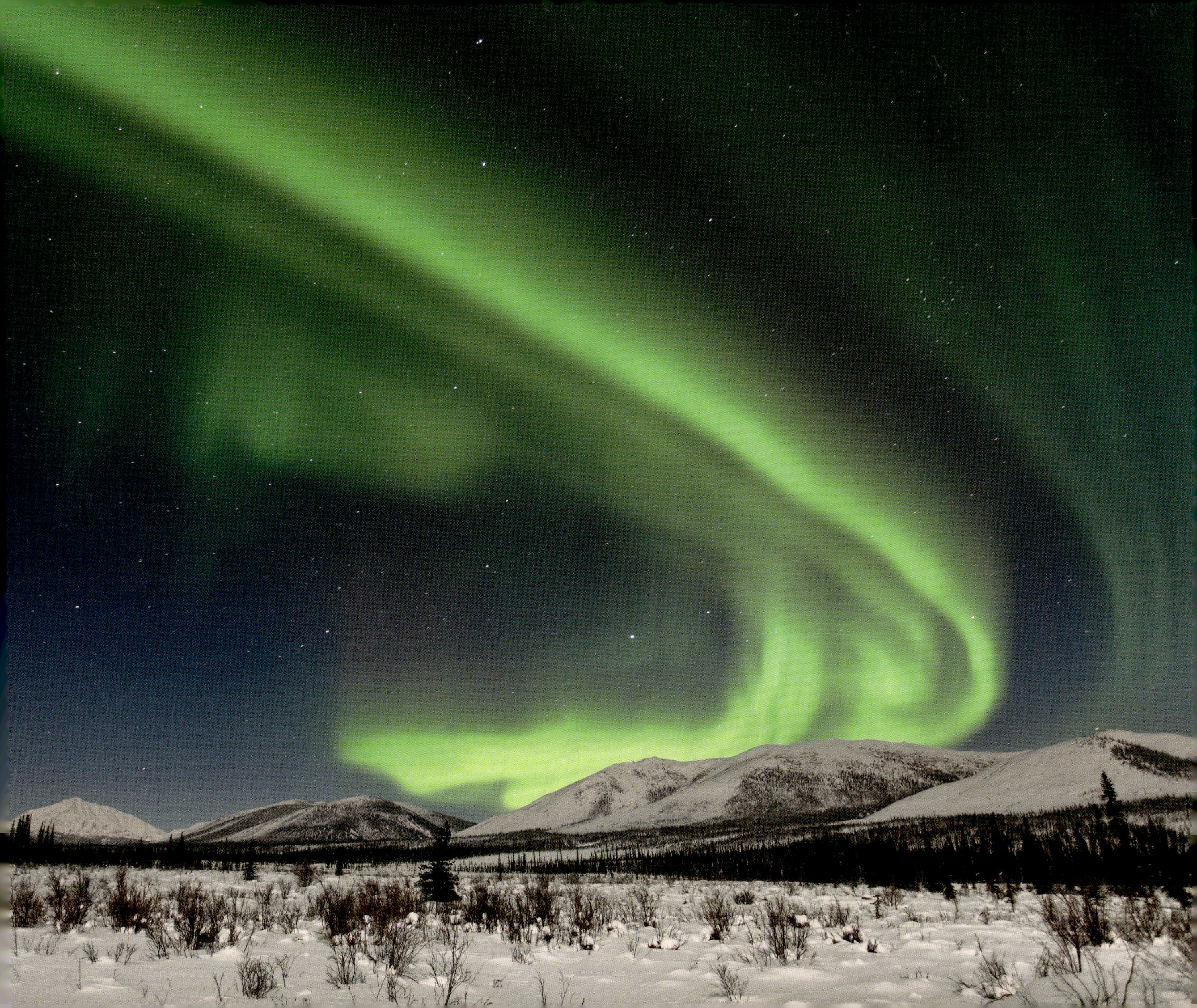

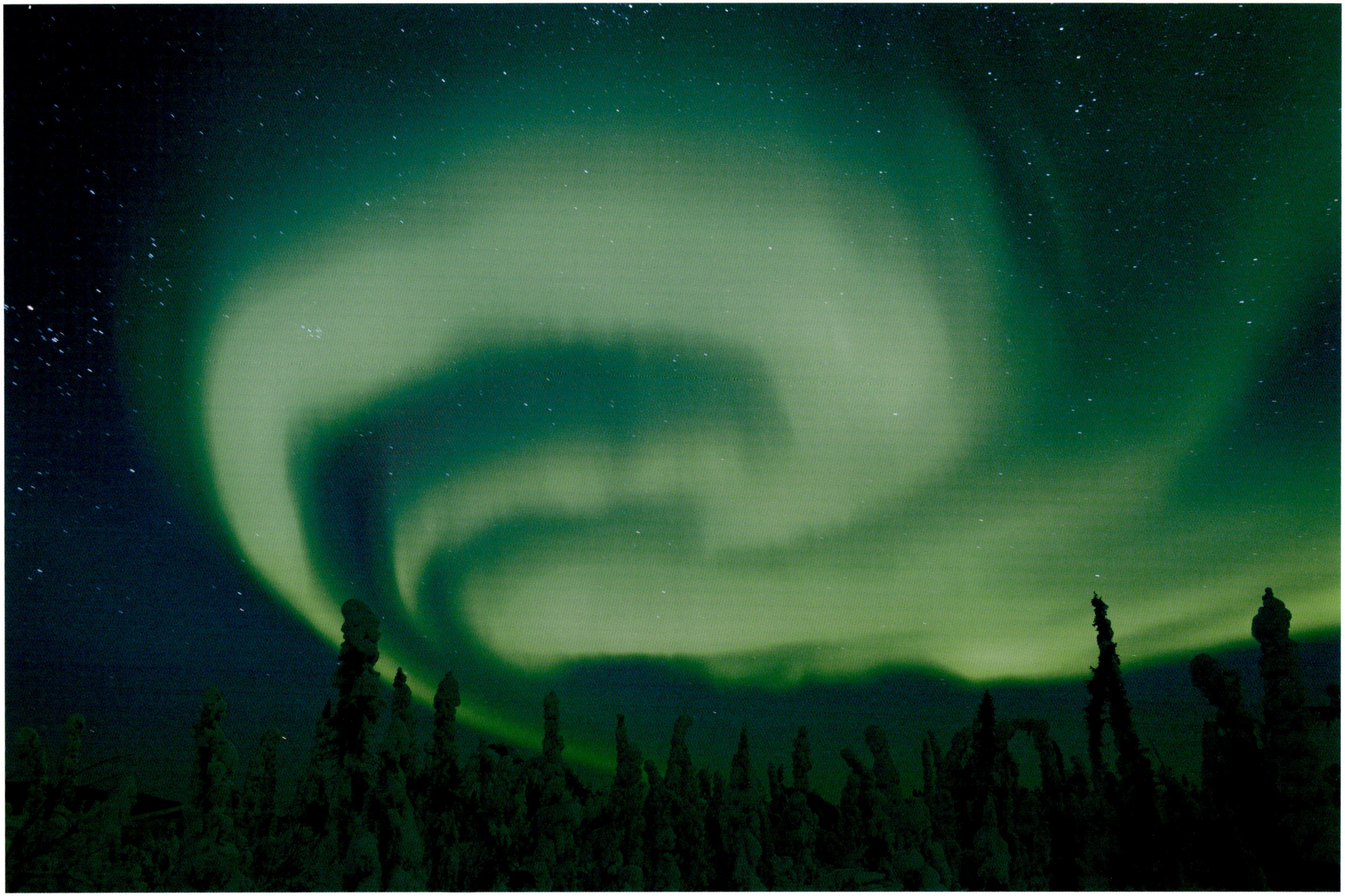

The northern lights are caused by solar winds. Electrically charged particles are repulsed by the sun and collide with the atoms of the outer atmosphere of our planet. The particles are redirected towards the poles by the earth's magnetic field, and discharged on collision, leading to this fascinating light display in the sky. Left: A northern-lights spiral over the taiga forest near Eagle Plains; right: an eruption of northern lights above the Richardson Mountains. Both in Yukon Territory, northern Canada.

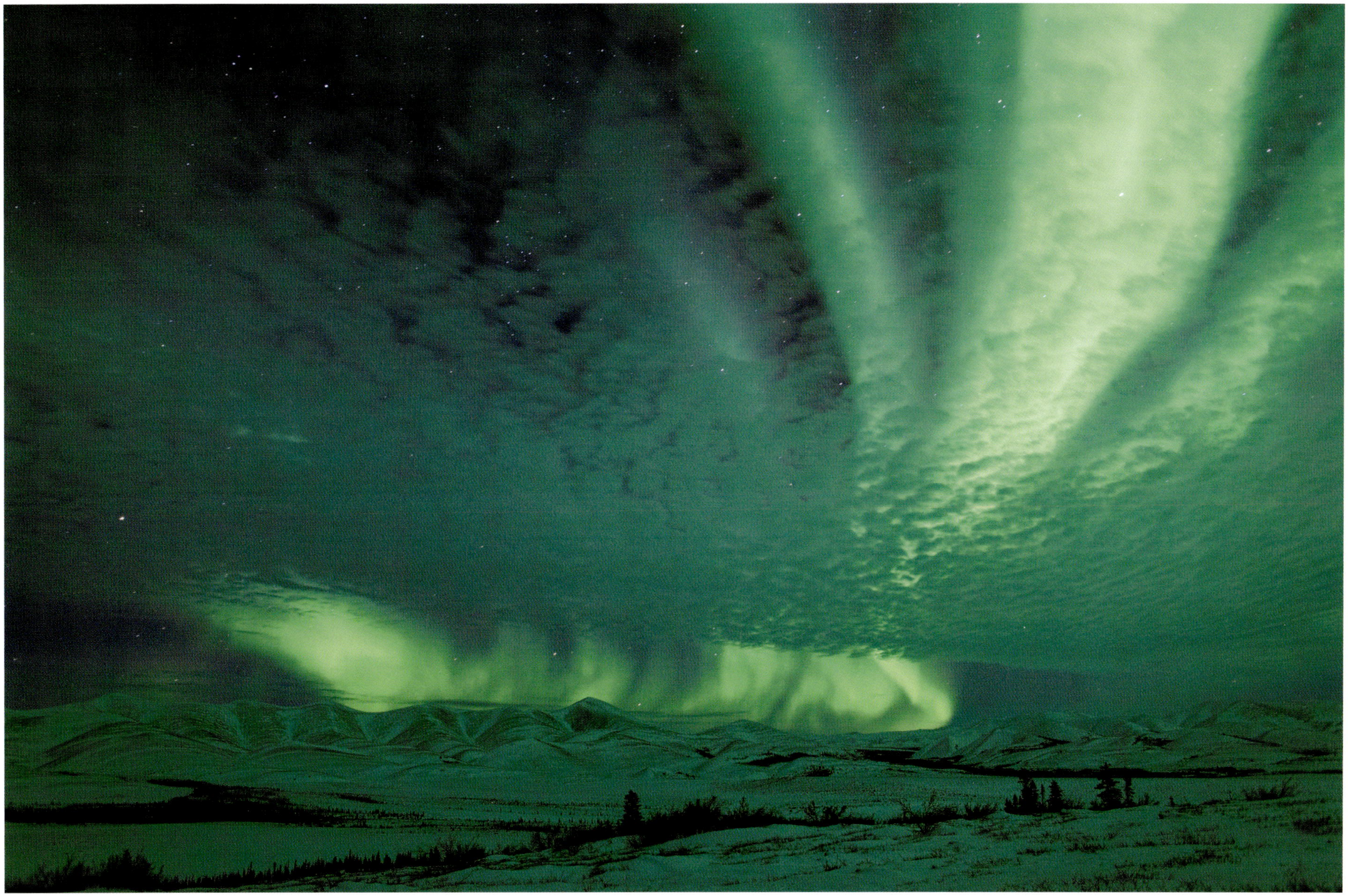

GREENLAND'S ARCTIC – A TREASURE TROVE OF SNOW AND ICE

Erik the Viking, also known as Erik the Red because of his red hair and red beard, was exiled from Iceland for three years in 982 AD. Because he was no longer welcome in the Norwegian fjords either, he travelled west by boat and finally came to the coast of a land unknown to him. Erik the Red named the newly discovered coast "Greenland". It is not known whether he did so because of the copious vegetation in the south of the country, or whether his aim was simply to lure settlers to the new country upon his return to Iceland.

The first Inuit from Alaska and Canada had arrived on the west coast of the vast island approximately 5,500 years beforehand. There were two further phases of settlement by the Inuit. The Thule Inuit arrived in the southwest around the year 1000, like the first Vikings; the Polar Inuit came to the far north approximately 500 years later. The Polar Inuit are the northernmost people in the world, and have retained their original way of life to this day.

Greenland was already a veritable treasure island for the inhabitants of the time, despite the difficult living conditions. It remains so, to an even greater degree, to this day as a result of its great importance to the stability of the Earth's climate. The south of Greenland has immeasurably rich vegetation, with over 3,500 plant species; its waters contain large fish stocks, while its birdlife is composed of more than 200 species. Its west coast has a unique glacial landscape that also includes the largest ice fjord in the world: Ilulissat Icefjord. During the summer months, the Sermeq Kujalleq glacier calves almost daily, and often in a spectacular manner, into a roughly 40-kilometre-long fjord, so that the latter is filled with icebergs. The ice fjord has even been awarded the status of UNESCO

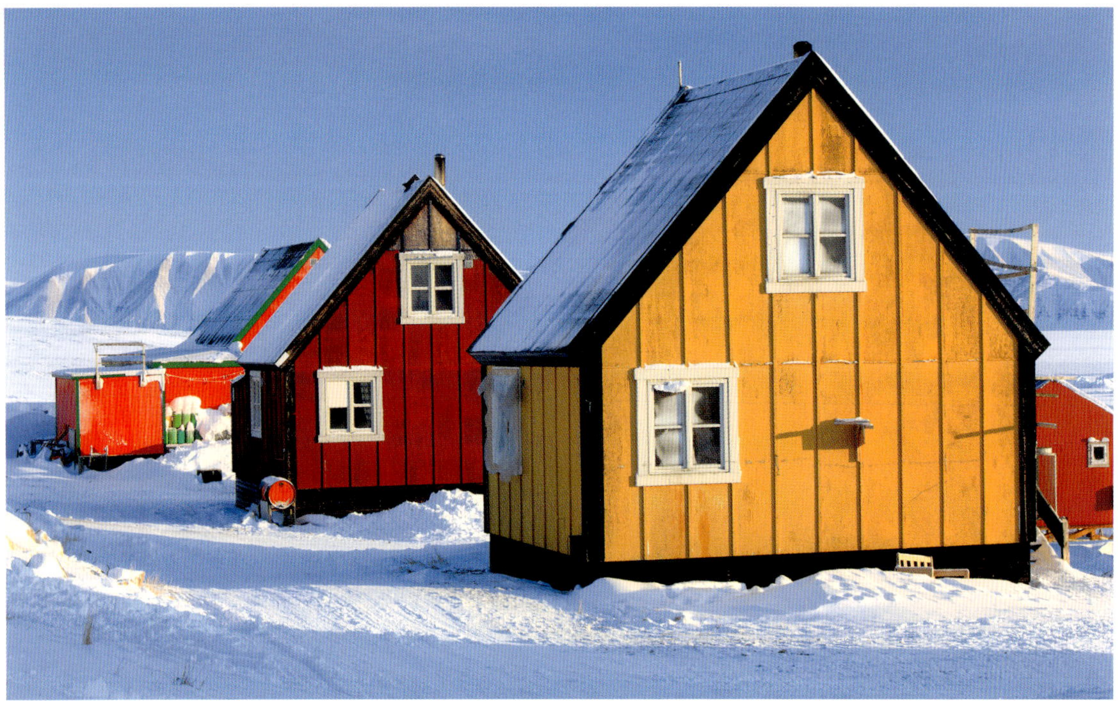

Typical residential houses in Qaanaaq, northern Greenland.

World Heritage Site because of its particular importance and uniqueness.

The icebergs can be surprisingly big and drift slowly south once they have passed through the fjord. Some even reach New York. Incidentally, it was one of these that spelled doom for the *Titanic*.

The flow velocity of the Sermeq Kujalleq glacier in particular has increased dramatically in recent years as a result of climate change, and has even doubled. With a velocity of 40 metres per day, the glacier is one of the most active and therefore, sadly, also one of the "fastest" in the world.

Climate change has also caused another of Greenland's giant glaciers, the Petermann Glacier, to achieve a sad fame. In the summer of 2010, an iceberg over 260 square kilometres in size – the largest ever to have been observed in the northern hemisphere – broke free. The iceberg, almost the size of the city of Munich, or four times the size of Manhattan, has been drifting through the Arctic Ocean ever since.

Greenland is the largest island on earth: 2,650 kilometres long, up to 1,200 kilometres wide and with a surface area of almost 2.2 million square kilometres, it is about six times the size of Germany. And yet, with a population of about 56,000 inhabitants – or one person per 40 square kilometres – it is also among the most sparsely populated countries on Earth. Politically, it belongs to Denmark, although its structures are overwhelmingly autonomous. The "thickness" of the enormous island is even more impressive than its incredible expanse. Although it lies almost entirely at, or even below, sea level, Greenland juts more than 3,000 metres out of the sea because about four fifths of the island are encased with a gigantic ice crust, the largest ice mass outside the Antarctic. (The ice masses on Antarctica are considerably larger, but Greenland's ice constitutes one of the largest freshwater reservoirs on the planet. The ice on mainland Greenland is equivalent to about 20 times the quantity of water in all the rivers and lakes on Earth.) This ice crust has formed over the course of the last millennia through snowfall and the resulting compression of snow crystals to ice alone; it now weighs an unimaginable 230 billion tons and has a volume of 2.34 million cubic kilometres.

The weight of the several-kilometre-thick ice pushes the enormous country downwards so that most of the mainland lies below sea level. Without the ice, the island would rise continuously over time and jut up to 600 metres out of the sea. And this process has already started: Greenland now rises by up to five centimetres each year because more ice melts – than is formed through new snowfall – an unimaginable 280 cubic kilometres per year as a result of the continuous increase in temperature of the Earth's atmosphere.

The more ice Greenland loses, and the more it rises out of the sea as a result, the closer many other countries come to their demise: the melting ice causes the sea level to rise, centimetre by centimetre, worldwide.

If all of Greenland's ice were to melt, as could be the case in as little as 300 years, according to the most recent measurements – this could lead to a worldwide rise in sea level of six or more than seven metres. This would have incalculable consequences for countries with coastlines, as well as for oceans and for the world climate. The huge quantities of fresh water that would flow into the sea might influence the sea currents to such a degree that even the Gulf Stream, one of the engines of the global climate, would change, possibly resulting in climate chaos in large sections of the world.

Greenland is a crucial element in the stability of the global climate system and of the world's oceanic environment. Preserving Greenland's treasures is absolutely no longer just a question of nature conservation or of the regulation of existing means. It is a question of survival on our planet.

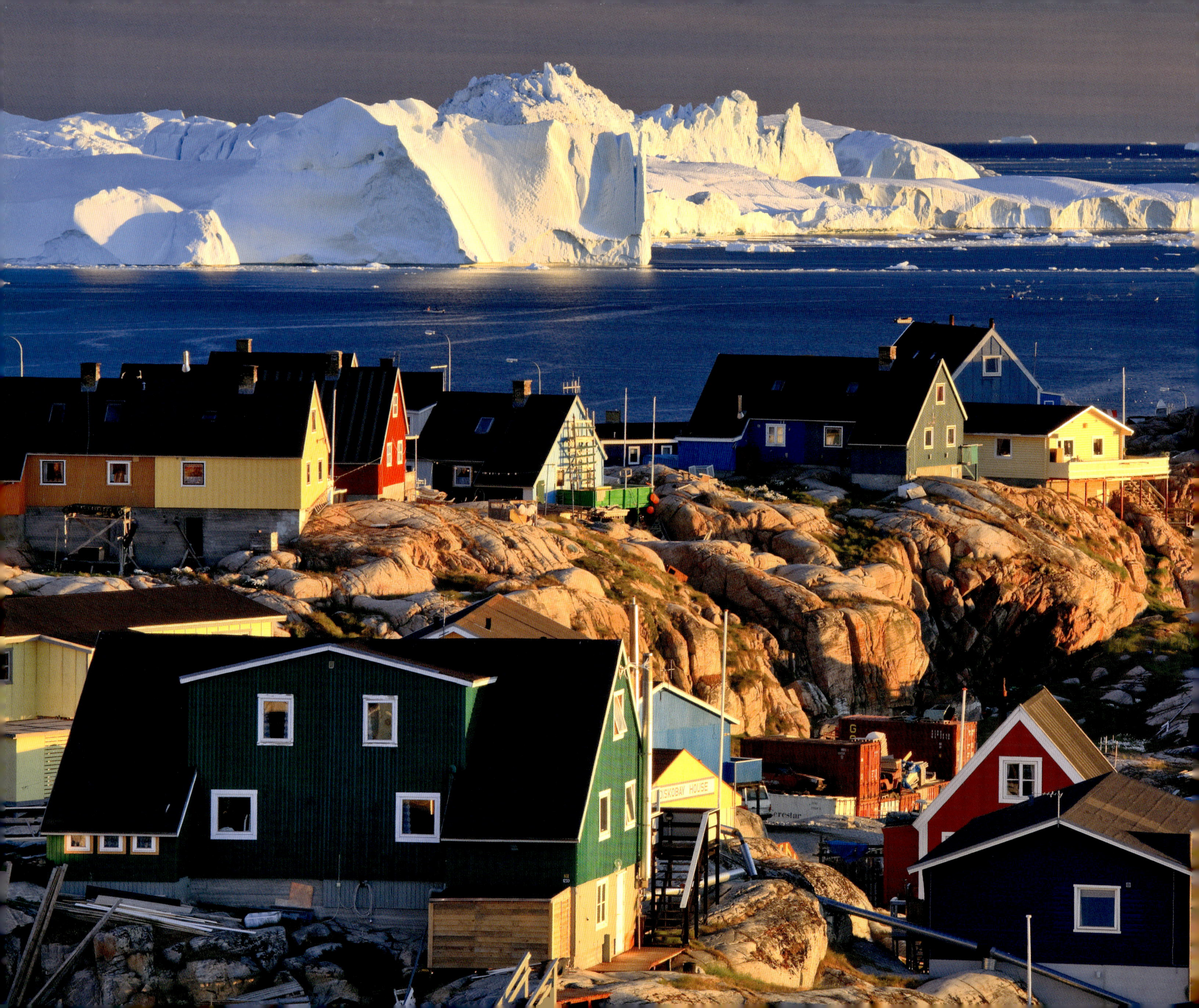
DISKOBAY HOUSE

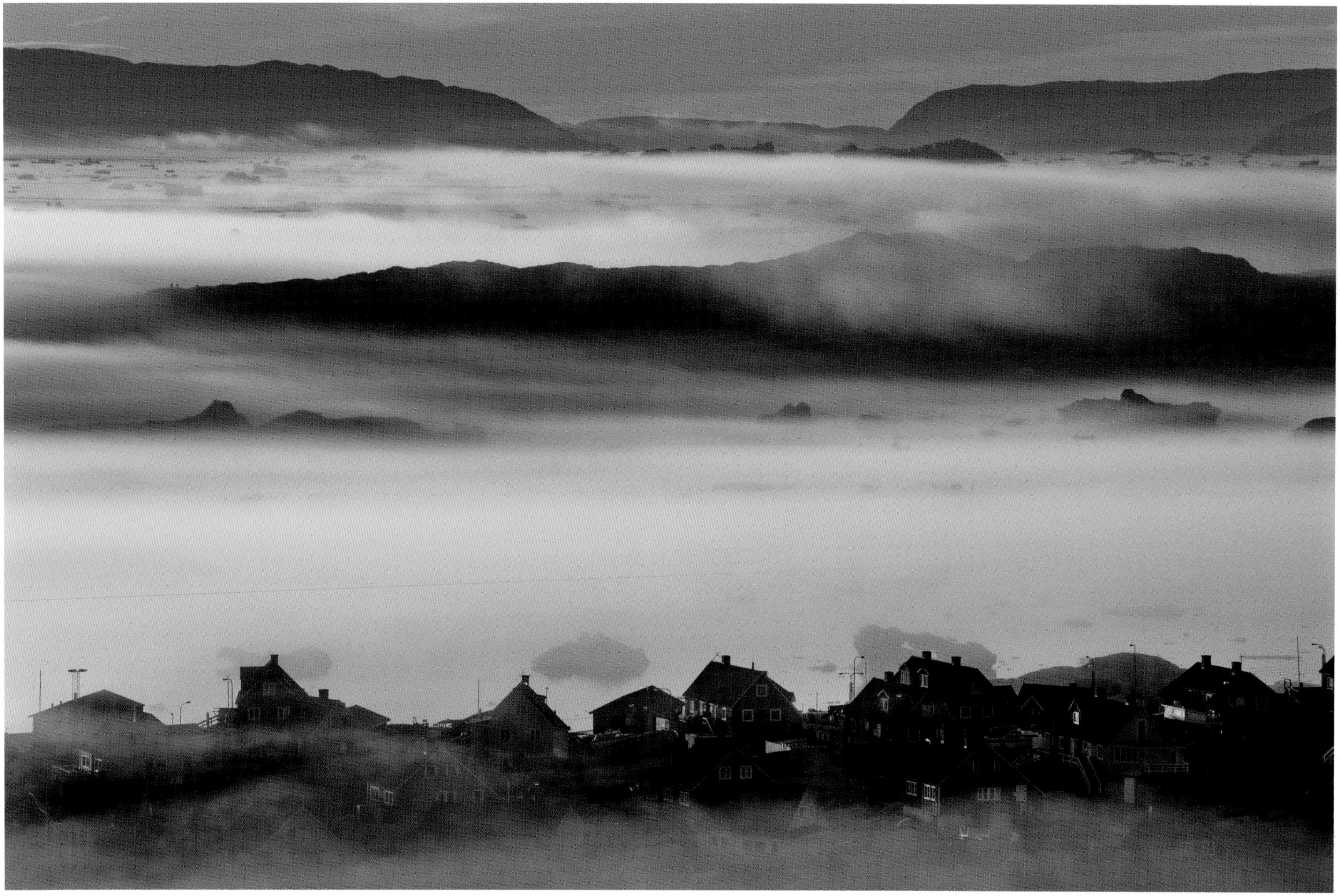

With a population of just under 4,500, Ilulissat is the third-largest settlement in Greenland. This small town is located in western Greenland, on the edge of Disco Bay. The famous Ilulissat Icefjord, inscribed as a UNESCO World Heritage Site since 2004 (and the only ice fjord to be listed to date) is the main attraction.

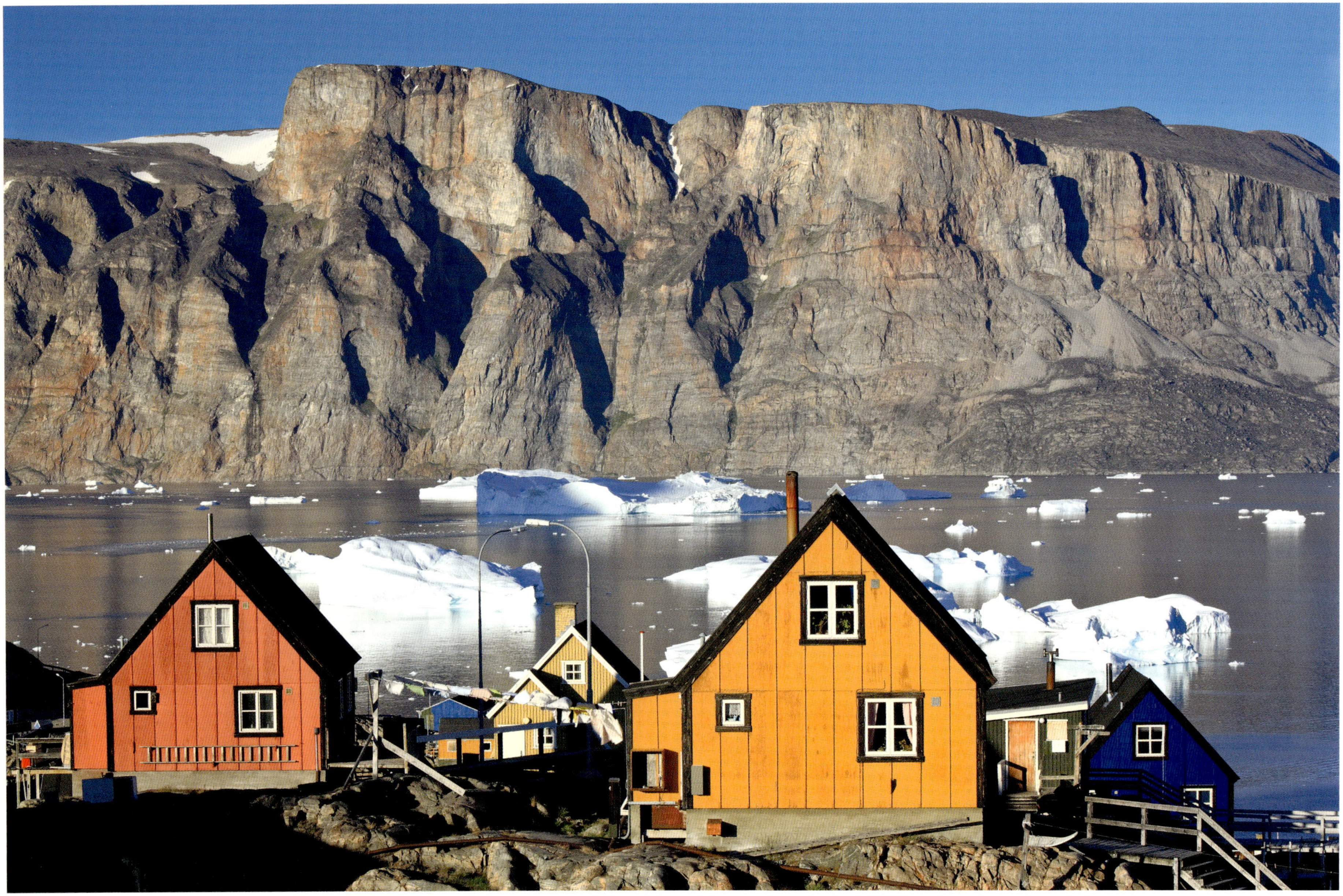

Uummannaq has a population of 2,800 inhabitants and lies about 600 kilometres north of the polar circle. It is one of the most beautiful settlements along the entire west coast. During the short summer months, air-dried cod can be found all over town. Considered a delicacy, it is hung to dry in front of the small wooden houses.

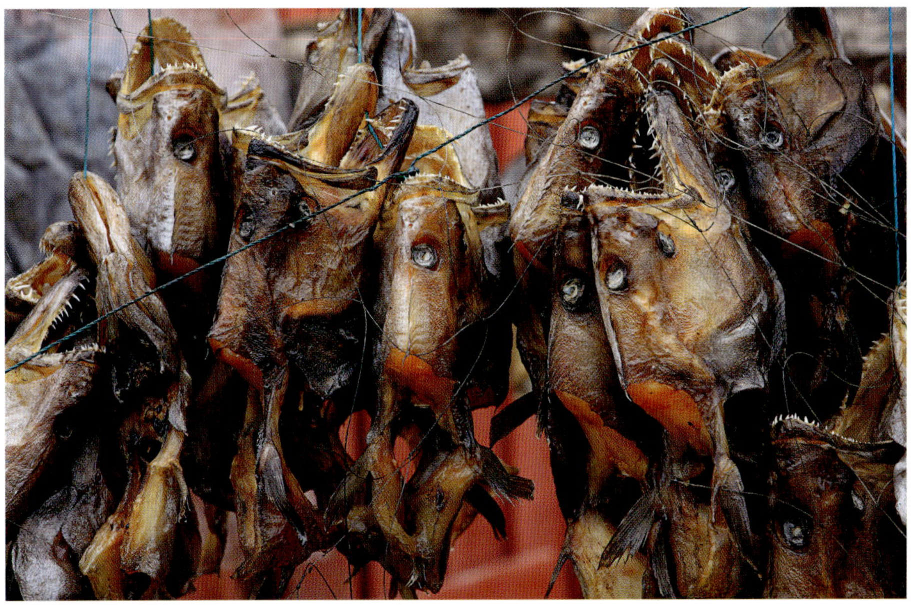

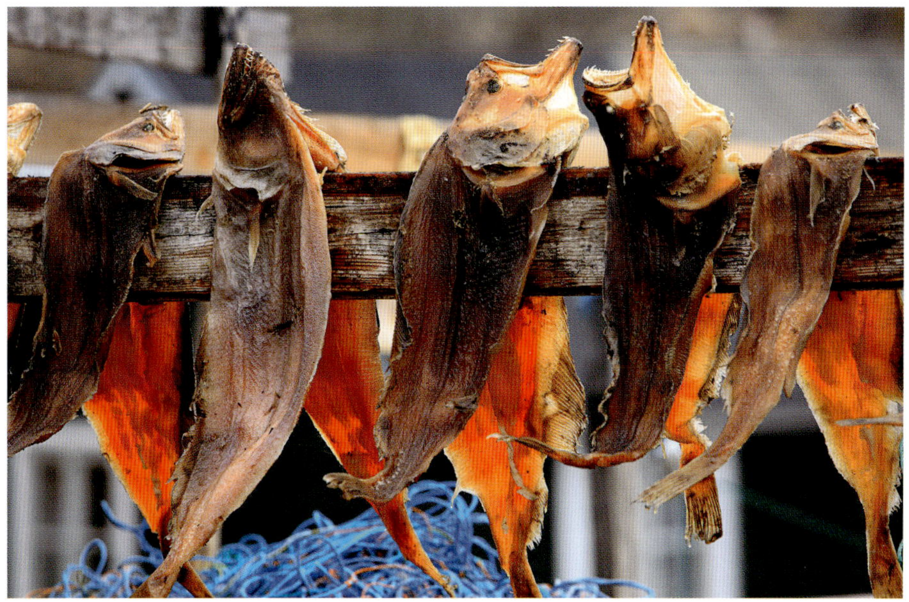

Sledge dogs have a long tradition in Greenland, although they are only to be found in certain parts of the country. Only the region north of Sisimiut on the west coast and the length of the east coast are "sledge-dog areas". In the north of Greenland, in contrast to Canada or Alaska, for example, dog sledges continue to be frequently used forms of transport. Sledge dogs are primarily working animals, rather than pets, in Greenland. And so they often lead a fairly miserable life, attached to a chain, during the summer months.

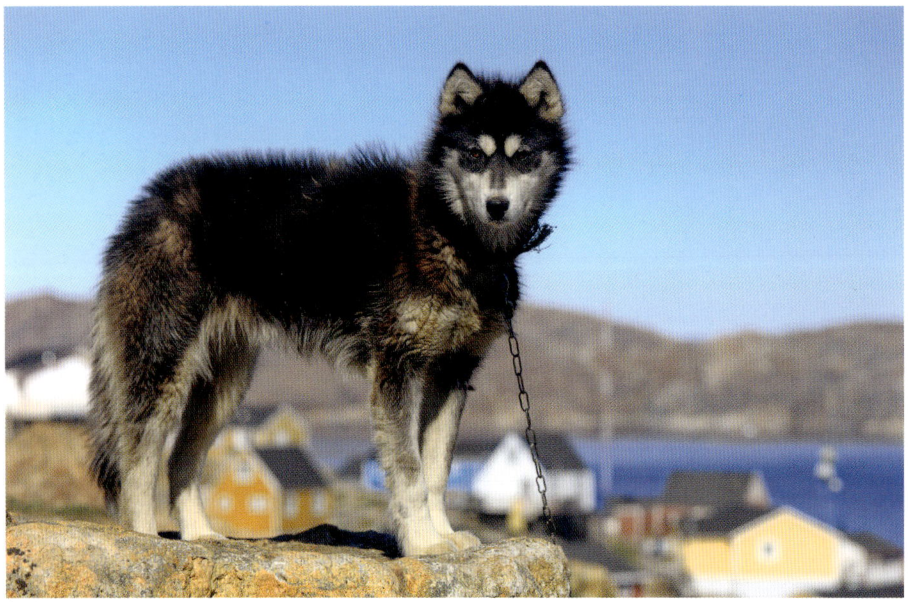

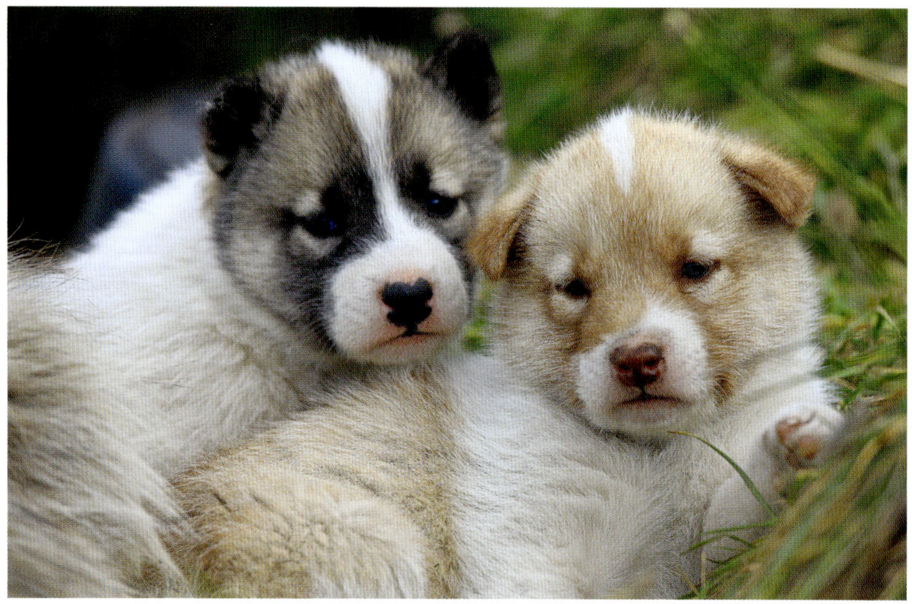

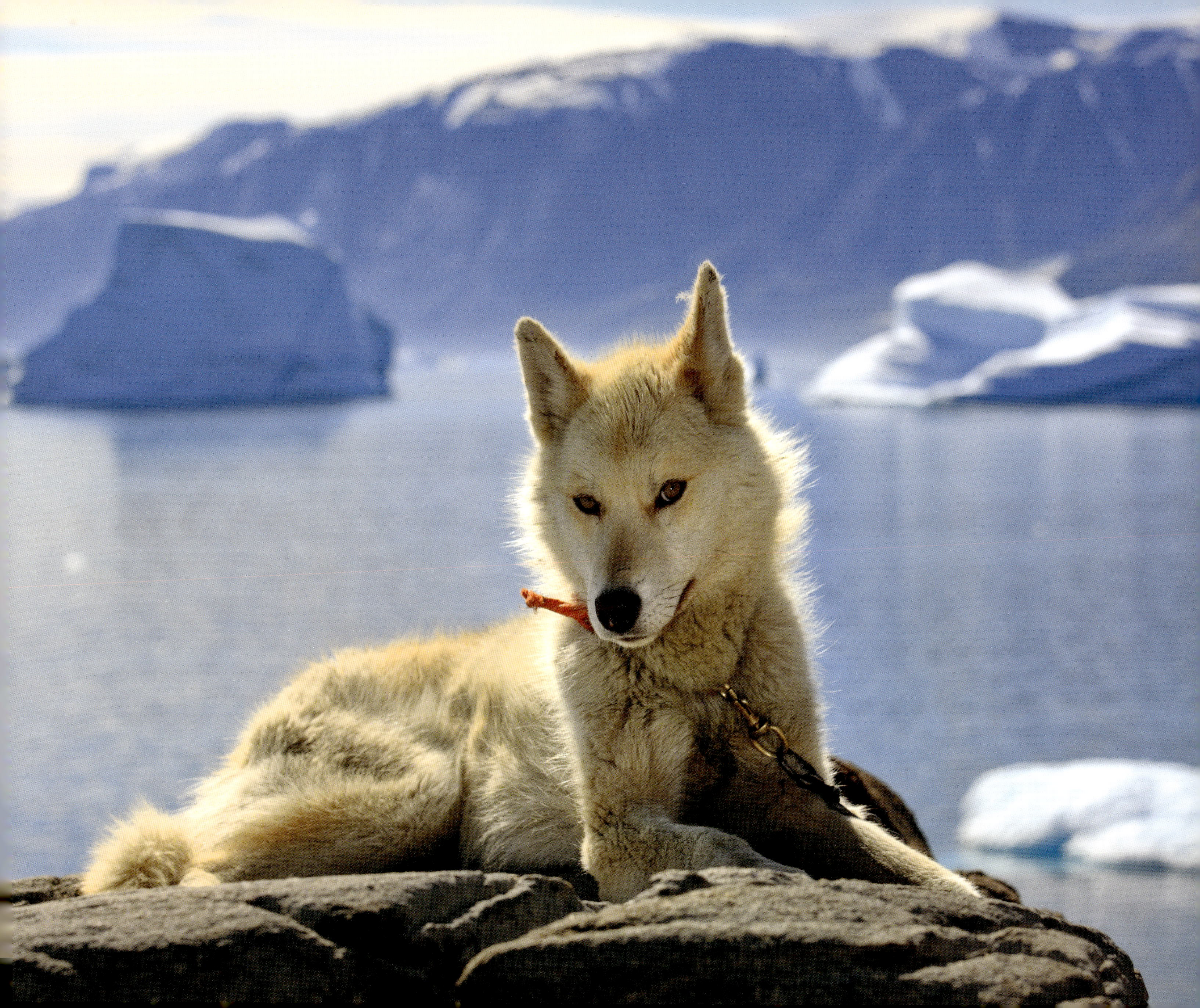

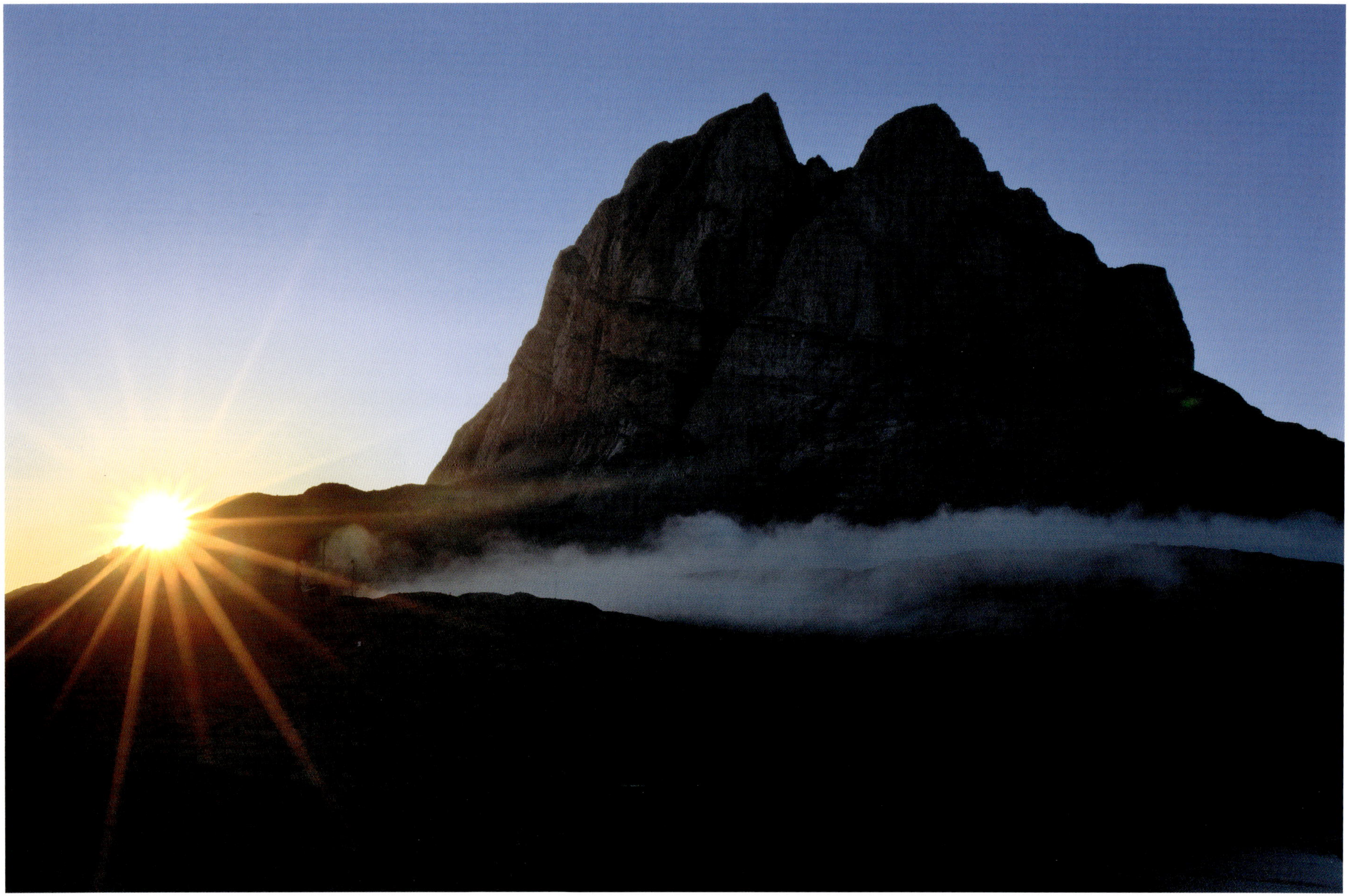

The seal-heart shaped Uummannaq Mountain is the emblem of Uummannaq. Situated right behind the small town, the mountain reaches 1,175 metres into the sky over Greenland.

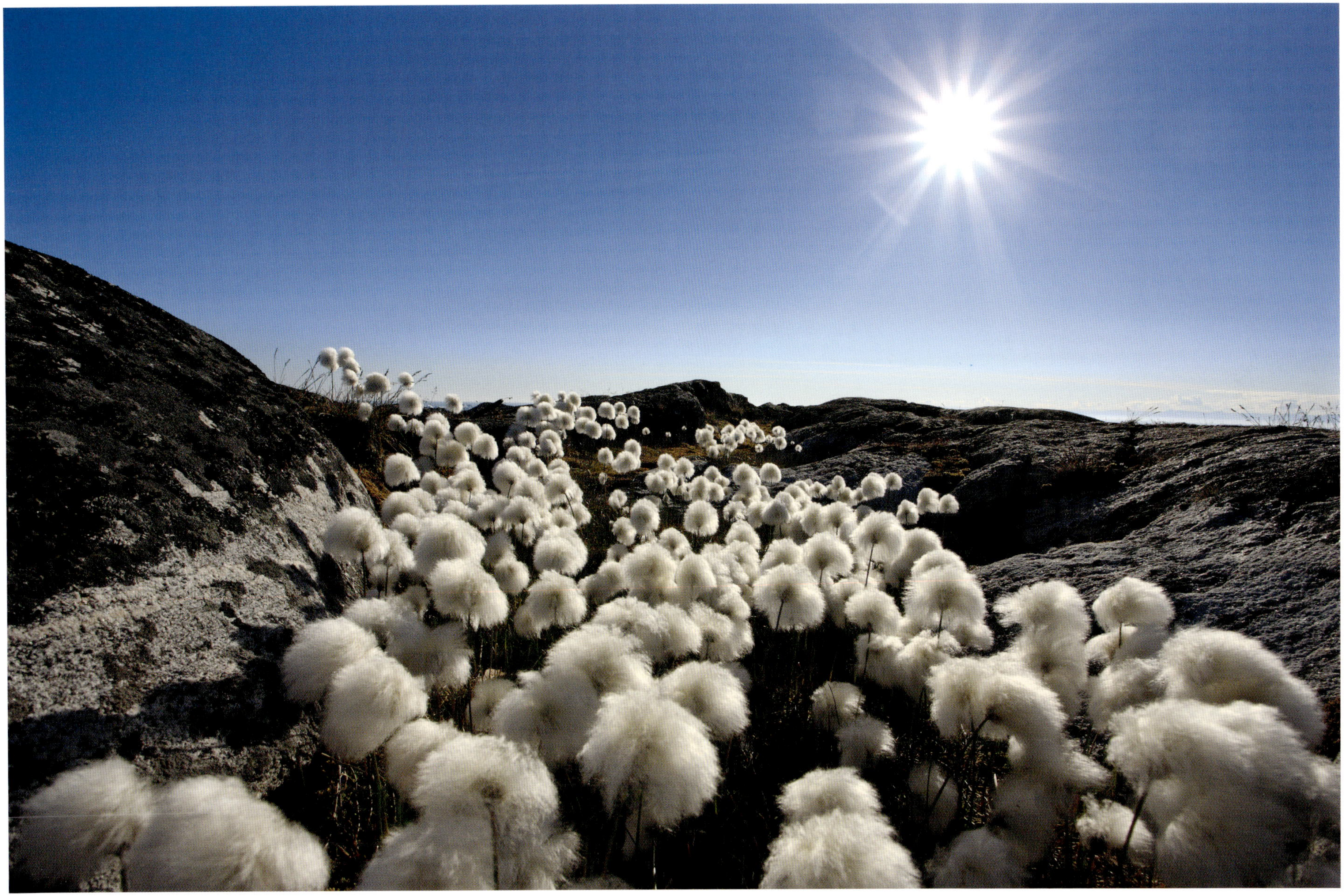

The picturesque cotton grass in Ilulissat, northwest Greenland, comes to life during the summer month and thrive in the damp tundra soil.

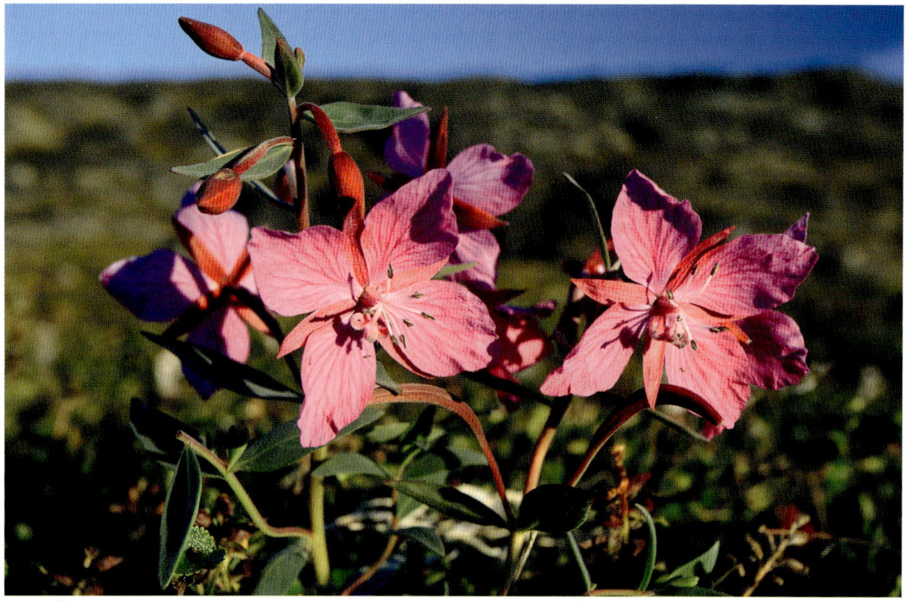

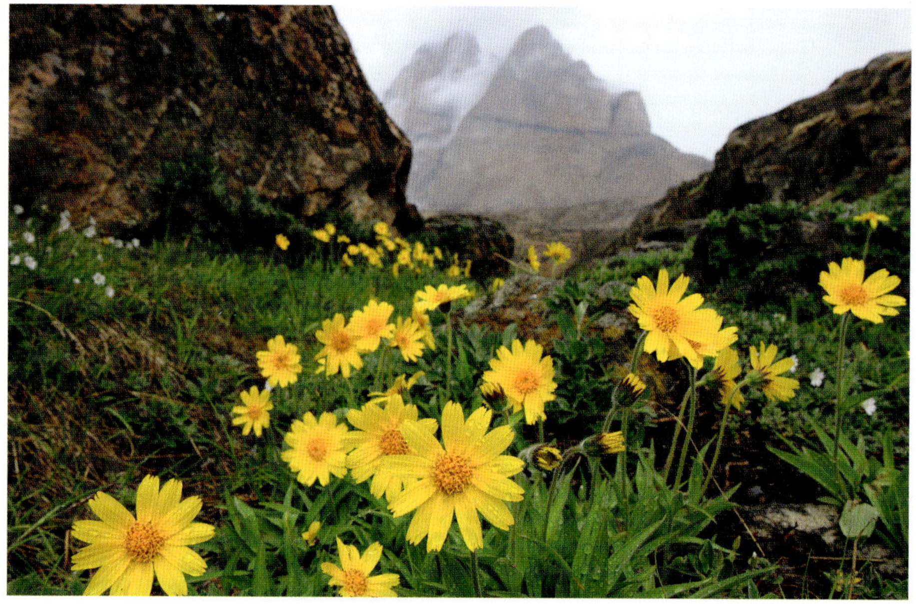

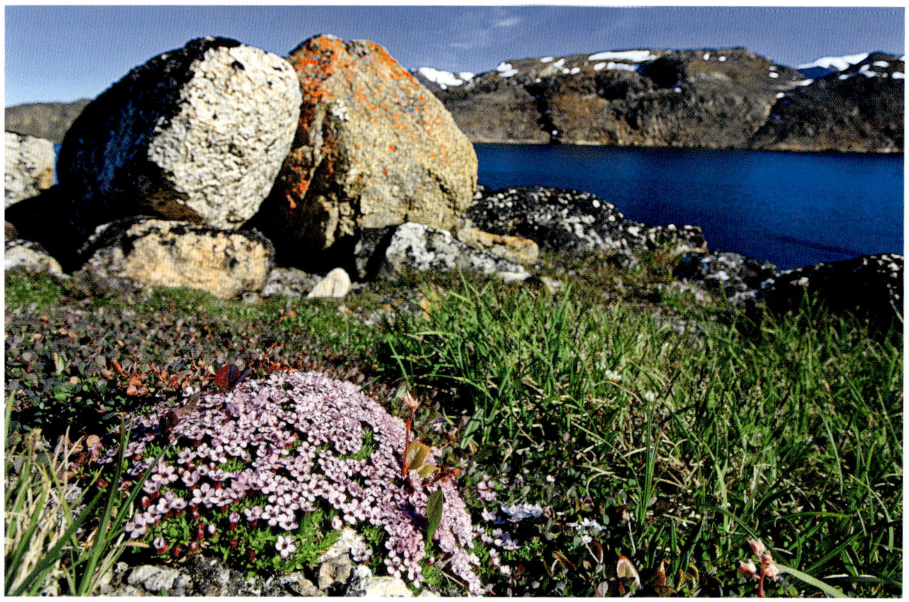

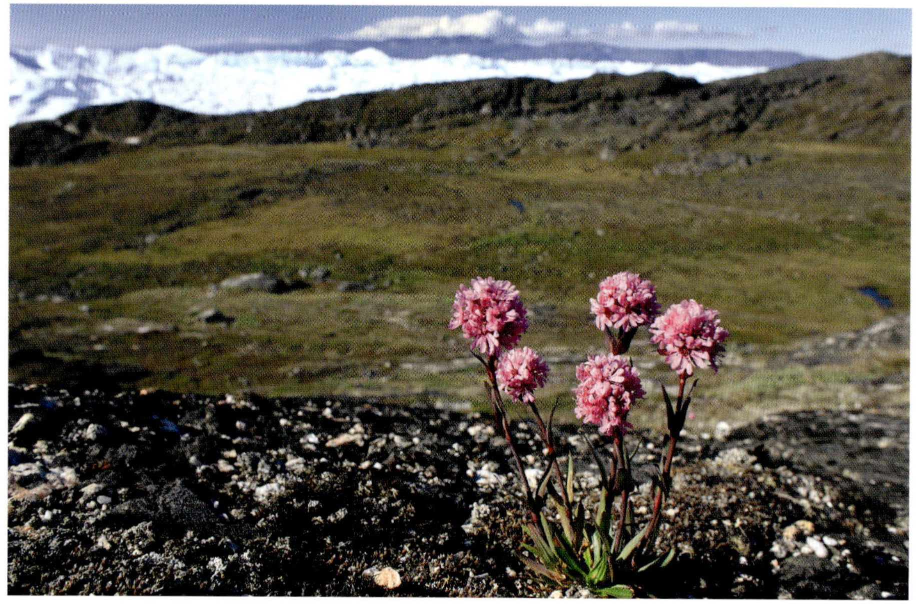

You would be mistaken to think that Greenland is a cold ice desert all the year round. During the short summer in July, the Arctic shows itself in a colourful light with hundreds of species of flowering plants. Ilulissat, northwest Greenland.

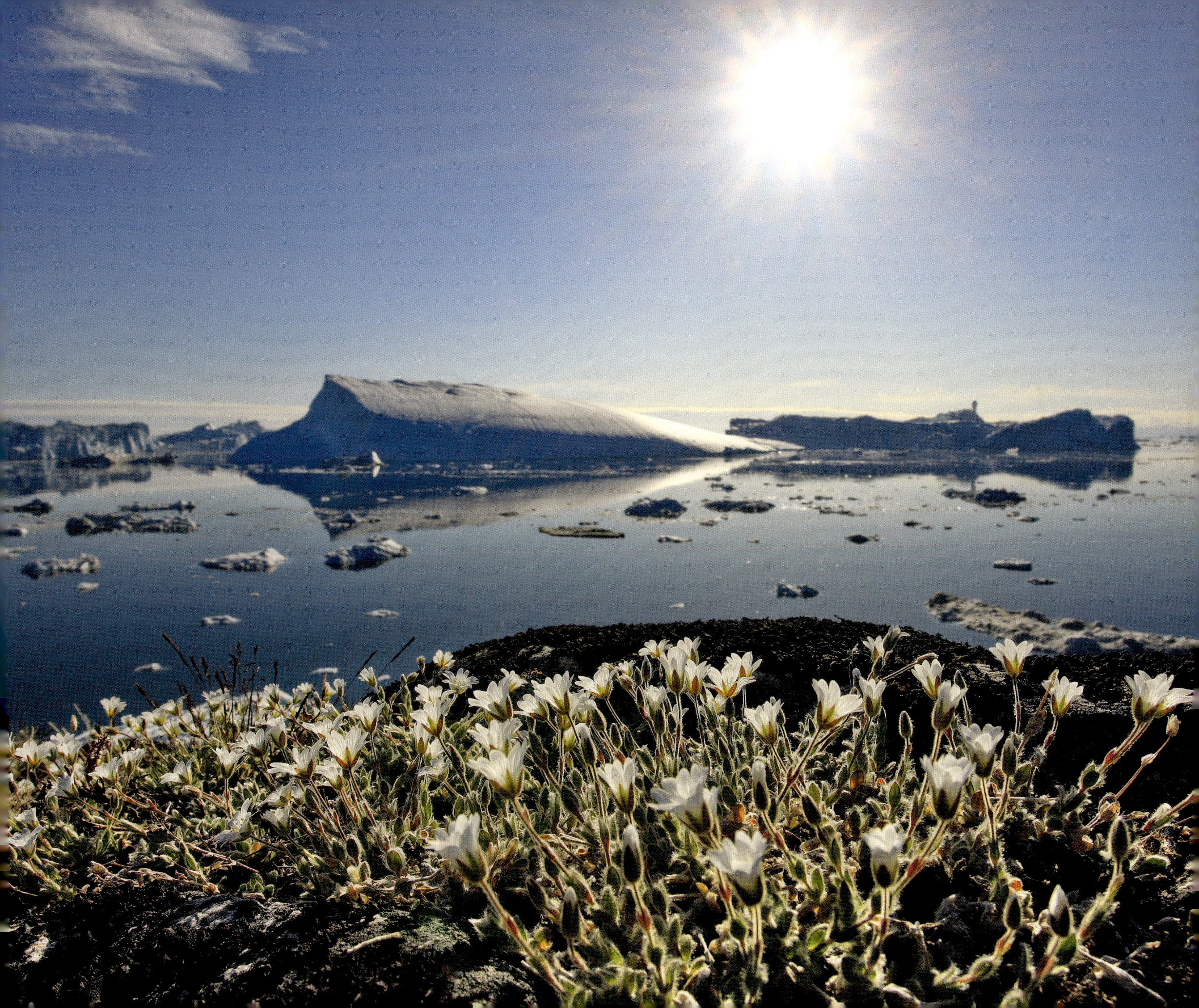

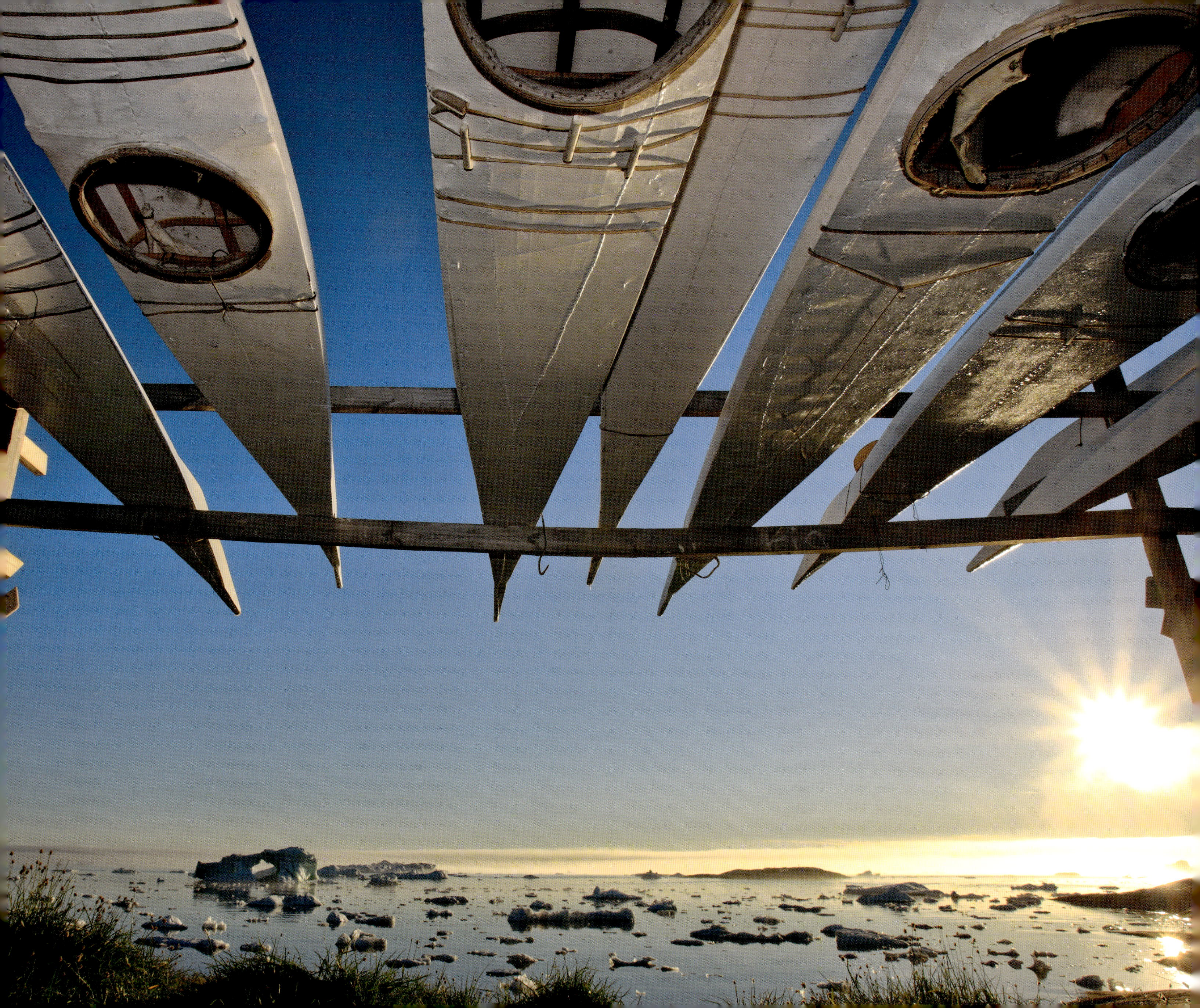

The word "kayak" derives from the Greenlandic word "qajaq". Kayaks are canoes that were developed by the Inuit. They are, primarily, fast boats that can be easily manoeuvred, and are used to hunt marine mammals such as seals, or even whales. The frame of the kayak is made of wood or animal bones and is covered with stretched seal skin. In Greenland, too, the kayak is increasingly being replaced by motorised boats. Only in the far north do the Polar Inuit continue to hunt seals by kayak.
Ilulissat, northwest Greenland.

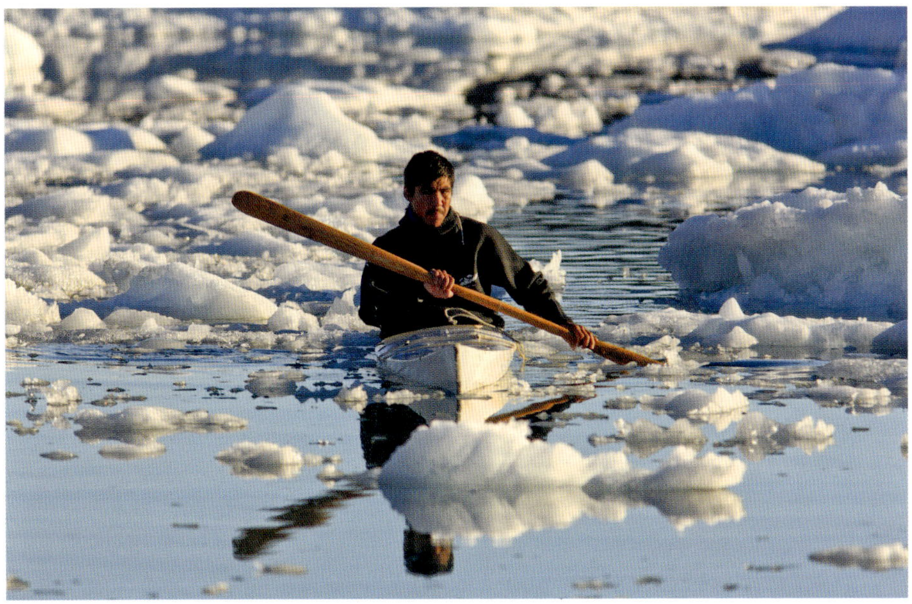

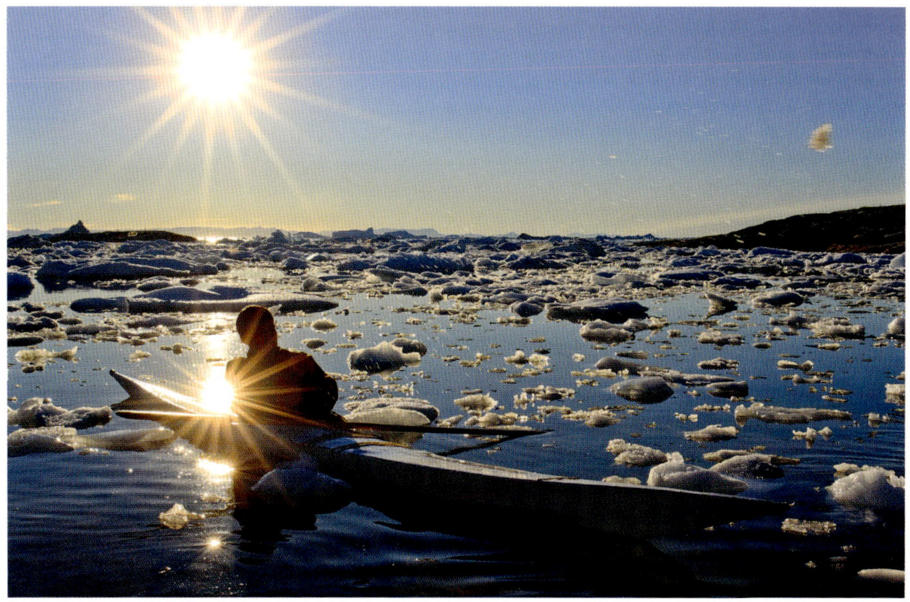

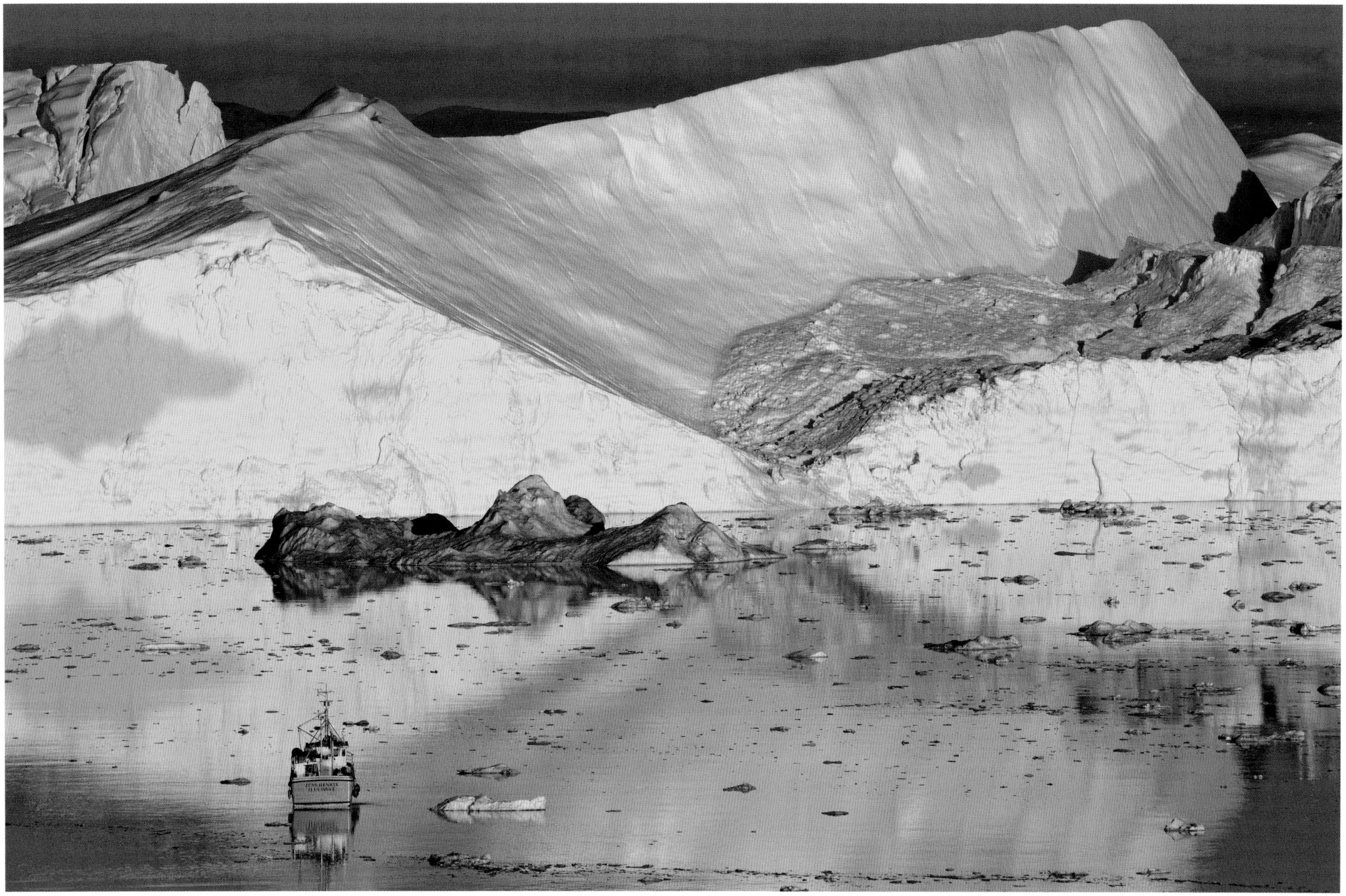

The Ilulissat Icefjord is the largest ice fjord in the world. The Sermeq-Kujalleq glacier, one of the fastest and therefore one of the most active glaciers in the world, ends in the sea here. The enormous glacier calves into the fjord and leaves behind icebergs that can be up to several hundred metres in size.

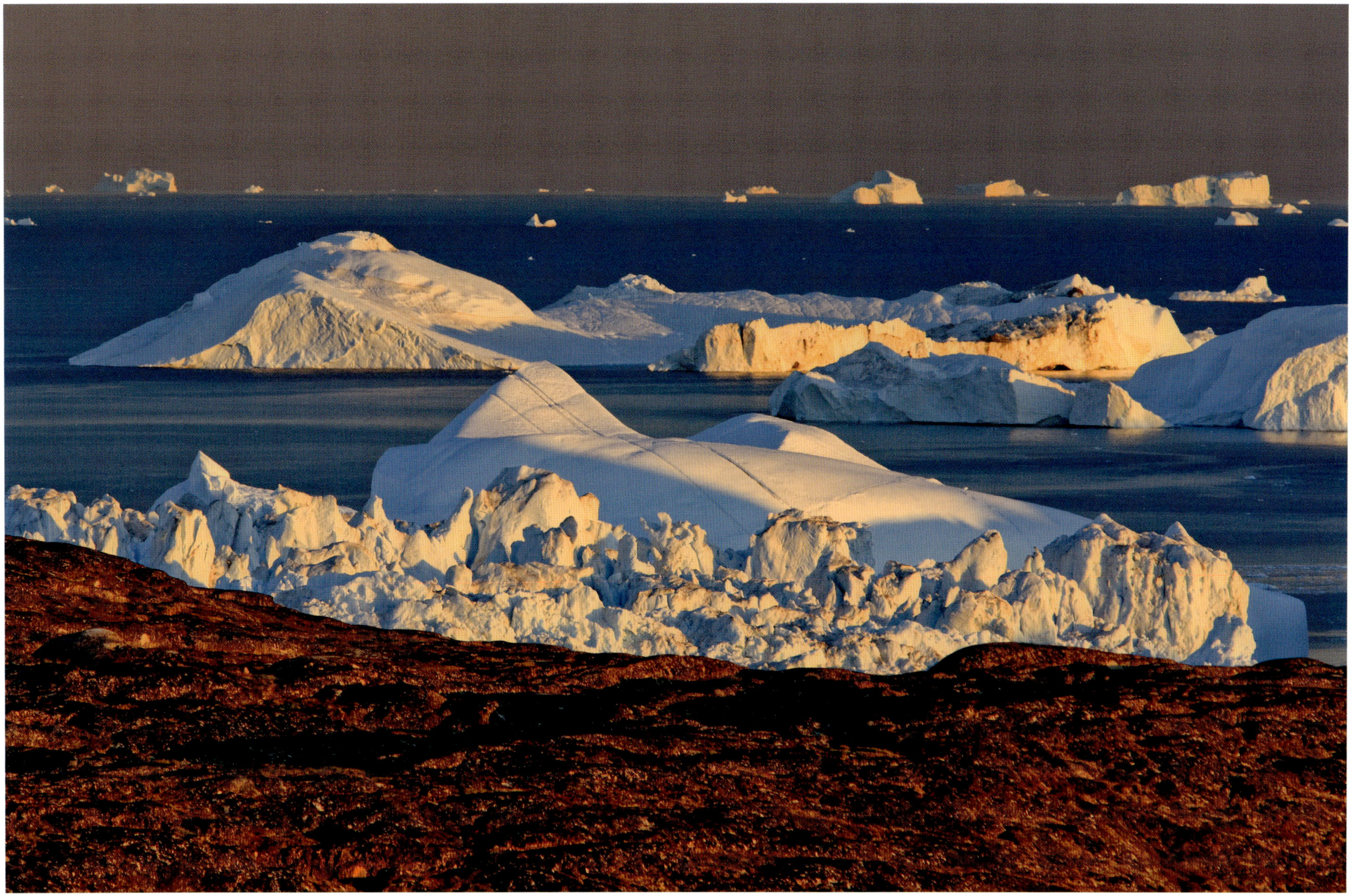

Pages 92/93: Fog has descended. The midnight sun casts a magical light over the ice fjord at Ilulissat.

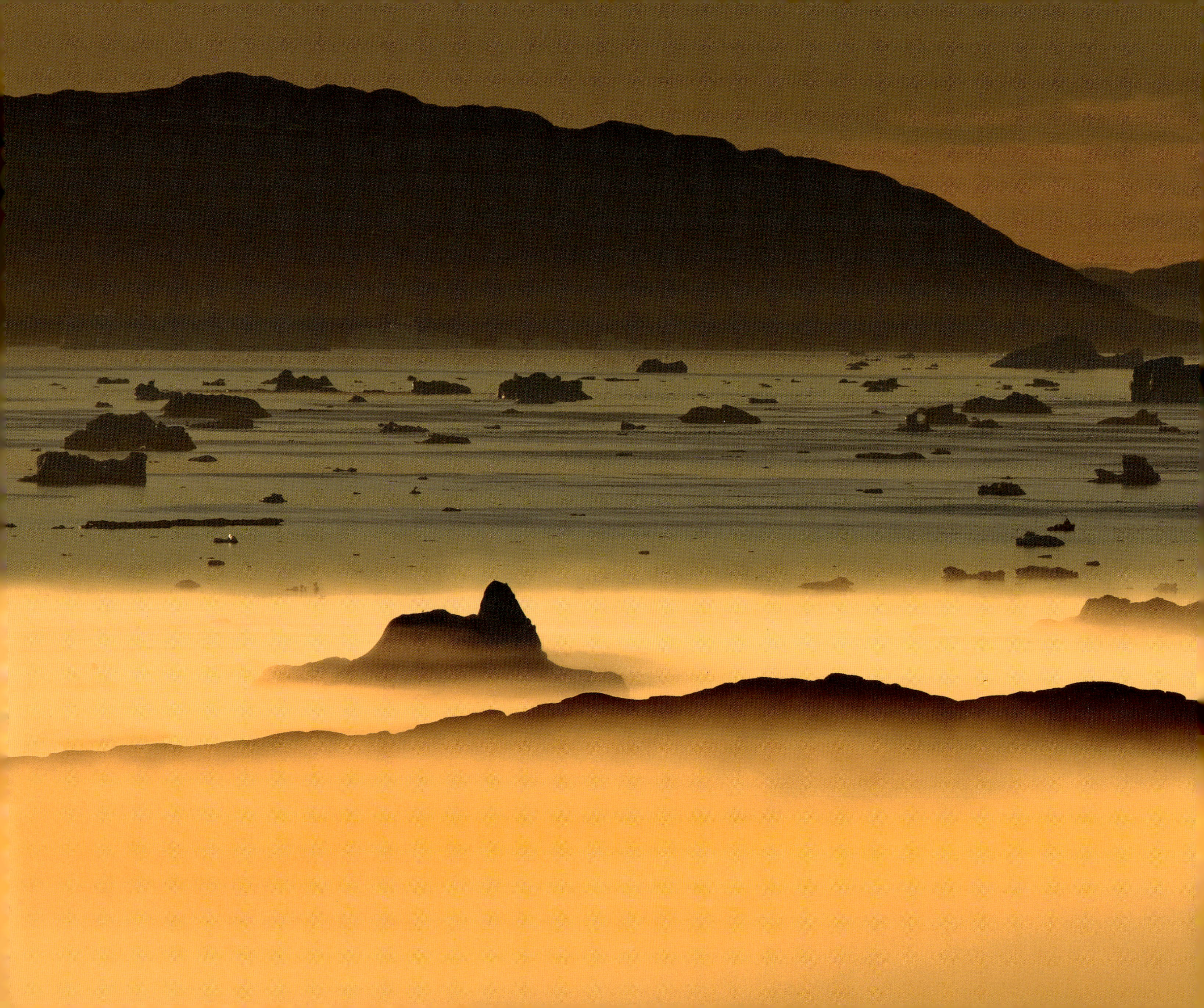

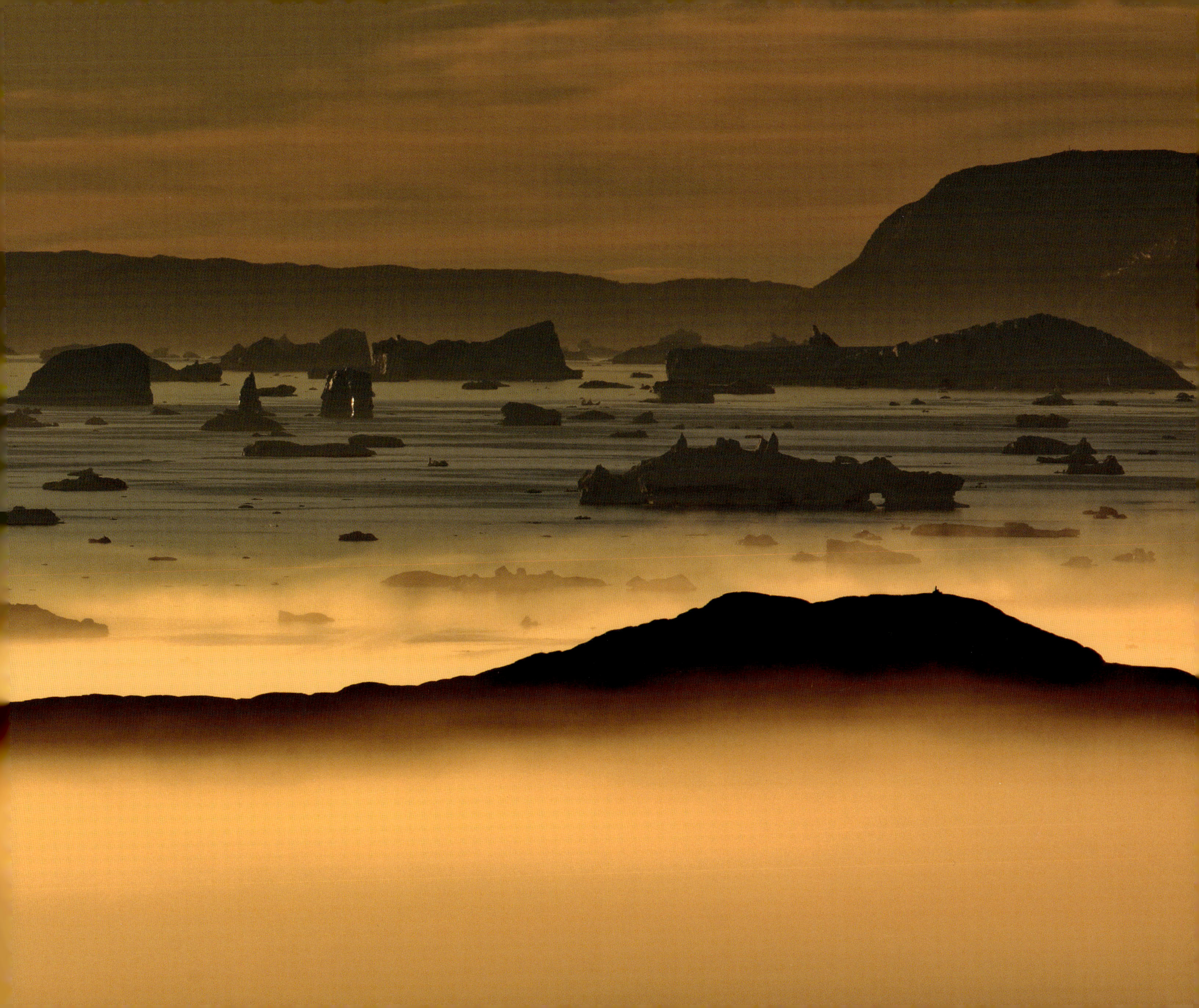

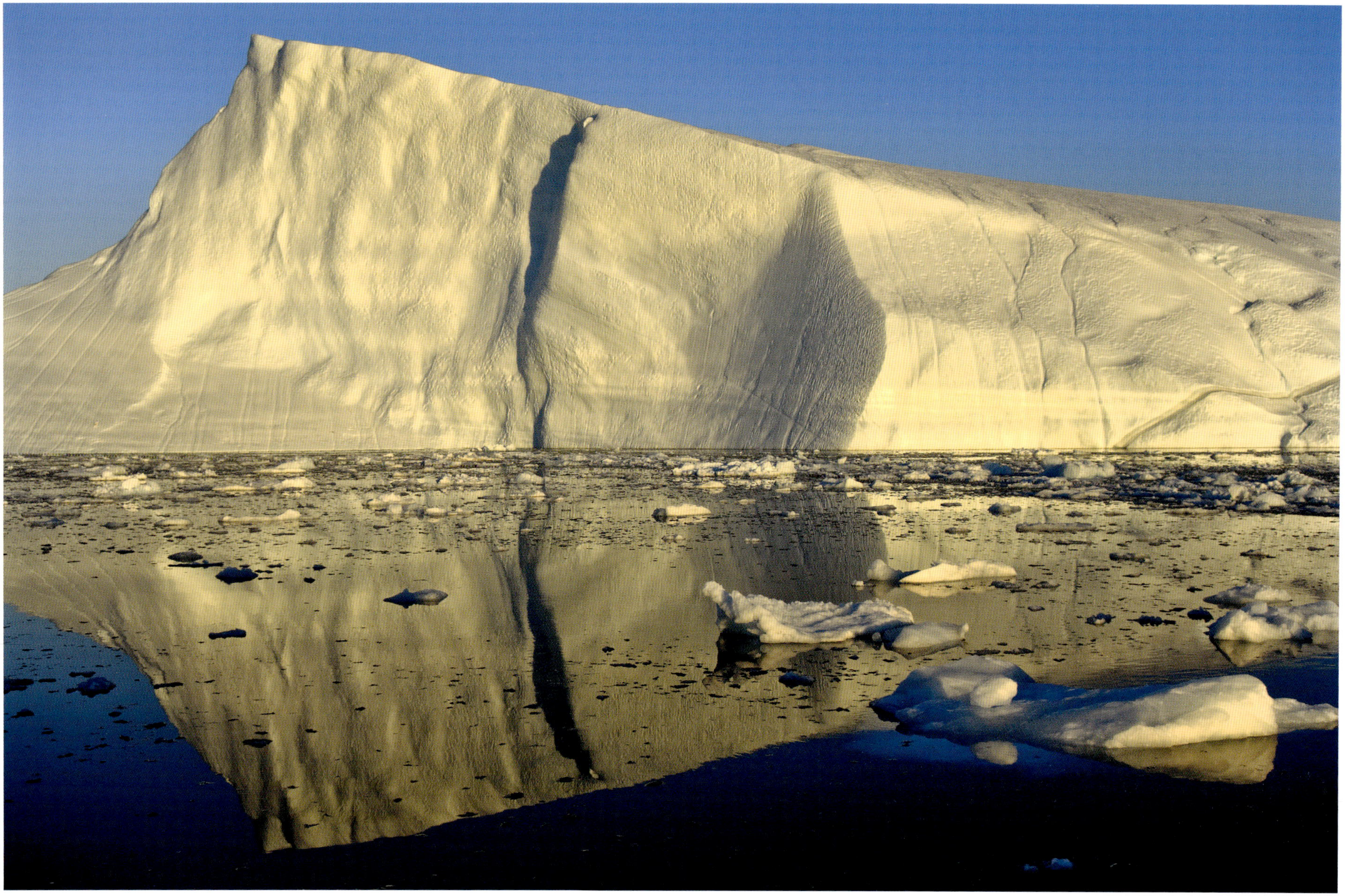

The floating icebergs of the Ilulissat Icefjord need roughly twelve to fifteen months to pass through the shallow fjord (in which they run aground again and again) and reach the open sea. The ice monoliths drift onto the open sea and then head south. Icebergs from Ilulissat have been spotted off the coast of New York.

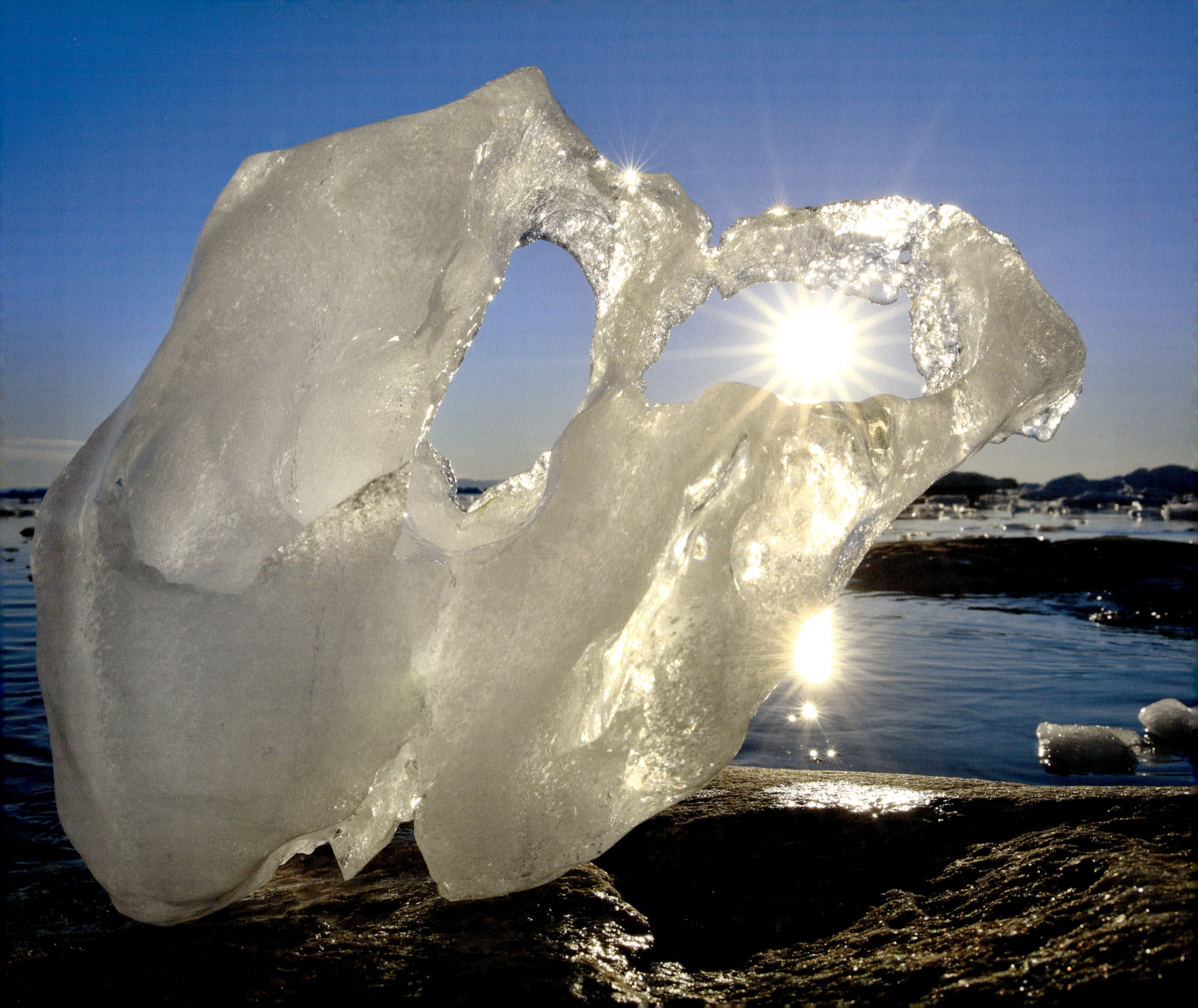

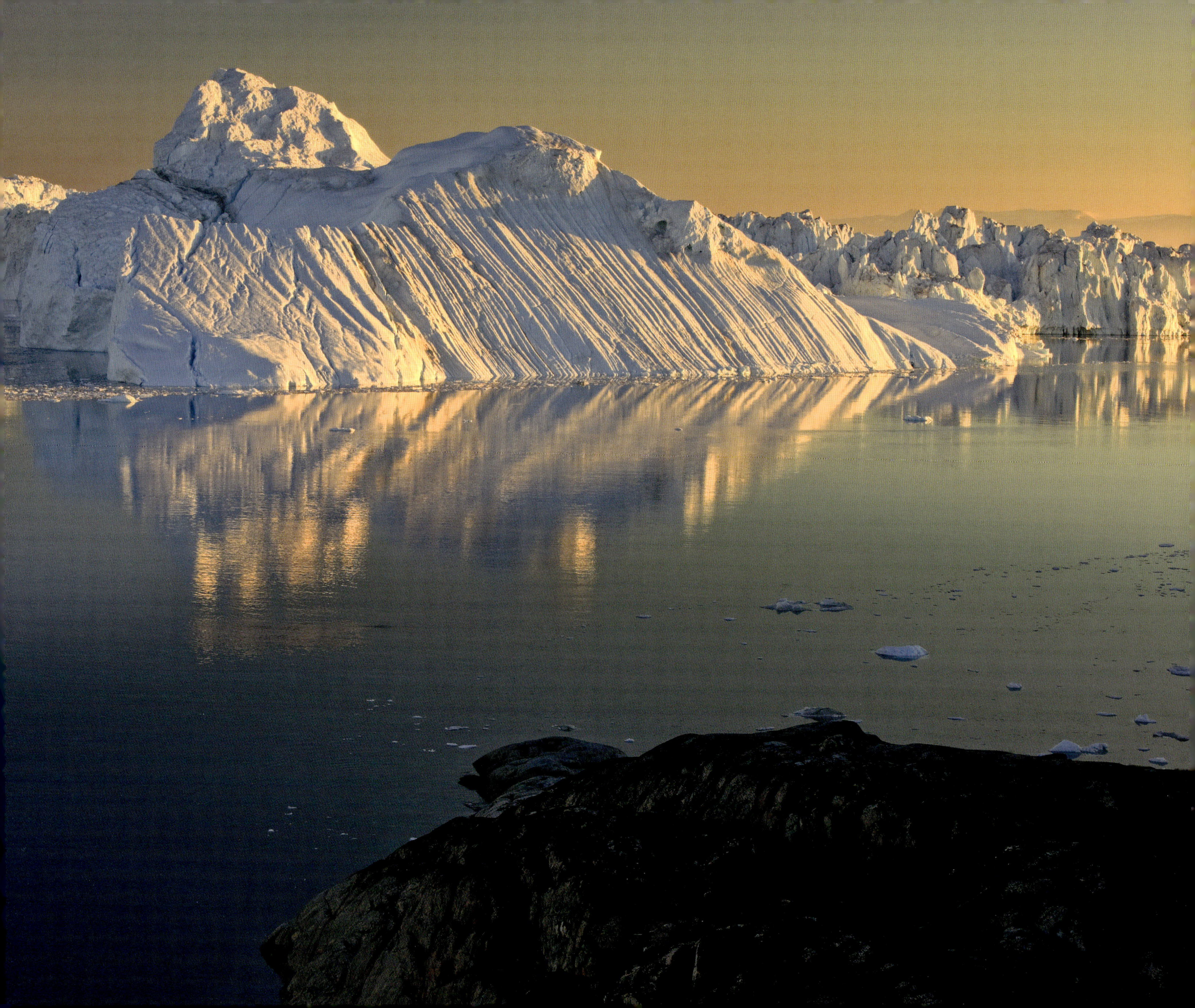

"Our fishing boat slowly chugged forward towards the icebergs. We were ten 'ice tourists', and our captain came from Ilulissat. Everyone on board was chattering away excitedly; our nocturnal excursion would carry us deep into the world-famous ice fjord. The weather was perfect, and the light of the midnight sun bathed the landscape in a golden light. After a journey of about 20 minutes, we reached the first enormous icebergs. The temperature immediately dropped by a few degrees. We glided past the huge mountains of ice. Time and again we were startled by loud cracks and thuds. Icebergs must be treated with respect. Whole walls of ice can suddenly break off and the flood wave is capable of capsizing small boats. I suddenly noticed how quiet it was on board; you could have heard a pin drop. We stared in awe at the sparkling ice. Everyone was entranced by the magic of this magnificent natural wonder."

Bernd Römmelt

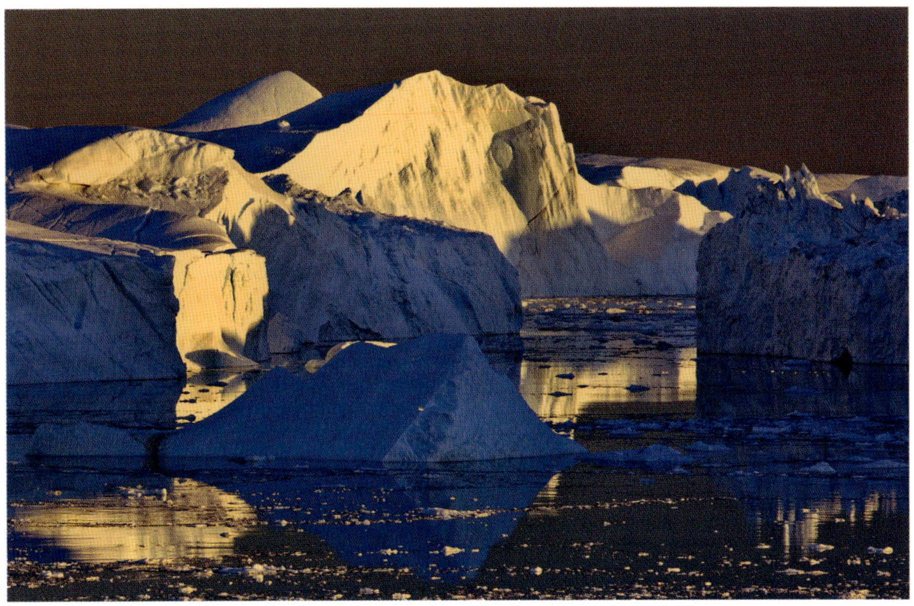

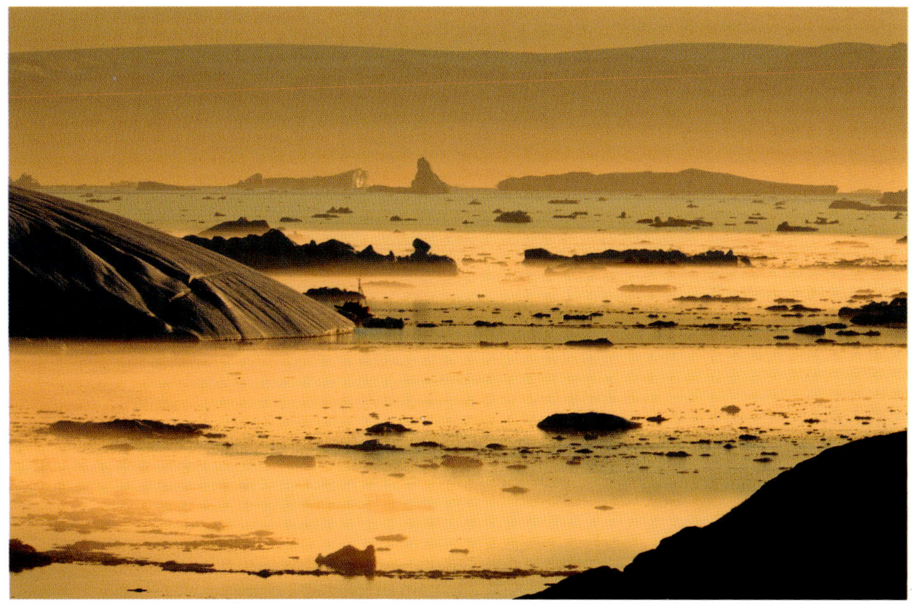

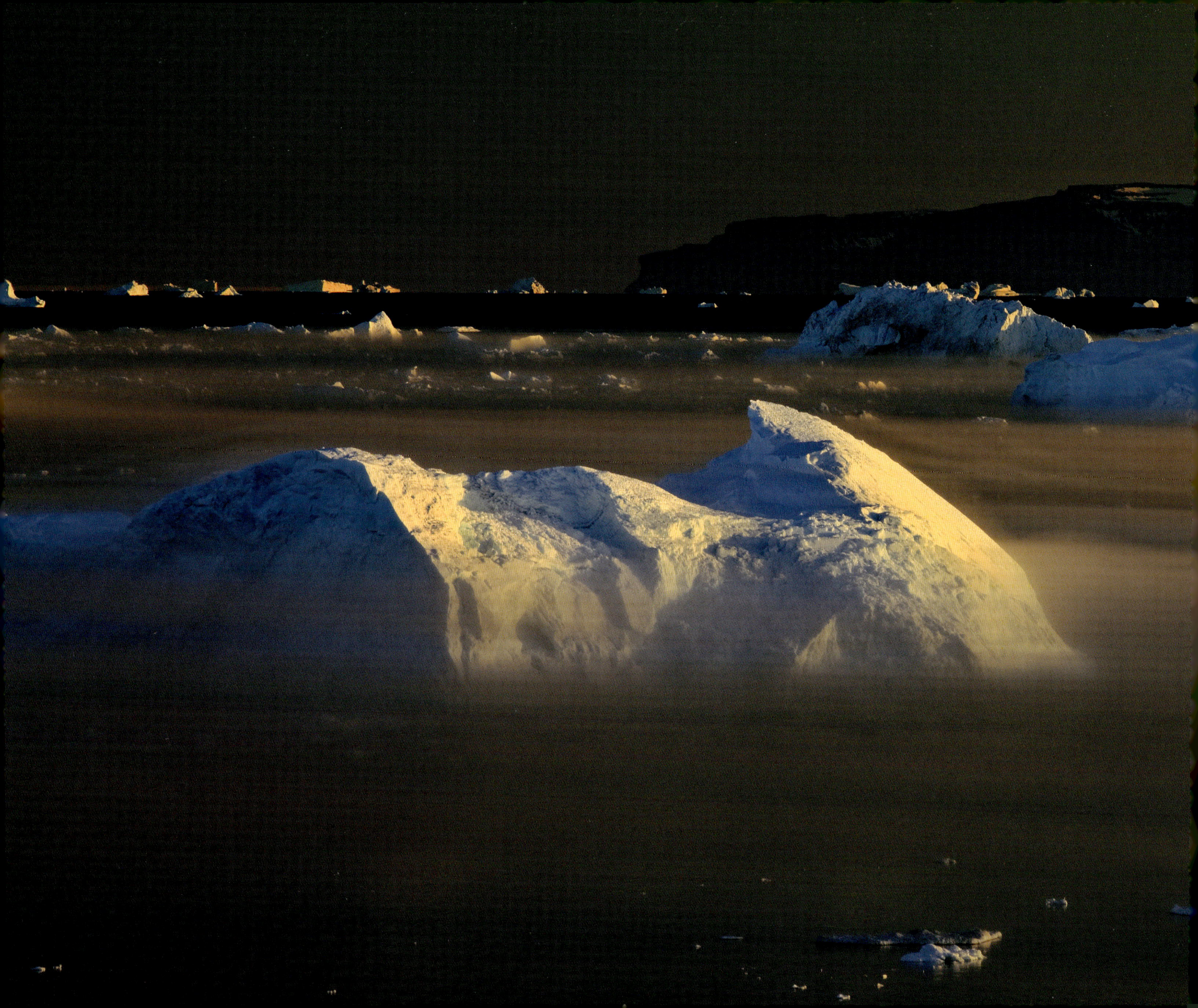

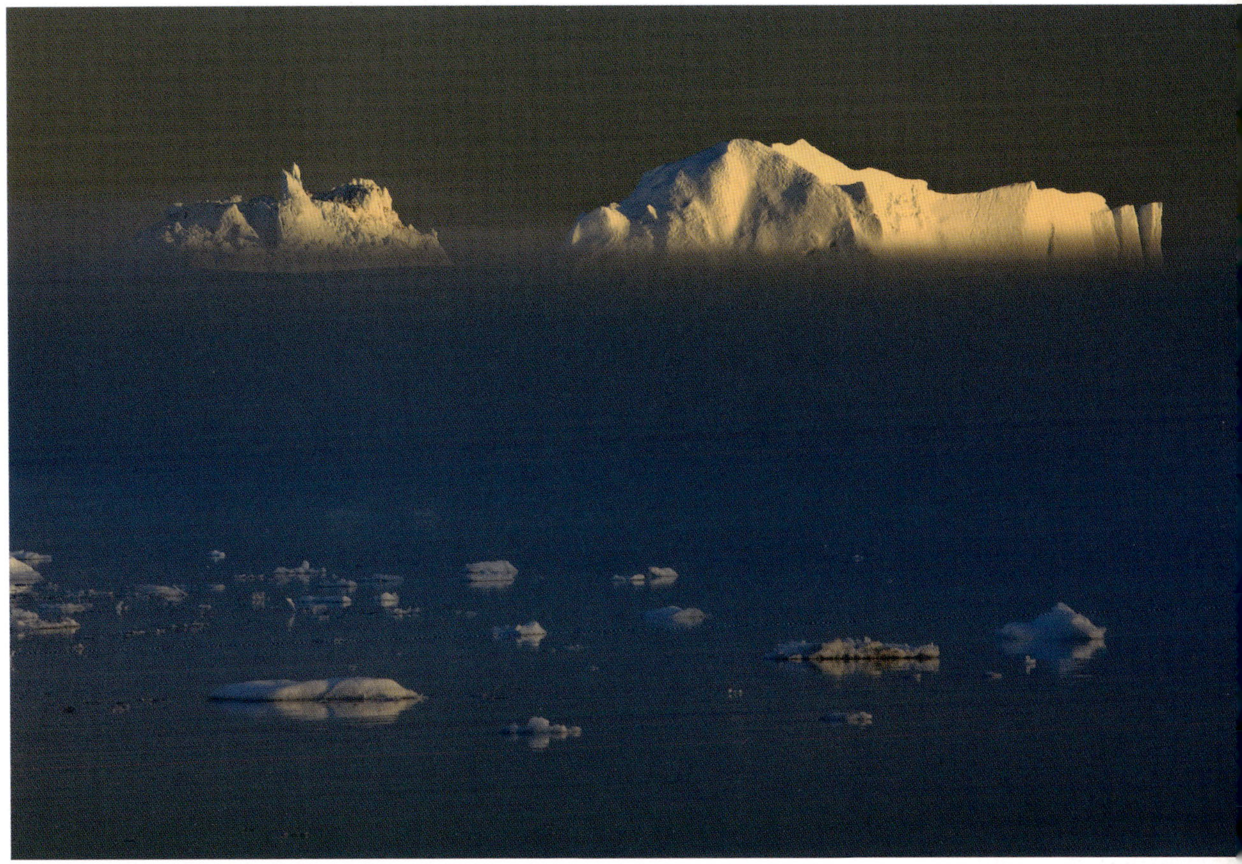

The Sermeq-Kujalleq glacier retreated by about ten kilometres between 2001 and 2007, while the speed of the ice flow doubled from 20 metres to 40 metres per day. It cannot be ignored any longer: Greenland's ice is beginning to melt. And it is doing so at a dramatic rate and with serious consequences for the rest of the world, as the sea level rises.

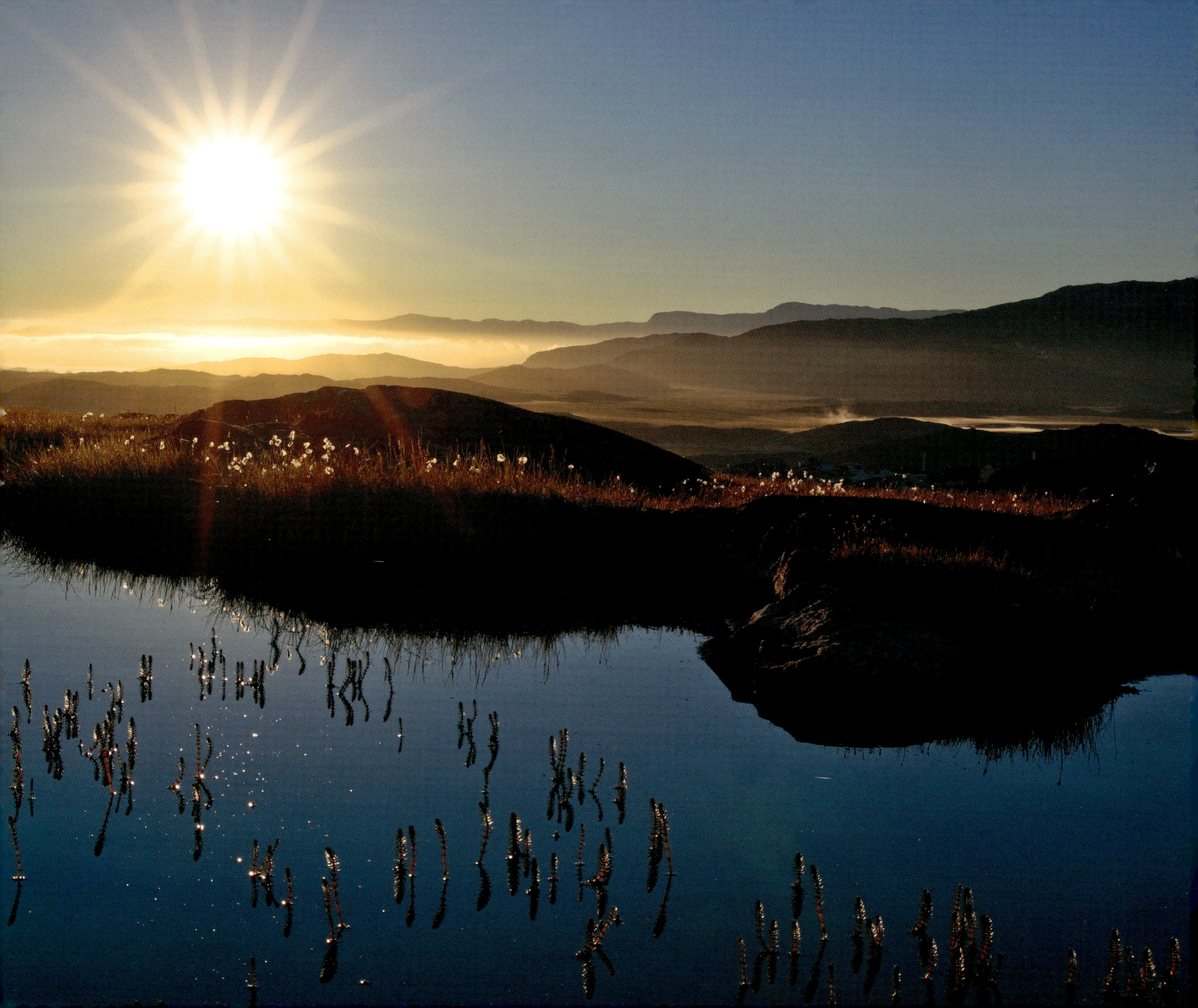

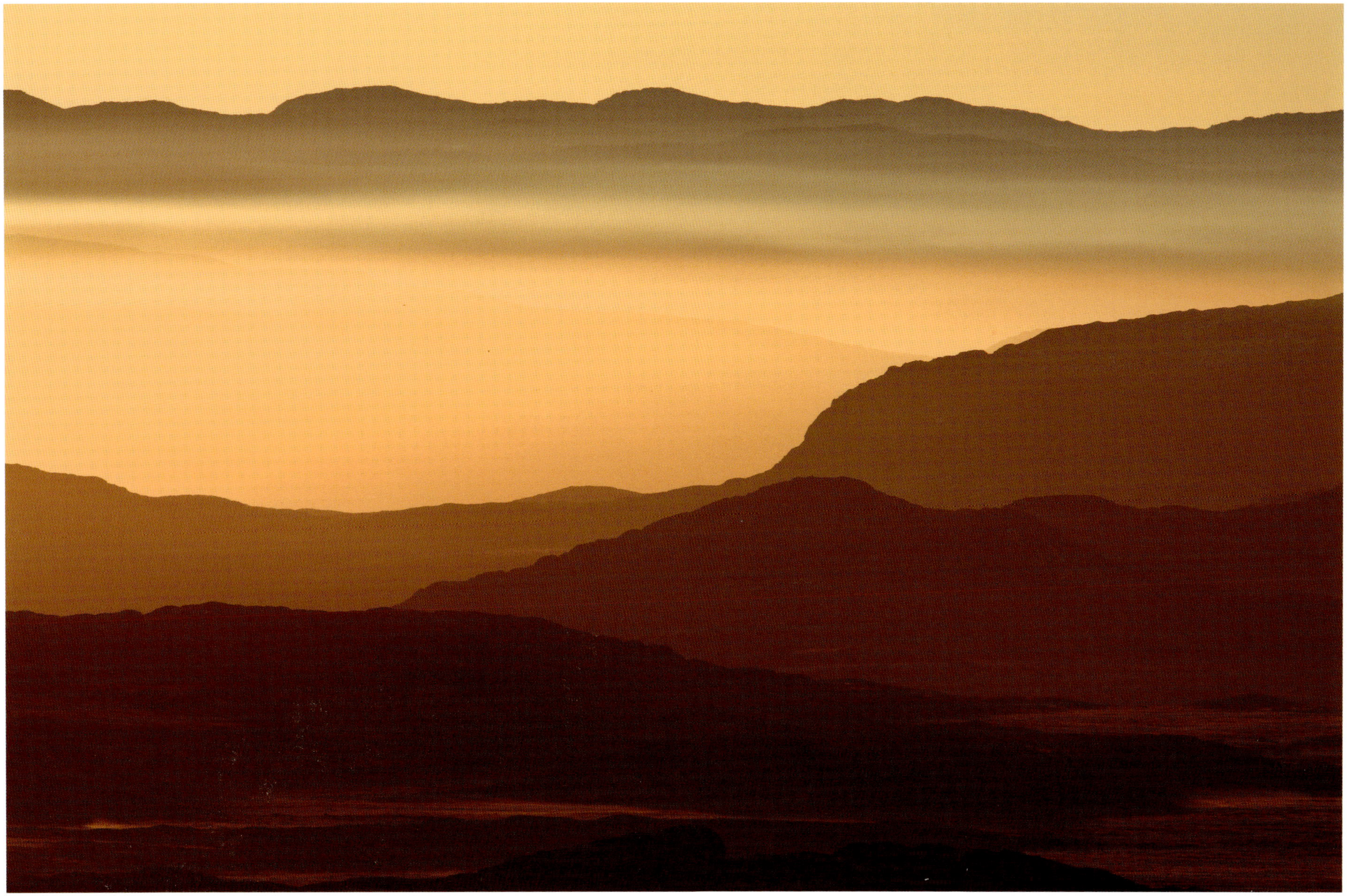

In July, the sun begins to rise again at about 2 o'clock in the morning. Those who have experienced the magical hours between 11 o'clock at night and 2 o'clock in the morning in the high Arctic will never forget the fantastic light there. Ilulissat, northwest Greenland.

Only a small number of tourists make their way to the settlement of Upernavik, in the far north of Greenland, which has a population of 1,157. Upernavik lies on a rocky island south of the Upernavik ice fjord. Some of the biggest icebergs on earth calve into the fjord.
Graves cannot be dug into the ground because of the permafrost. The deceased are therefore covered with big stones and the graves decorated with plastic flowers.

Pages 104/105: View of the Inglefield fjord near the settlement of Qaanaaq. It is still entirely frozen in the month of March.

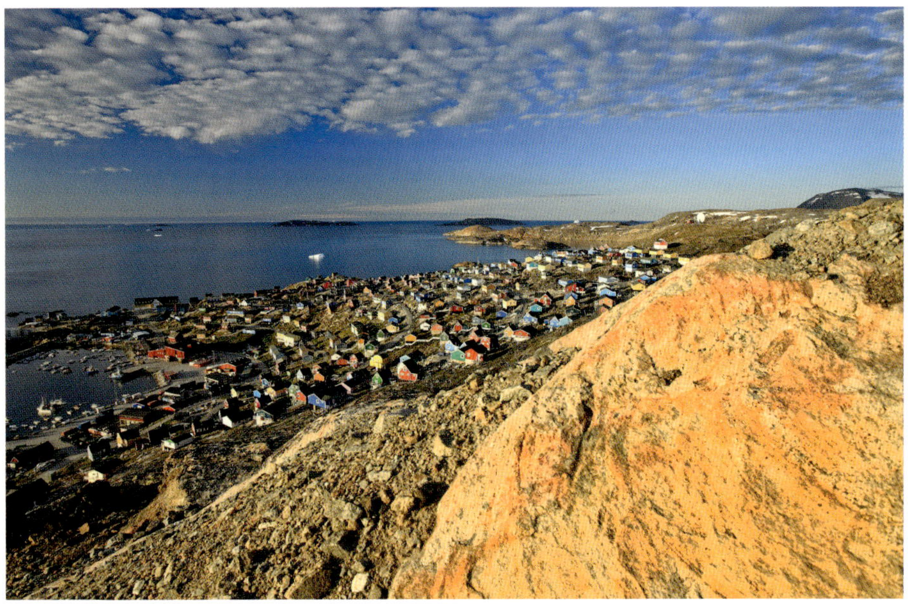

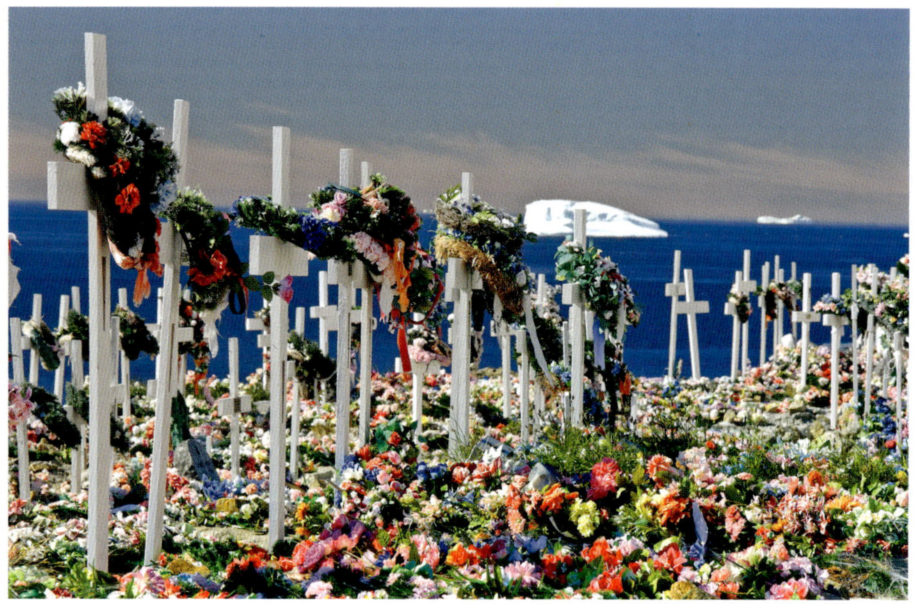

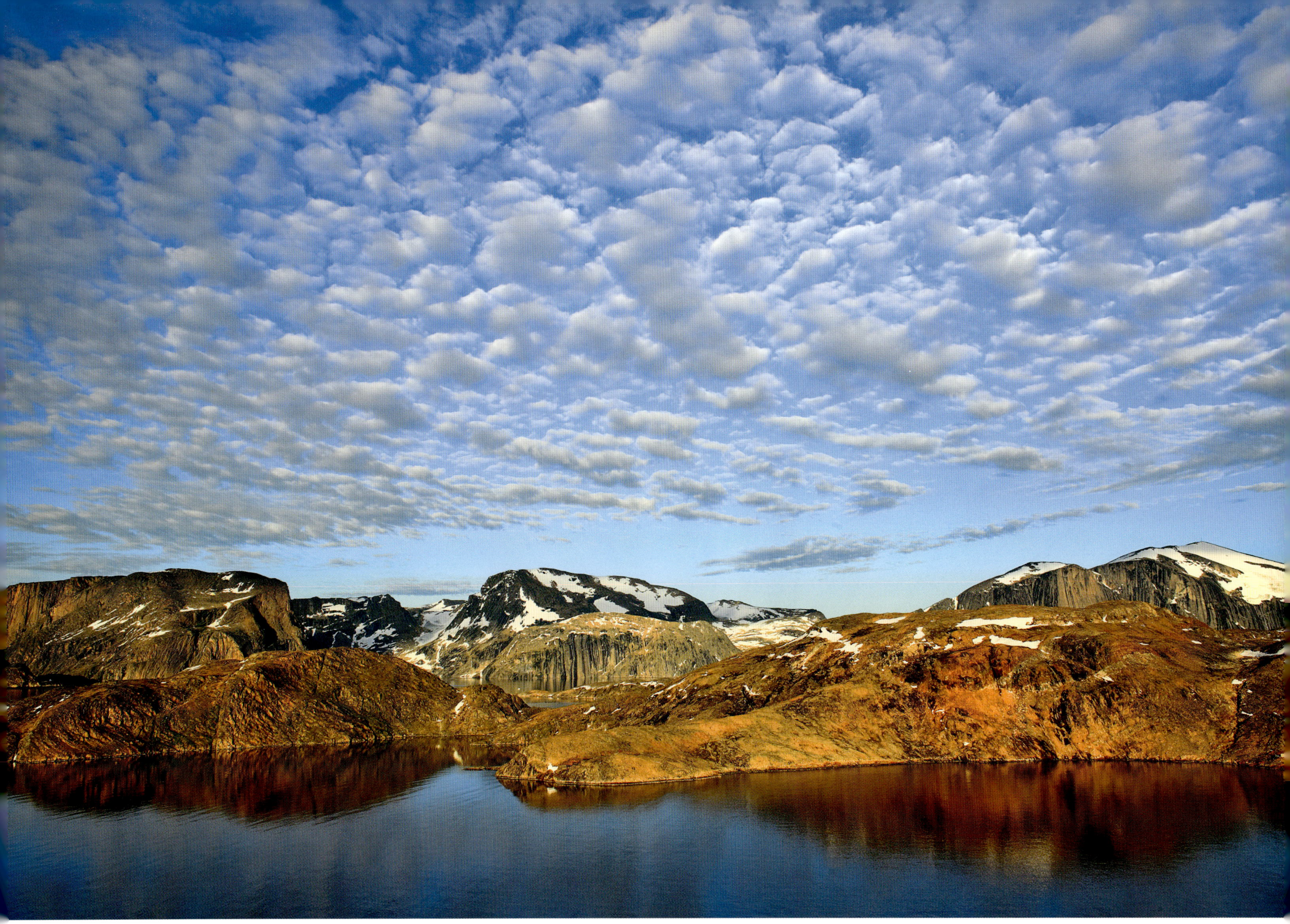

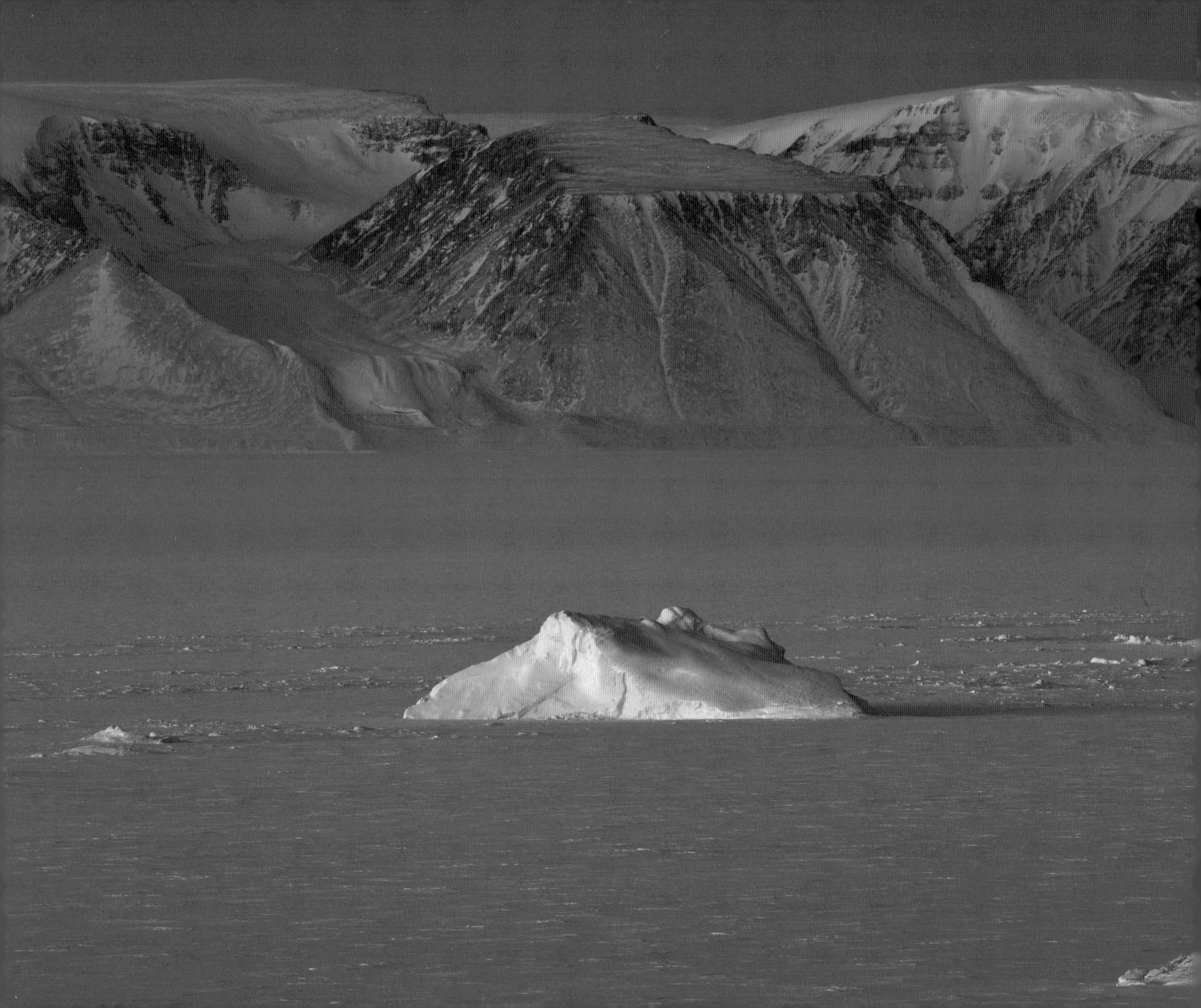

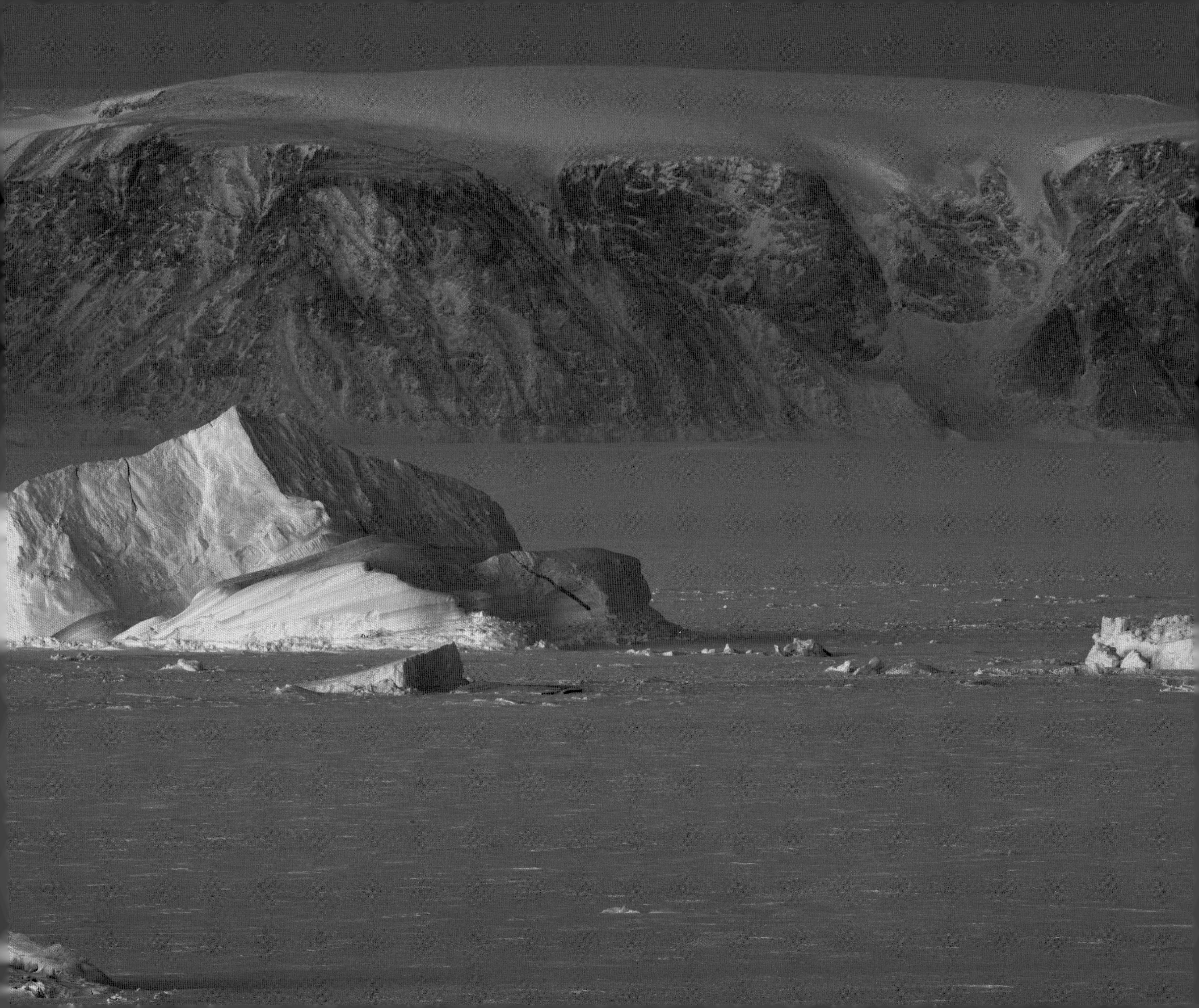

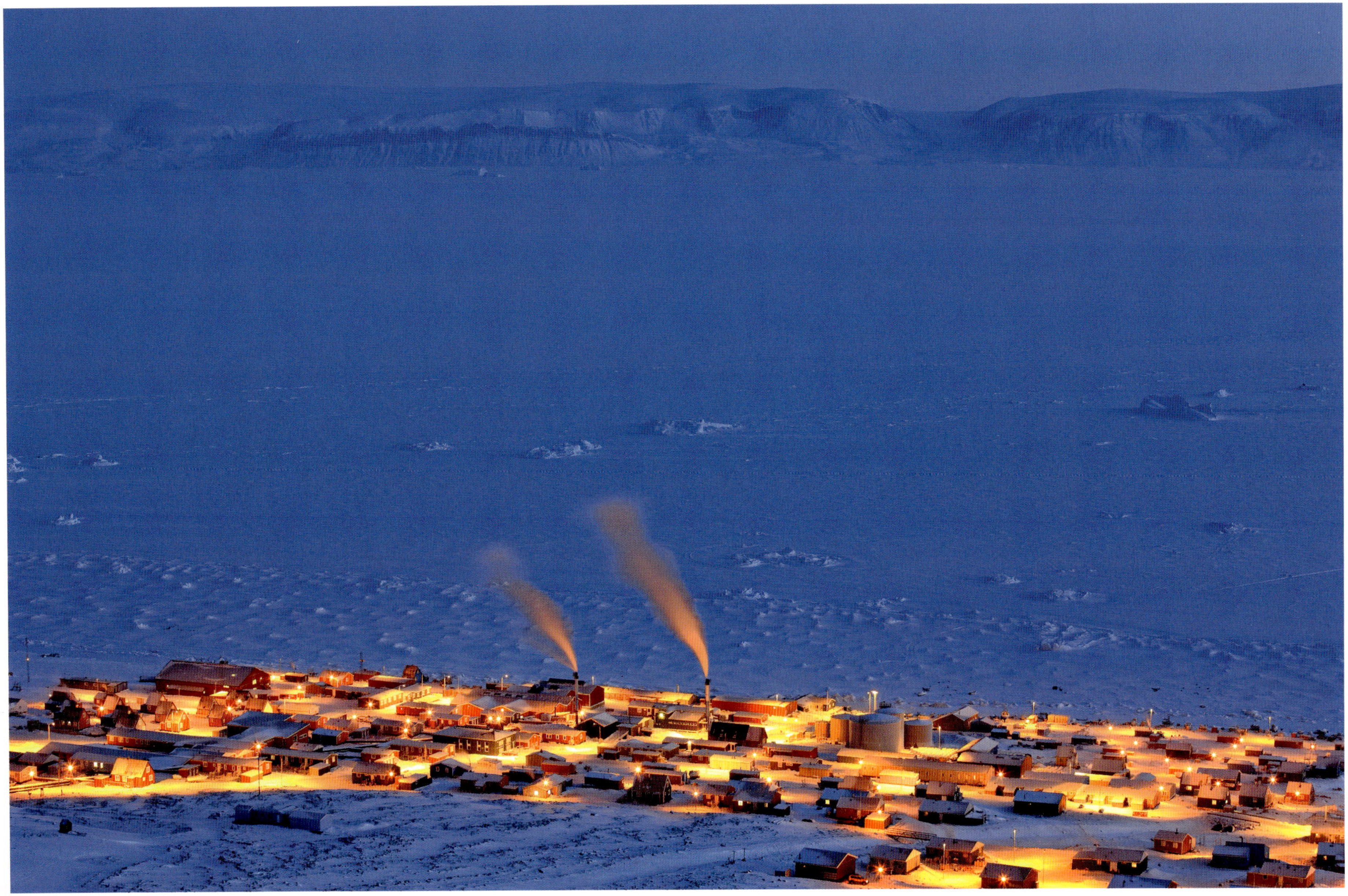

The small settlement of Qaanaaq is situated by Baffin Bay, in the far north of the country. It is just 200 kilometres southwest of the geomagnetic North Pole.

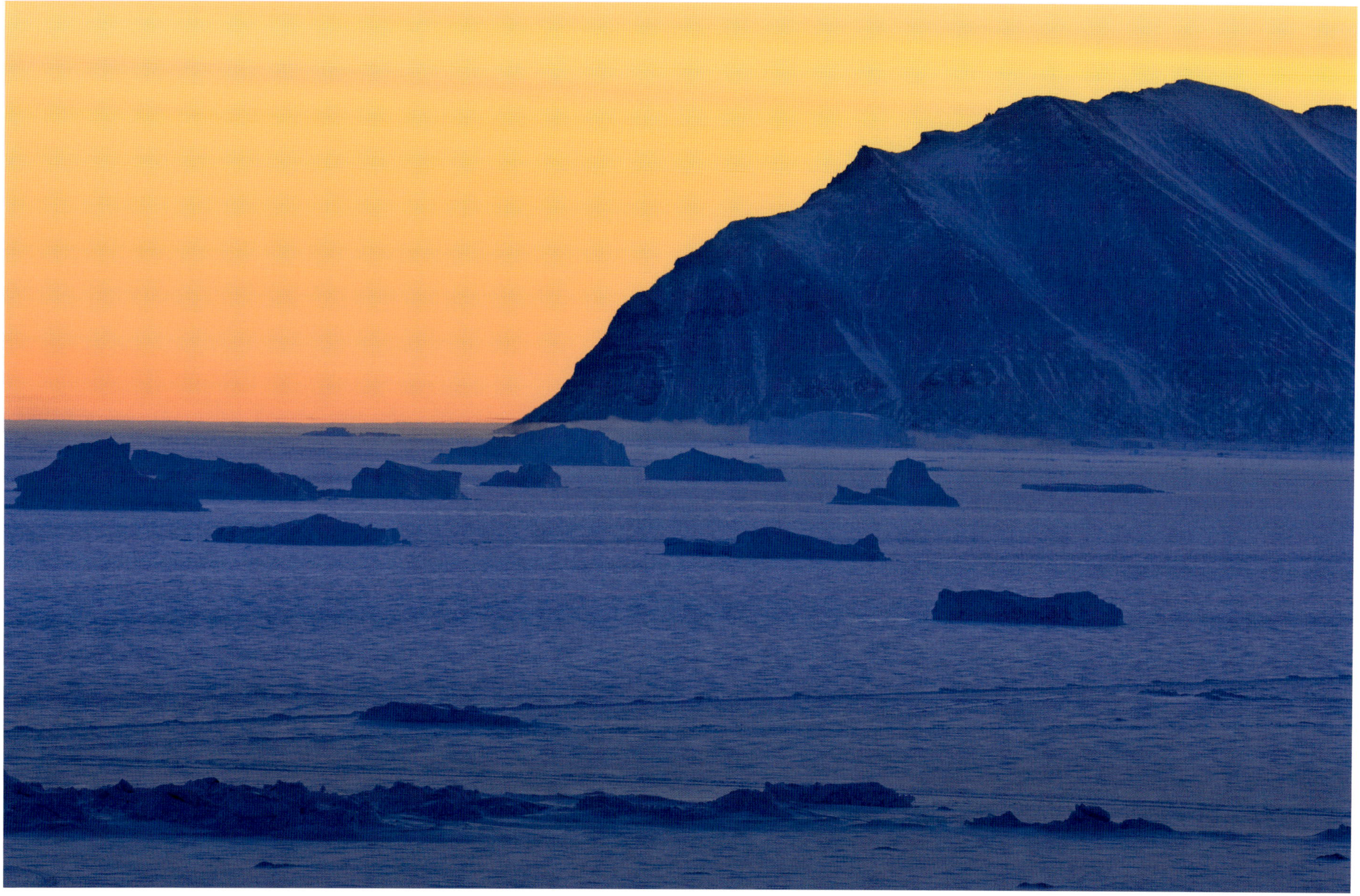

The polar night occurs here between November and February. By February it is no longer completely dark, however, and long periods of twilight conjure fantastic colour spectacles onto the Arctic sky.

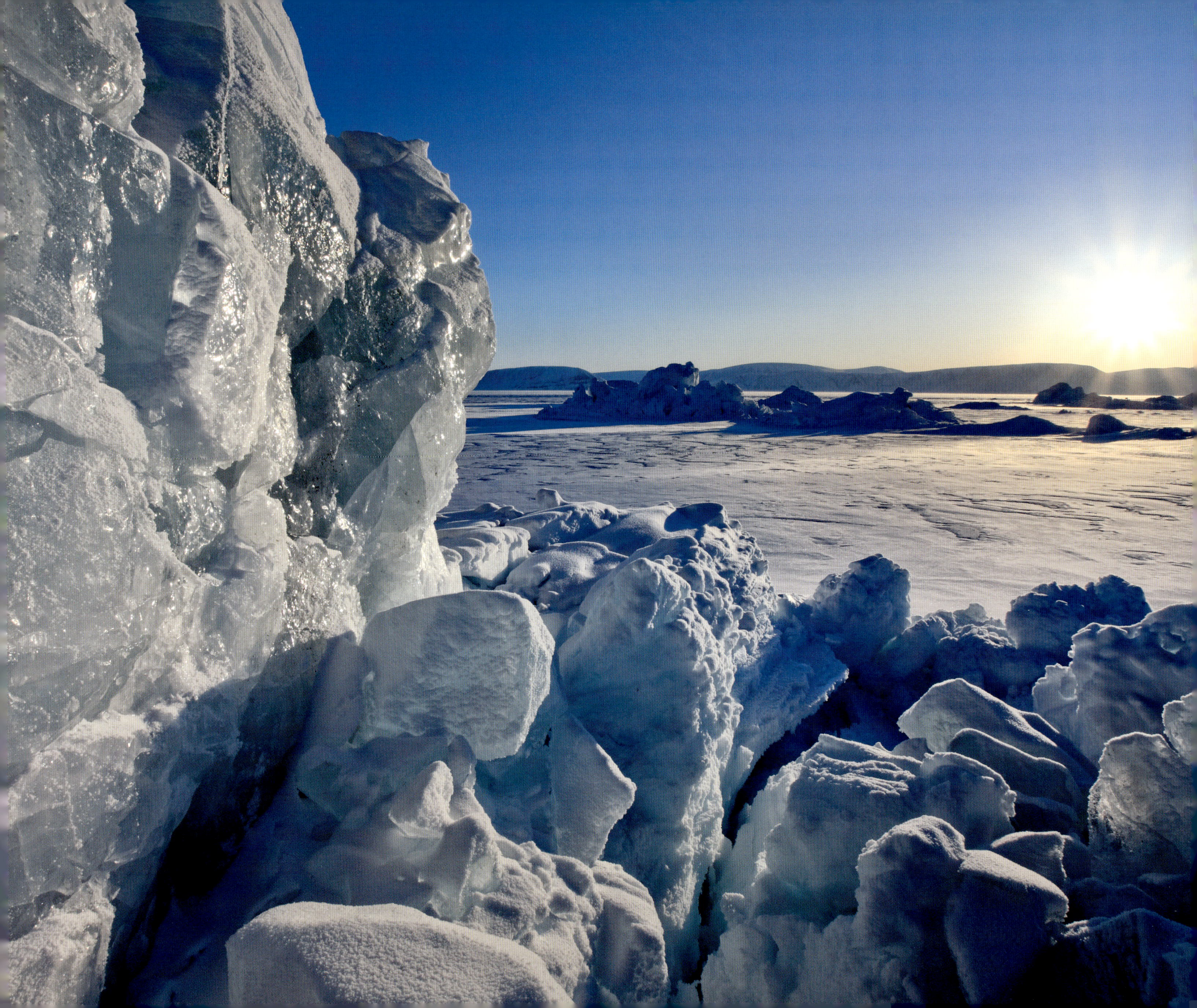

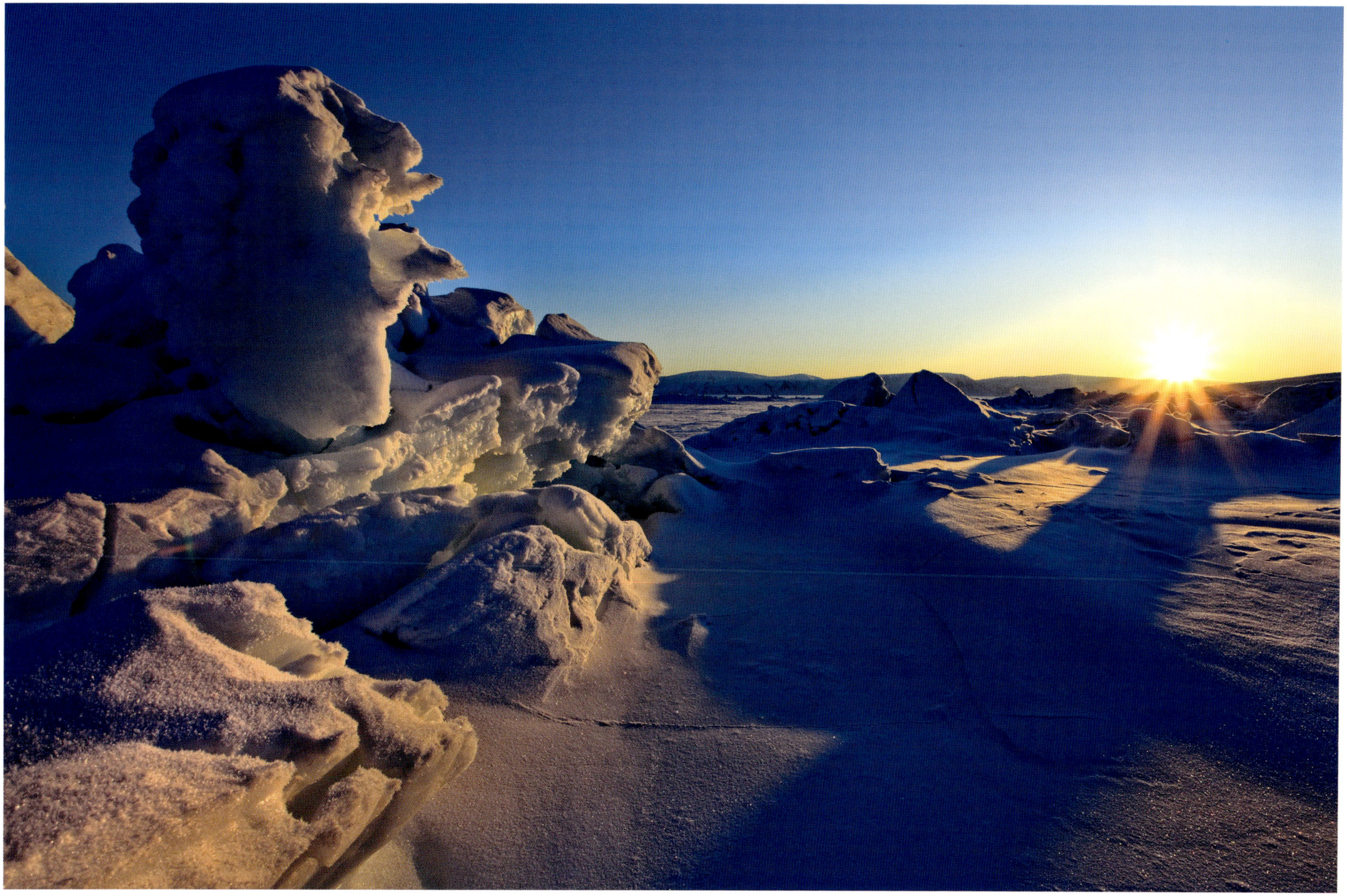

As early as the end of April, just two months after seeing the polar nights of February, one can admire the midnight sun above the pack ice. The metre-thick pack ice will not disappear completely until July.

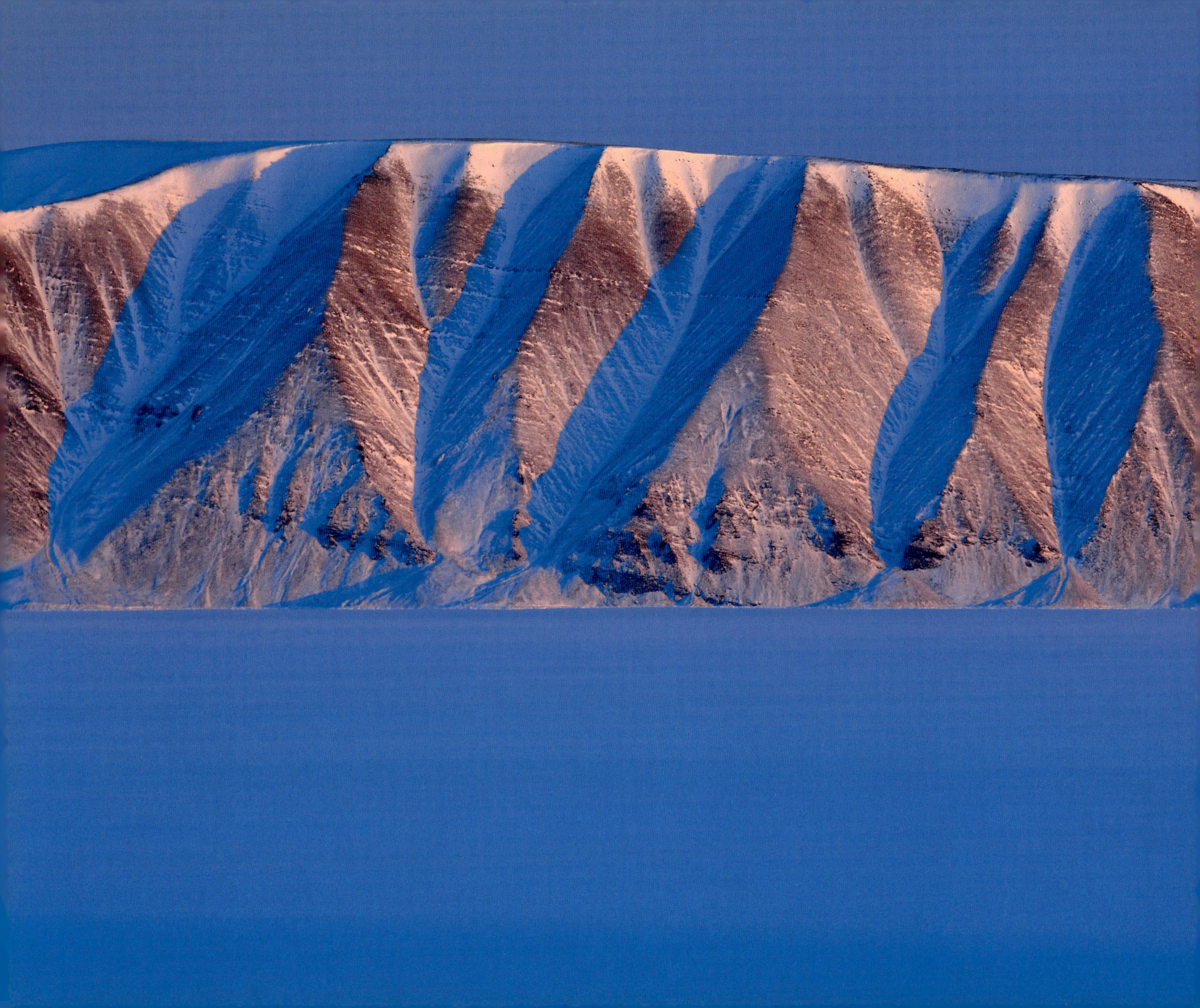

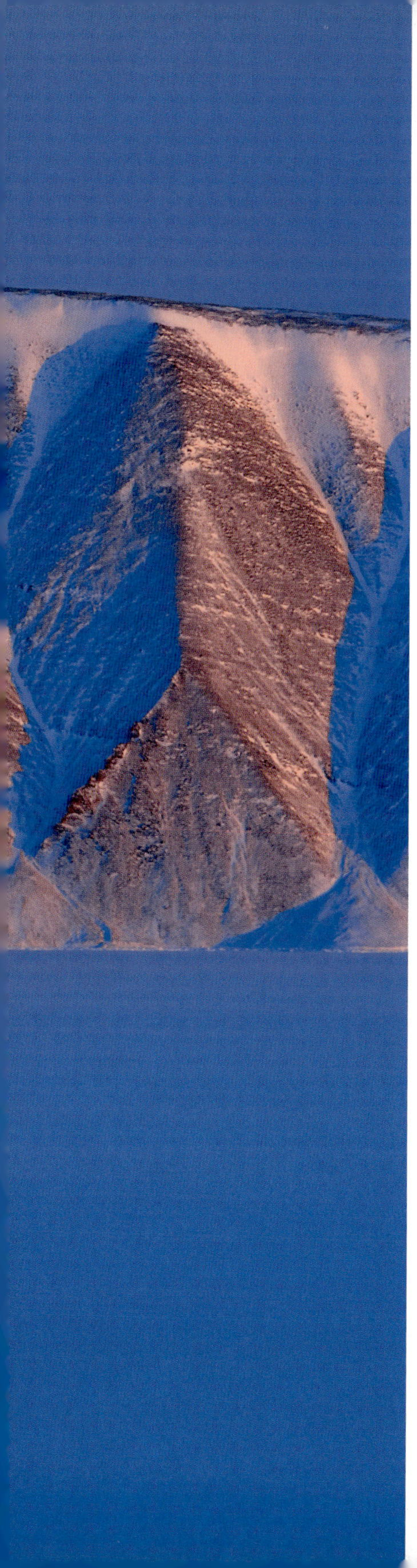

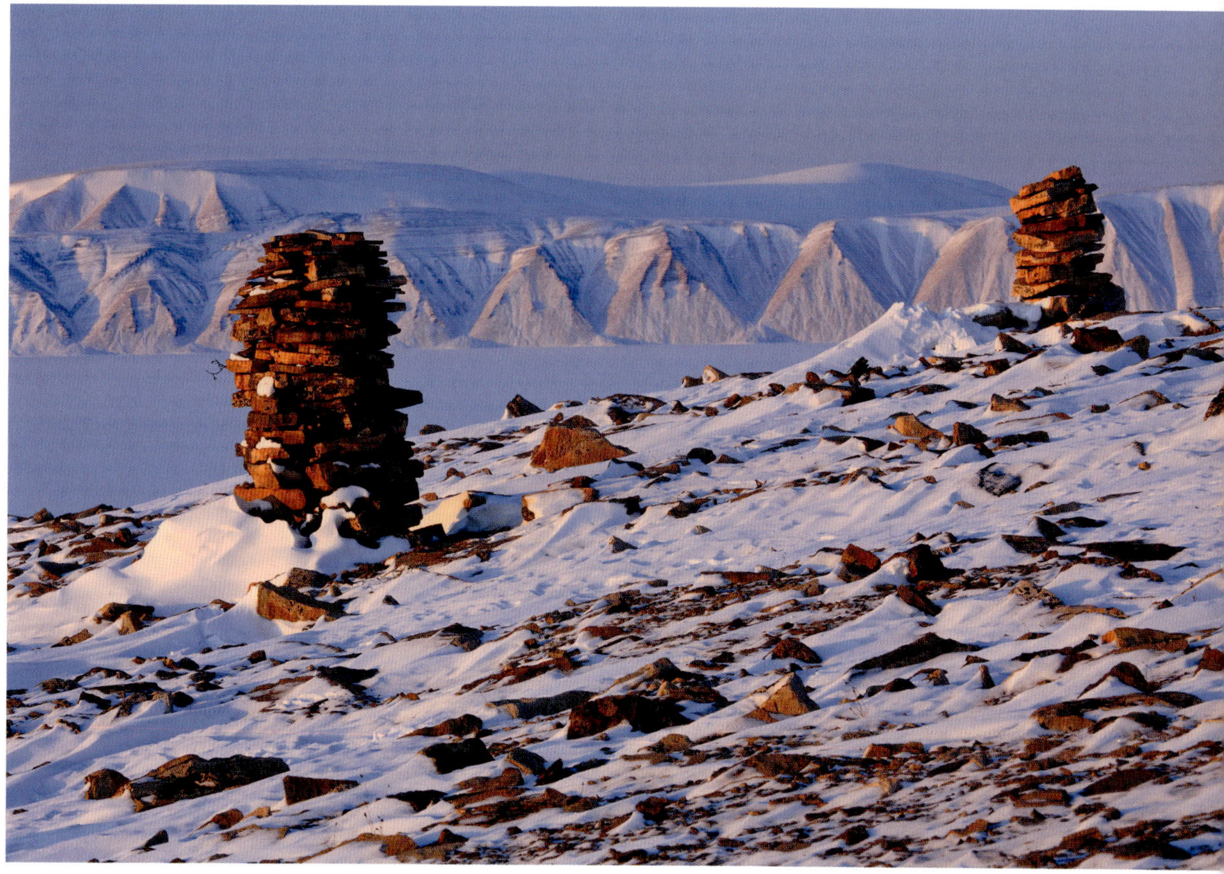

The Inuits' stone signposts are used mainly for orientation in the treeless expanses of the high Arctic.

For the inhabitants of northern Greenland, the first day of the year on which the sun appears above the horizon – 17 February in 2011 – is a festive day. They have had to get through 22 weeks without the warm rays of the sun.

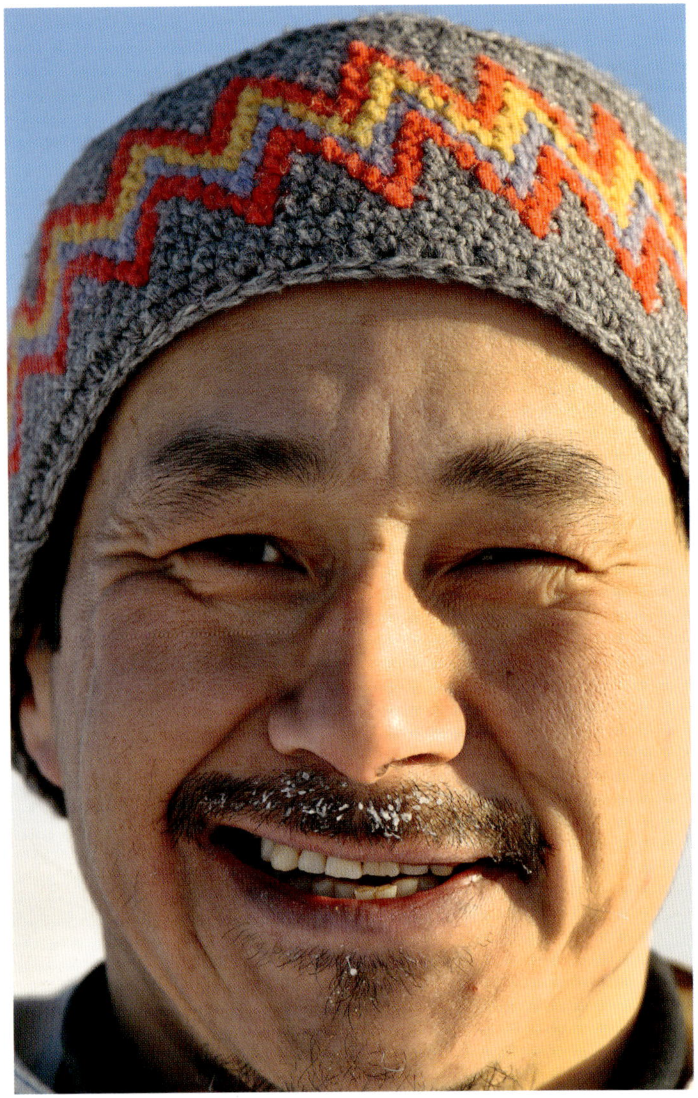

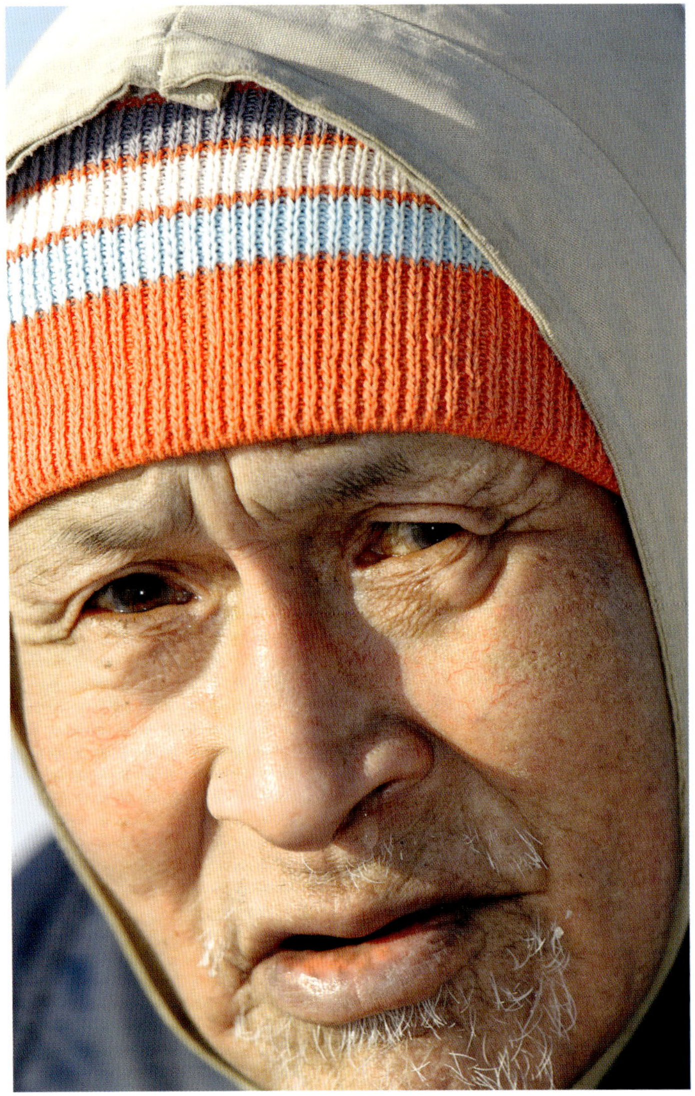

Cheerful, friendly faces that tell many a story: Qillay Danielsen, Knud Qujaukitsoq and Mads Ole Kristiansen, Qaanaaq.

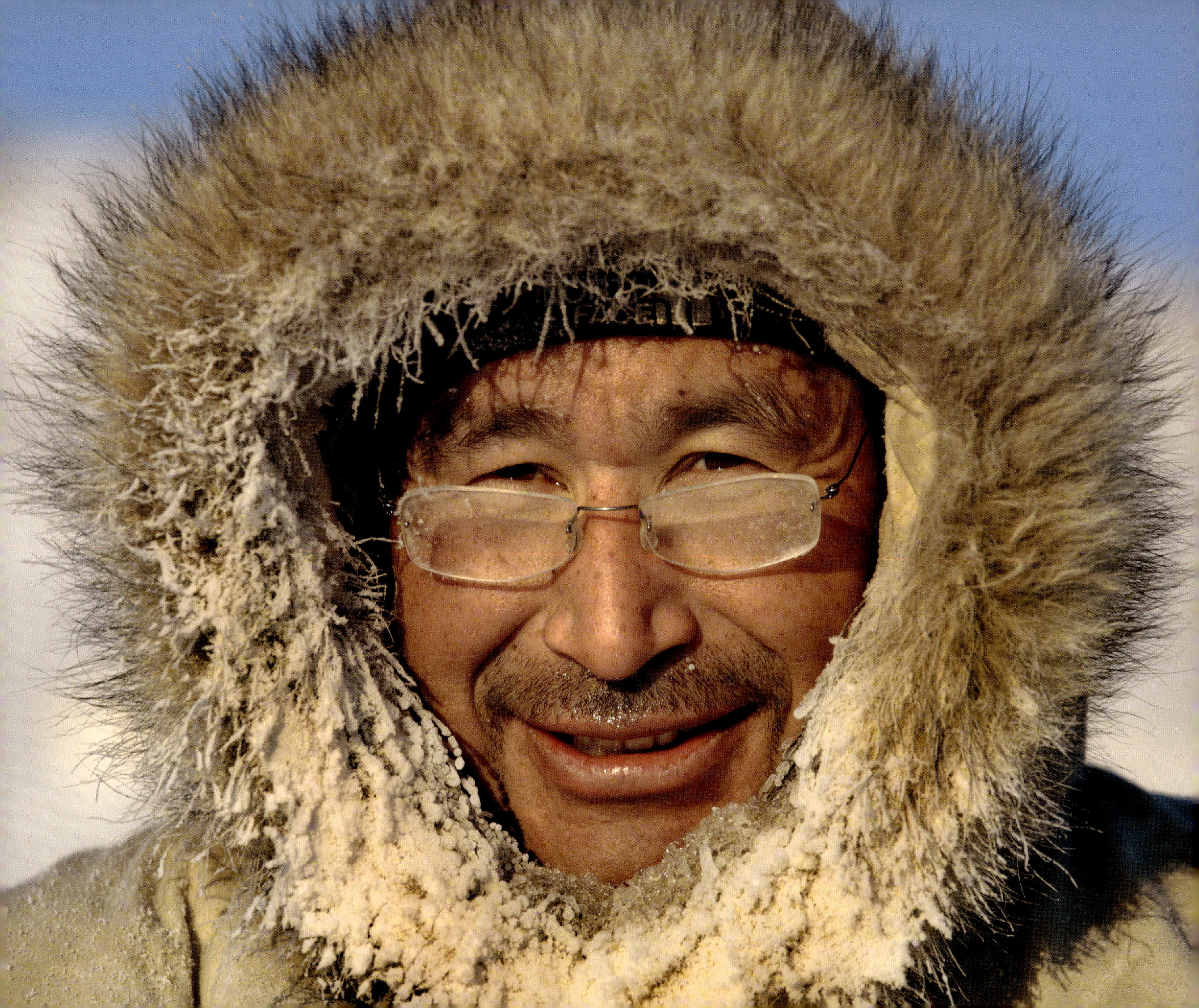

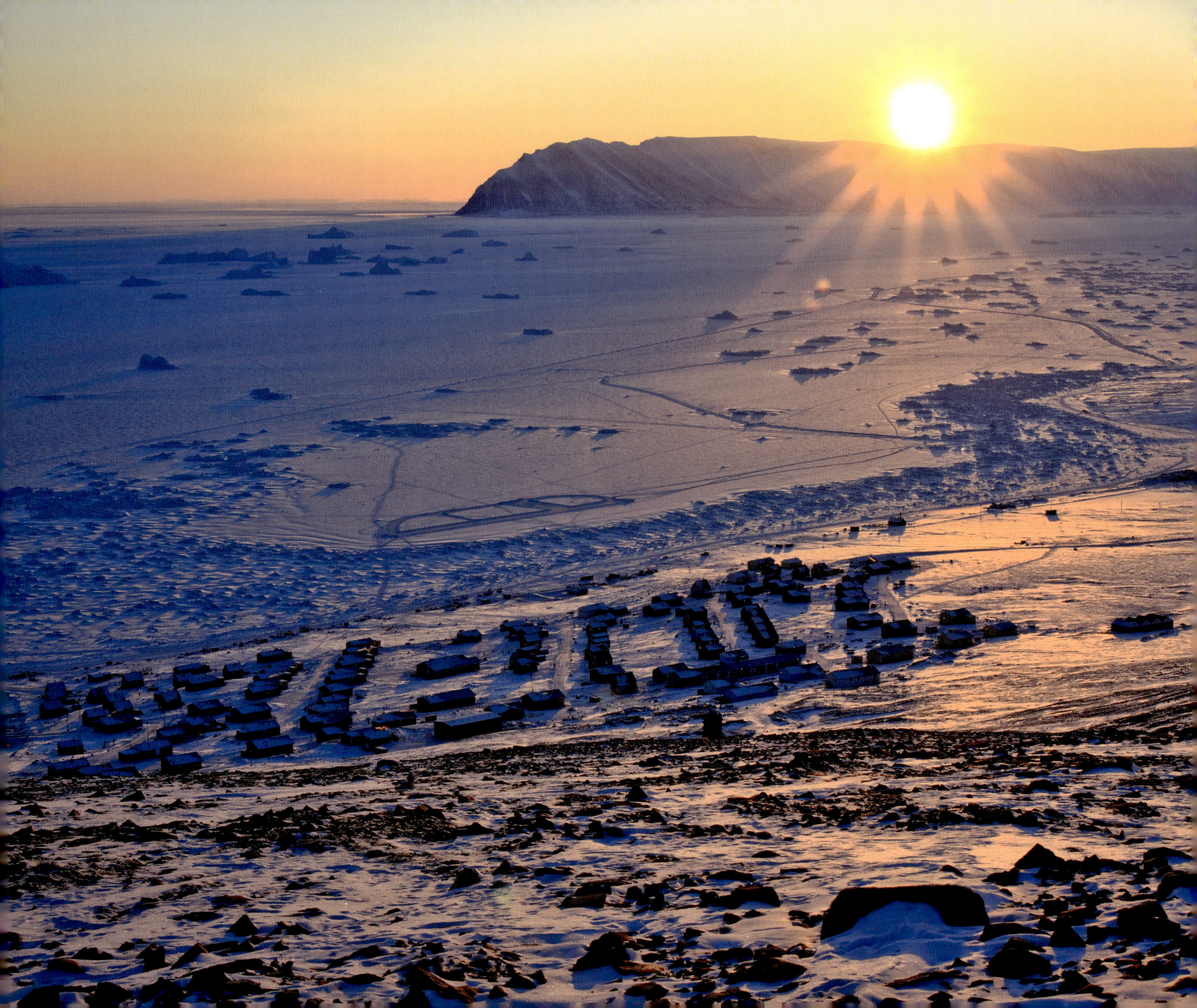

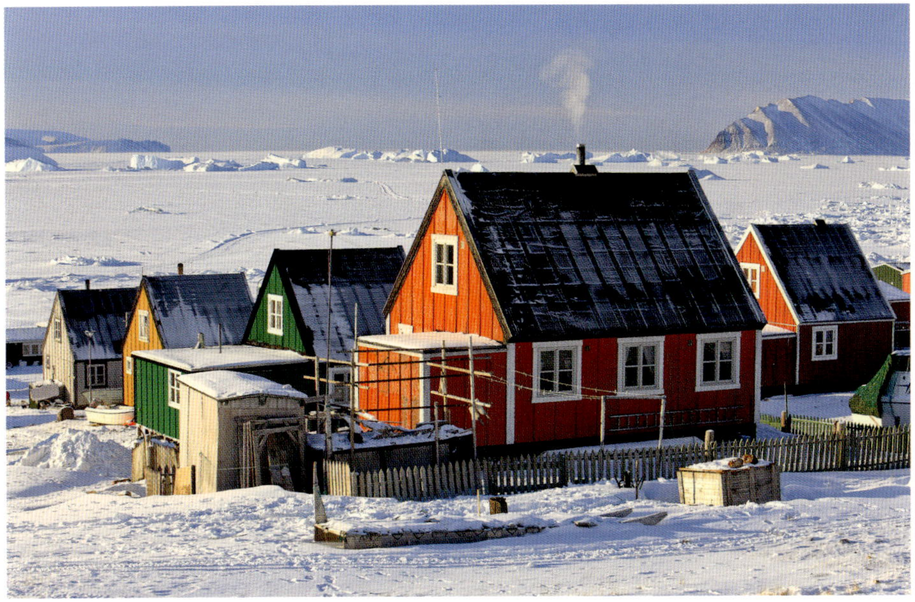

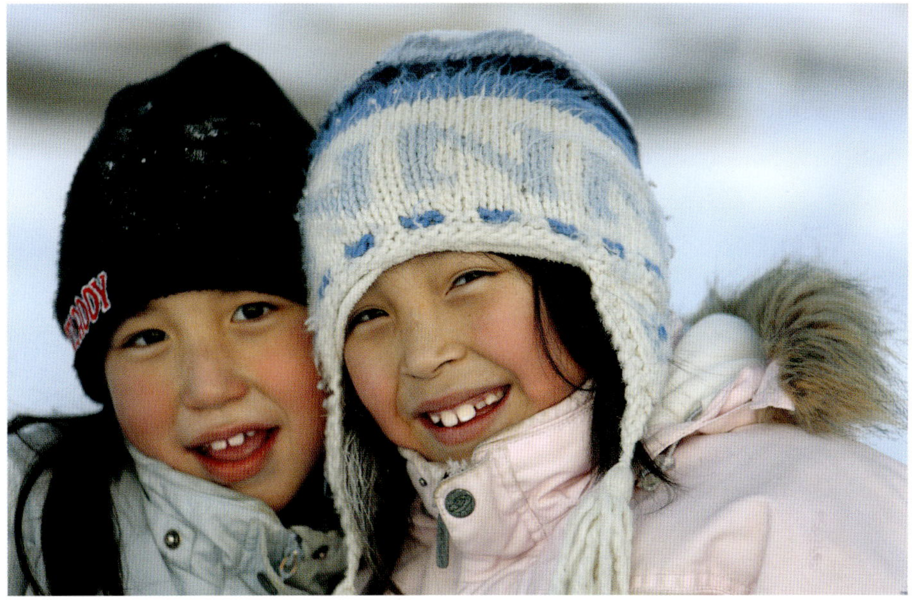

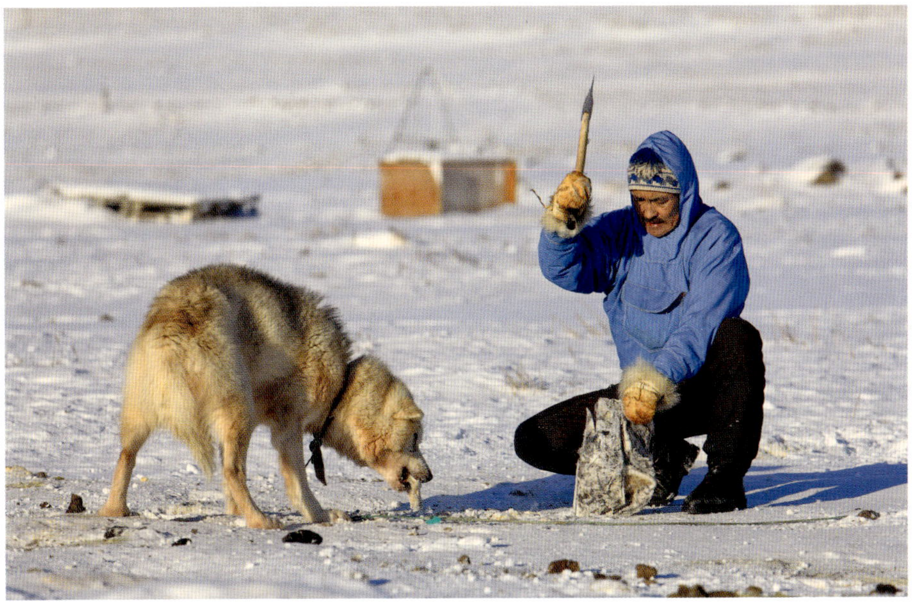

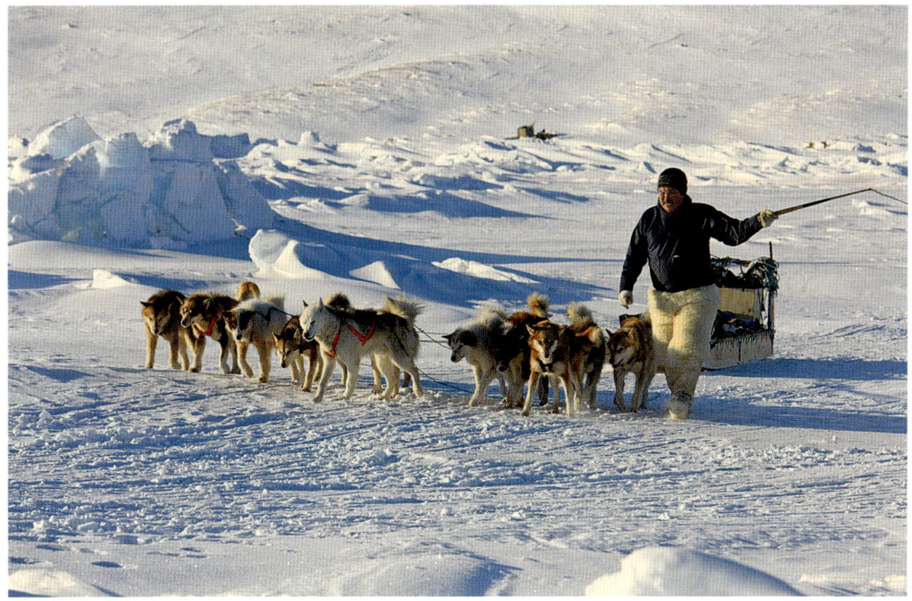

Qaanaaq was founded quite recently. In 1953, inhabitants from the town of Uummannaq (Dundas) were forcibly relocated to Qaanaaq because the USA had just established the Thule military base nearby. Qaanaaq (left), approximately 90 kilometres away as the crow flies, became the new home for many people. Village life is quite lively, even during the winter months.

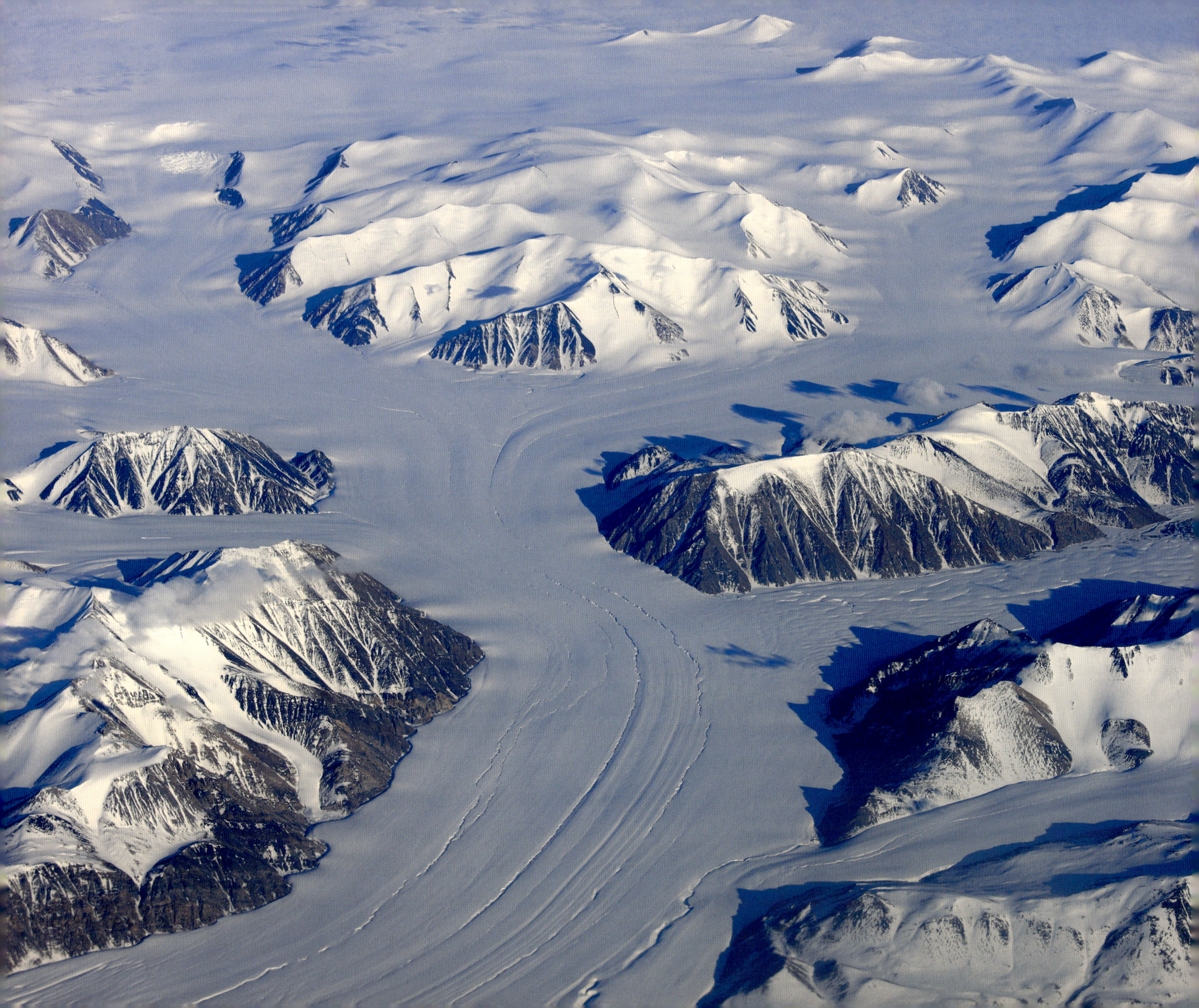

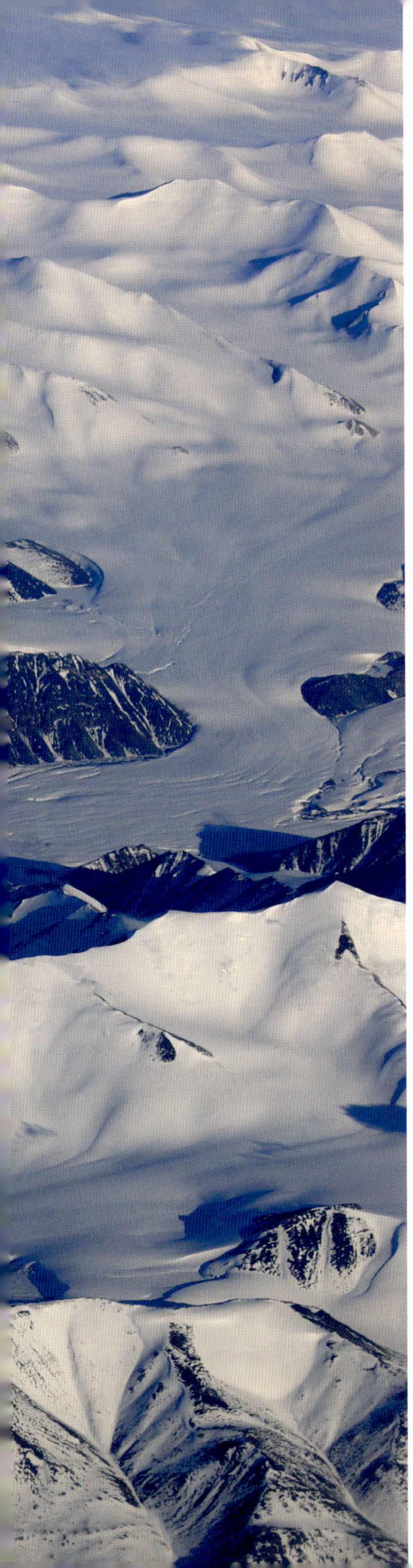

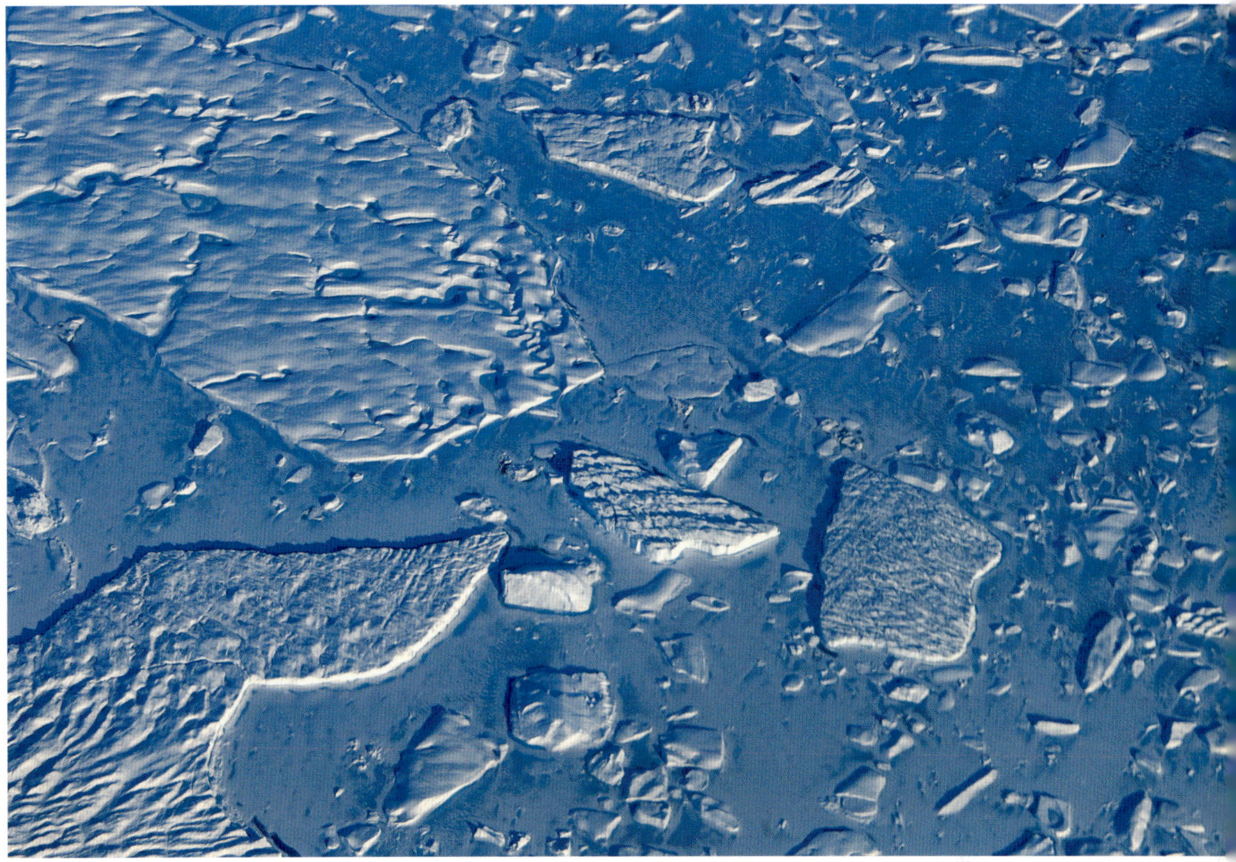

A bird's eye view of northern Greenland from a height of approximately 10,000 metres.
Left: In the valleys, enormous glaciers flow slowly towards the sea.
Right: Pack ice, viewed from above.

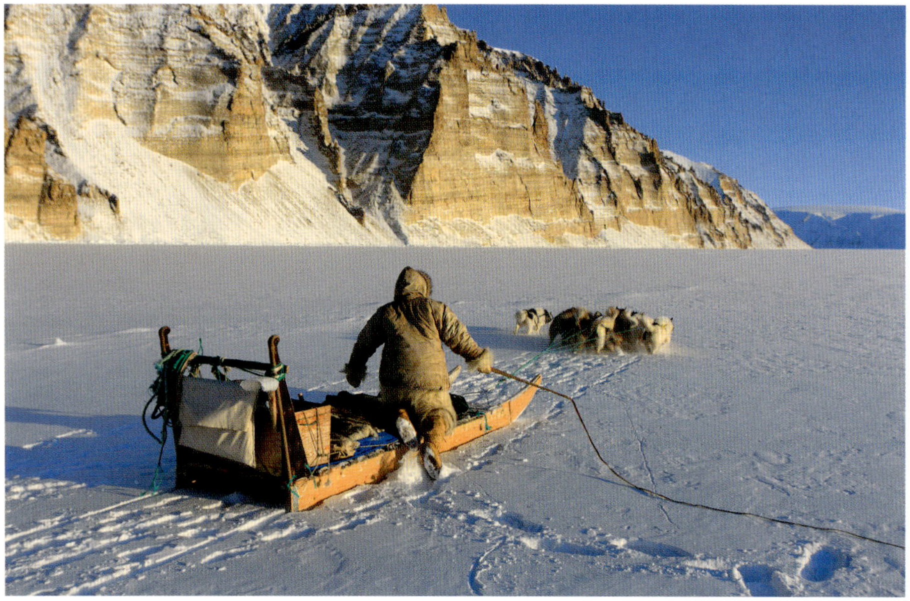

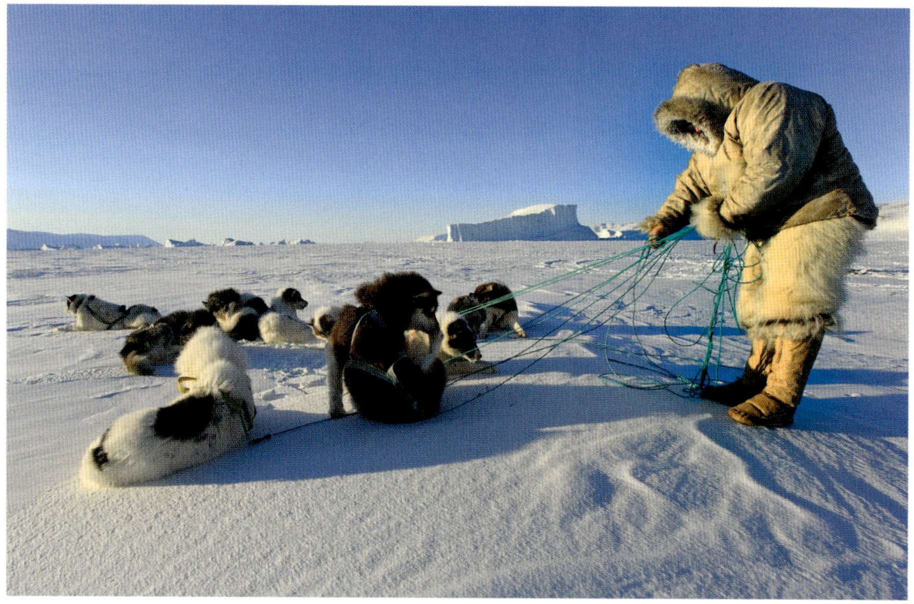

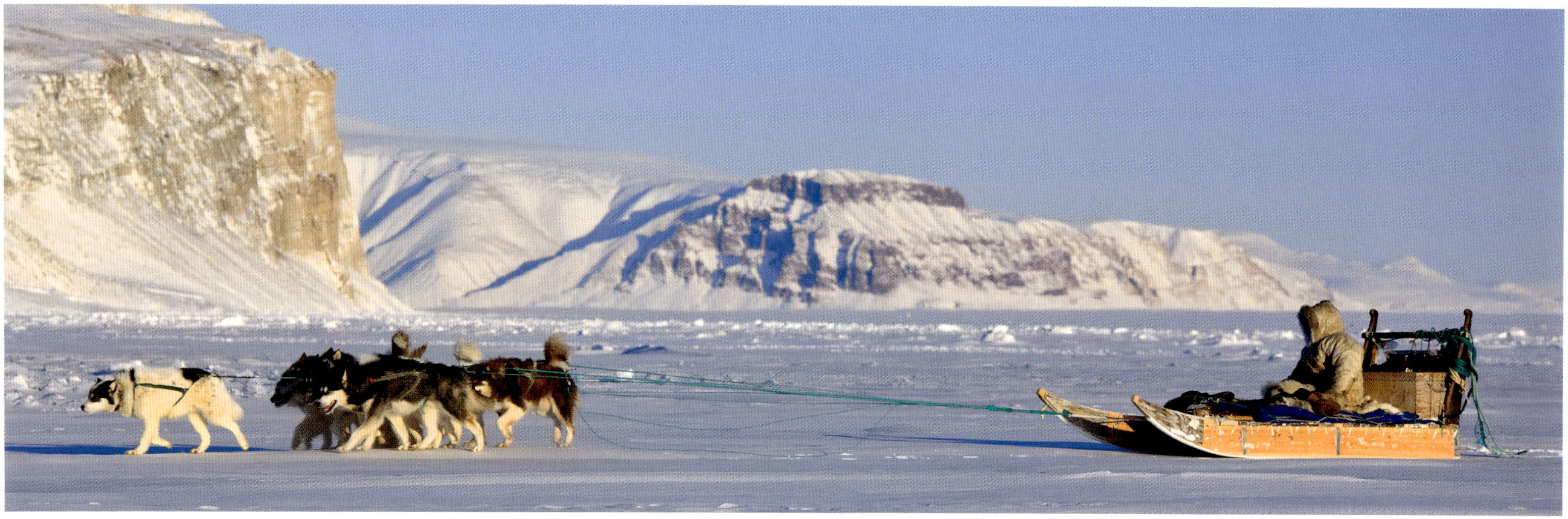

The inhabitants of Qaanaaq belong to the so-called Polar Inuit. The Polar Inuit continue to lead a very traditional life. For example, they refuse to use motorised snowmobiles, preferring to use their dog sledges to hunt. Their clothing appears to be from another era. When hunting, they wear trousers made of polar-bear fur, and shoes and jackets made of seal hide. It is their experience that "nothing keeps the cold out better than that which is worn by the animals too" (Mads Ole Kristiansen).

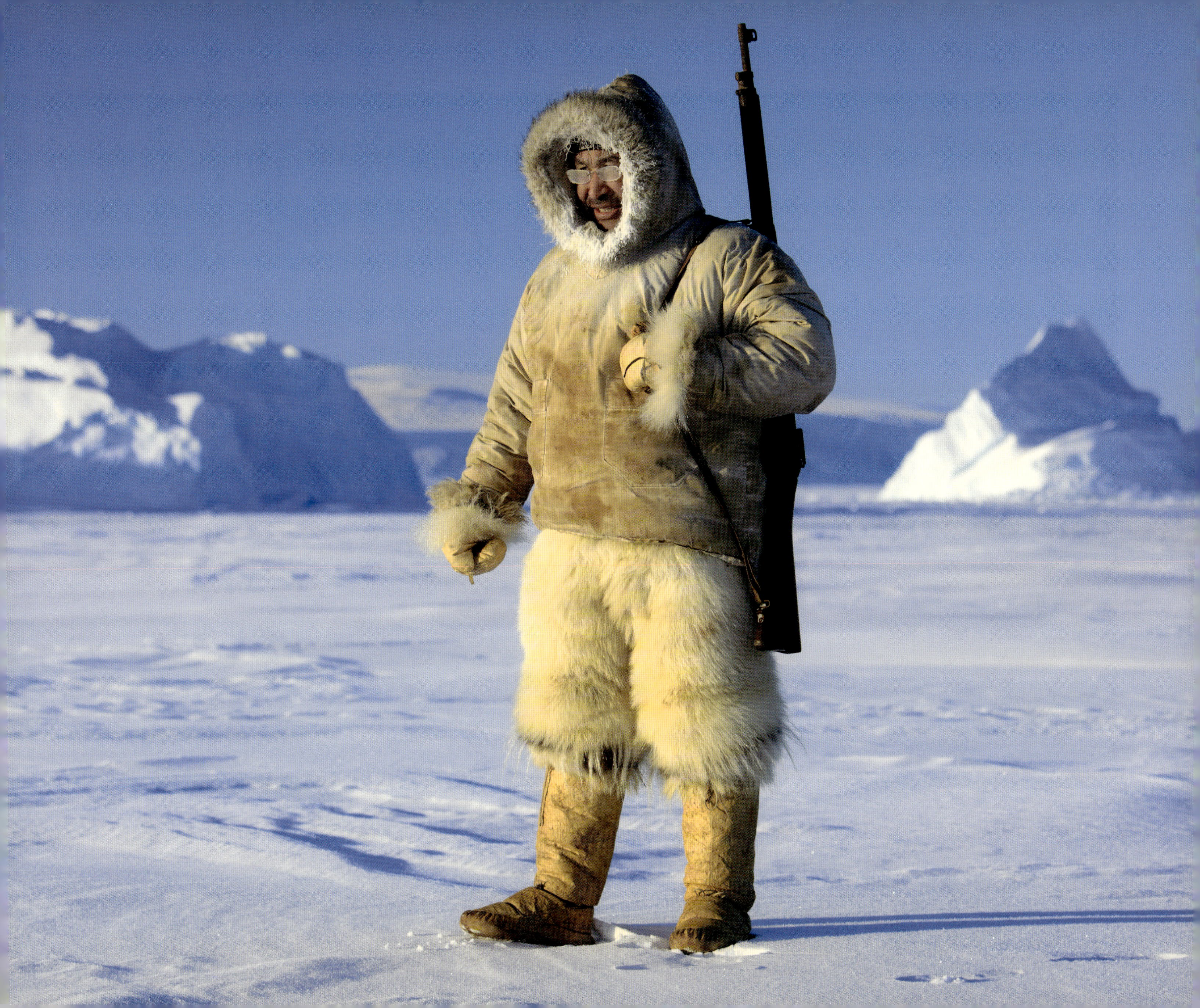

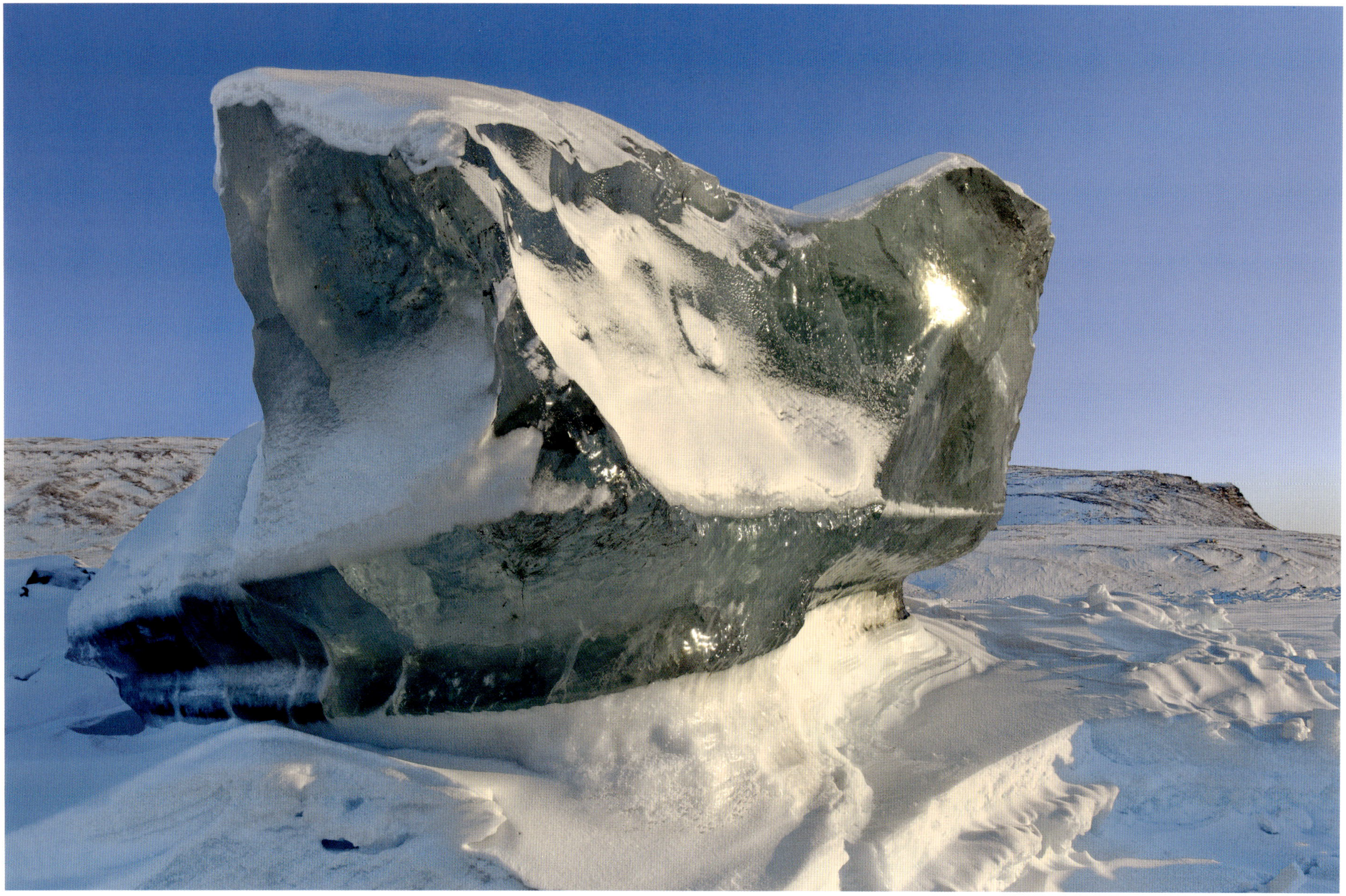

Going for a walk between the glistening pack-ice floes on the frozen sea is an impressive experience. Pack ice, which is formed out of freezing seawater, can become up to three metres thick in the winter. This ice is not static, but subject to a constant drift determined by marine currents and the wind. Inglefield fjord near Qaanaaq.

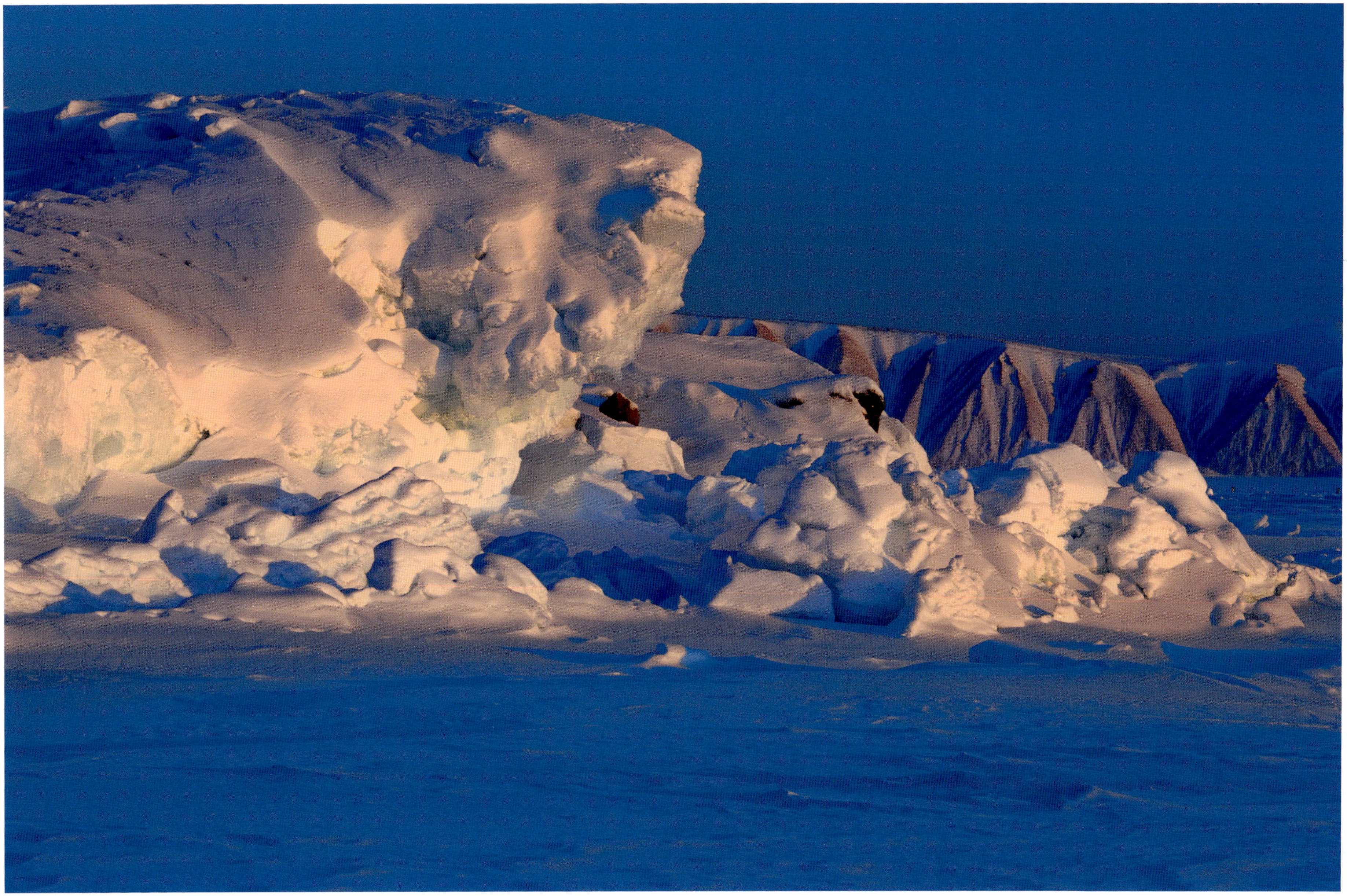

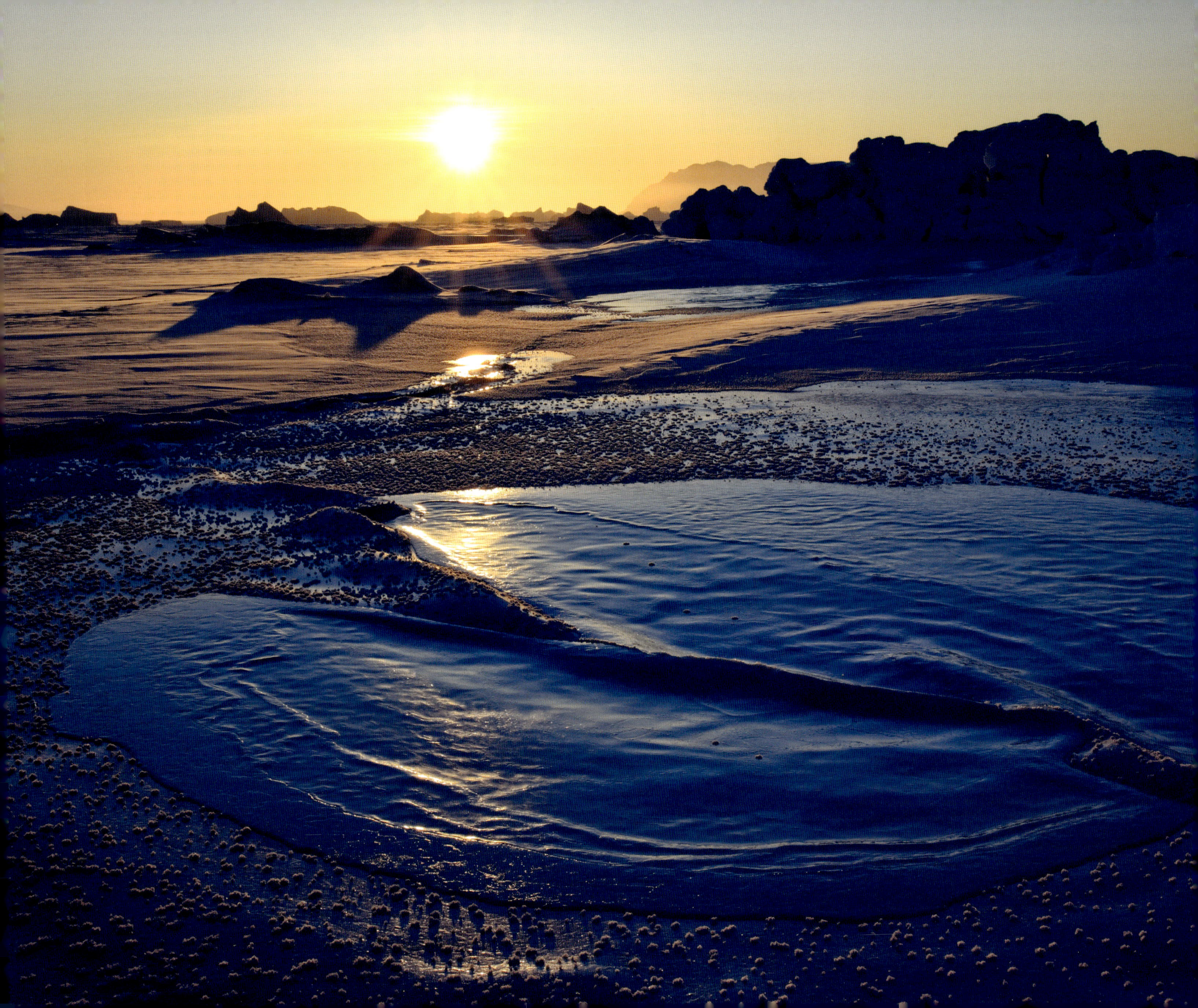

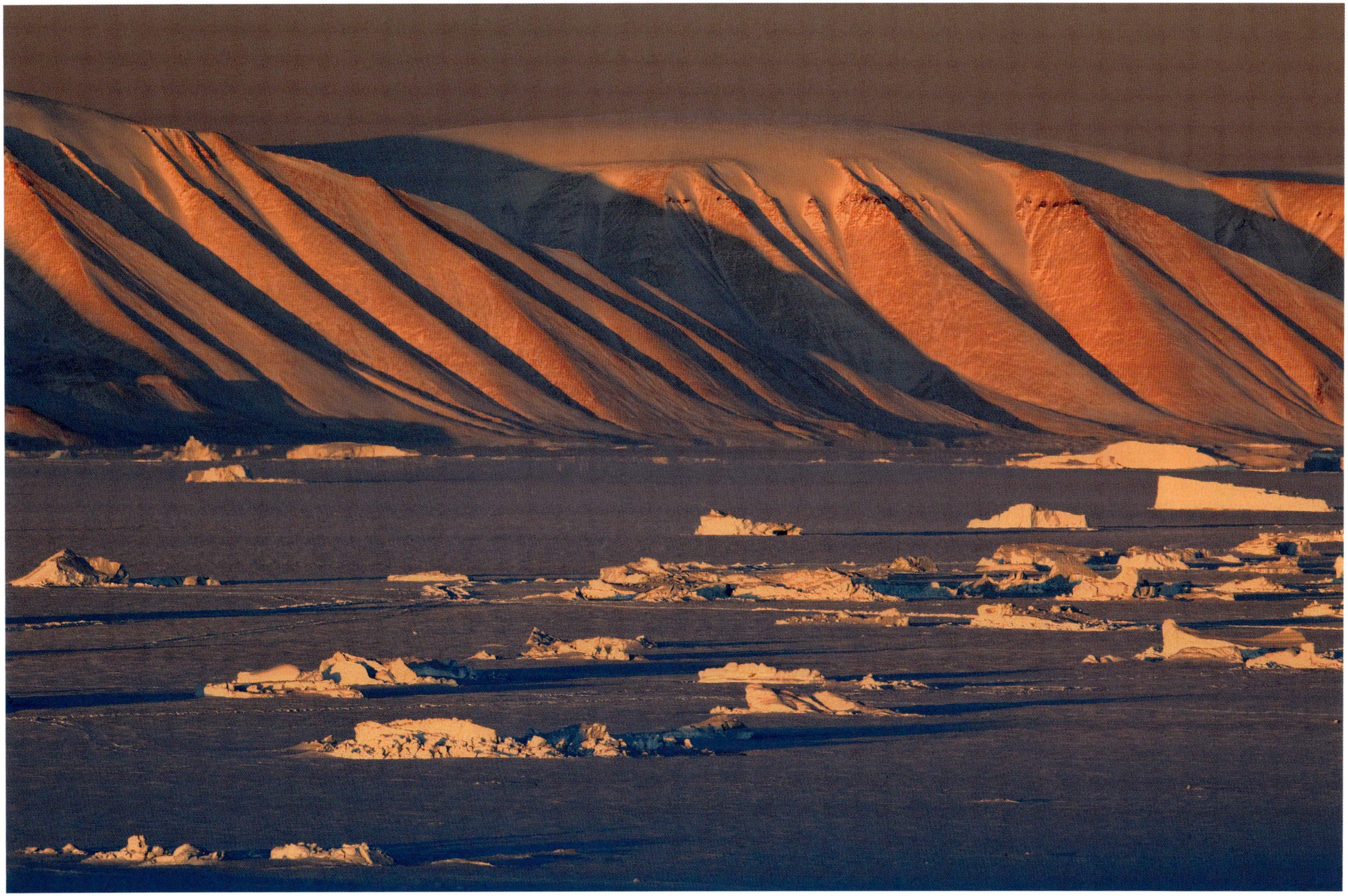

In recent years, the pack ice in the high Arctic has receded considerably. In the summer of 2007, more of the perennial ice (that is, ice that does not usually disappear in the summer) melted than ever before. The winter pack ice no longer achieves the thickness or expansion it reached in the past, either. If climate change continues at the present pace, there will be no more summer pack ice in ten to 20 years' time. Inglefield fjord near Qaanaaq.

EUROPE'S ARCTIC – THE CONTINENT'S WILDERNESS

Europe is considered to be the richest continent: rich in terms of wealth and industrial development. And yet it is simultaneously the poorest continent: poor in terms of wilderness, and poor in terms of nature largely free of human influence. There are not many large, natural wilderness areas left in Europe: a few mountain regions in Romania's Carpathian Mountains or the Caucasus, or the dense, wild forests in the northwest of Russia. Most importantly, the far north: the Arctic.

According to the political definition, the European Arctic includes Greenland and parts of Russia, but it is defined here as consisting of Iceland, Svalbard and Lapland. These three Arctic areas are geographically quite close to one another, but the differences between them are great.

Iceland is the largest volcanic island on Earth, and lies in the middle of the north Atlantic, with its northern coast squarely on the polar circle. Because of the more than 30 active volcanoes and countless hot springs, some parts of the island are so warm that banana trees thrive there. The birdlife on the island is acknowledged to be exceptional. Although Iceland was completely deforested during the centuries when settlement occurred, the birdlife continues to be abundant. It consists primarily of birds that live on the surrounding sea, including auks, gannets and Atlantic puffins. There is an abundance of fish, linked to nutrient-rich marine currents.

In the north of Scandinavia, between the Lofoten archipelago in the west and Karelia in the east, lies Lapland. This enormous area, which consists of areas both to the north and to the south of the polar circle, is characterised by fjords and mountain ranges, tundras and forests, lakes and moors. Many types of large predator, such as bears and wolves, lynxes, wolverines, eagles and eagle owls still live in this sparsely populated region. It is also home

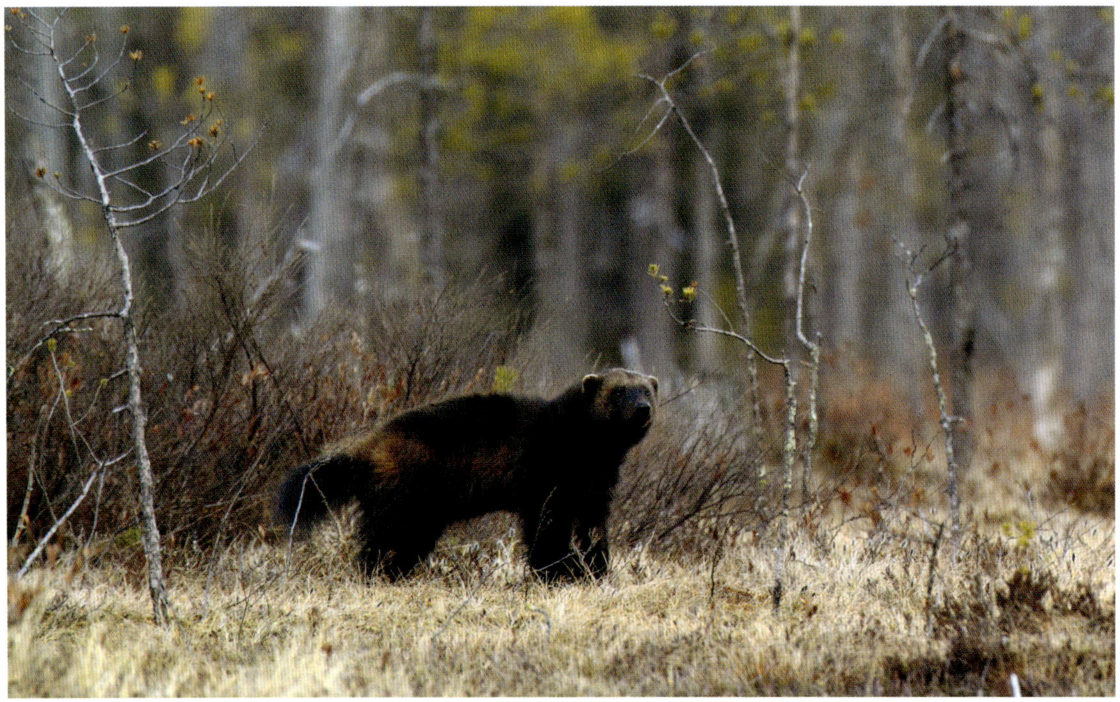

A wolverine in the Finnish-Russian borderland, near Vartius.

to traditional reindeer breeders, the Sami, a European people at home throughout Lapland. Counting approximately 100,000 members, this is one of the largest population groups in the far north.

Because of the harsh winters, reindeer, and the now rare Finnish forest reindeer, in particular, are dependent on the dense growth of lichen, which only occurs in intact forests. This means that forests are essential to survival in this polar region. And yet they have been the focus of a heated debate for several years. The forestry industry, driven particularly by the Swedish-Finnish paper industry, are opposed by the majority of Sami and by environmental protection organisations, who demand protection from deforestation for the few remaining virgin forests. The agreement of 2010, which states that most of the remaining intact forest areas may not be cut down, is an important step towards ensuring the survival of the reindeer and, consequently, that of the traditional way of life of the Sami themselves.

The third region, Svalbard, is a very different part of the European Arctic. Geographically, it is part of the high Arctic, and lies just 1,200 kilometres from the North Pole. 60 percent of Svalbard is covered by glaciers, including the largest glacier in Europe: the Austfonna glacier.

Administered by Norway and with a population of just 3,000 people, this archipelago is the only European territory that is home to the polar bear. A self-contained population estimated at 3,000 bears lives here and on the surrounding Franz Joseph Land islands. The polar bear, the Svalbard reindeer and the polar fox are the largest land mammals of this island world.

Despite its remoteness, Svalbard has experienced many periods of intensive exploitation. The earliest took place during the 17th century with the large-scale hunting of whales and walruses, from which the populations have not recovered to this day. This was followed by the hunting of seals and other animals with valuable furs. In the 18th century, this was succeeded by the hunting of reindeer and Arctic foxes. Since the early 20th century, the rich supply of coal has been exploited by the Russians and Norwegians, while research and tourism are of importance nowadays. Svalbard is considered to be the biggest research laboratory in the Arctic, where an increasing amount of research and climate research, is carried out.

Svalbard is also home to the largest plant-seed bank in the world. Up to 4.5 million seeds, mainly of agricultural crops, from more than 170 countries, are safeguarded here, deep in the permafrost ground, for the use of future generations.

Europeans should, actually, have a strong interest in retaining an intact Arctic. Not

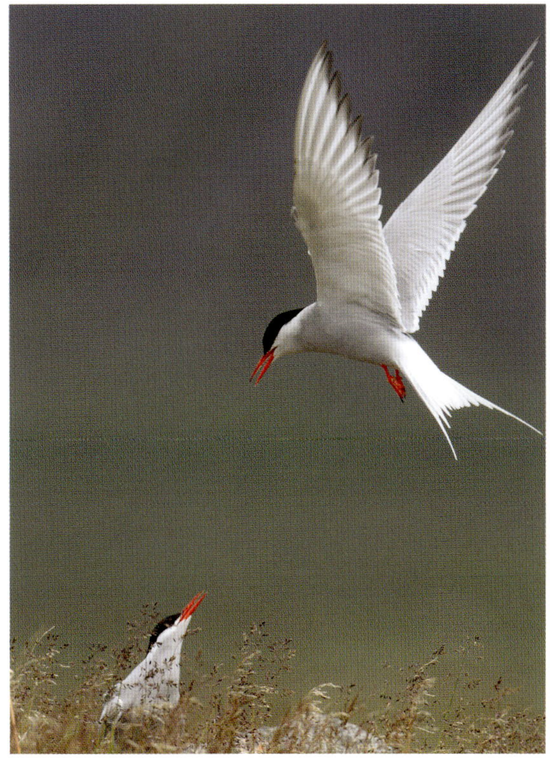

Arctic terns feeding. West Fjords, Iceland.

simply because five (or even six, if one counts Russia) of the altogether eight Arctic states are in Europe. In reality the fish stocks are exploited and most of the forests have been cut down. The search for oil and oil production threaten the seas, and climate change, long ago reached even high-Arctic regions. Europe's last wilderness areas are nature's treasure troves, repositories of the diversity of species, and consequently part of the biological inheritance of a continent which must be passed on to later generations as intact as possible.

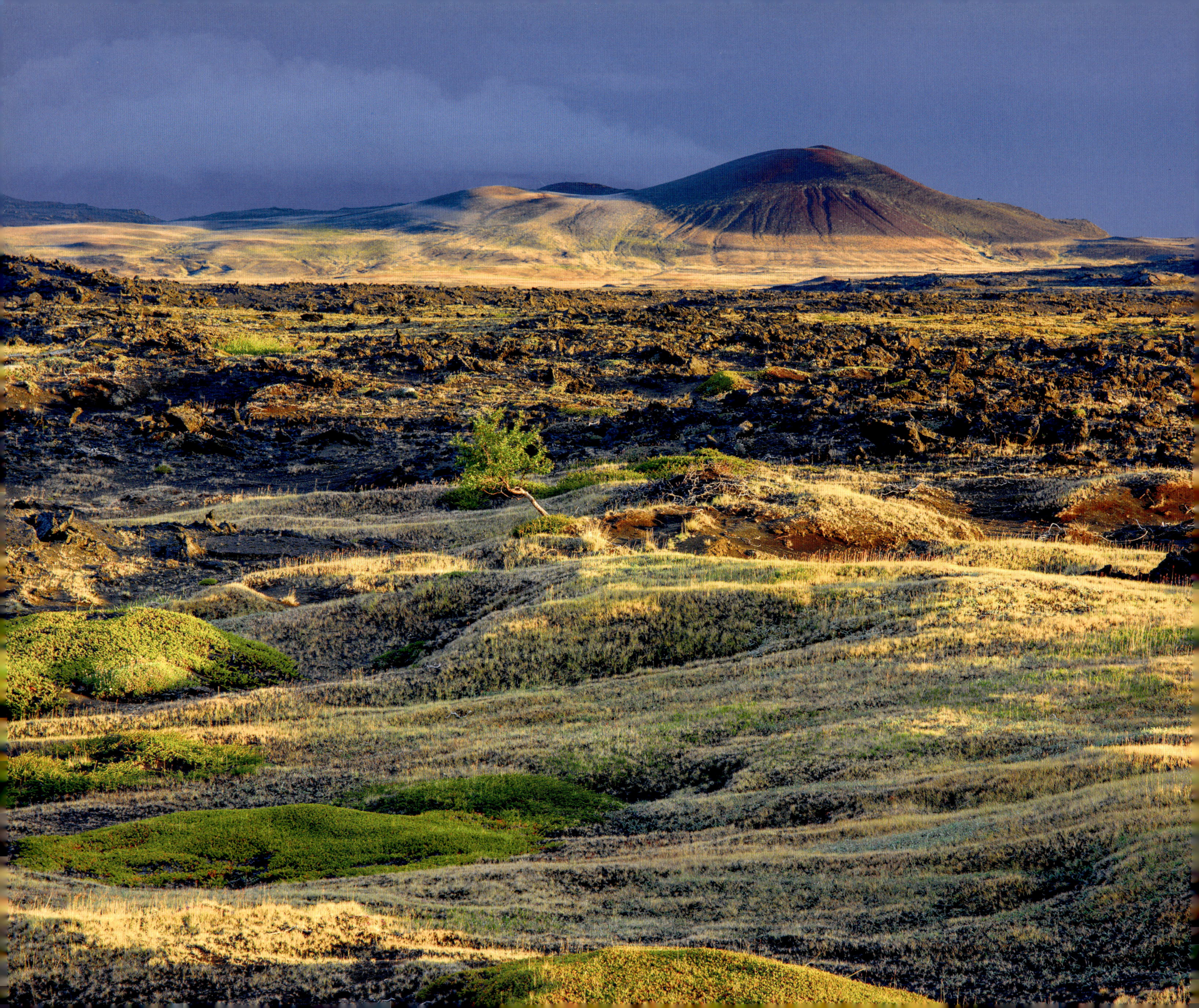

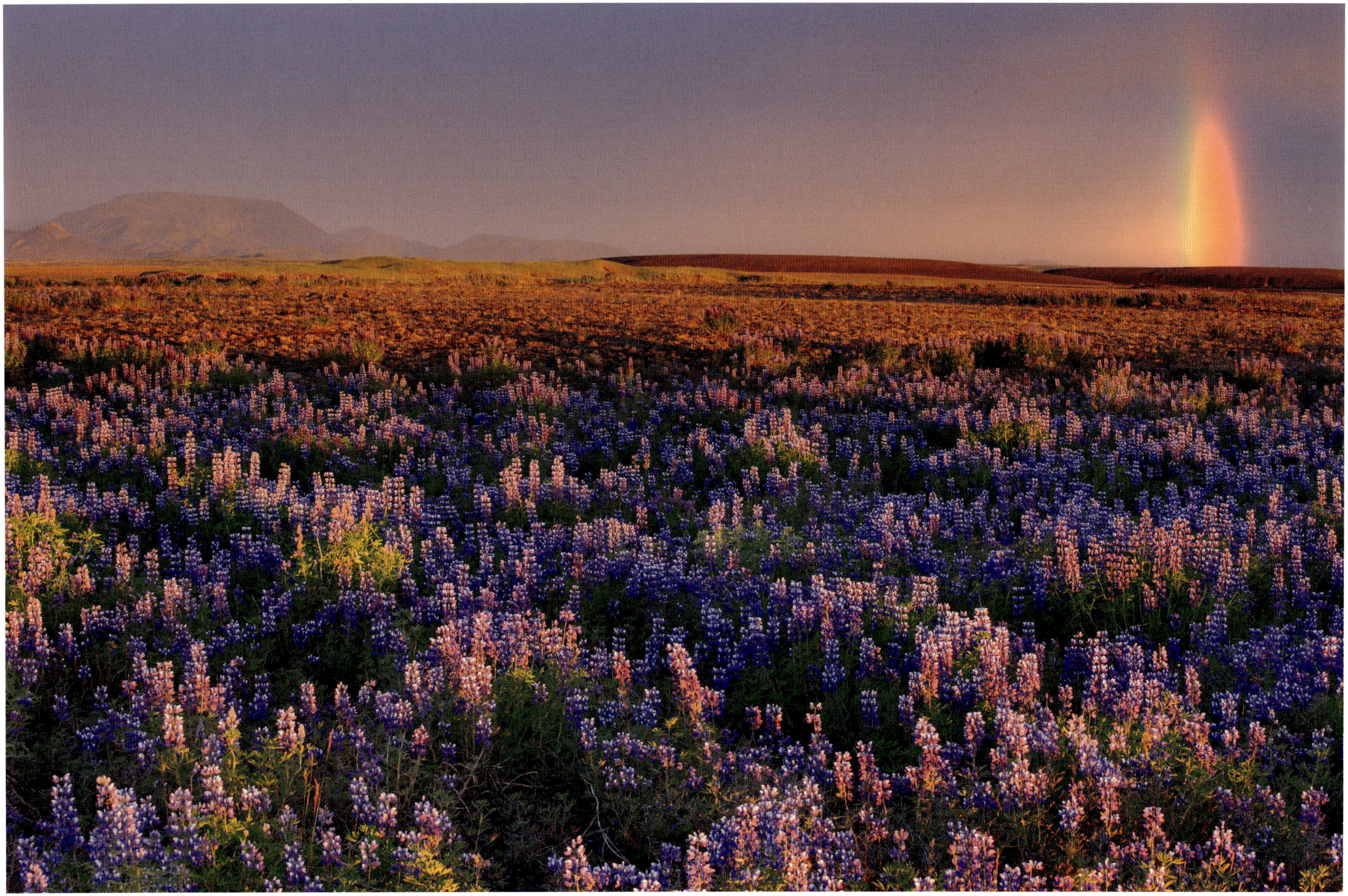

Left: Volcanism is omnipresent in Iceland as there are approximately 30 active volcanoes, which continuously reform the land. Solidified lava near Myvatn Lake in northeastern Iceland.
Above: Lupins are particularly important after volcanic eruptions as they supply the ground with nitrate through the bacteria living in their roots. Near Myvatn Lake, northeastern Iceland.

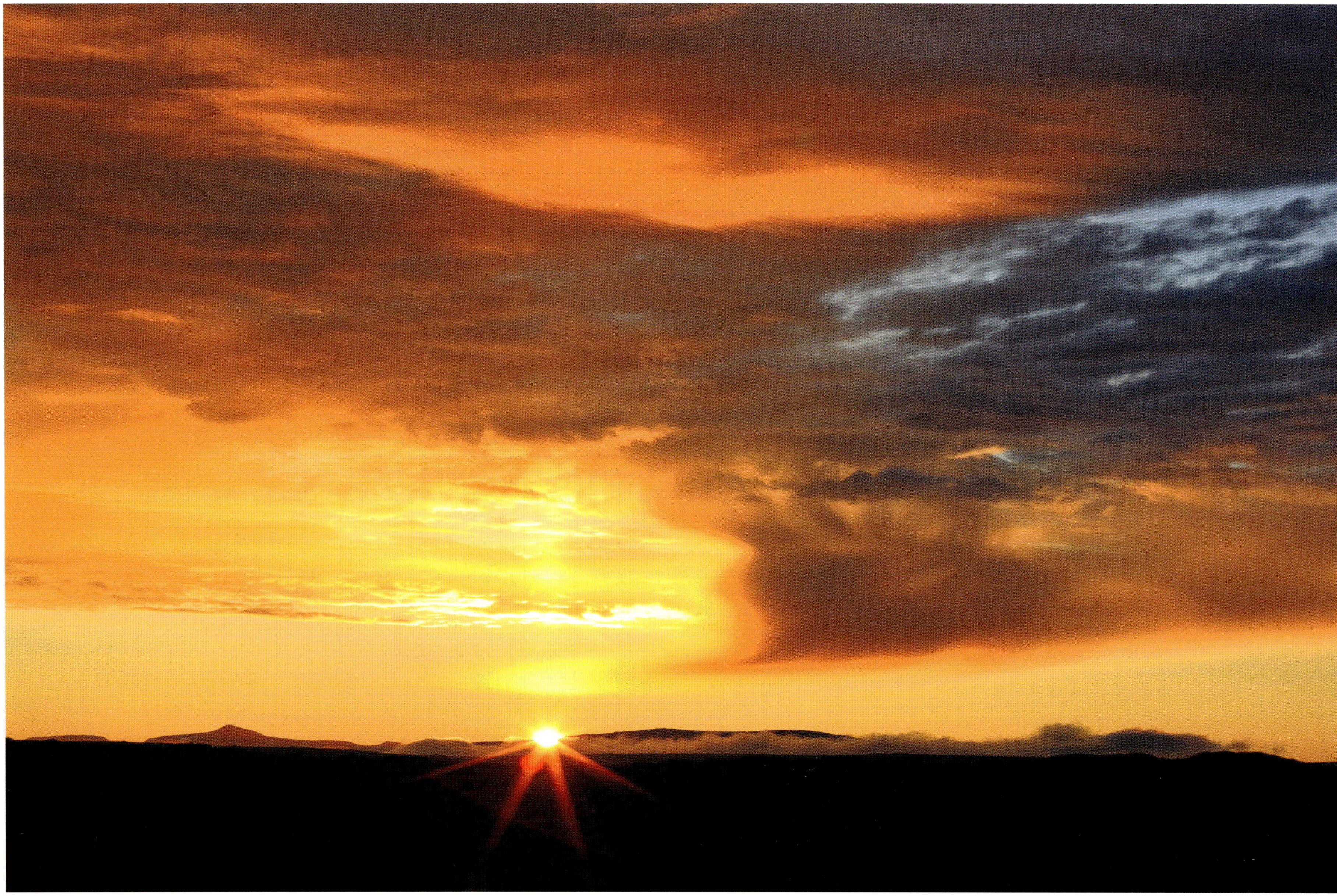

In July, the sun disappears behind the horizon for just one hour or so, conjuring up fantastic colour displays in the night sky. Northeastern Iceland.

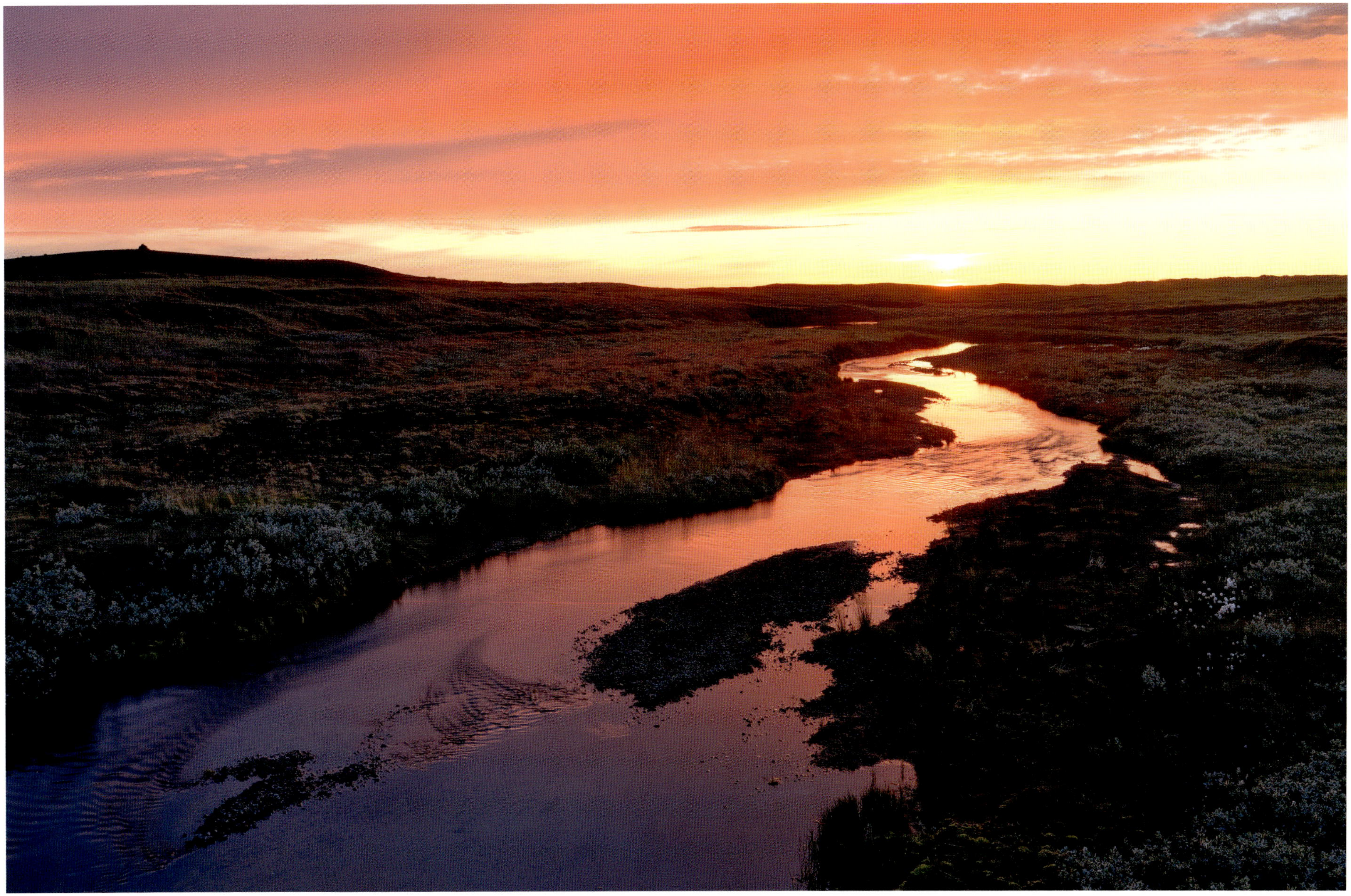

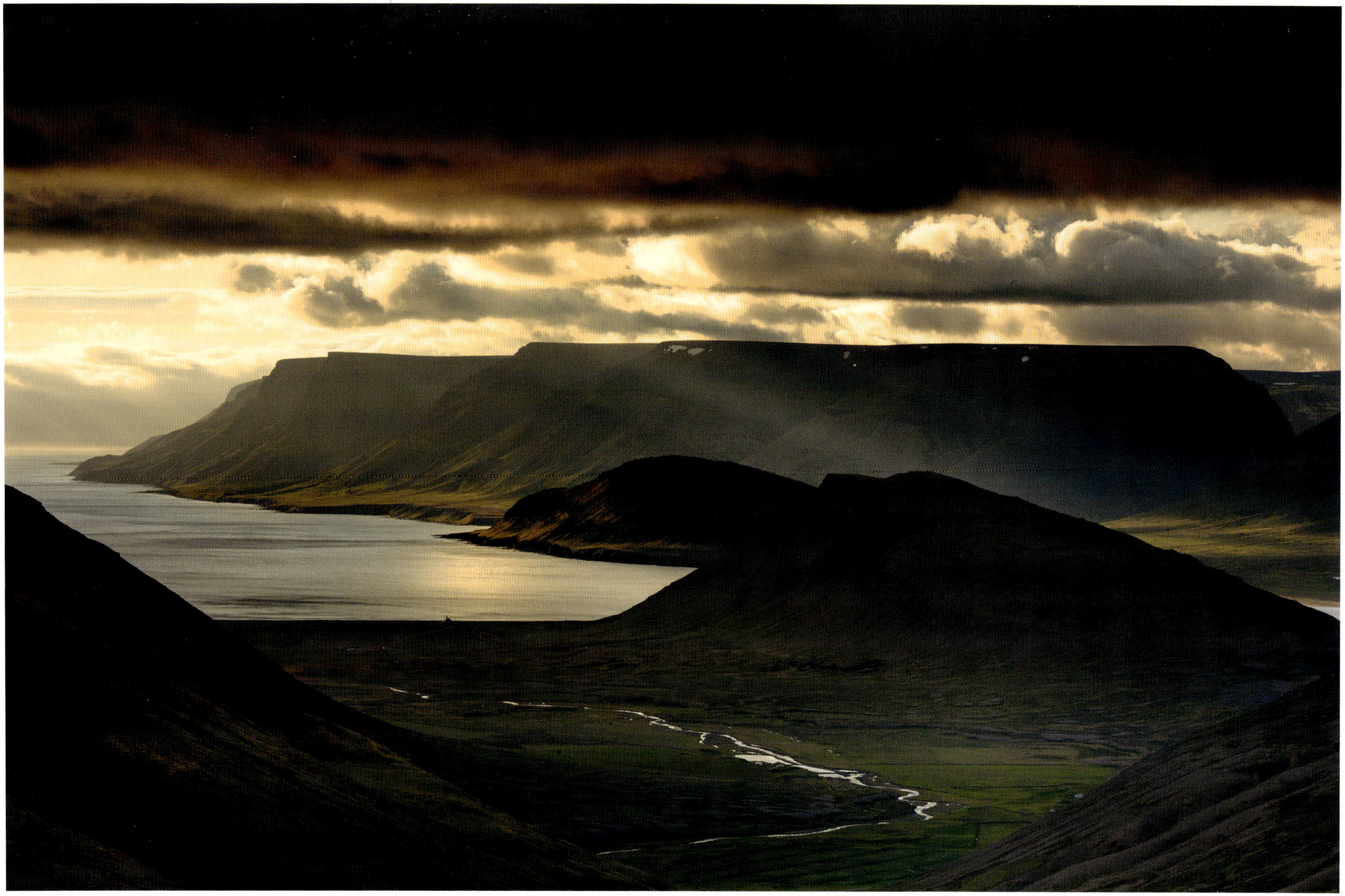

In Iceland's West Fjords, bright sunshine and heavy rainfall alternate, each phase often lasting, just a minute. The world of the fjords is resplendent in this magical light.
Right: Seljalandsfoss, one of Iceland's highest and most beautiful waterfalls. Southwestern Iceland.

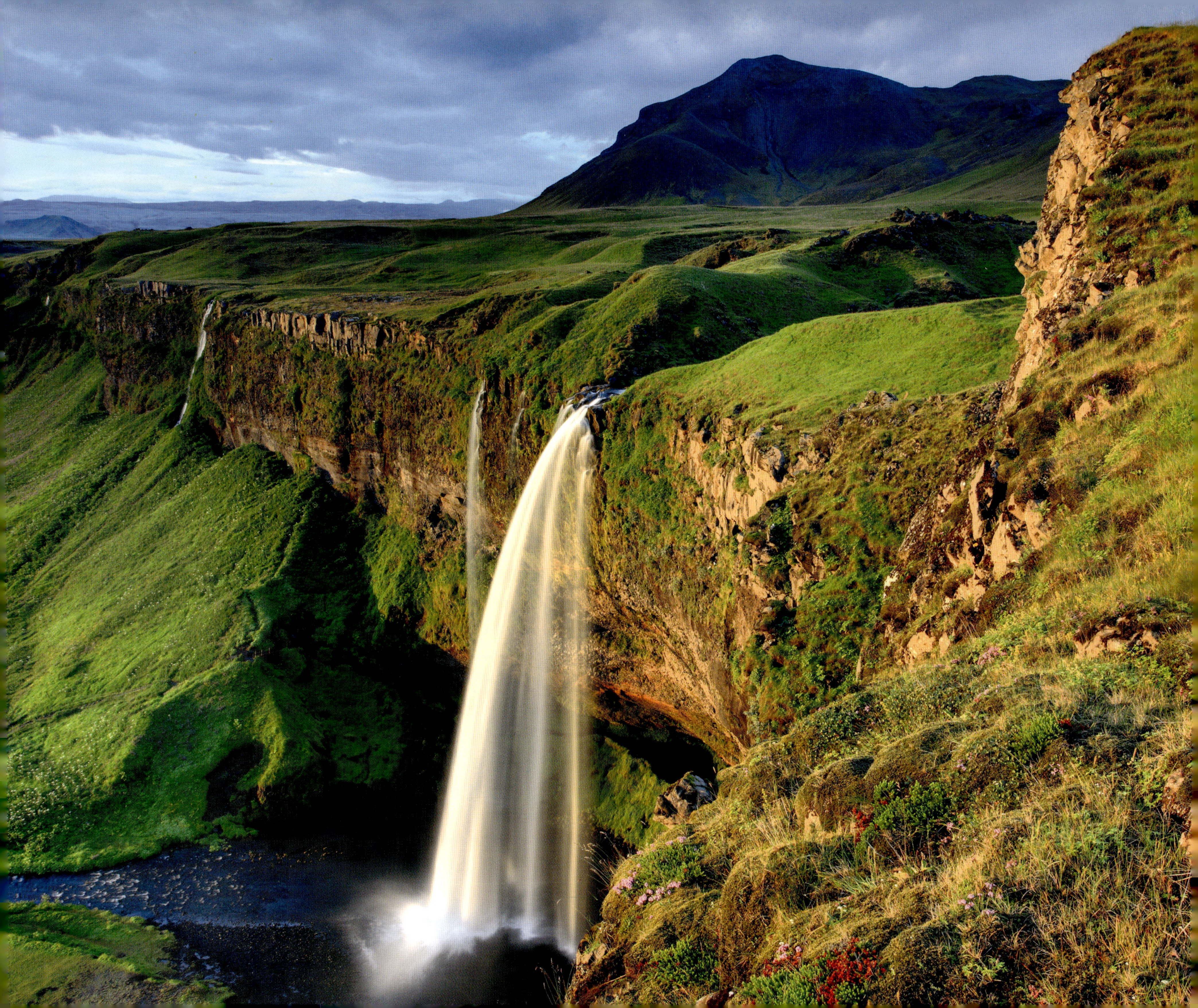

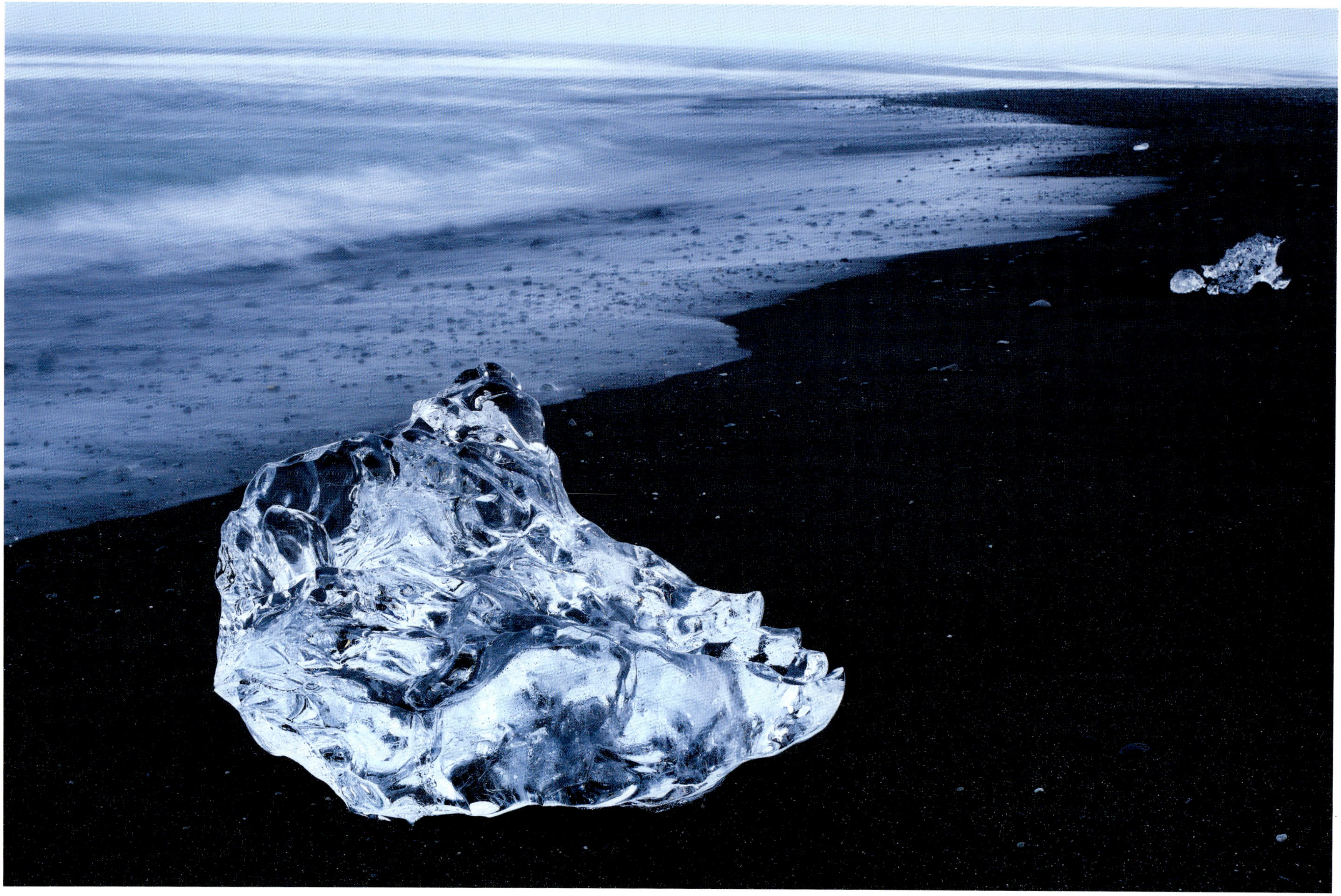

The tongue of the Breidamerkurjökull glacier calves into Jökulsarlon, a large glacier lake, in southwestern Iceland. The lake is connected to the sea through a narrow channel along which large chunks of ice float into the sea, and sometimes end up on the black beach.

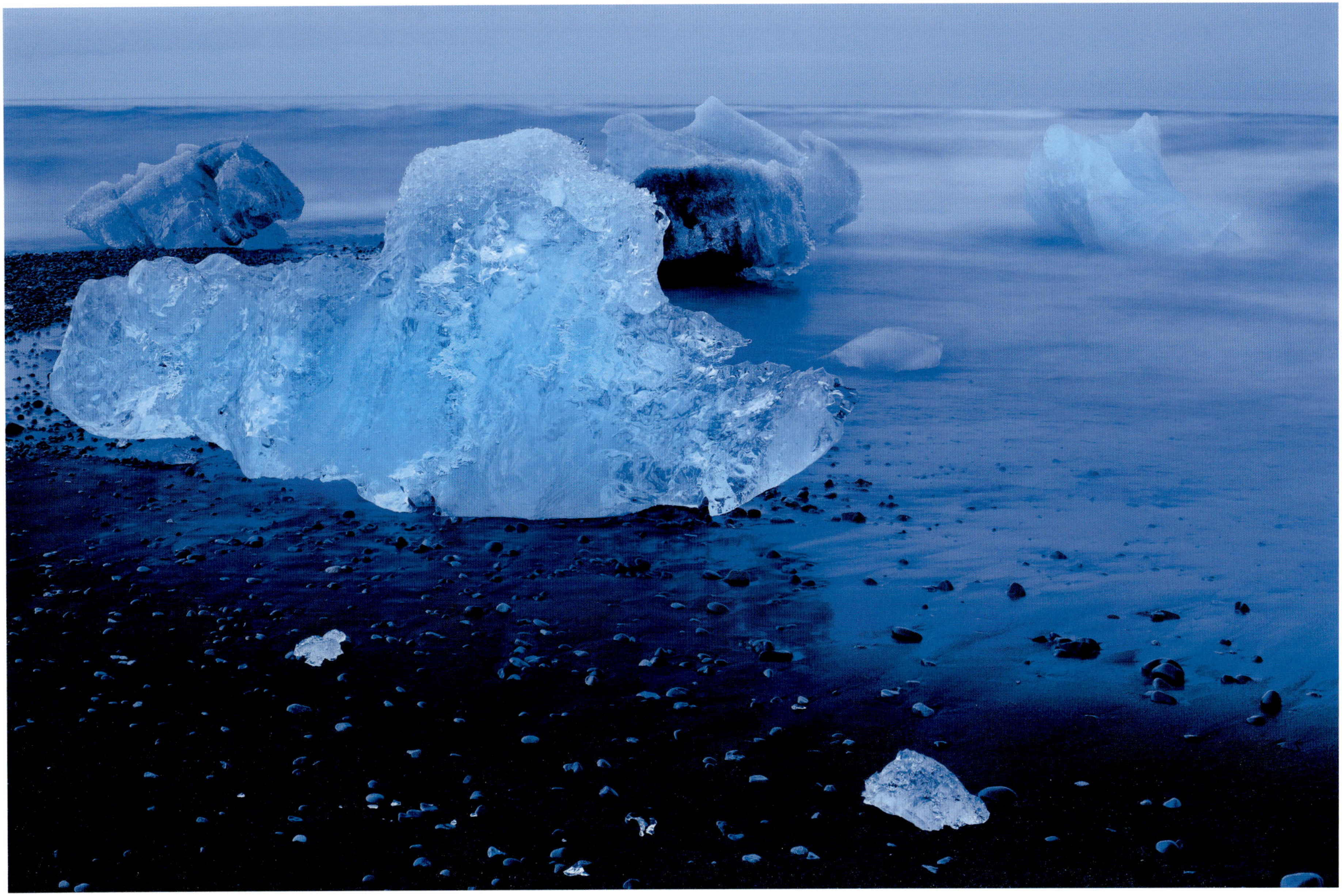

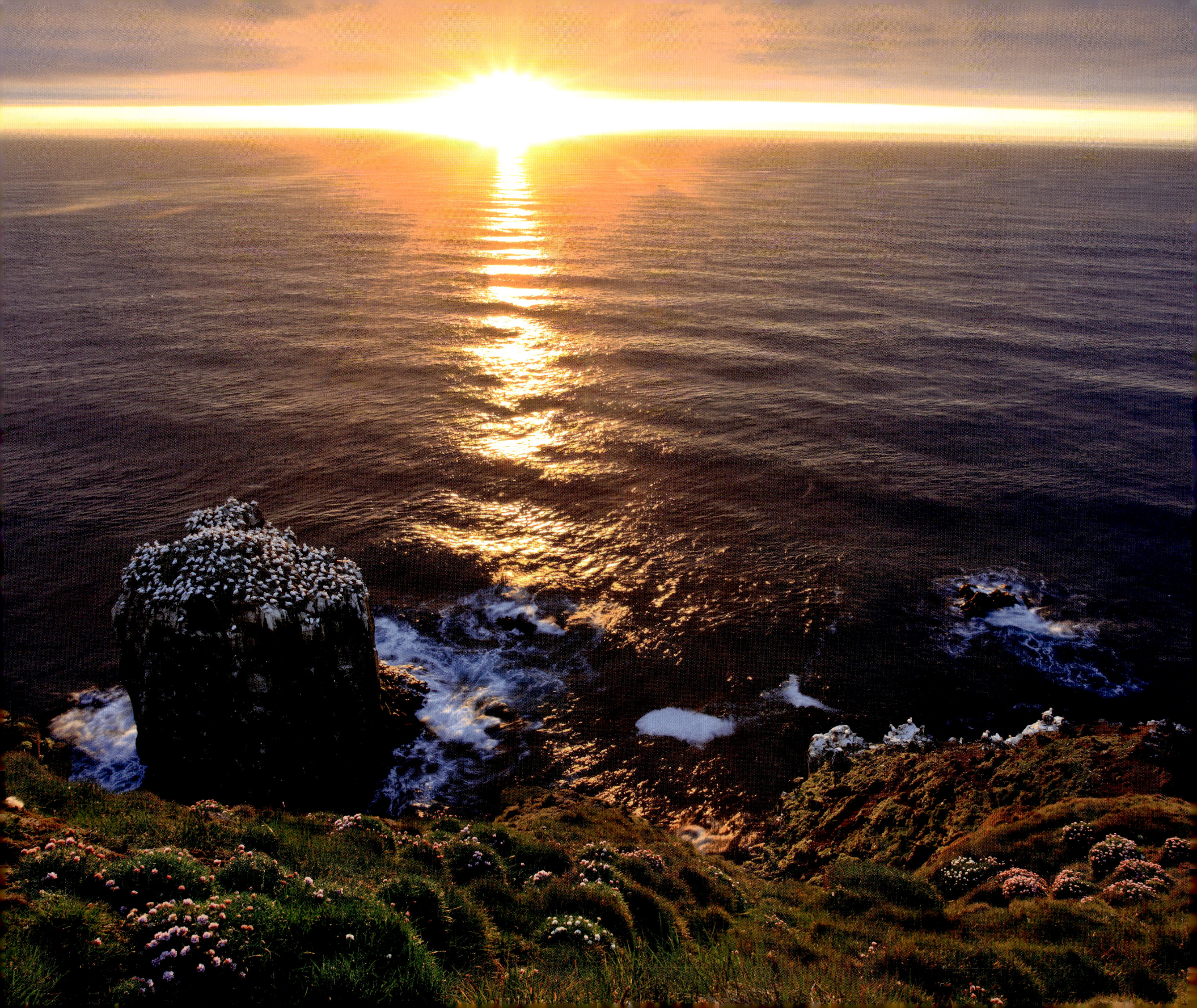

The Langanes Peninsula in the far northeast of Iceland is home to a large colony of northern gannets, the largest members of the gannet family. They can weigh more than three kilograms. Northern gannets favour steep rocky islands off the seacoast for their nests. This provides better protection for them and their young against predators in general, and Arctic foxes in particular.

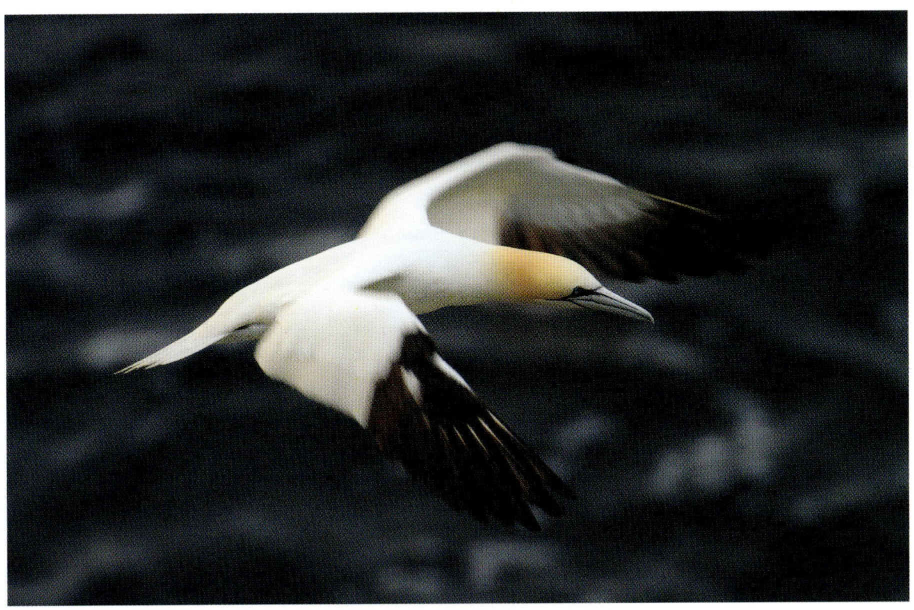

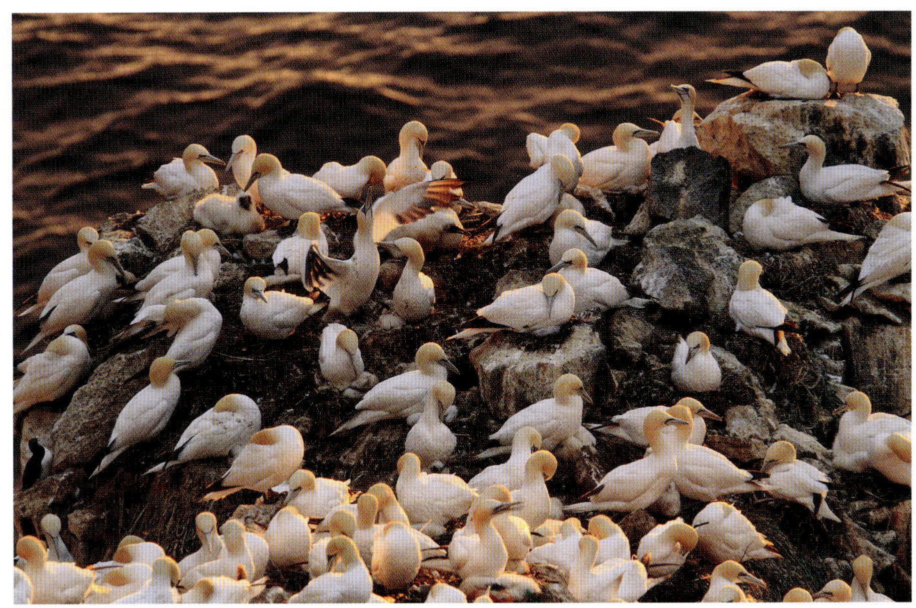

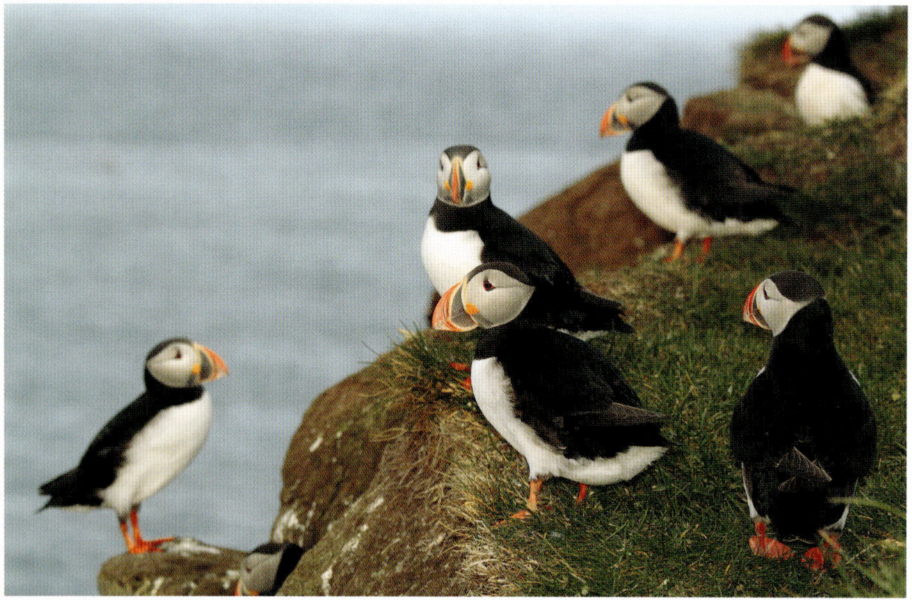

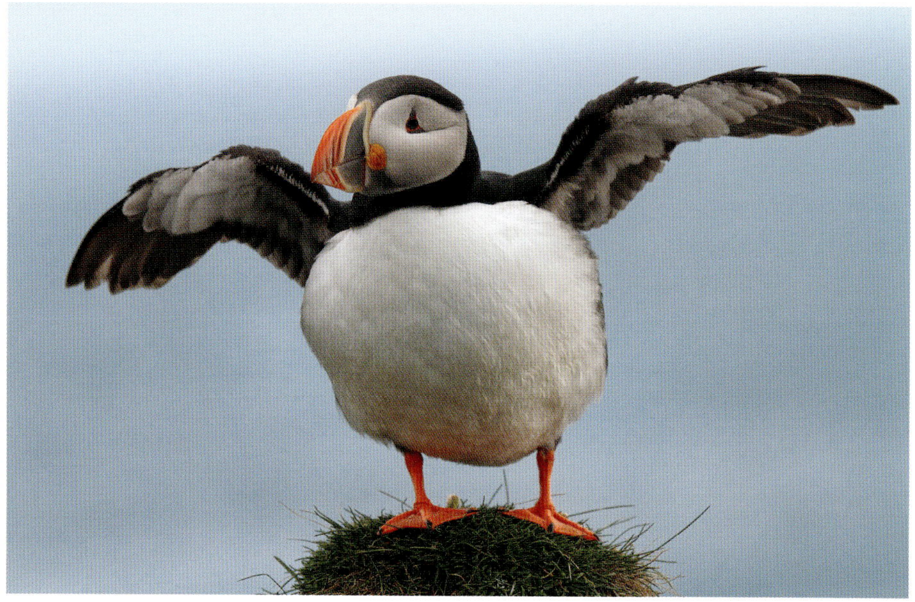

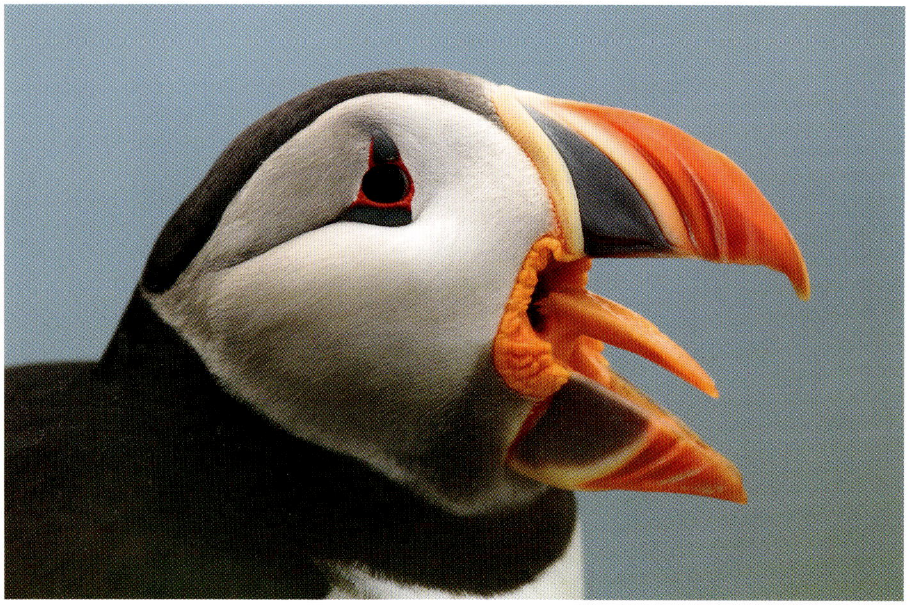

Atlantic puffins are known as flying clowns not just because of their colourful beaks and dark eye markings, but also because of their ungainly flying technique. These small seabirds spend a large part of the year on the water, where their main food consists of the lesser sand eel. If the lesser sand eel is overfished, as it has been in the past, entire colonies of Atlantic puffins can starve to death. These swift divers only really come ashore to breed and raise their young. They usually lay their eggs in caves they have dug themselves. Nowadays, roughly half of all Atlantic puffins breed on Iceland's steep, grassy cliff sides. Latrabjarg in northwestern Iceland.

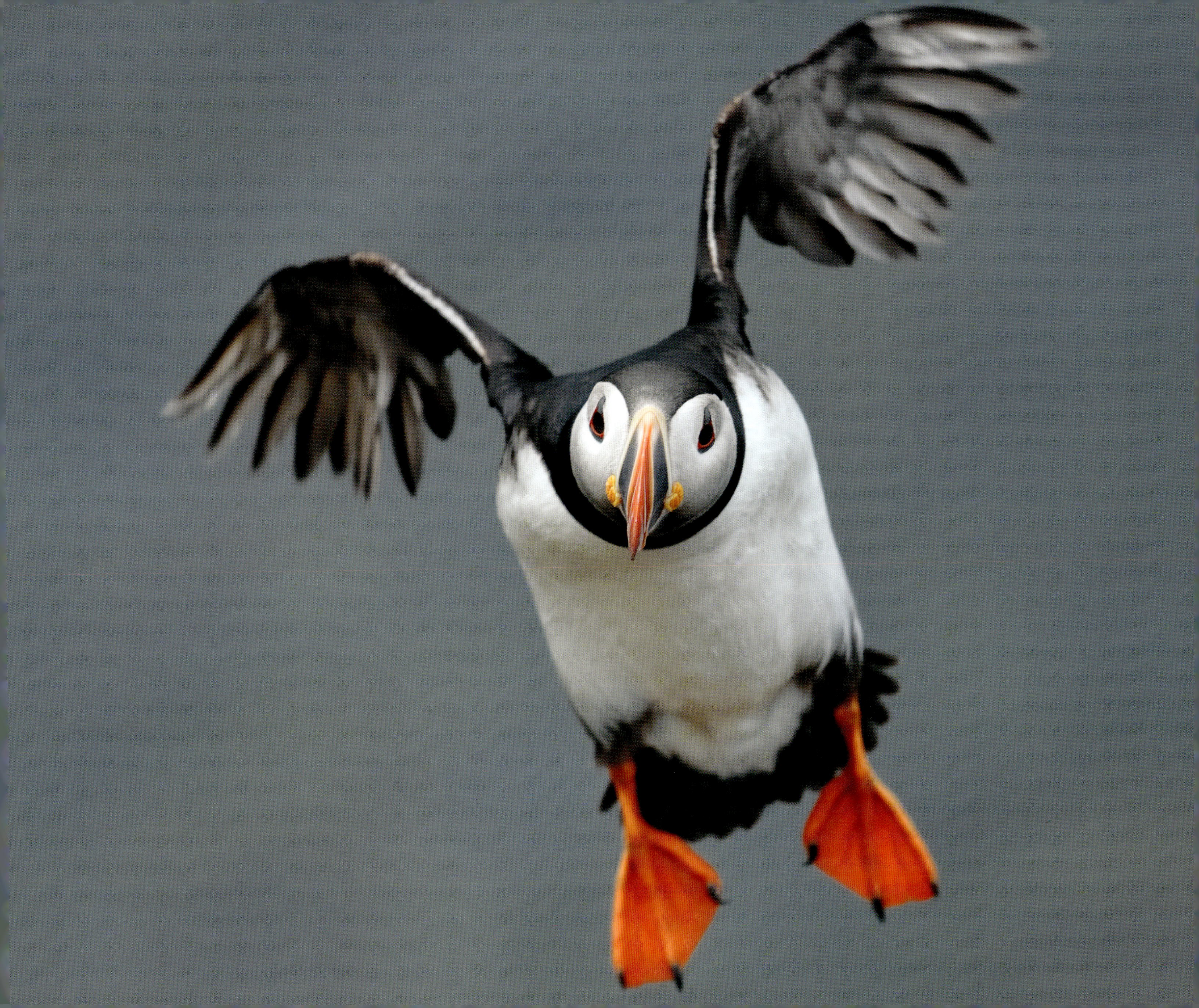

Iceland is famous for its birdlife.
The Eurasian golden plover (left) population, which likes to breed in wetlands, has long been in sharp decline.
This is due to the loss of its habitat such as the sweeping moorlands. Langanes Peninsula, northeastern Iceland.
The whimbrel (center) population on Iceland alone is estimated at 100,000 to 250,000 breeding pairs.

A young Arctic fox with grey summer fur. As soon as Iceland's foxes are mature, birds and bird eggs become their main prey. The Arctic fox may be the only land mammal on Iceland to have lived here before the arrival of the first humans. Hornsund, northwestern Iceland.

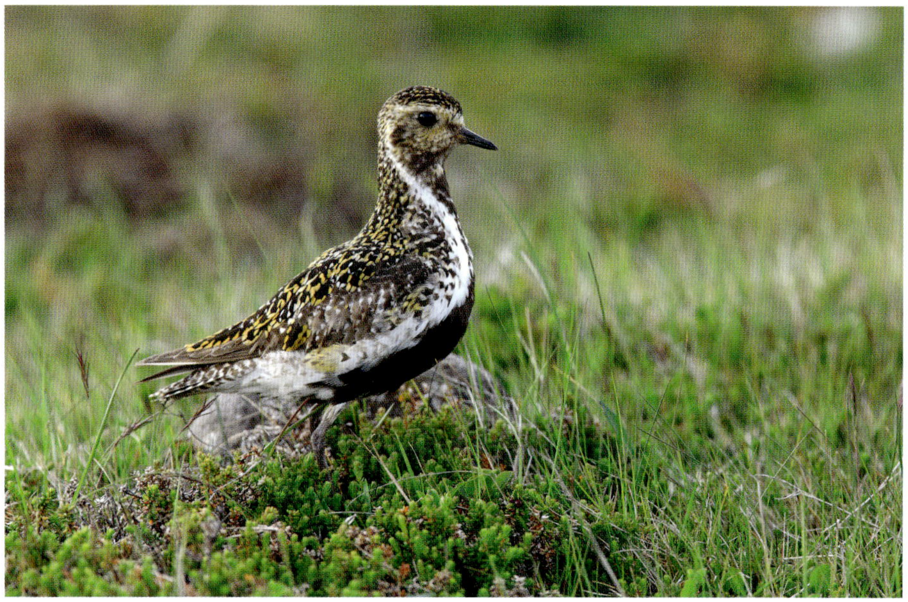

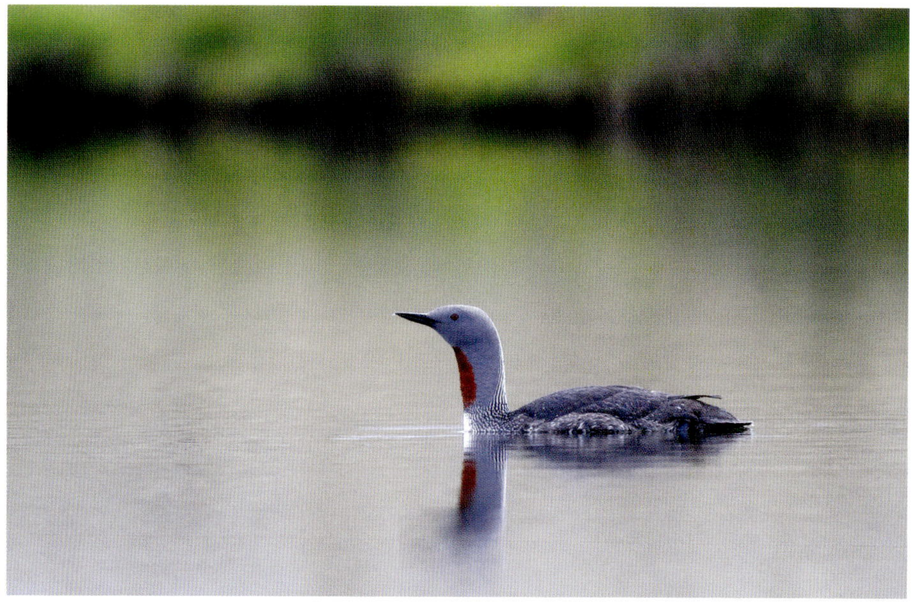

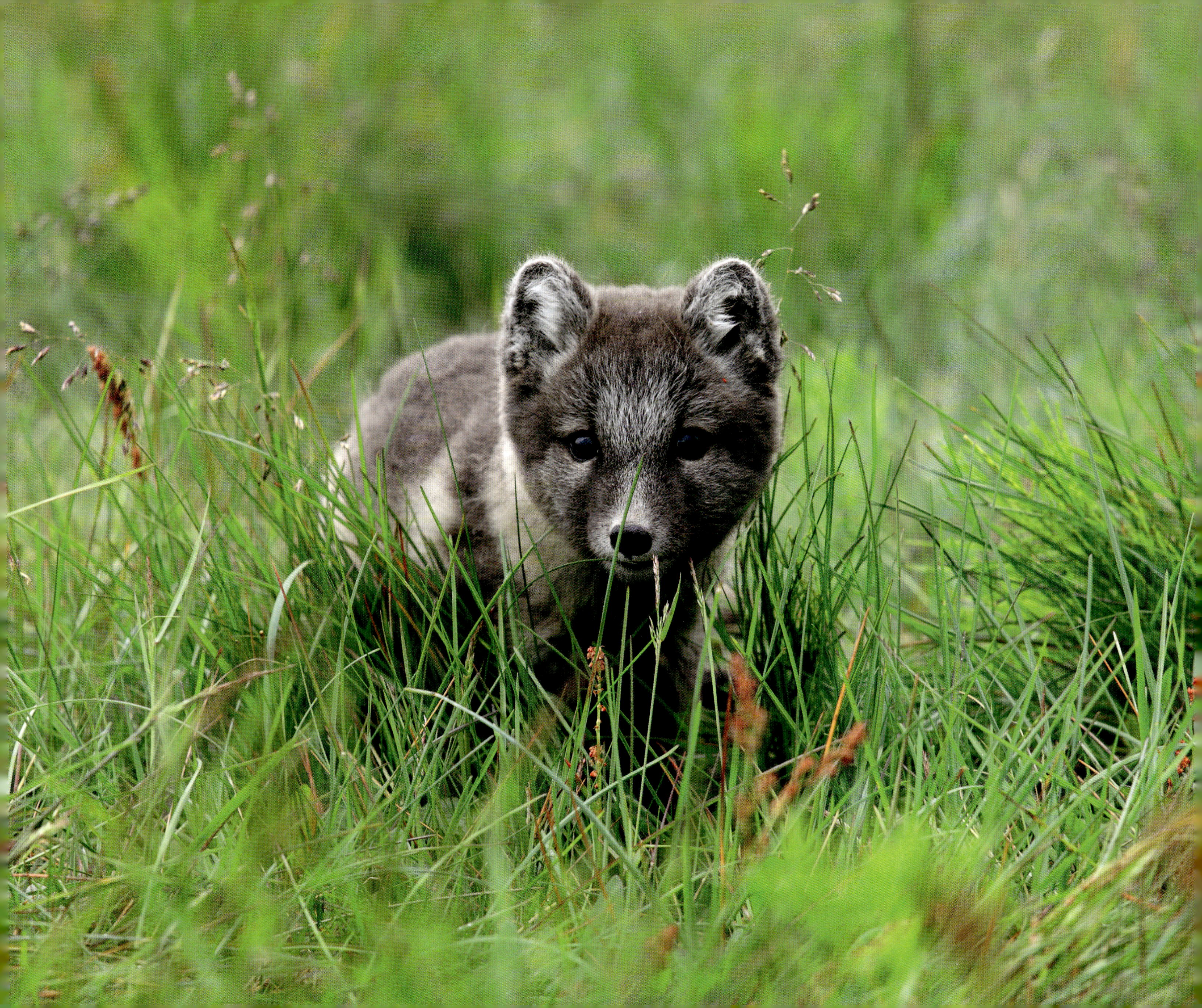

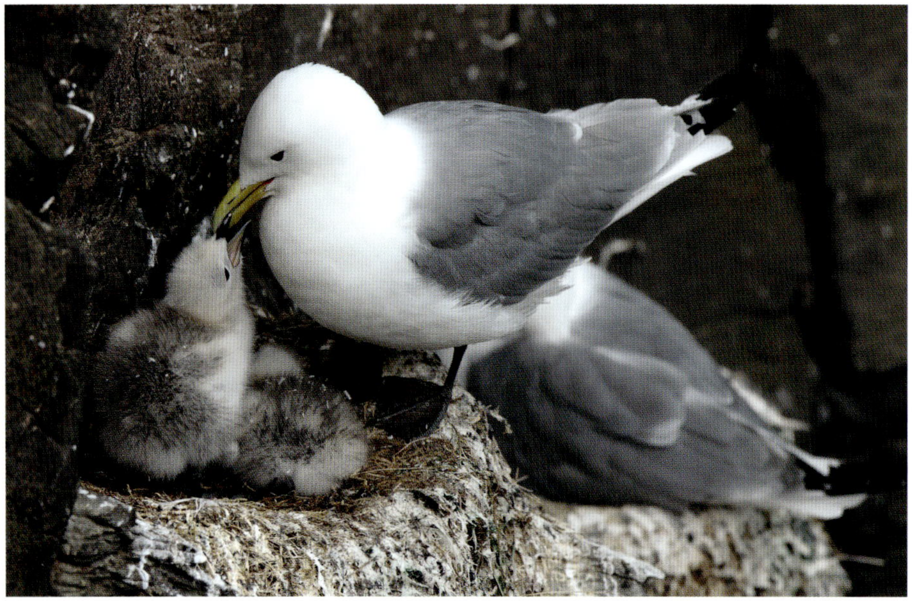
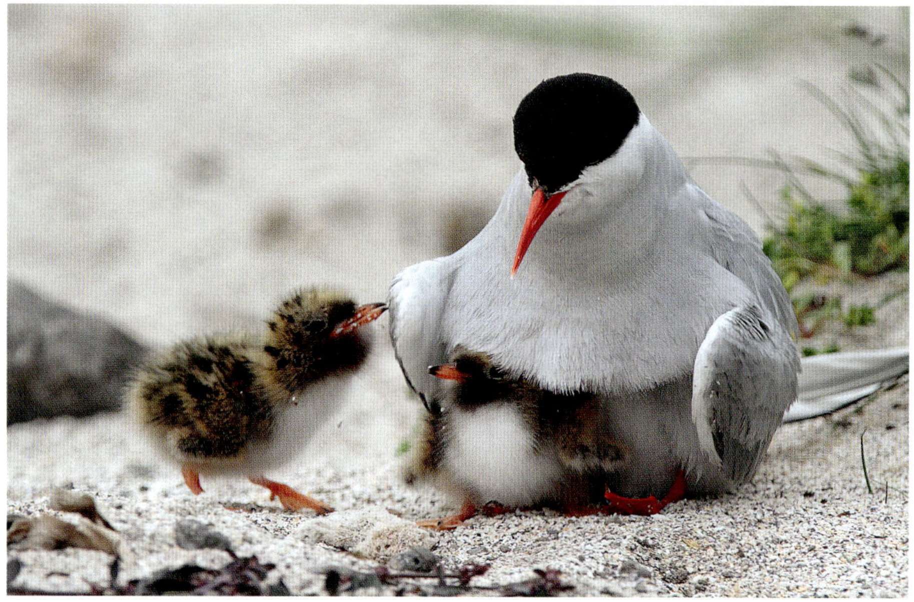
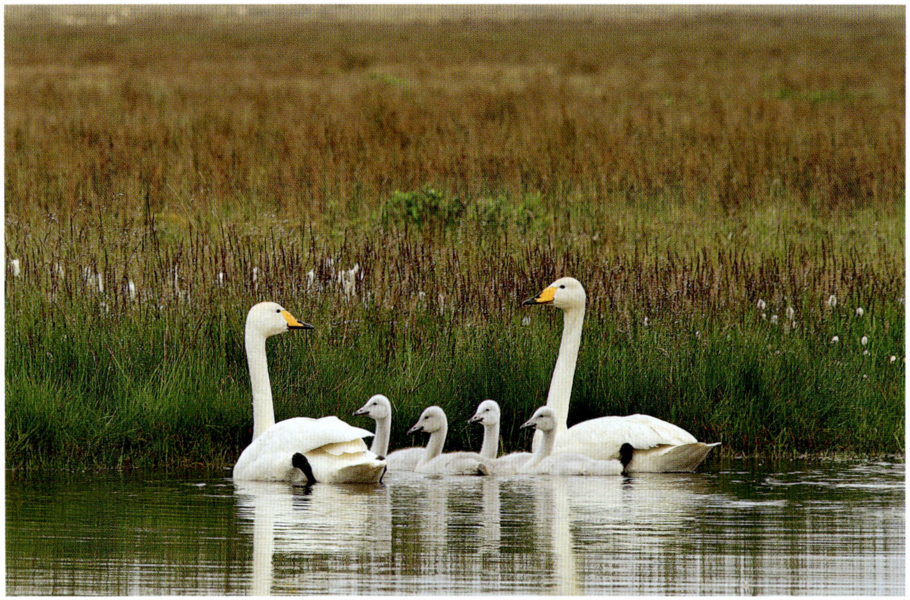
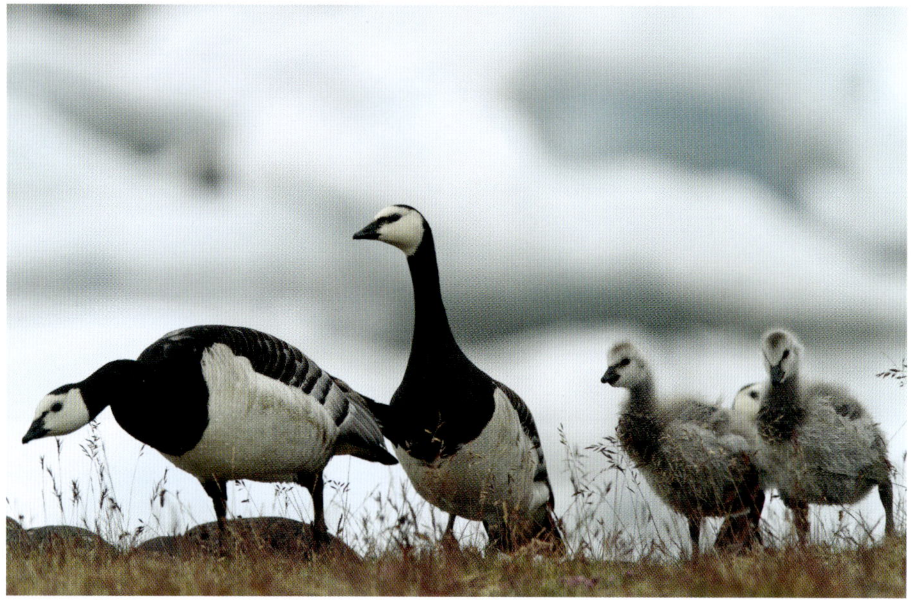

Birds and their young. Clockwise from top left: Black-legged kittiwake gulls on the Bird Cliffs of Latrabjarg, northwestern Iceland; Arctic tern, northwestern Iceland; barnacle geese, Jökulsarlon, southeastern Iceland; whooper swans, southeastern Iceland.

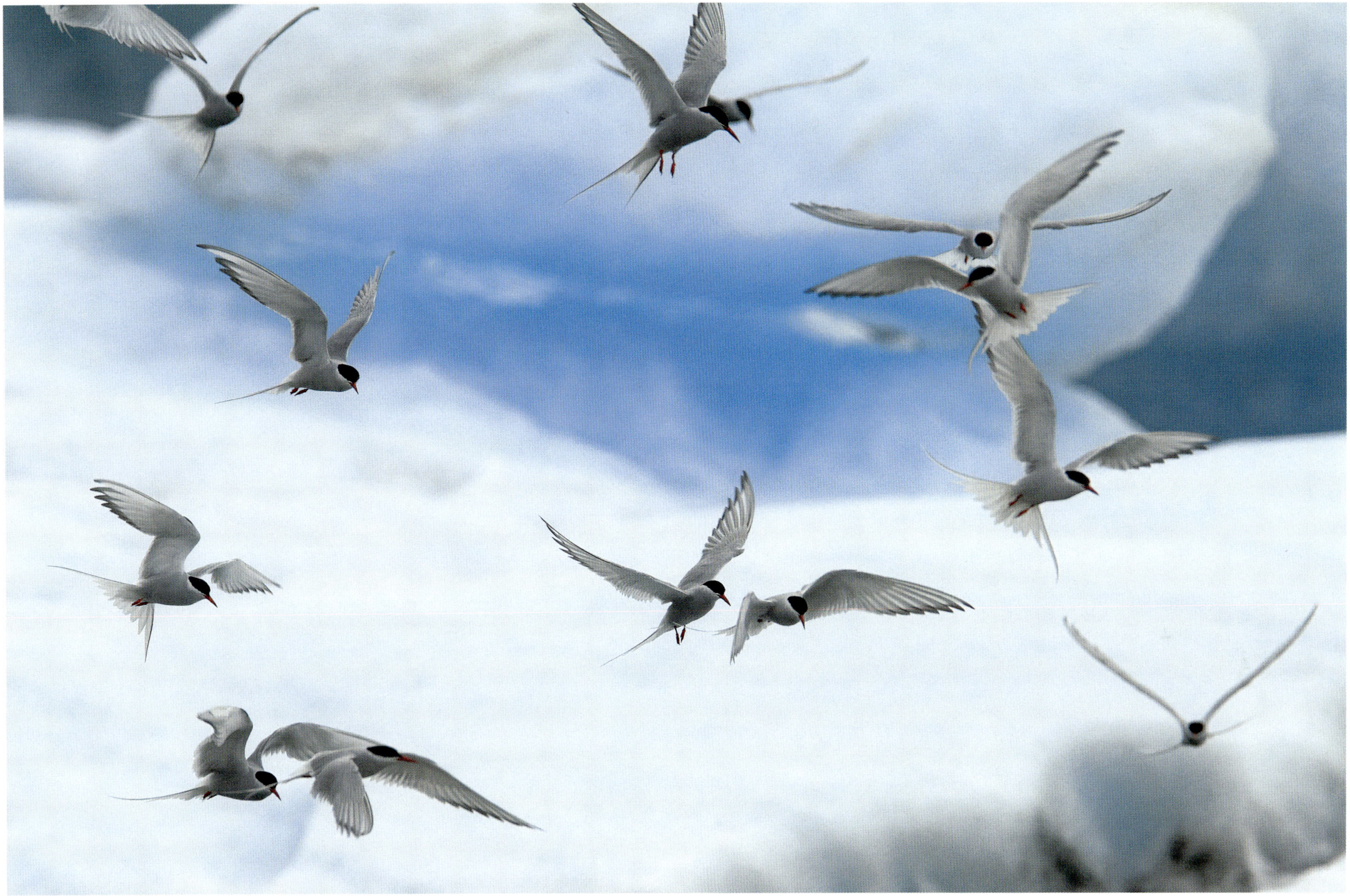

Arctic terns looking for food in the glacial lagoon of Jökulsarlon, southeastern Iceland.

Pages 142/143: Iceland's wild northeast is more austere than the rest of the island. The area around Myvatn Lake is one of the driest parts of the island because the rain or snow from the clouds that arrive from the south usually falls on the 8,100-square-kilometre Vatnajökull glacier.

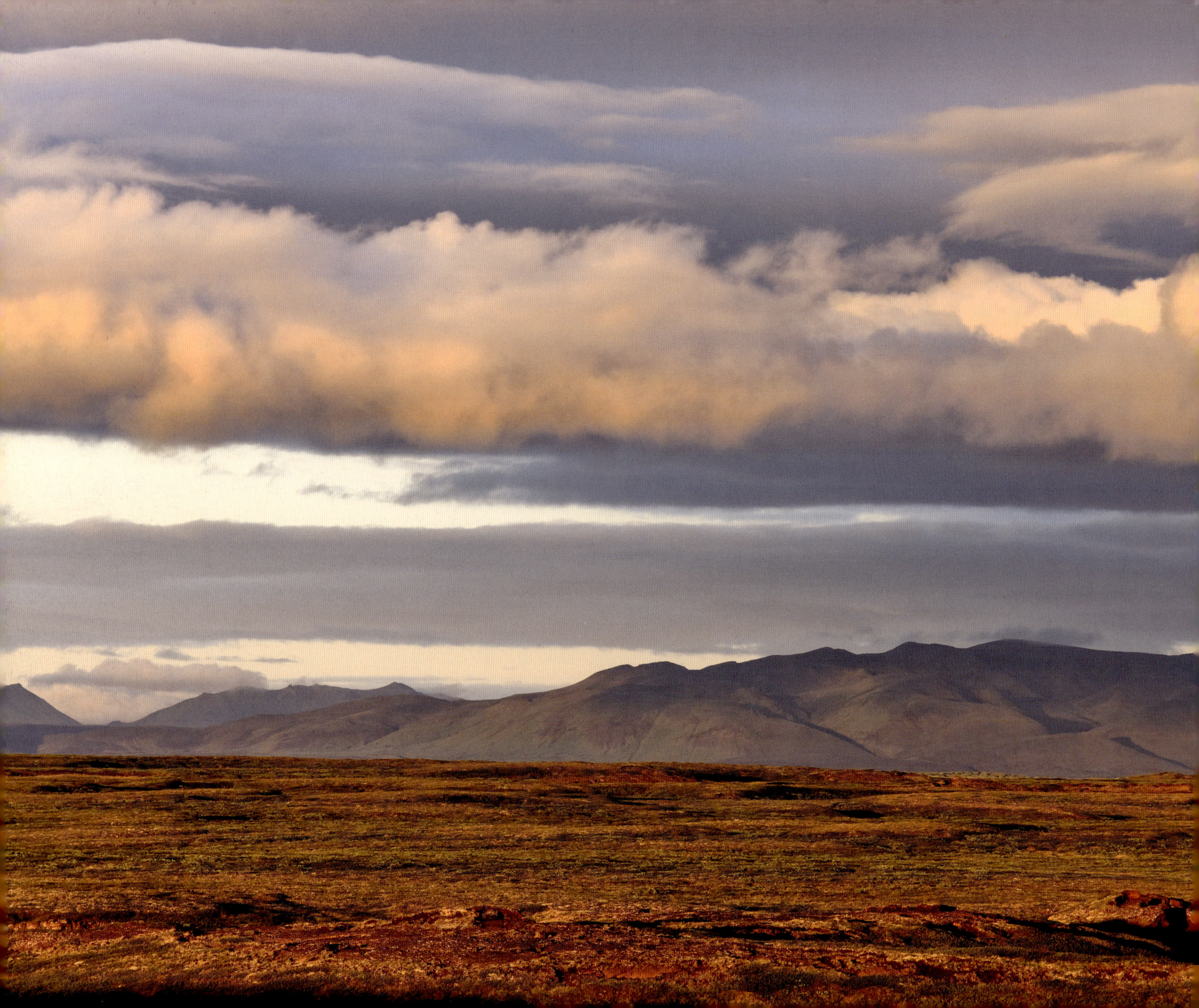

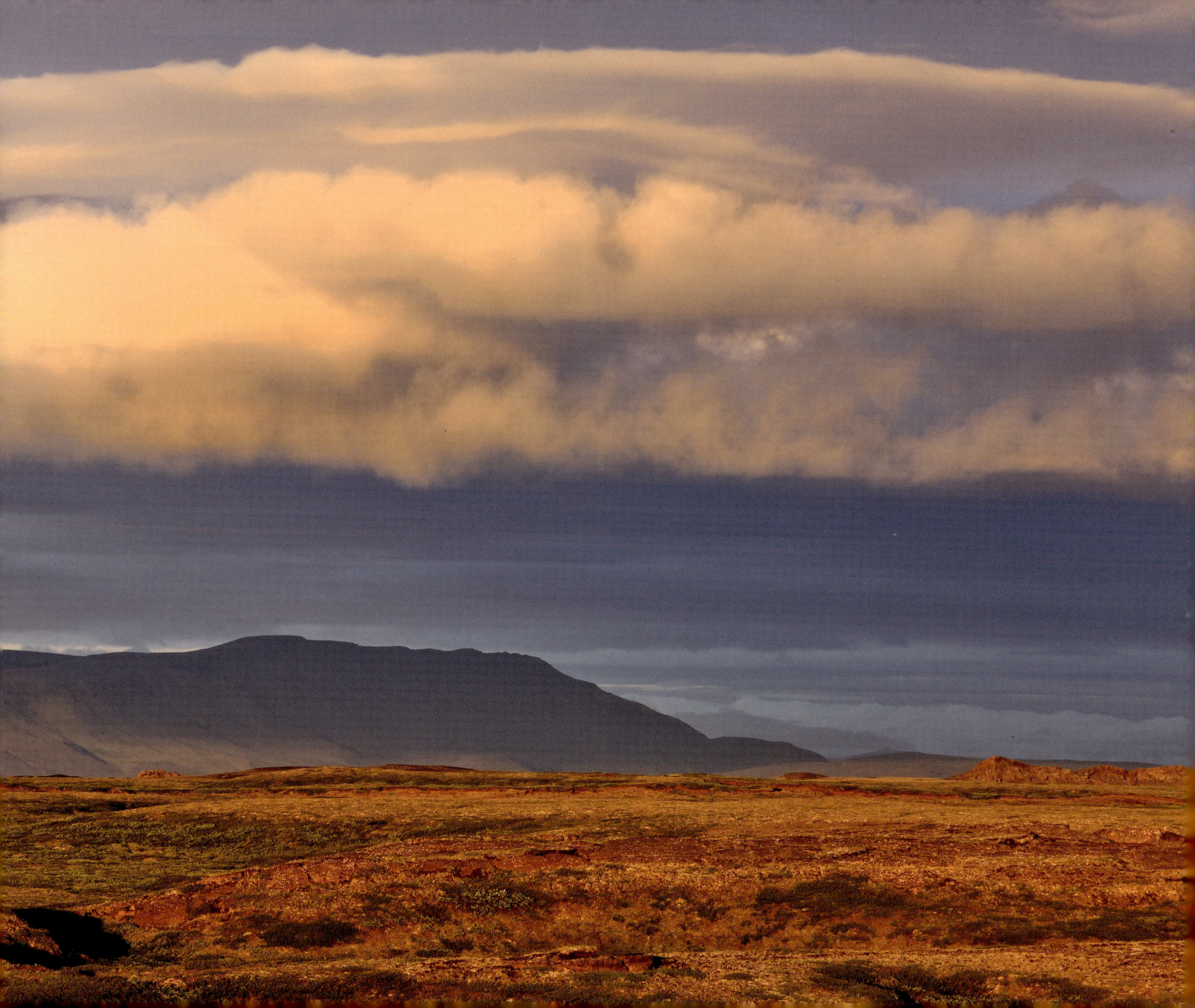

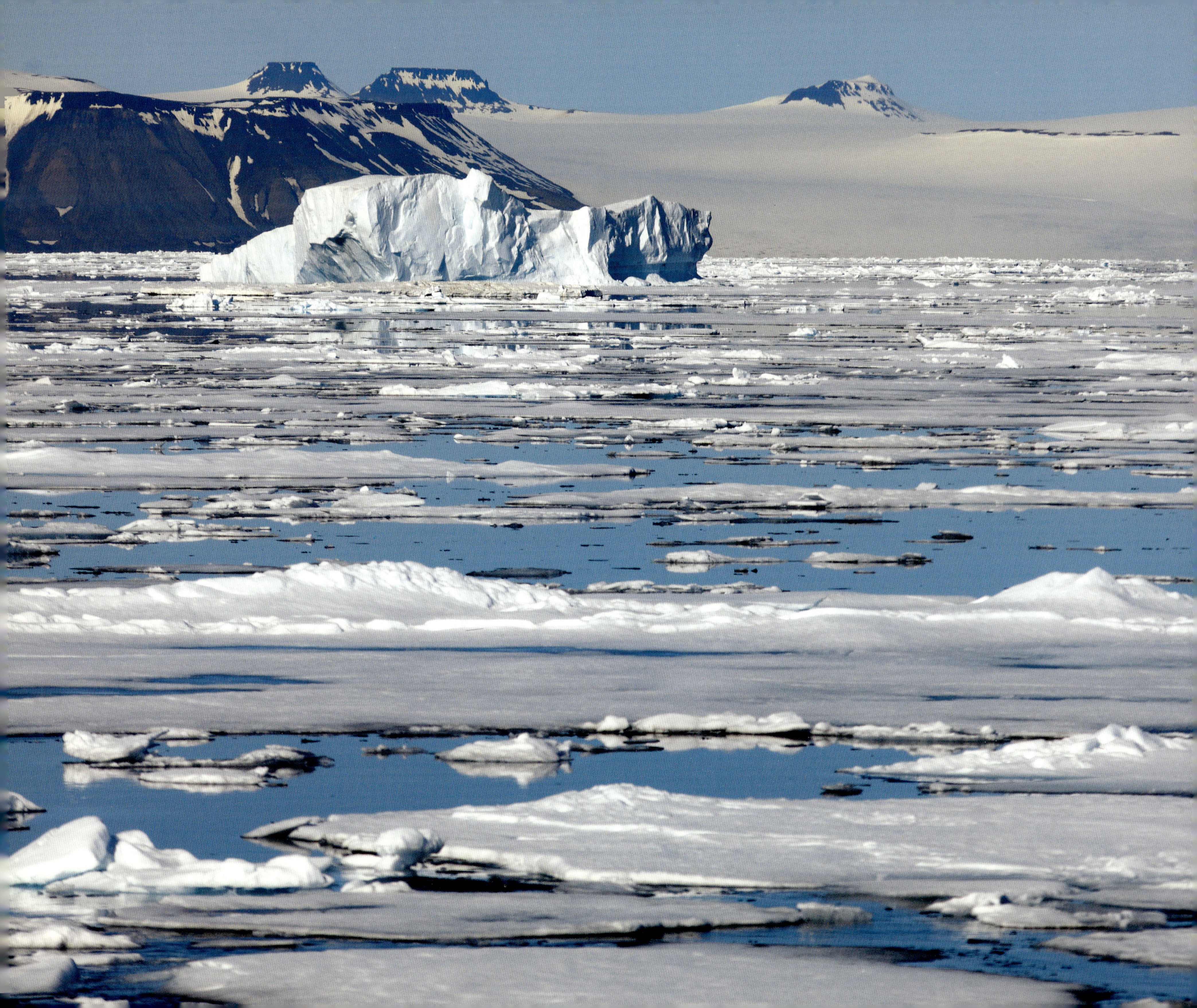

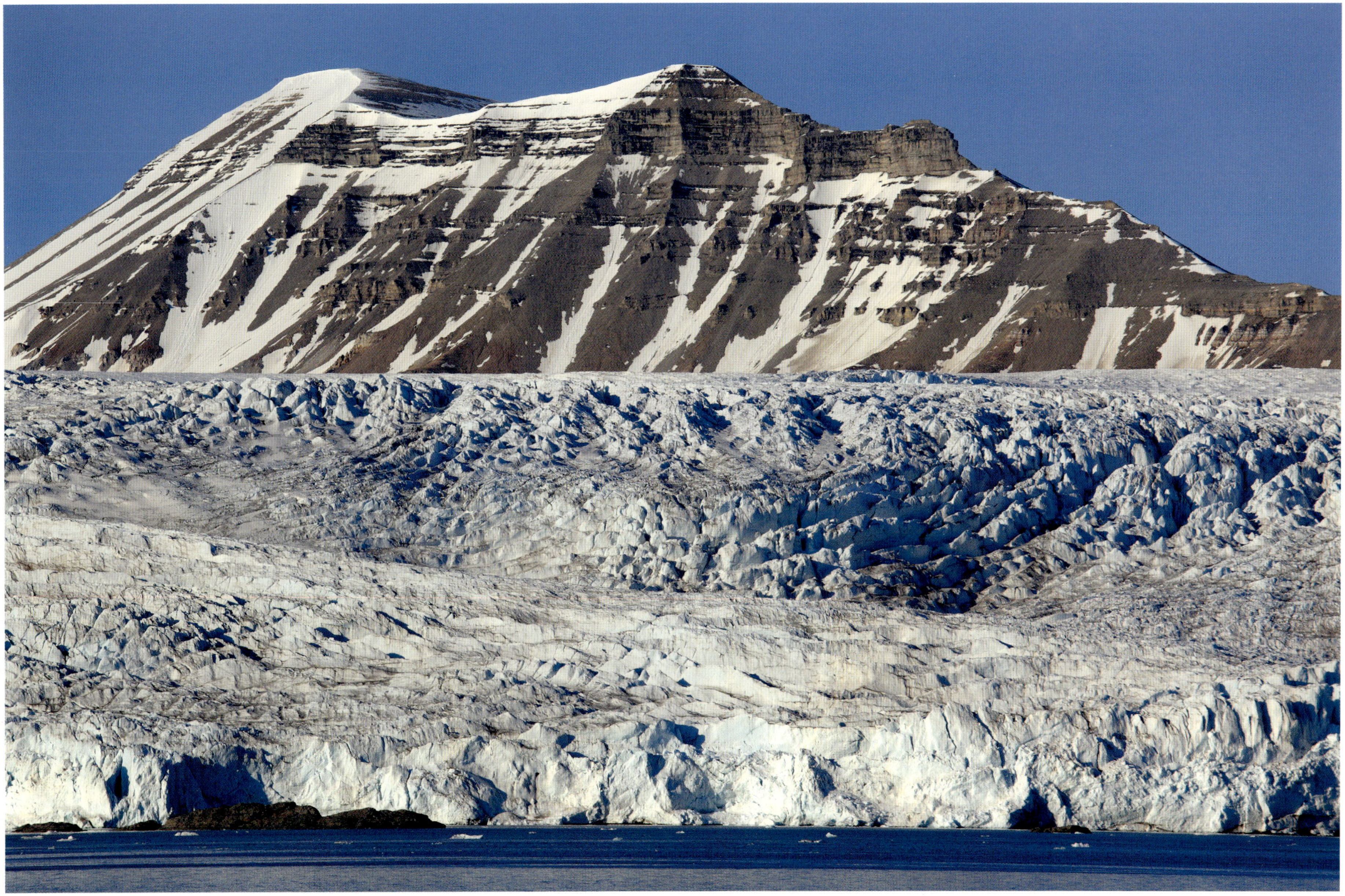

The Svalbard archipelago lies in the far north of Europe, between the 74th and 81st degree of latitude, making it part of the high Arctic. The local inhabitants call the archipelago Svalbard, or "cool coast", in reference to the Arctic climate. The north and east coast are covered with pack ice until the late summer. Only the west coast does not freeze up entirely because of a branch of the warm Gulf Stream.

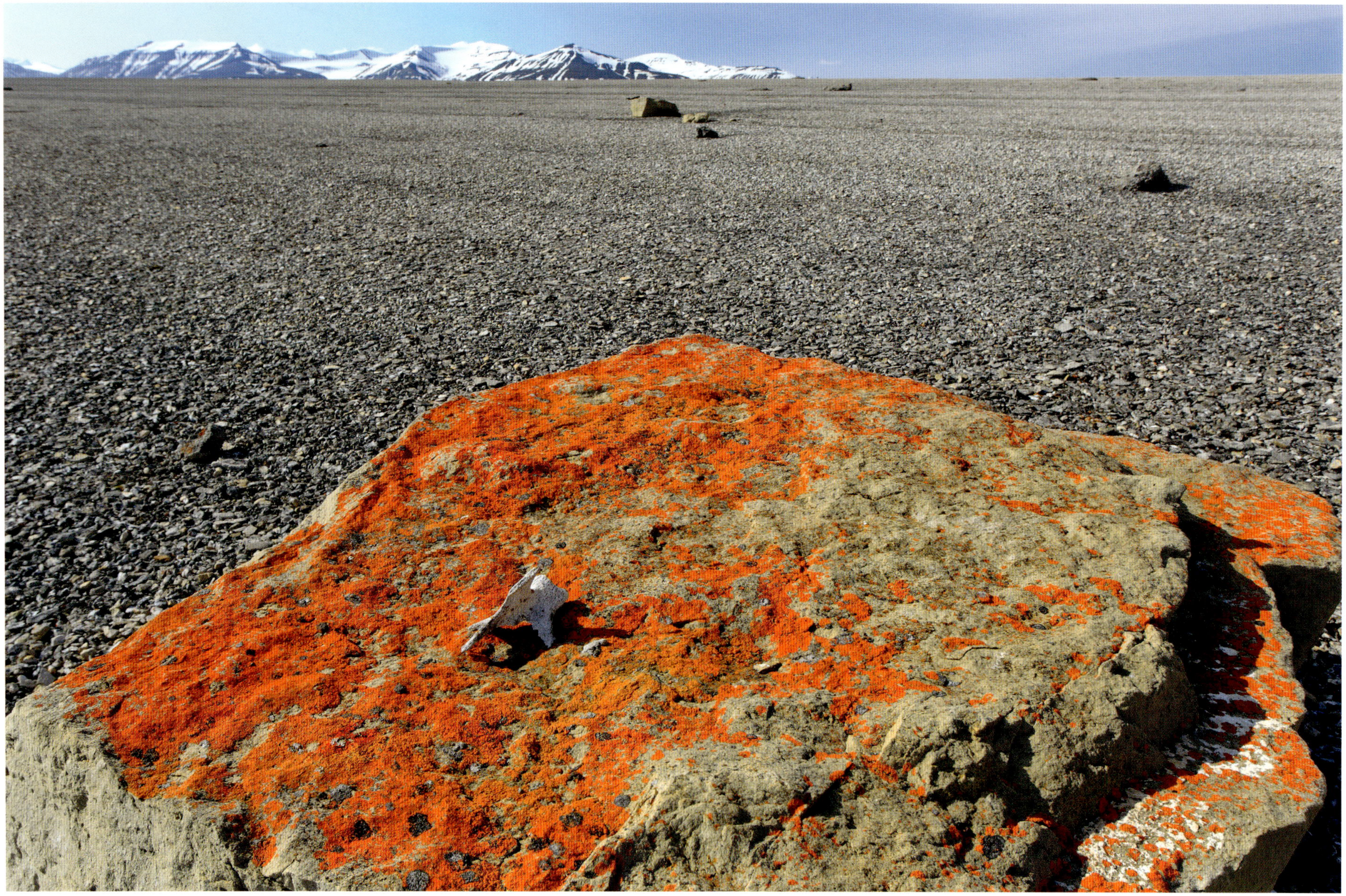

In some parts of Svalbard, lichen is virtually the only form of vegetation as there is almost as little precipitation here as there is in the Sahara. Along the edges of fjords in particular, mosses form dense padding, storing the desirable moisture like a wet sponge.

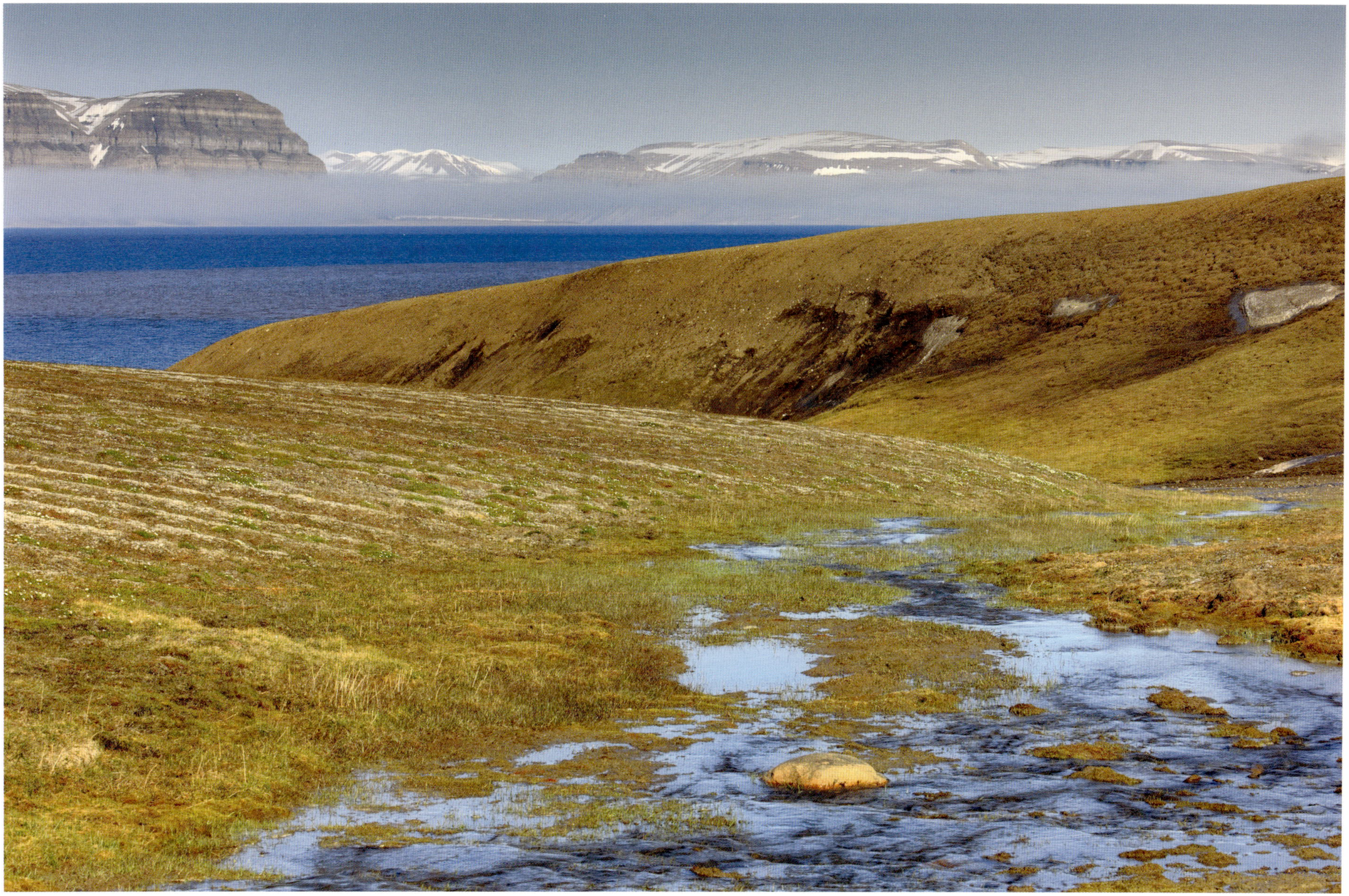

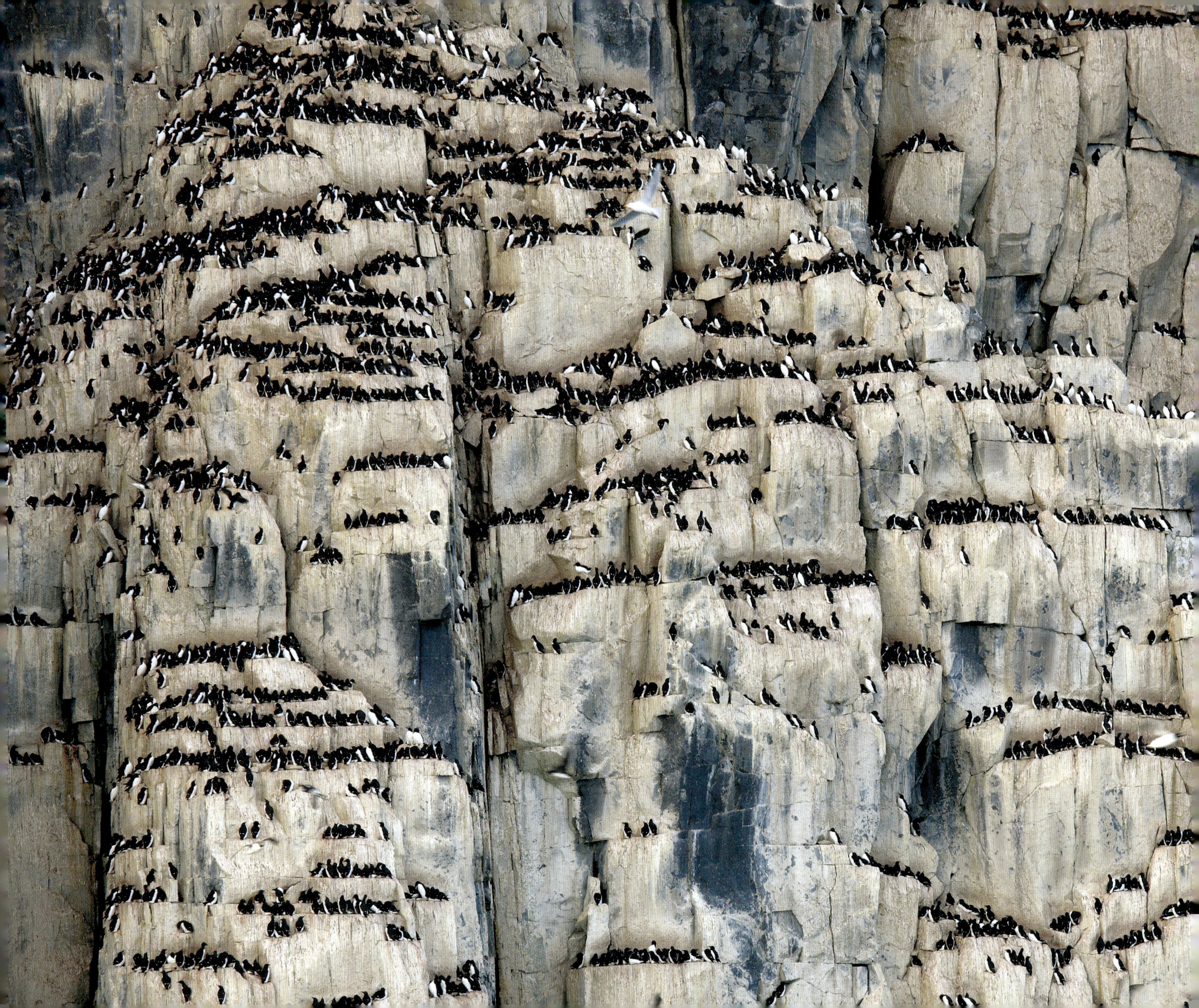

Thick-billed murres belong to the auk family and are somewhat more powerfully built than their near relatives, the common murre. They breed in large colonies on rocky coasts like this one by the Alkefjellet on Svalbard. Murres (left and centre photo) dive from the water surface to find food, which mostly consists of small fish, crabs, shellfish and squid.

The little auk (right photo) is the smallest member of the auk family. Little auks often gather in large flocks before going in search of food.

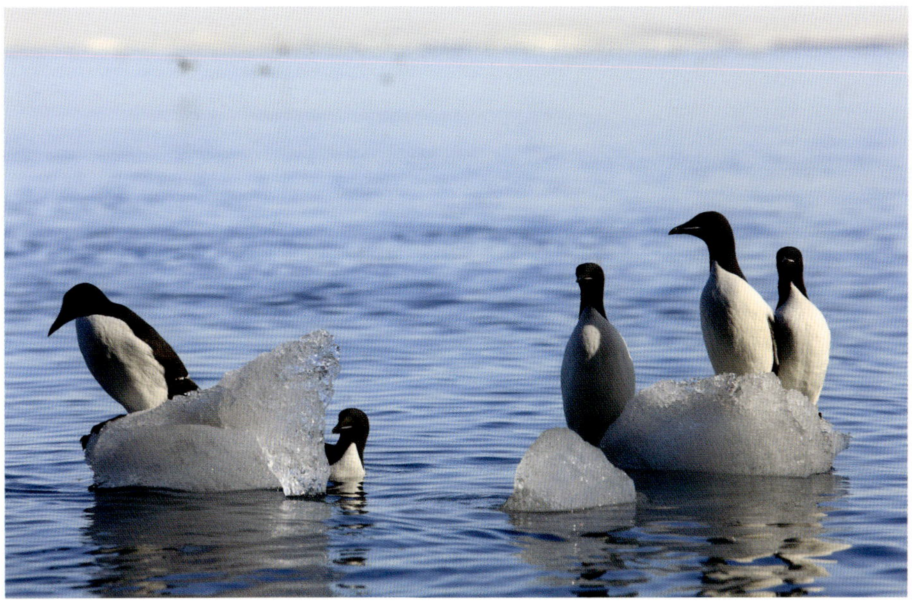

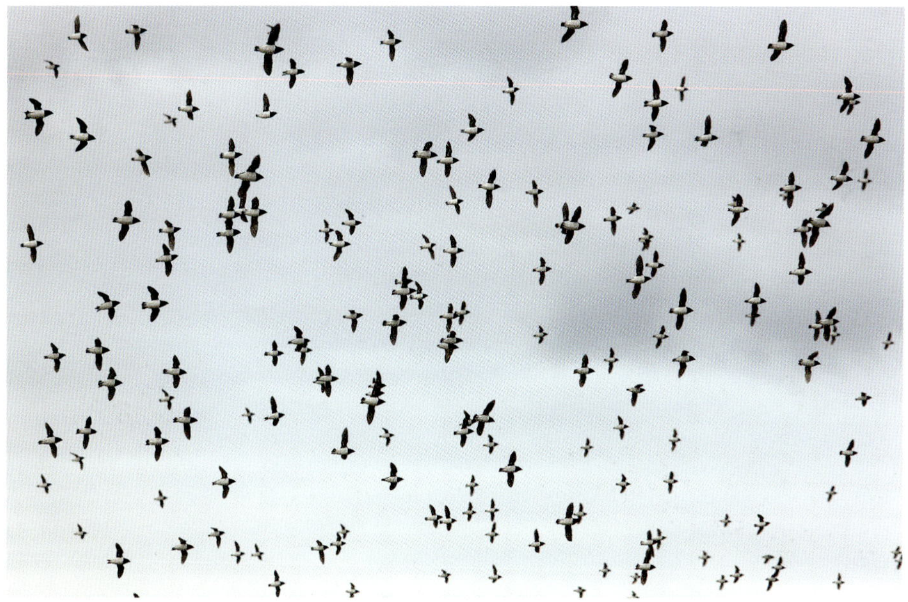

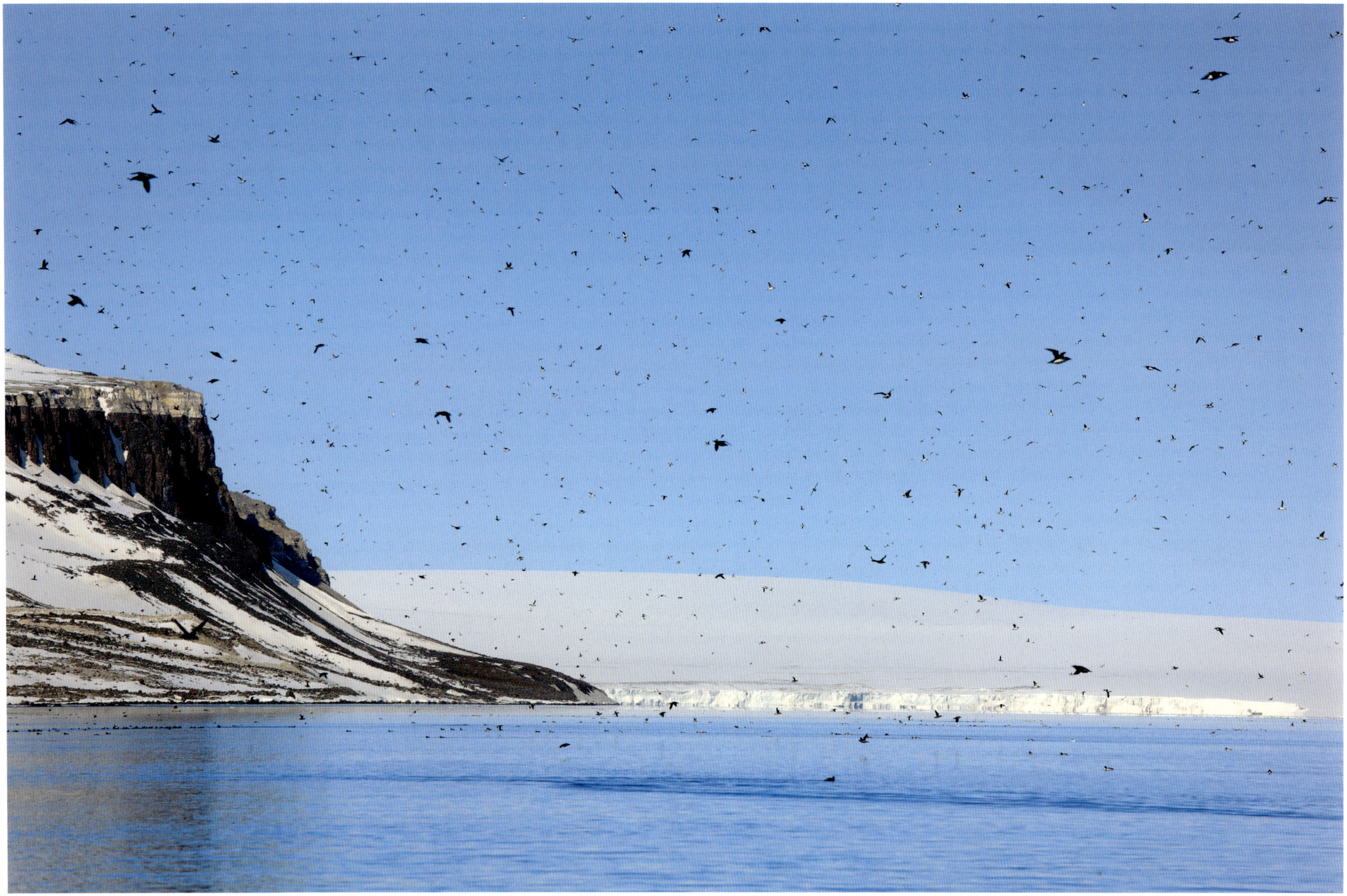

Thick-billed murres at the rocky coast of Alkefjellet.
Right: Little auks breed in large colonies on the steep coastal cliffs and on cliff faces near the coast, like this one by the Ingeborgfjellet on Svalbard. These small birds often form swarms that hunt for food, usually small crabs, together. When diving, they can cover distances of up to 25 metres under water.

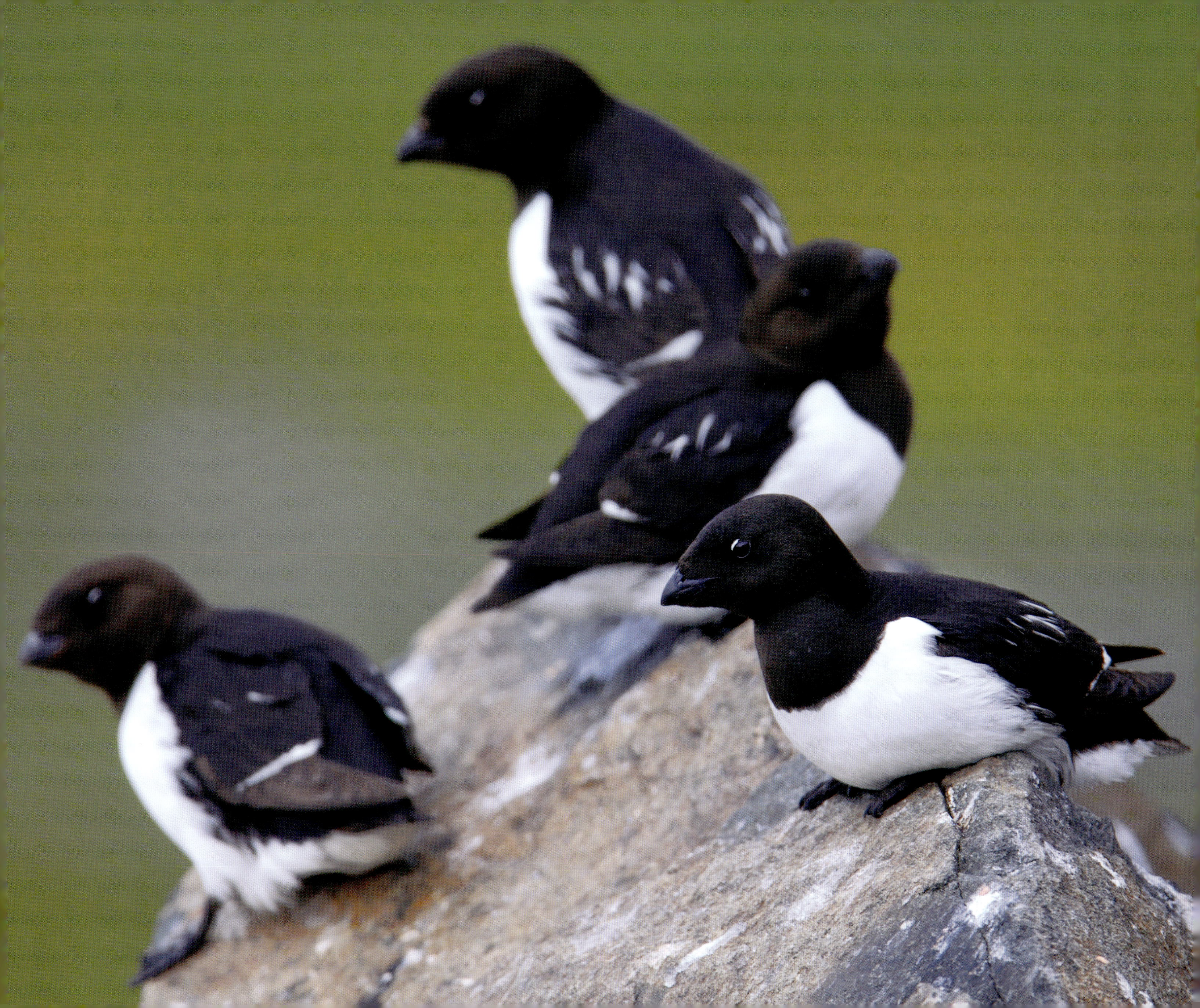

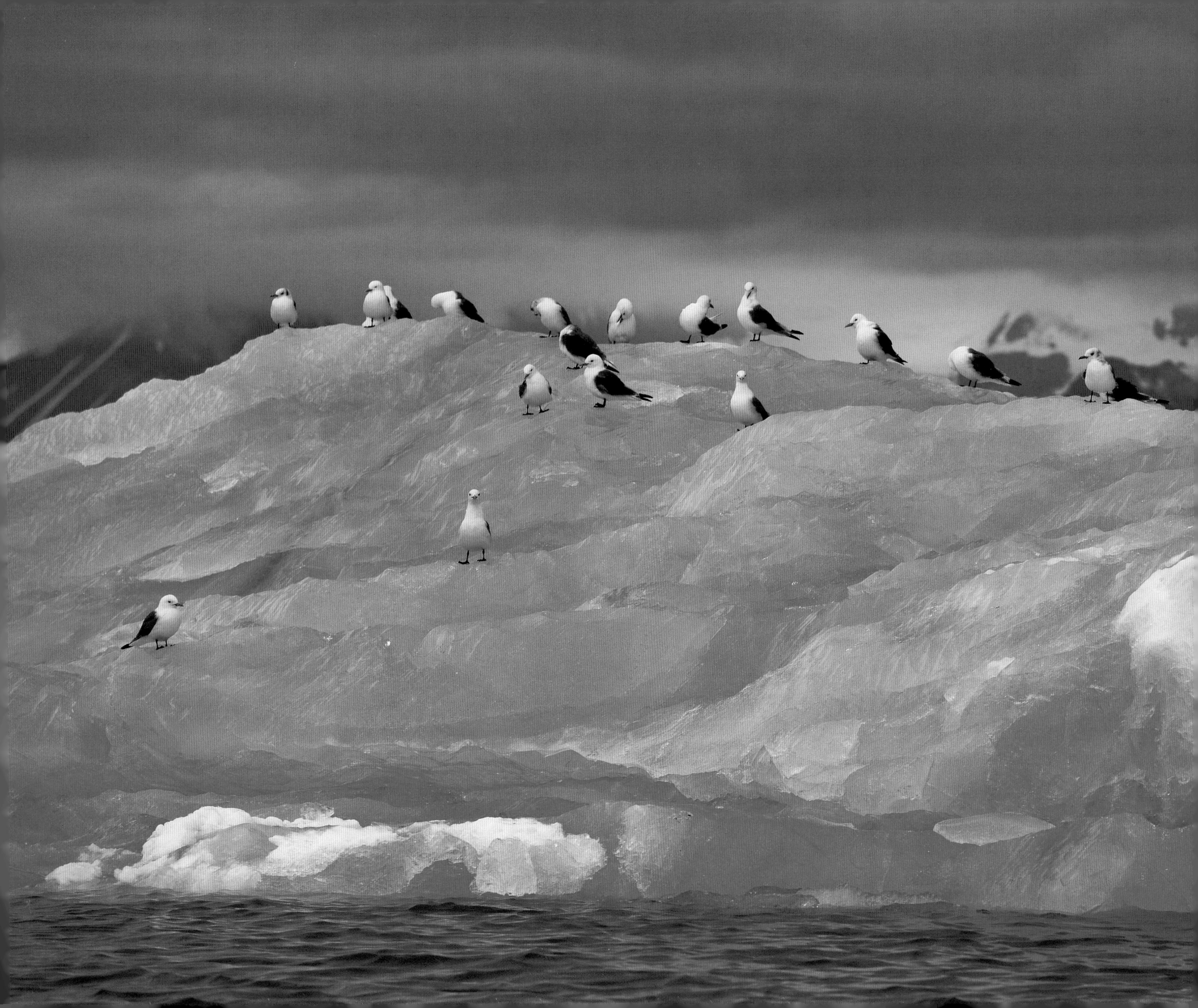

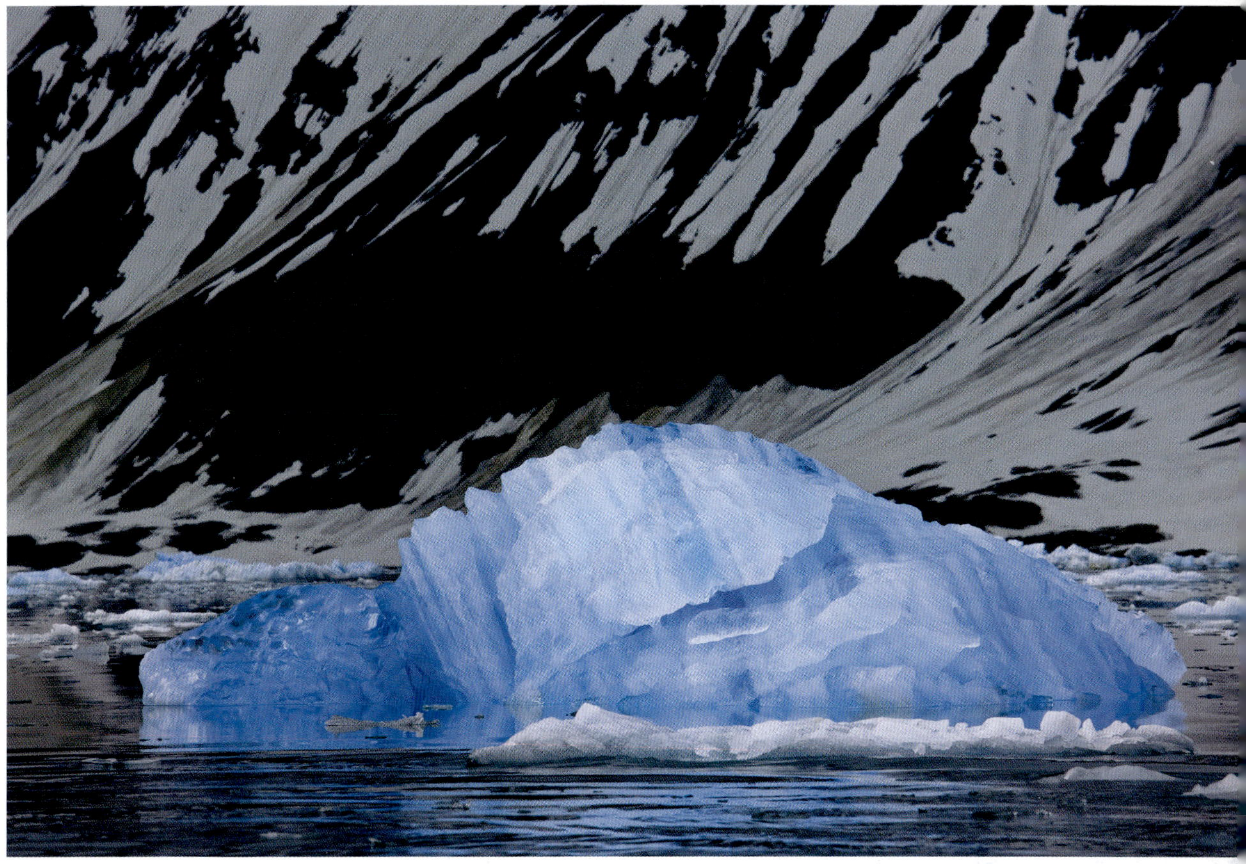

Hornsund in the southwest of Spitsbergen is one of the most beautiful fjords of the entire archipelago. The fjord slices 25 kilometres deep into the land. Active glaciers calve into almost all of the fjord's bays, so that the water is often covered with little icebergs.

For many, glacier ice is the most beautiful colour of blue on earth. It is formed by the immense pressure exerted by the ice masses, and the air that is trapped by this process.

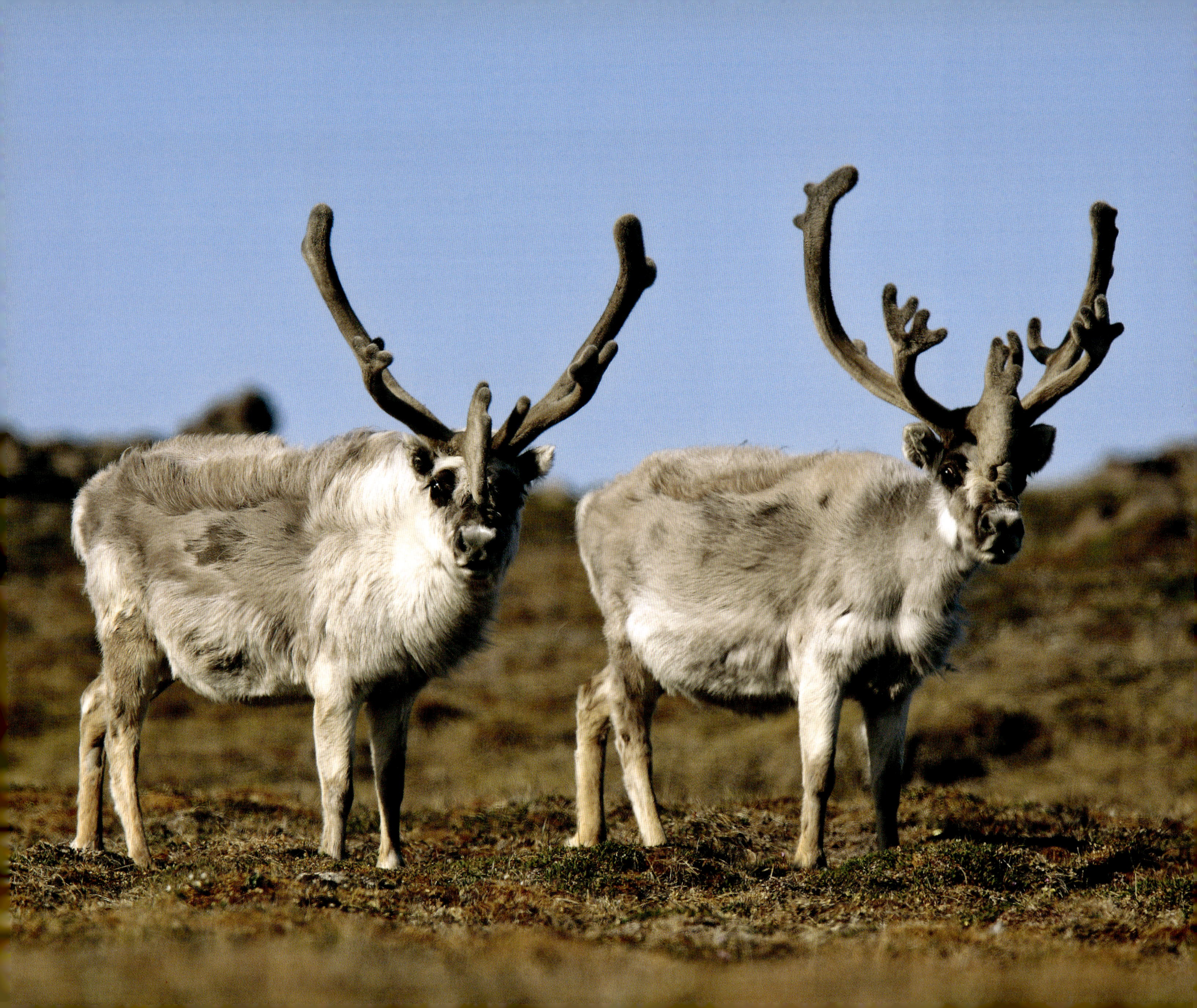

The Svalbard reindeer is a reindeer subspecies that is native only to Svalbard. The Svalbard reindeer is much smaller, lighter and looks more compact than its relatives on the Eurasian continent and North America. Its diet consists mainly of different types of lichen and moss. Sudden mild spells in the winter, during which it rains and the snow thaws, can be deadly for these animals. This is because they cannot break through the layer of ice that forms when the water on the surface refreezes, no matter how hard they scrabble at it. In this way, just one warm winter can spell the death of hundreds of animals.

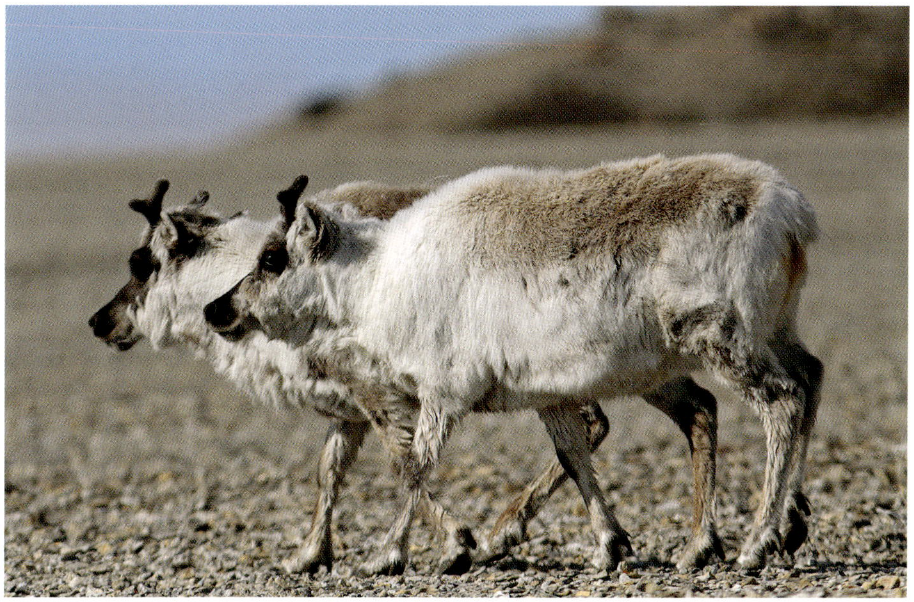

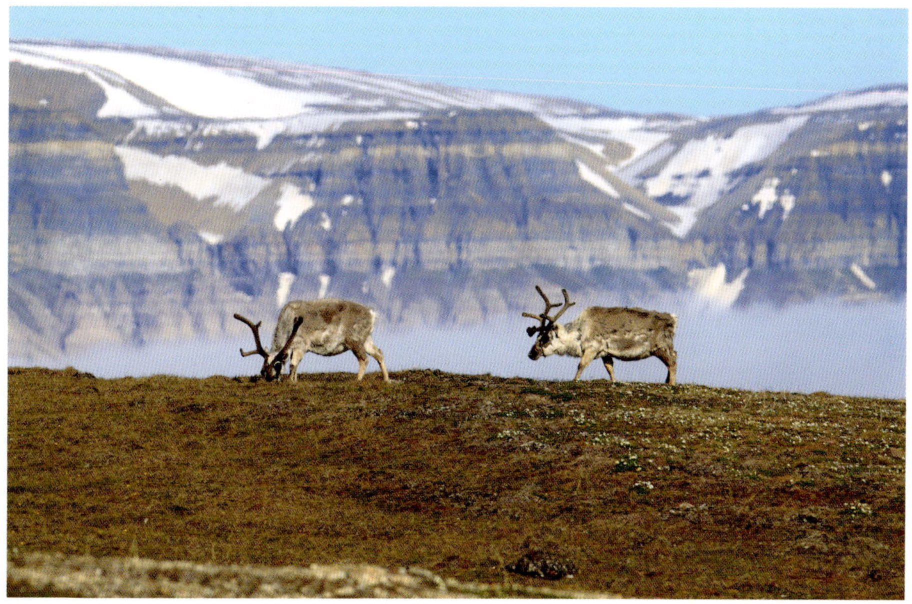

Walruses are the second-largest seals, second only to sea elephants. A fully grown male can grow to a size of almost four metres and weigh as much as 1,200 kilograms. Despite and because of their massive bodies, walruses are elegant swimmers and excellent divers. Their tusks have many functions: they help the walruses drag themselves forwards on land and to get out of the water, to open up breathing holes, defend themselves against polar bears, as status symbols for their owners, and even as headrests.
For centuries, walruses were hunted mercilessly on Svalbard, and came close to extinction. Only strict protective measures introduced in the middle of the last century saved the animals from complete disappearance. Nowadays, large colonies of walruses can once again be admired on Svalbard, especially along the Hinlopen Strait or on the north and east sides of Nordaustlandet.

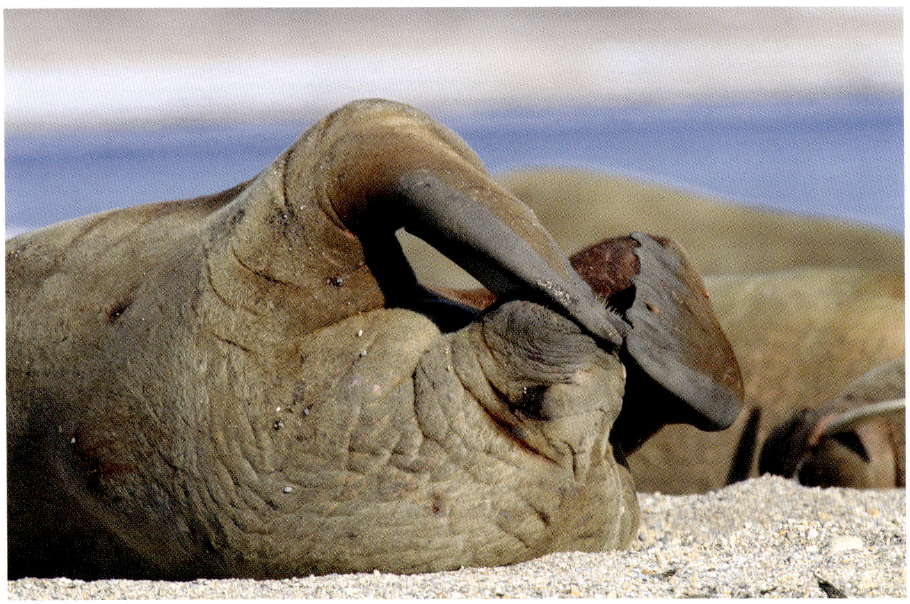

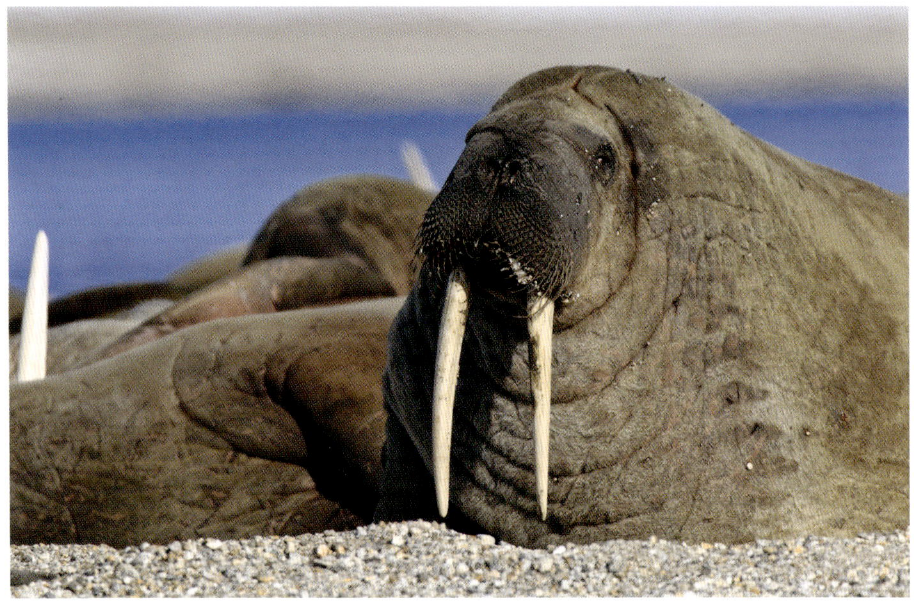

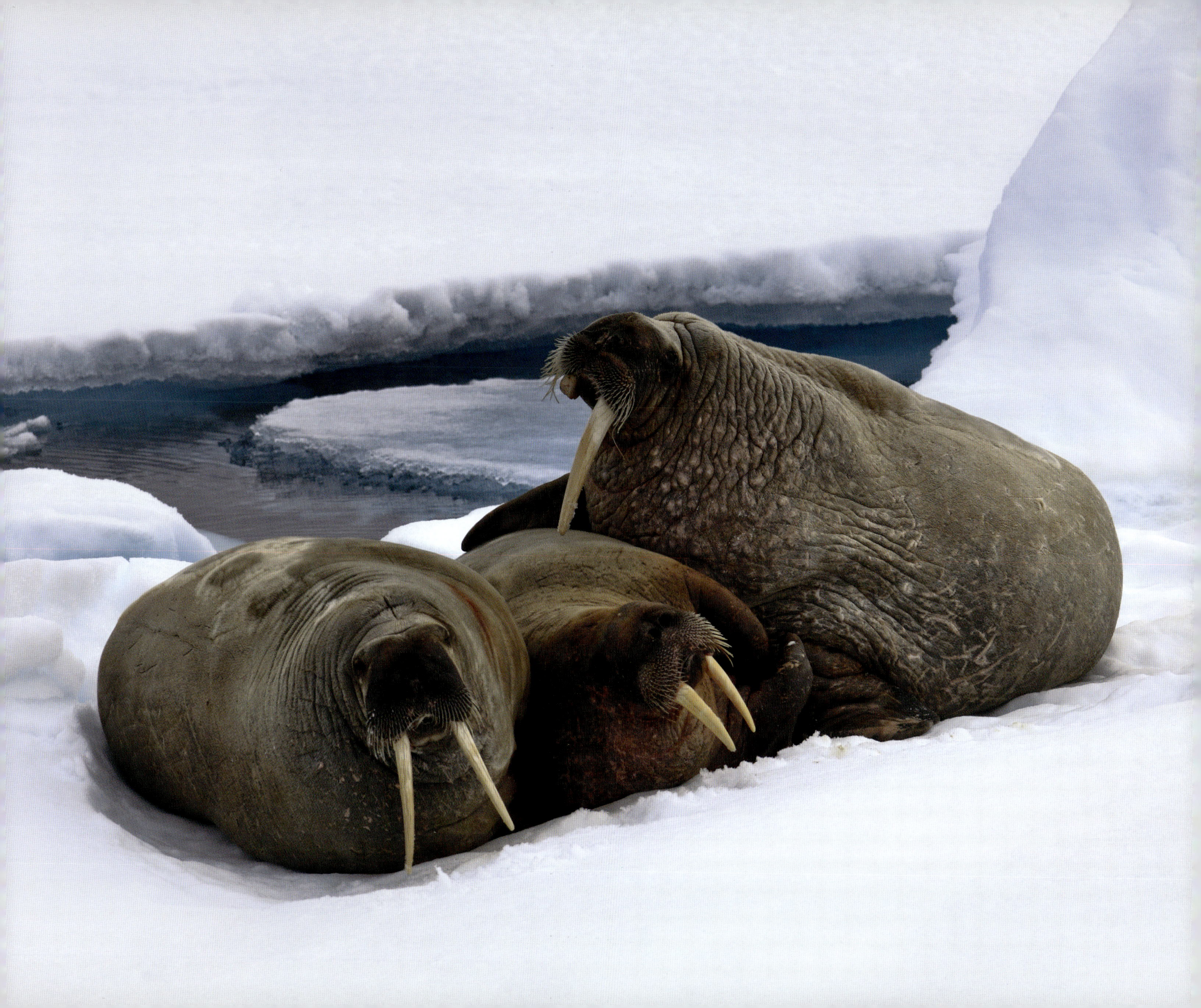

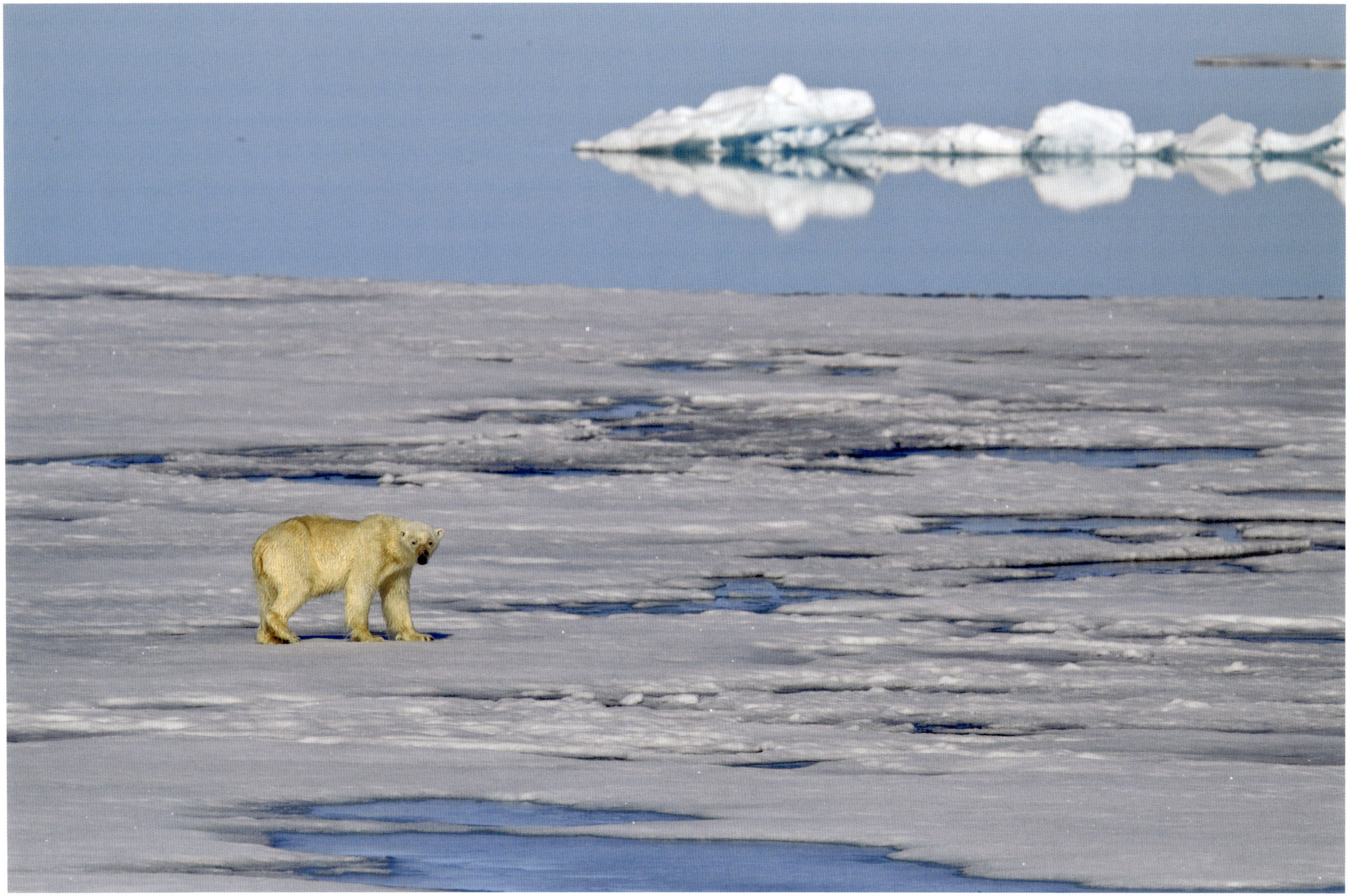

Polar bears are to be found almost everywhere on Svalbard, particularly along the north and east coasts as these regions are covered by pack ice for the longest period of time. Hinlopen Strait between Spitsbergen and Nordaustlandet.

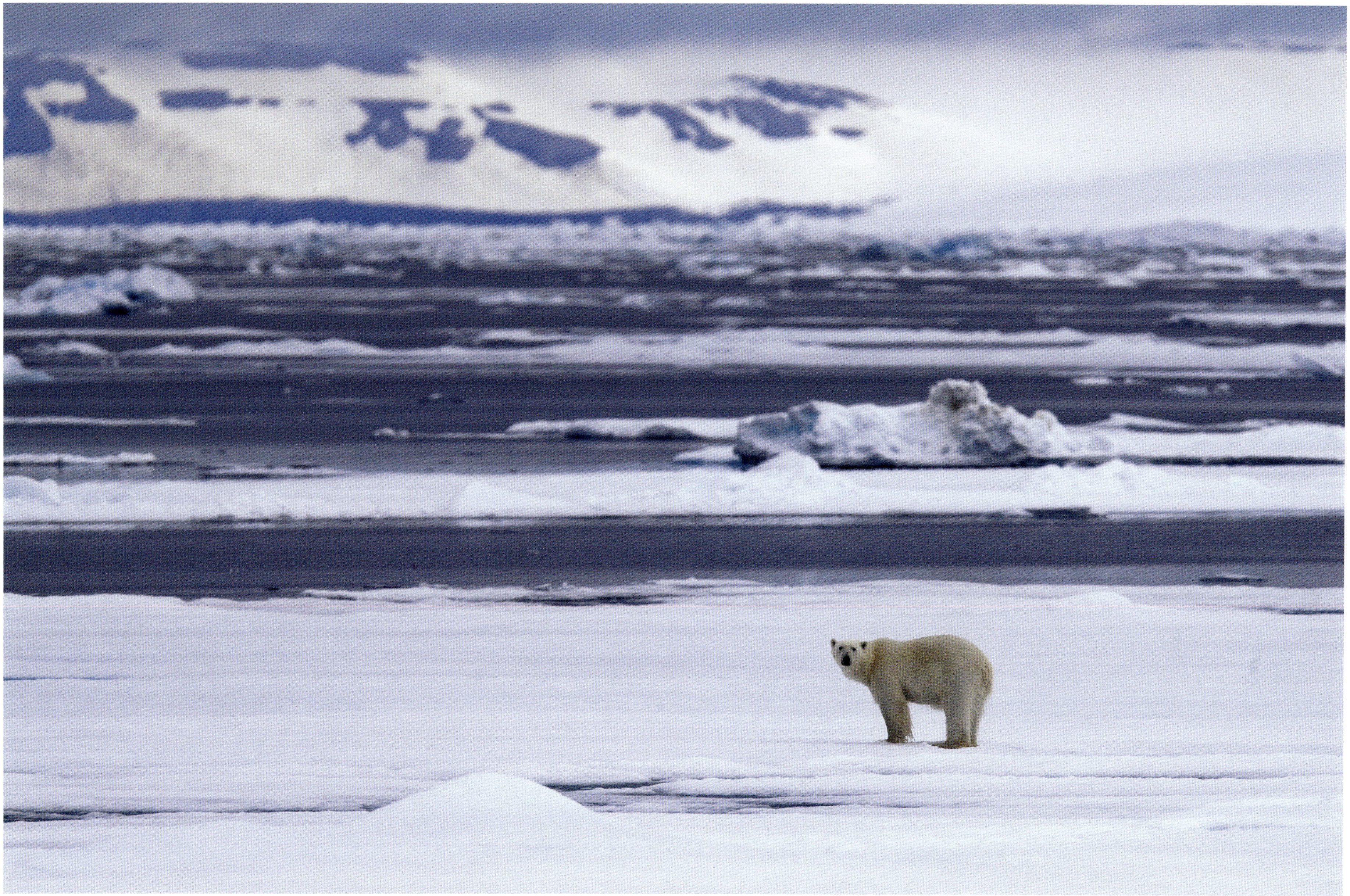

Pages 160/161: Tempelfjord on the west coast of Spitsbergen.

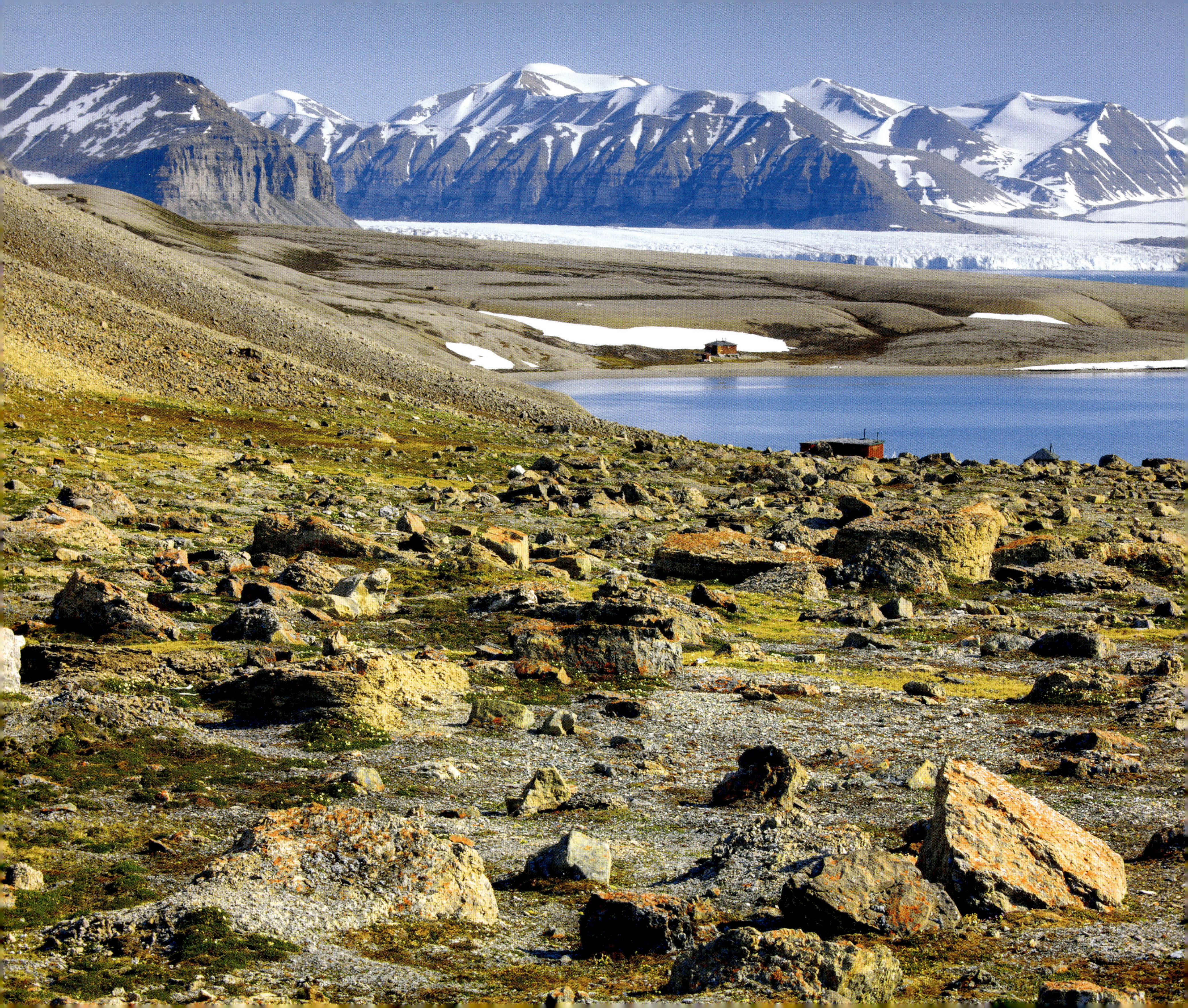

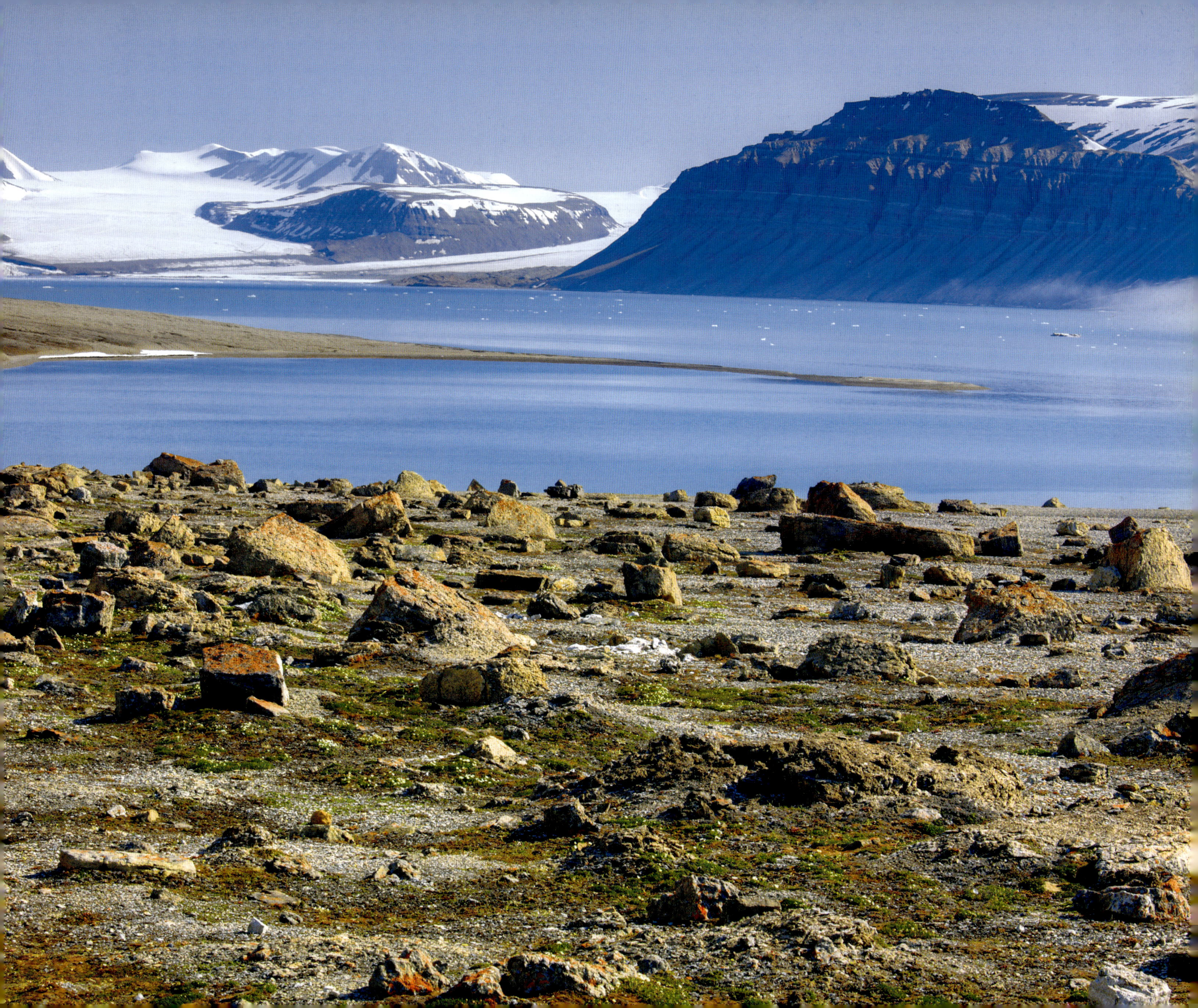

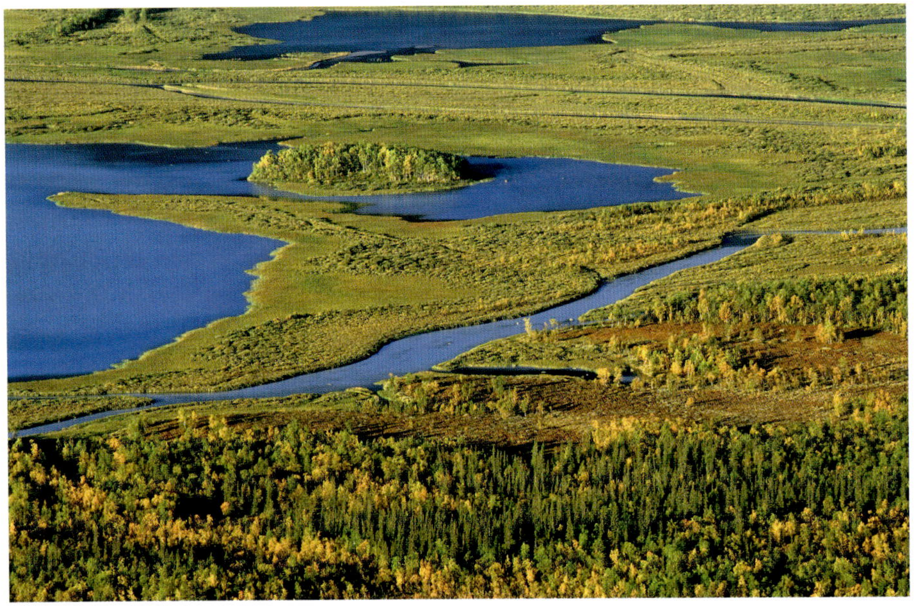

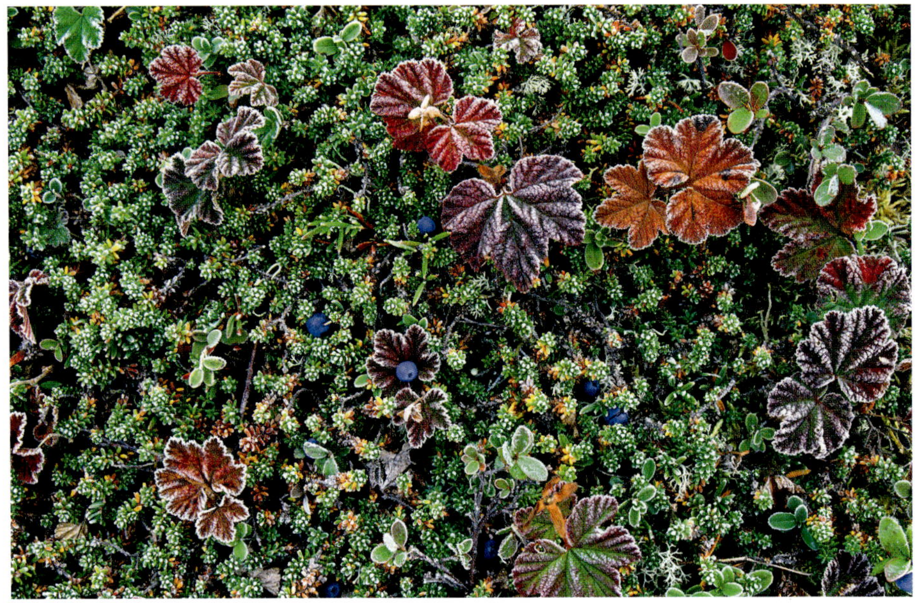

At almost 20,000 square kilometres, Sarek National Park in Swedish Lapland is one of the last big natural paradises left in Europe. Lynxes, bears, wolverines and elks (right) are still to be found here. Autumn is the most beautiful season in the park, and starts as early as the beginning of September.
Dwarf birch in Rapadalen, one of the most beautiful river valleys in the park, turn yellow-gold (centre) and the first frost descends on the land (left). Because of its great significance, the entire area covered by the national park has been part of the Laponian Area UNESCO World Heritage site since 1996. Sarek, which features more than a hundred glaciers, is an important part of the Scandinavian Arctic.

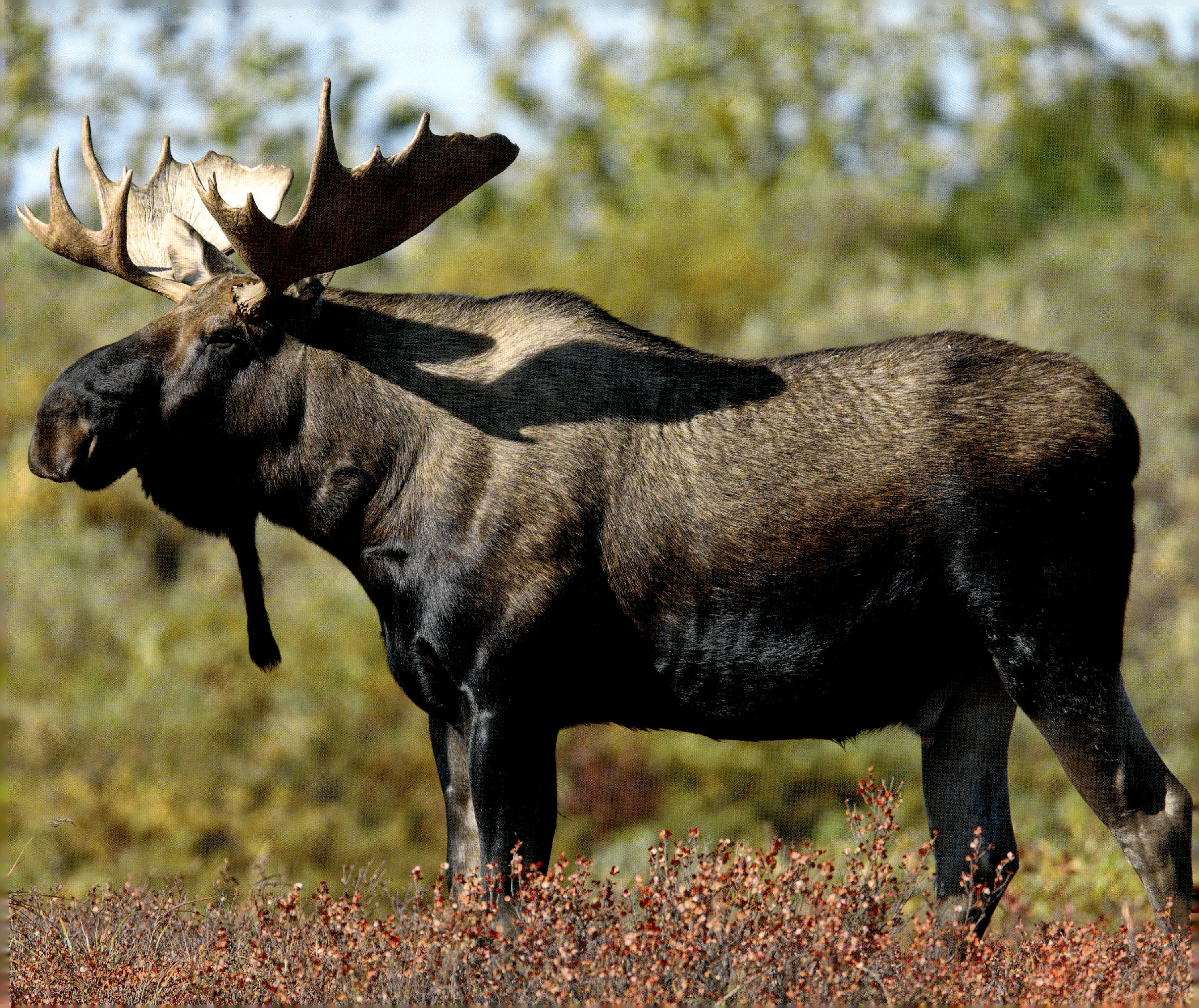

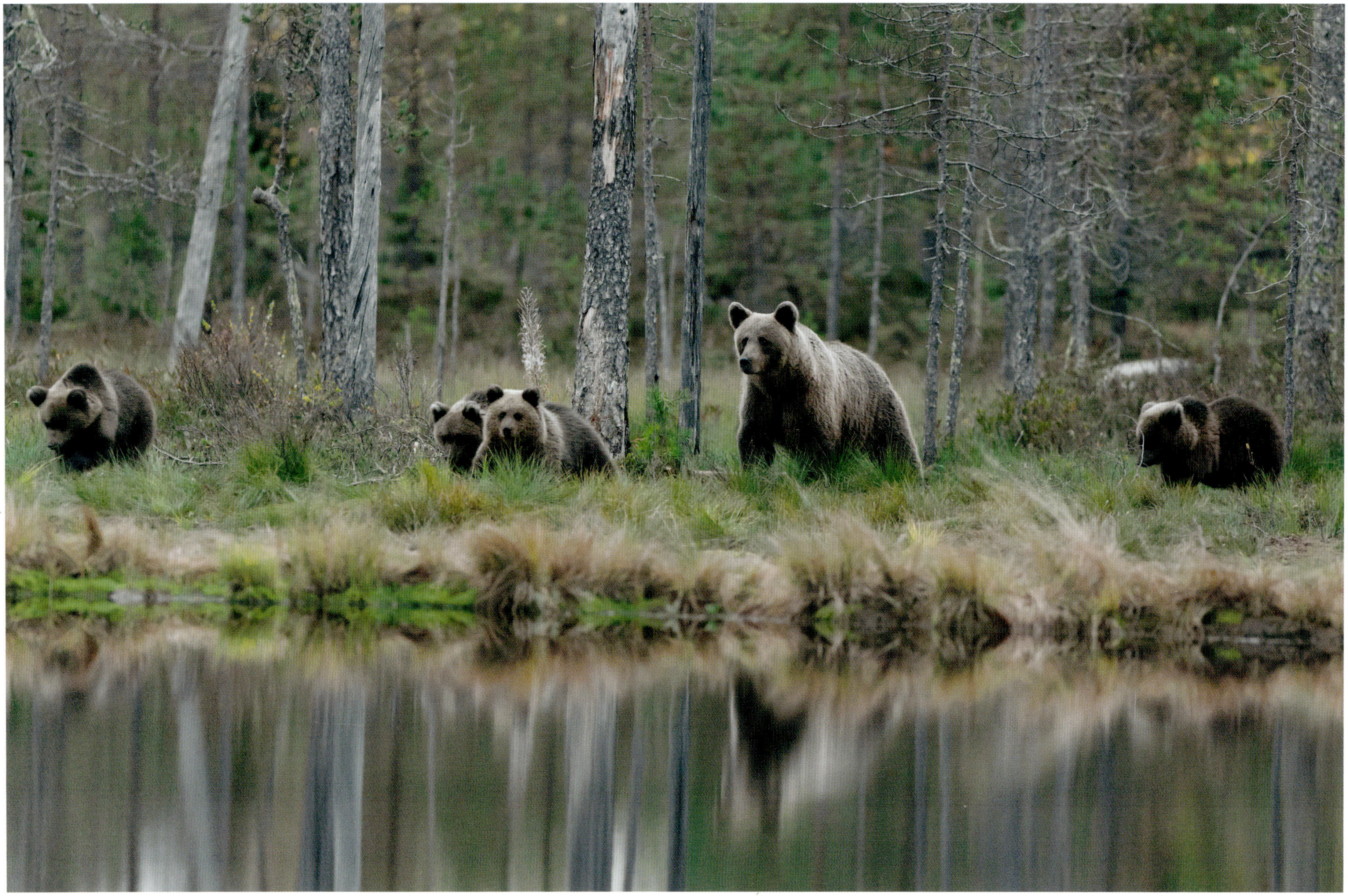

The European brown bear is a member of the same species as the American grizzly bear, although it is considerably smaller. Even in Lapland, brown bears have become very rare. Only a few thousand bears remain in Sweden, a few hundred in Finland and several dozen in Norway. Coming across a bear mother with as many as four healthy cubs – instead of the usual two or three – is therefore a doubly rare occurrence.

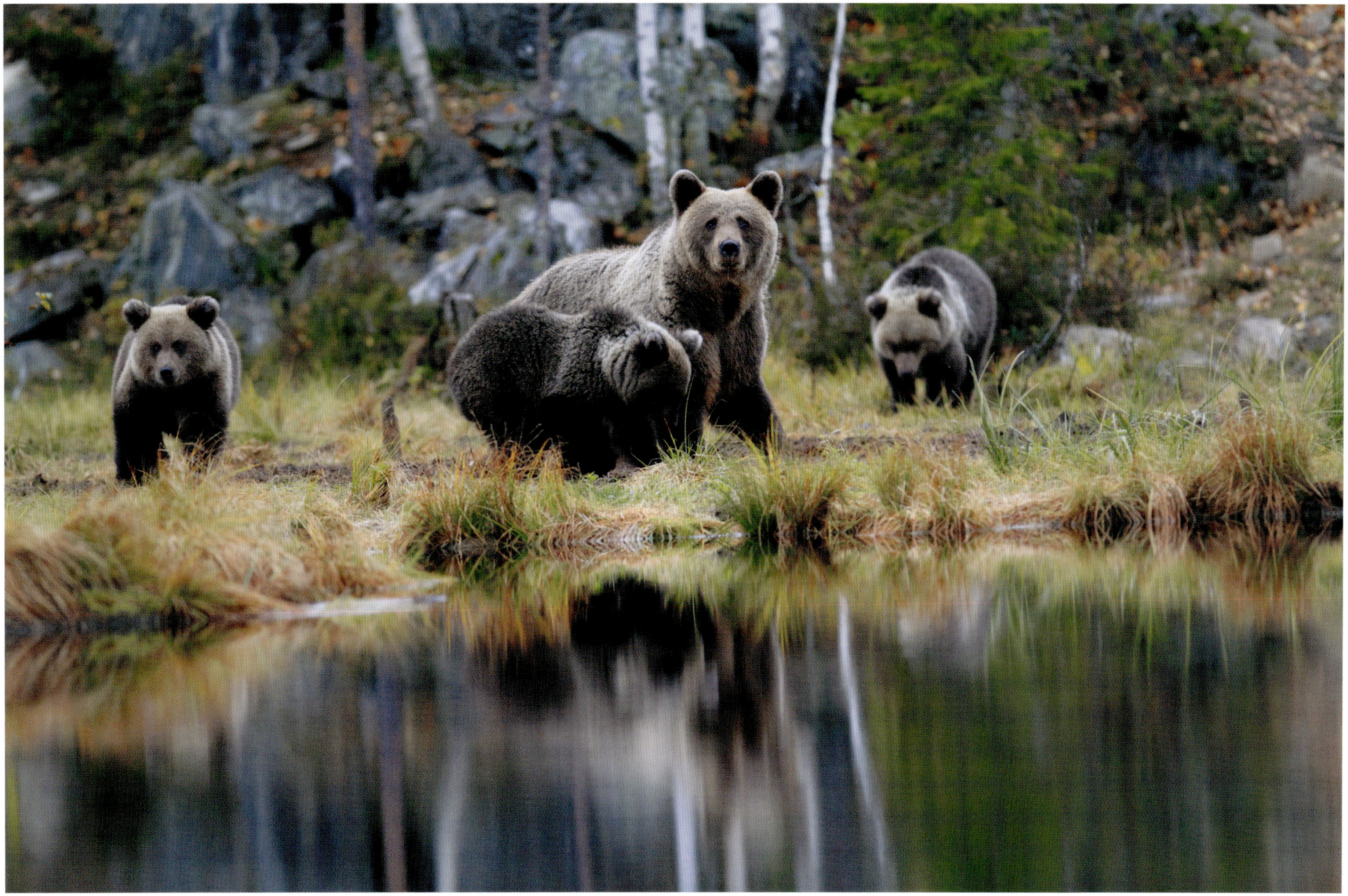

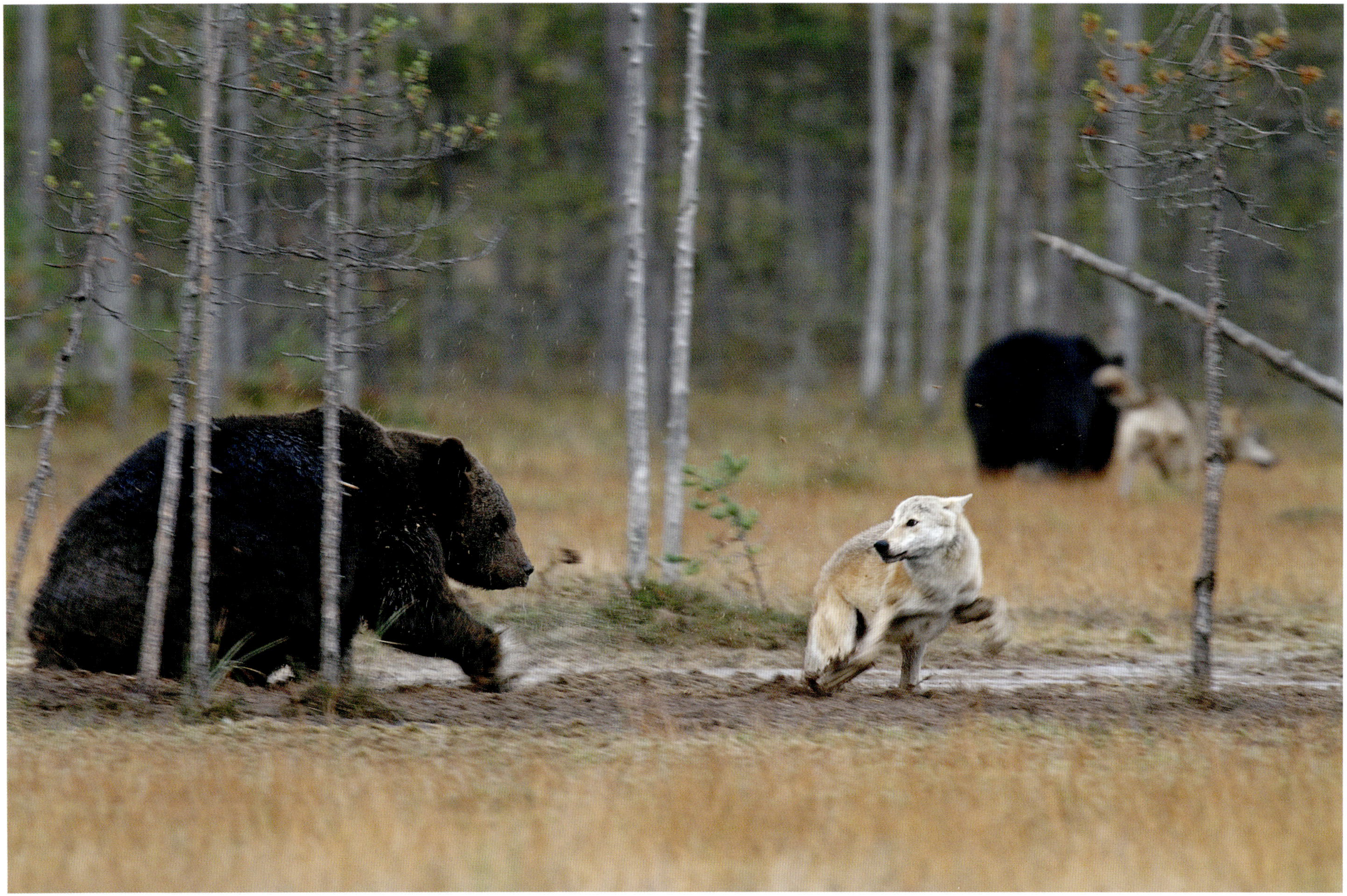

Wolves and bears occasionally have their sights set on the same prey. The wolf attempts to drive away the bear by "annoying" it constantly. The bear either reacts as the wolf hopes it will by wandering off, or uses unmistakably threatening postures to show the wolf which of the two of them is stronger, thus forcing its adversary to withdraw. There are never really any proper fights.

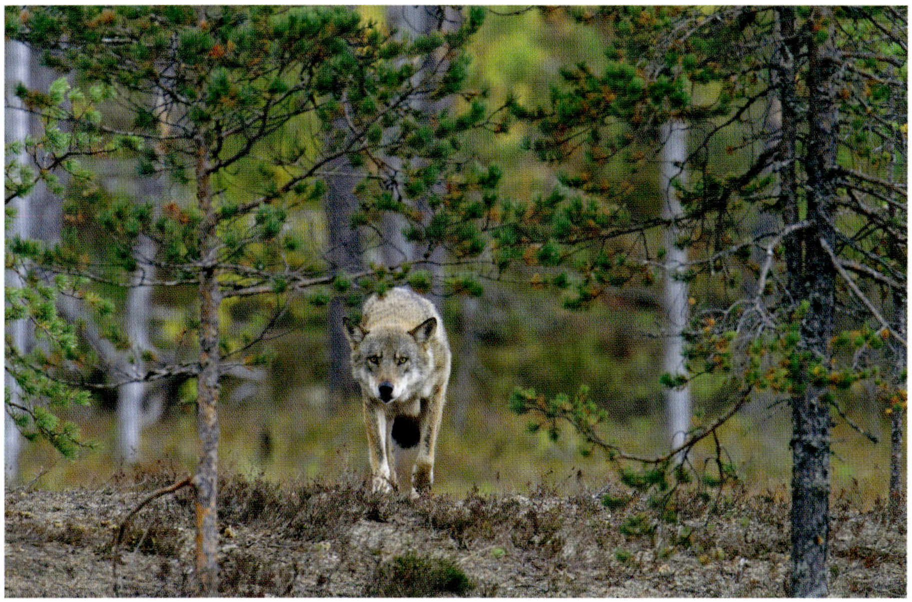

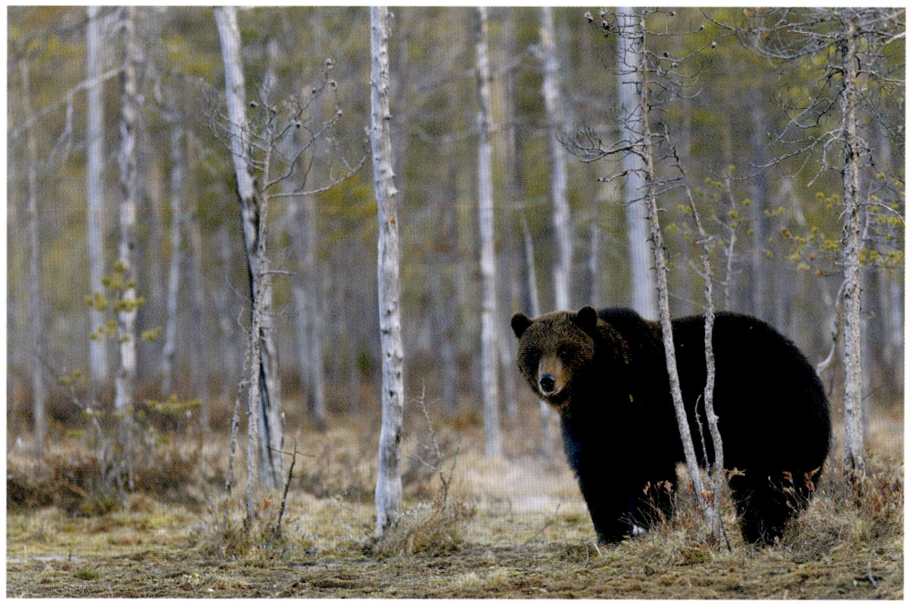

The Sami are the original inhabitants of Lapland and were probably the first people to live in northern Scandinavia after the Ice Age. At first, they lived as nomadic hunters and tended to use reindeer as beasts of burden and for transport. Over time, they became reindeer breeders, and followed the animals on their natural migrations: into the forests covered in a thick layer of snow during the winter and high up into the fjäll or the coastal regions of the Norwegian Sea during the summer. The Sami retained their own culture, even during the most difficult times of forced labour, slavery and famine. Reindeer have a prominent role in their lives to this day. In the past, reindeer supplied humans in the far cold north with virtually everything: food, material for clothing and shoes, and for all sorts of everyday utensils. Nowadays, only a small number of Sami make a living by breeding reindeer. Their special relationship with the animals remains palpable, however.

The Sami are also thought to be the inventors of a very special form of transport that is used throughout the world nowadays: skis. Kautokeino, Finnmark, northern Norway.

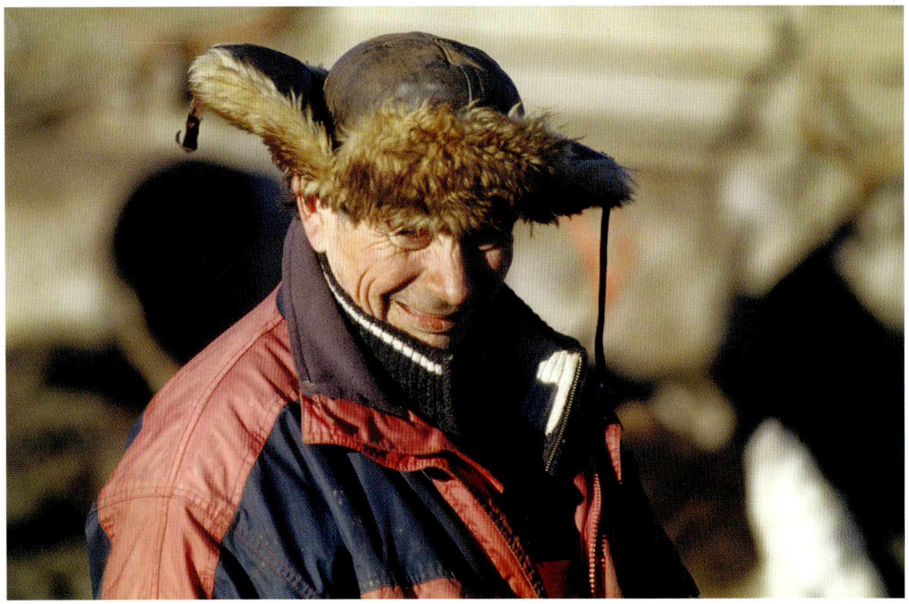

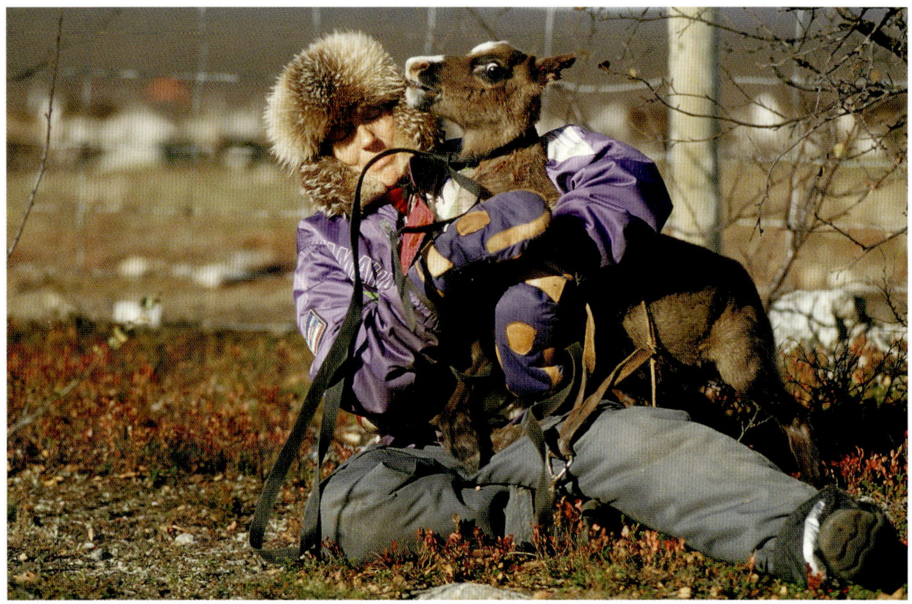

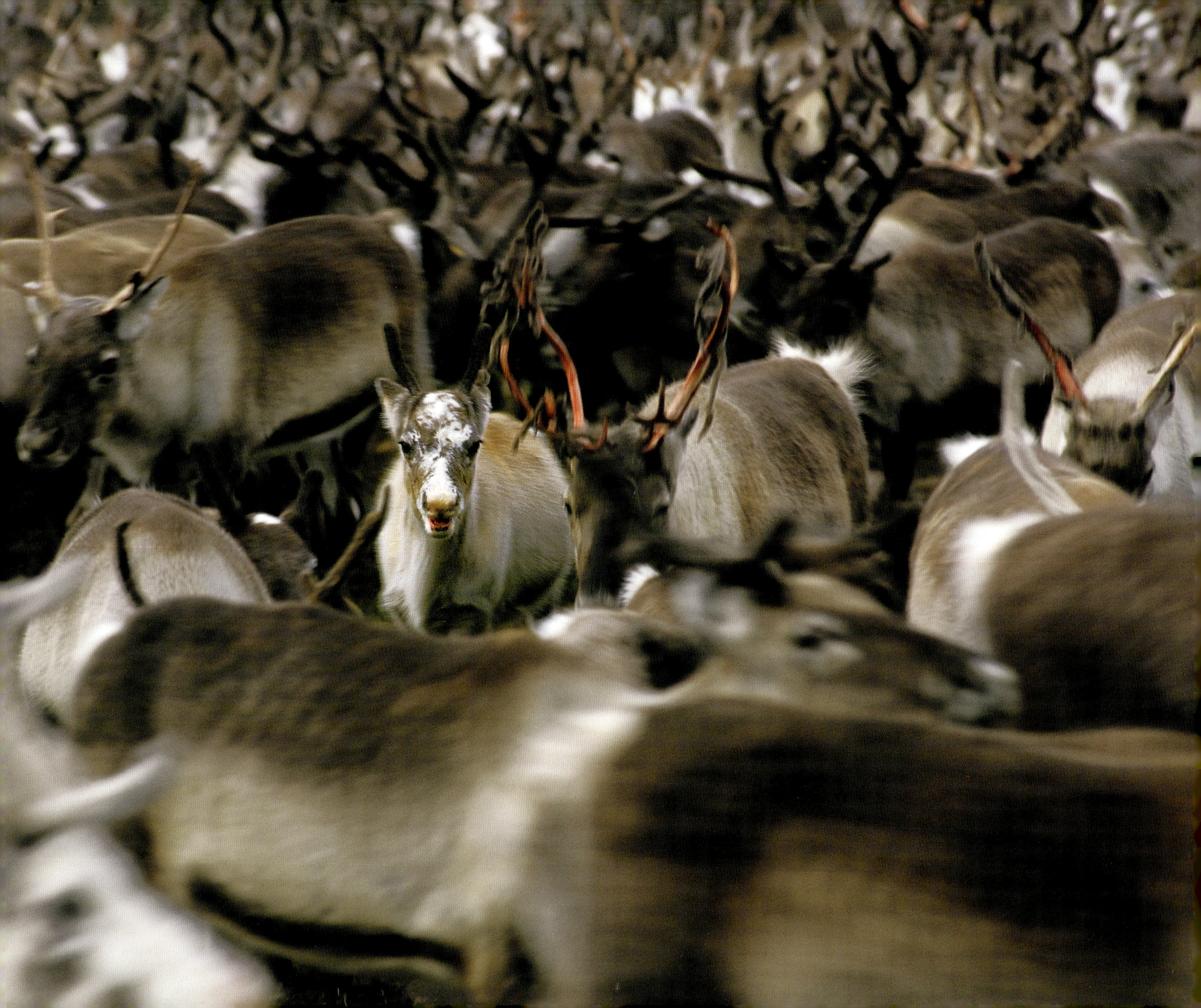

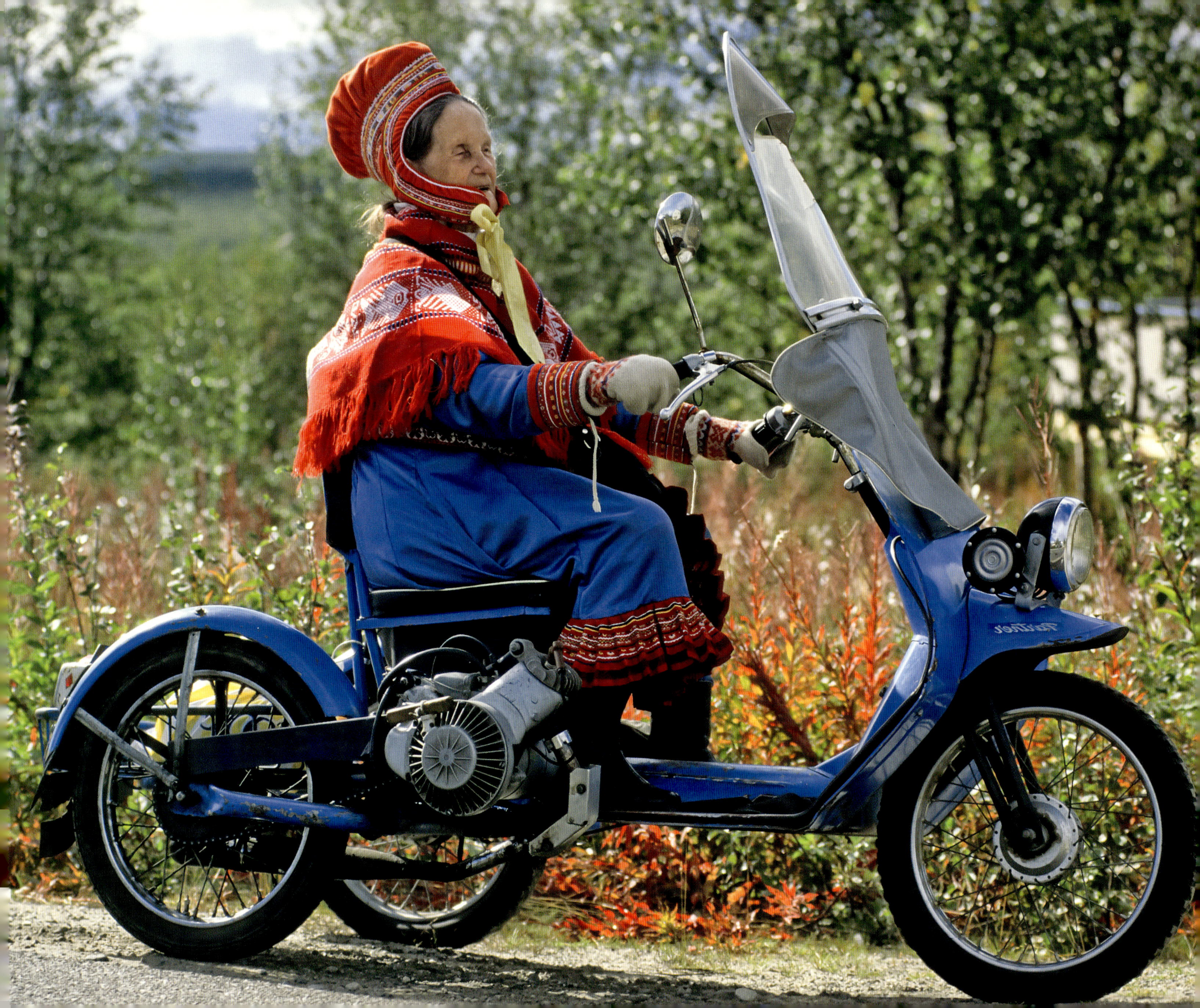

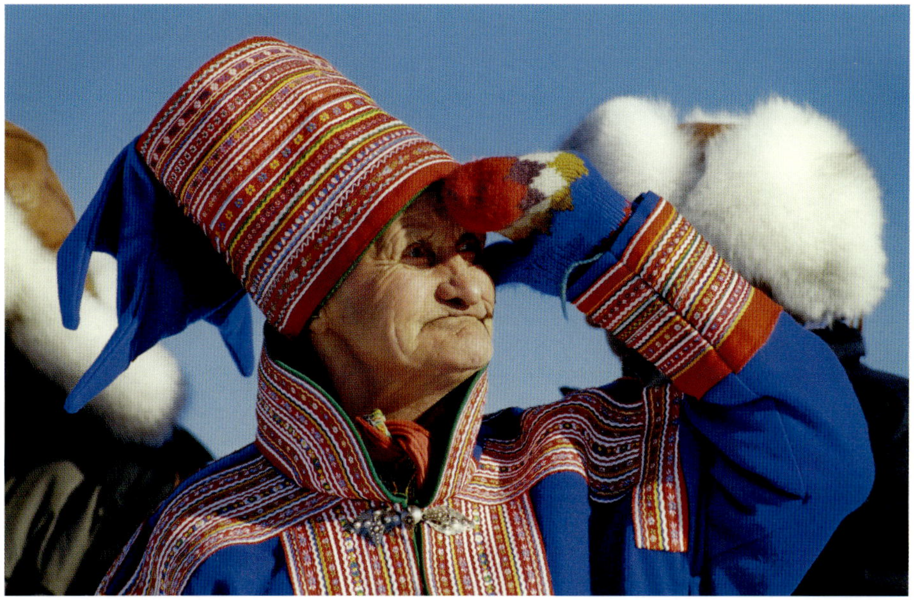

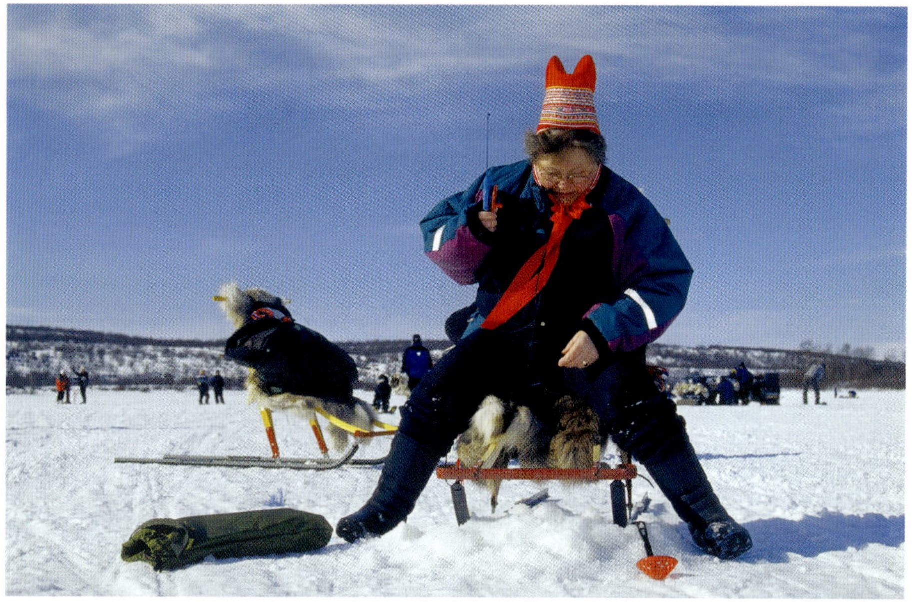

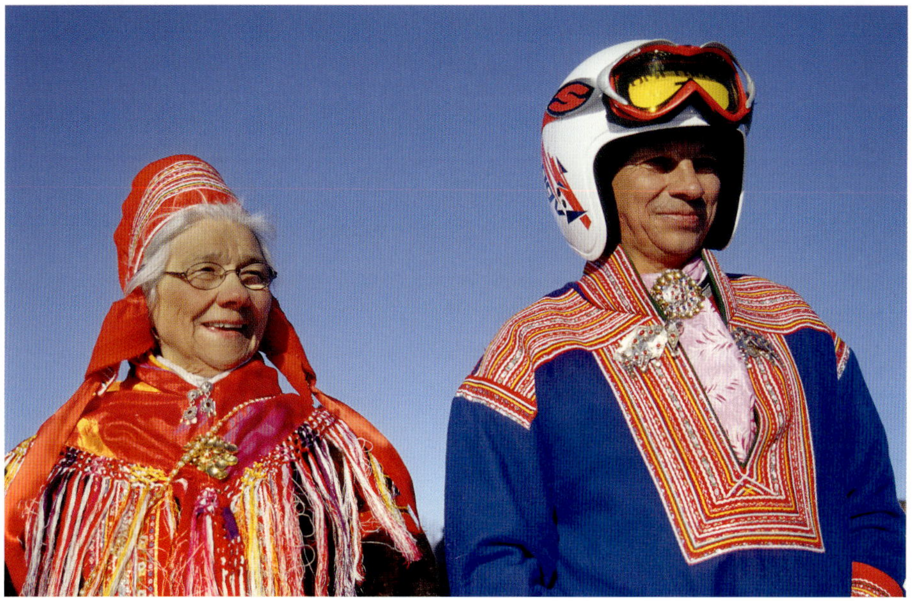

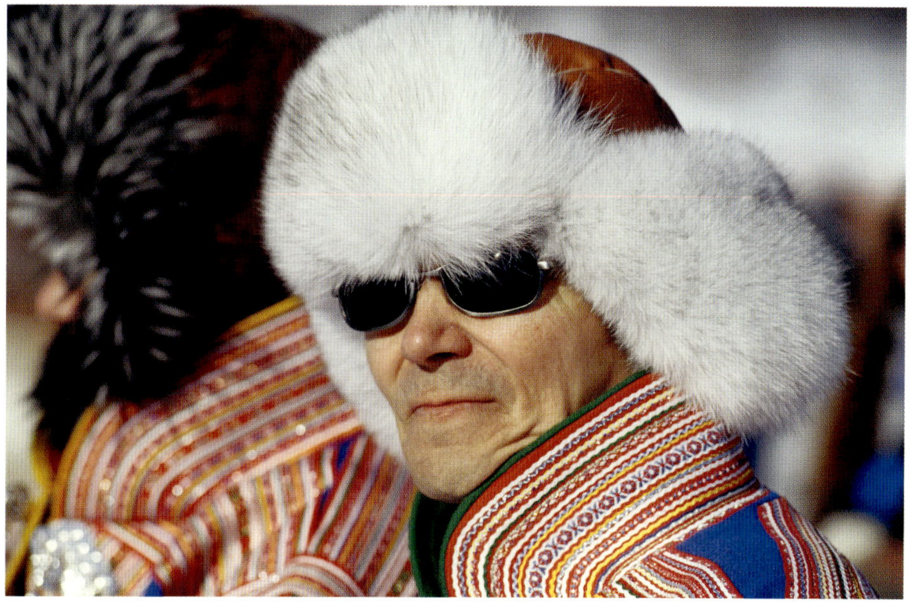

Easter (such as here, in Kautokeino, Finnmark, northern Norway) is one of the highlights of the year in the Sami culture. It is only on special occasions such as these that the Sami can now be admired in their colourful, splendid traditional clothes. Not only do many families get together during this period, but the majority of weddings and other festivities and ceremonial competitions take place around Easter. Examples include the reindeer races and Joiken, a special Sami form of singing.

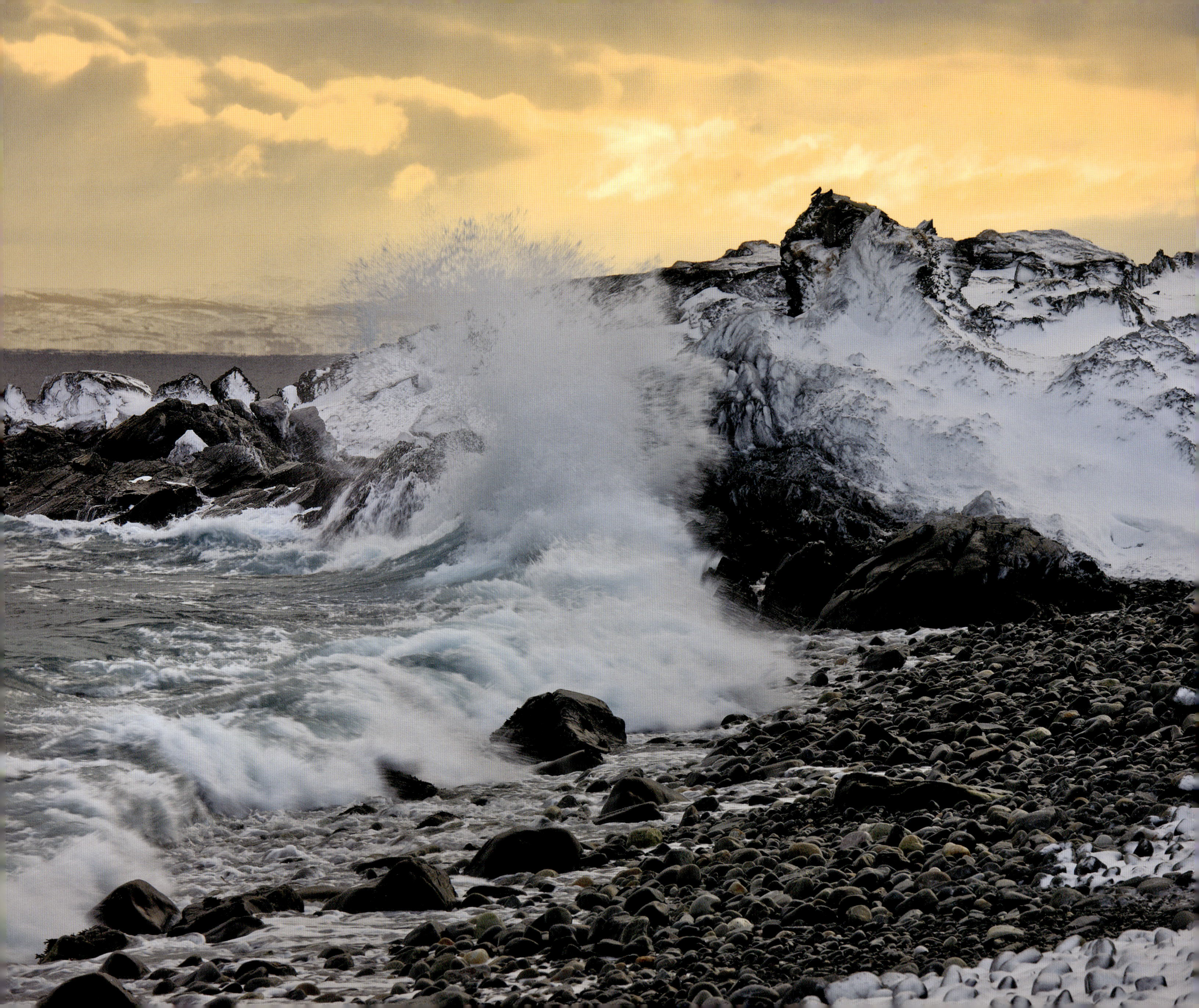

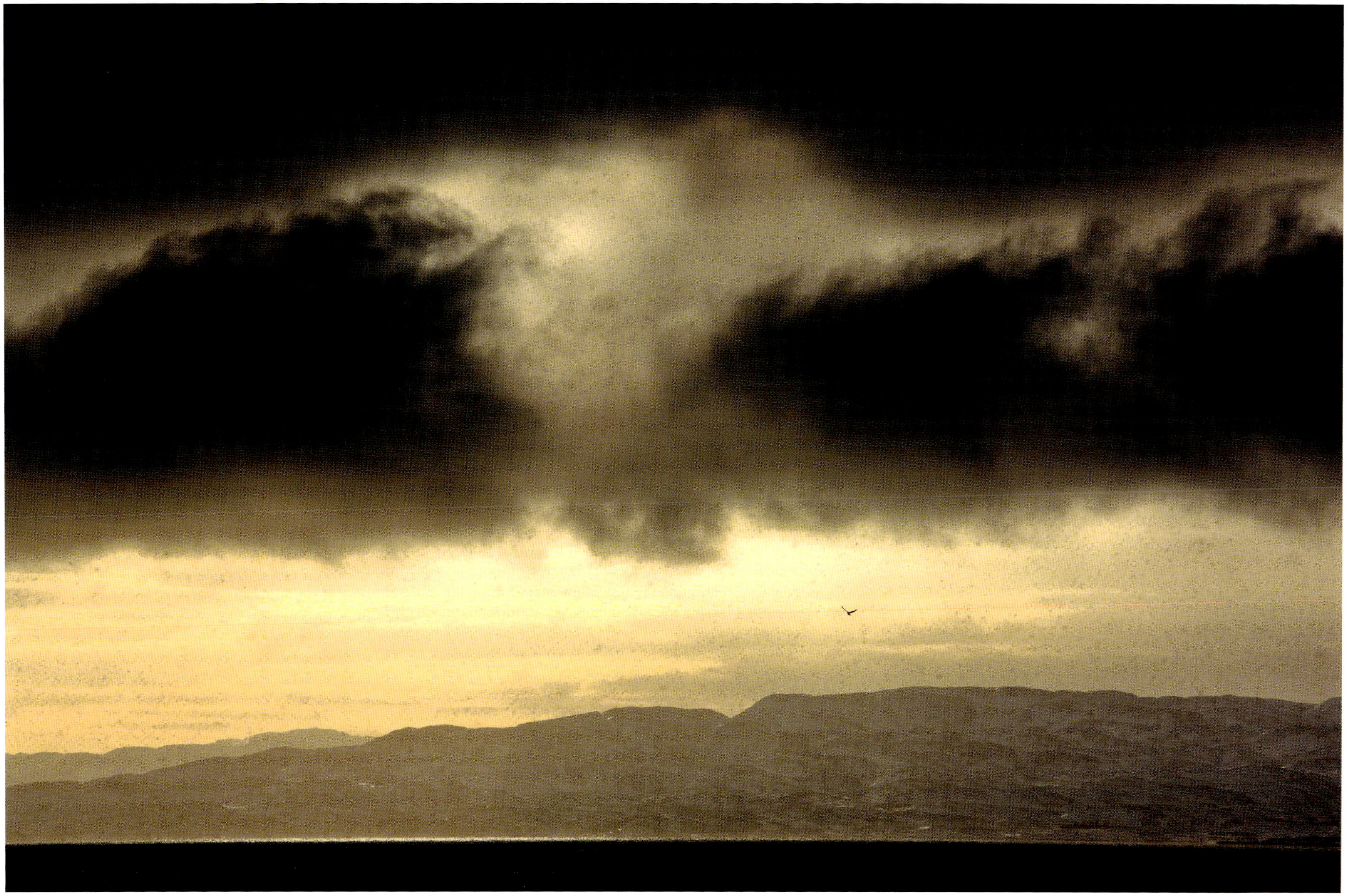

Heavy storms often pass over the coastal regions of Finnmark during the winter (left: over Porsangerfjord; right: over the Varanger peninsula). The streets then often remain impassable for days, until the snowplough has cleared the way again.

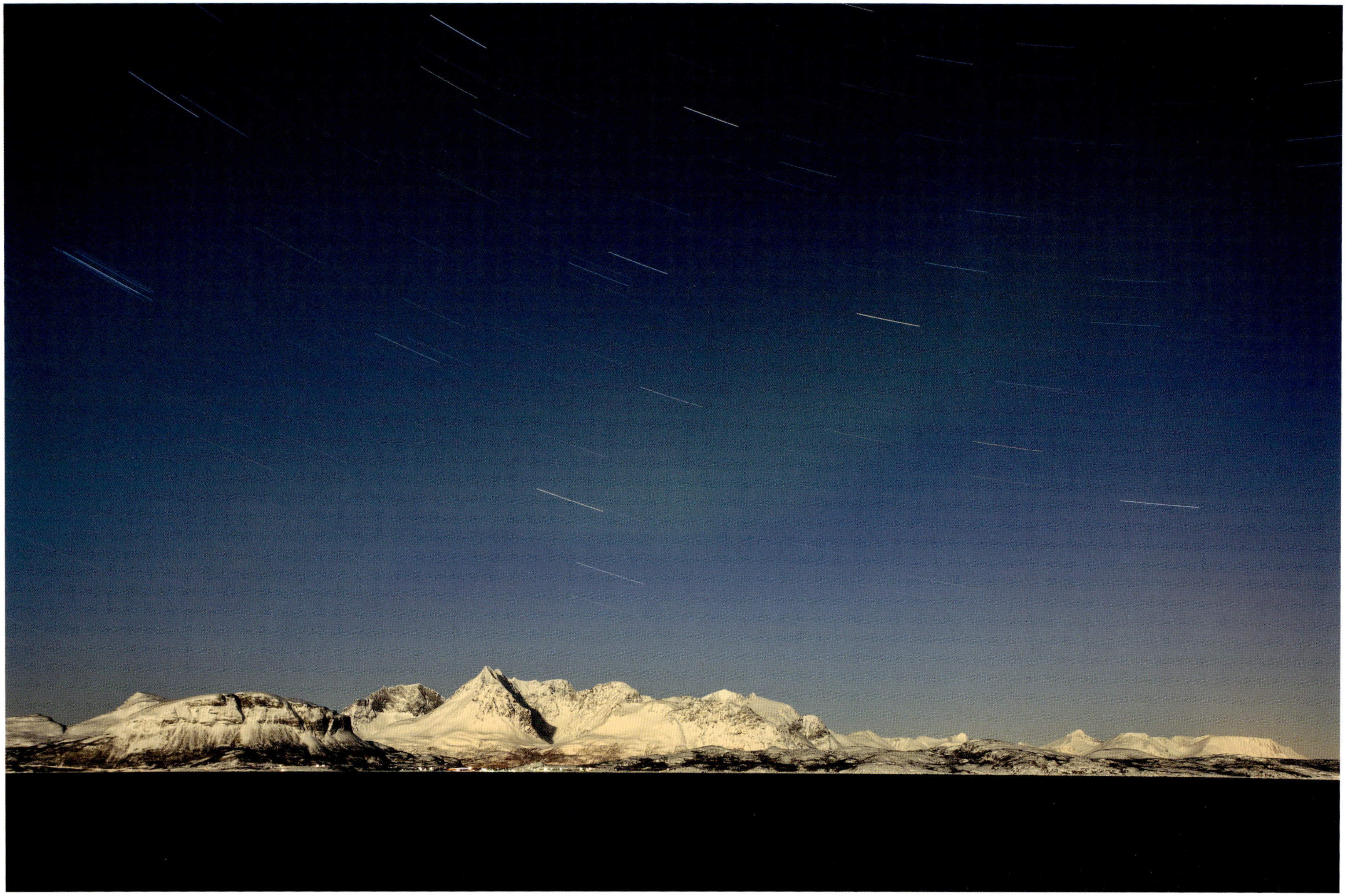

The moonlit Lyngen Alps in Troms county, northern Norway.

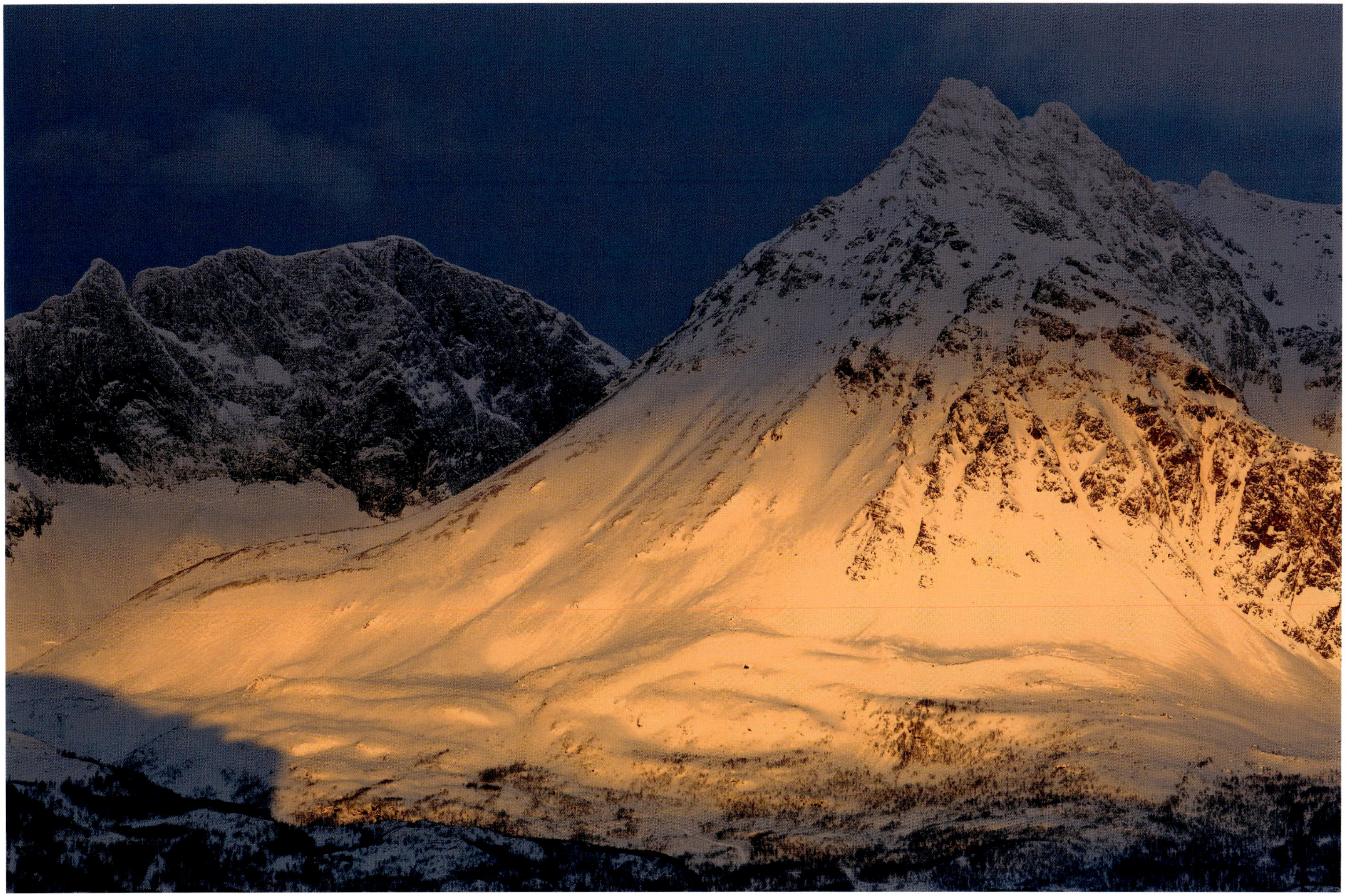

The light looks similar, although this is actually sunlight during a break in the bad weather. Lyngen Alps, Troms county, northern Norway.

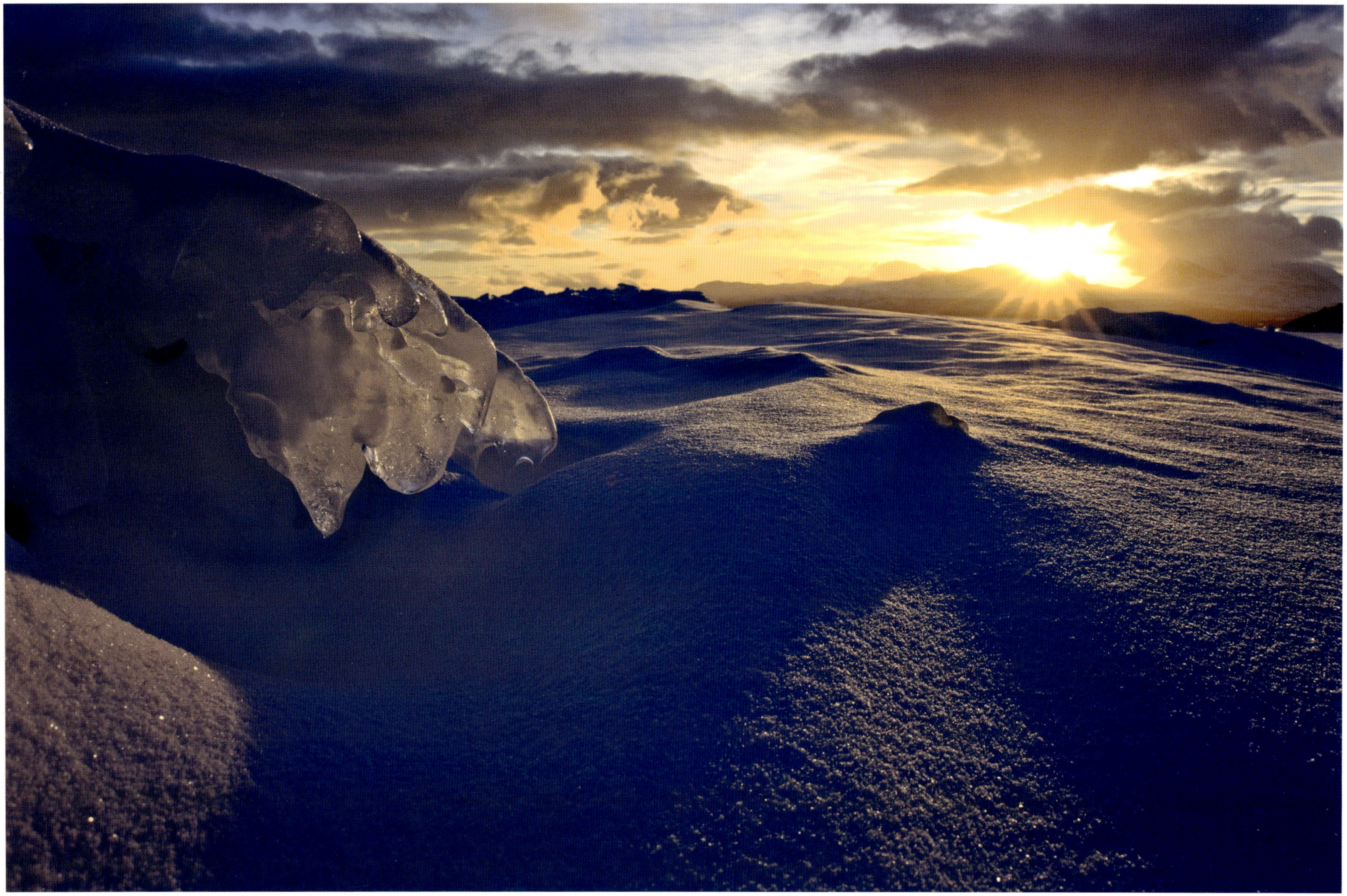

Torneträsk Lake is in Swedish Lapland, not far from the Norwegian border. With a surface area of 330 square kilometres, it is the seventh-largest lake in Sweden. From mid December until well into June, it is covered with metre-thick ice and snow.

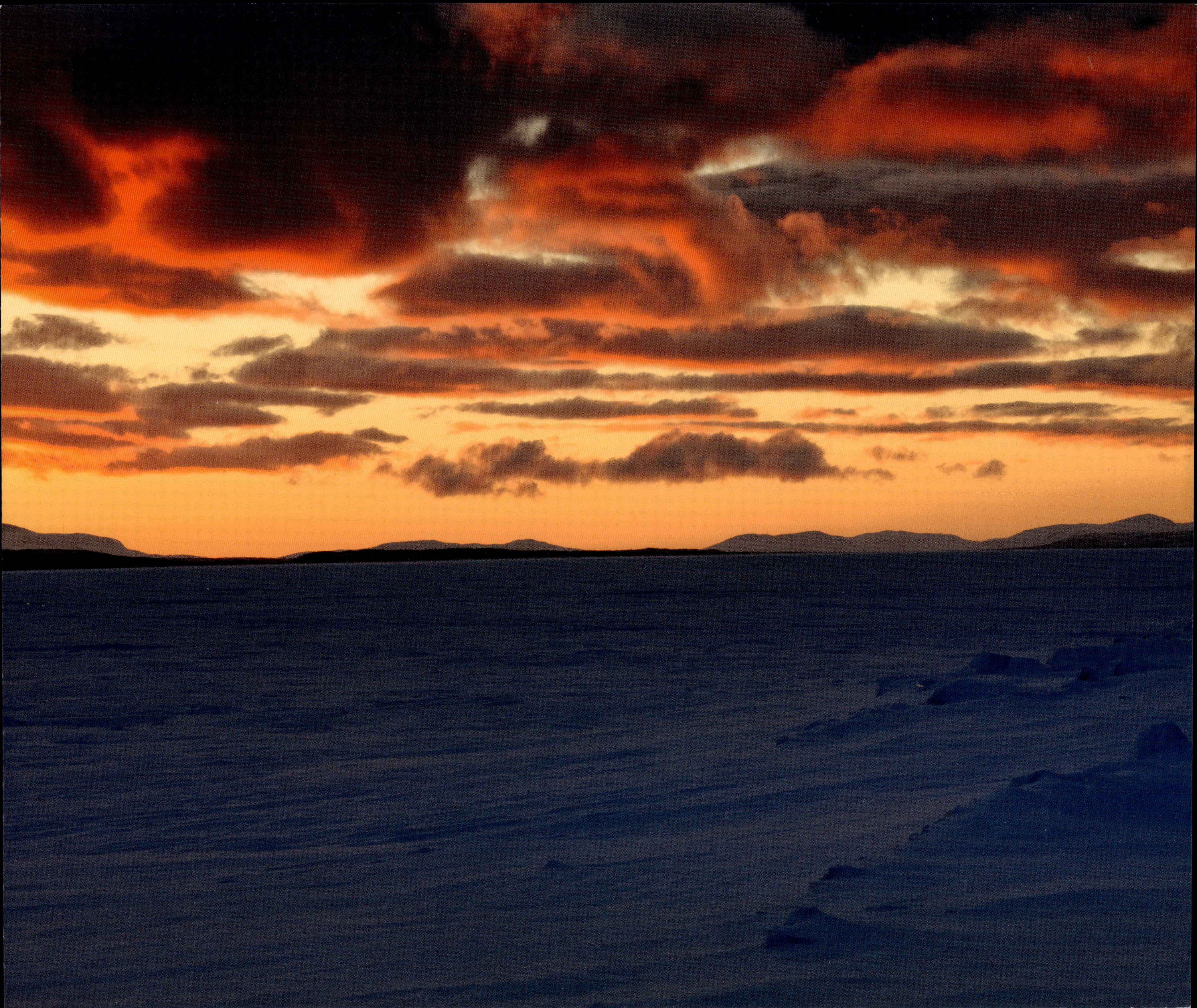

RUSSIA'S ARCTIC – TREASURE CHEST OF MANY ARCTIC PEOPLES

200 reindeer, 10 dogs and 26 wooden sleds carrying all of their belongings: this is how a "typical" Nenets family travels through the Arctic tundra in the far north of Russia year after year. At present, there are approximately 46,000 Nenets, and roughly 70 percent live as reindeer-breeding nomads. Their settlement area ranges from the autonomous region belonging to Arkhangelsk, in the far east of Europe, to the northwestern part of Siberia that is already part of Asia.

We think of reindeer and sleds mainly in connection with Santa Claus, but in Russia, these animals (which are to be found primarily in this region, where there are thousands of them) are also used to transport goods. Four specially trained reindeer pull one approximately three-metre-long sled carrying up to 150 kilogrammes, steered by one person. What is astounding is that the reindeer pull sleds all year round, whether the ground is covered in snow or not. With their incredible strength and their broad hoofs, the reindeer are well suited to navigate the low, herbaceous vegetation of the tundra.

The Nenets travel through the far north in family or small groups. In the spring, they usually travel to the coast of the Arctic Ocean, and back inland in the autumn. During these treks, they put up their big tent, the chum, every day. In its appearance, construction and assembly, it strongly resembles the large tipis of North American Indians, and is the Nenets' only accommodation. Six to twelve, and even as many as 20 people can cook, eat, sleep and spend time there, protected from the elements.

The enormous chum are erected toget-her, and at rapid speed. Every movement is coordinated, and the stove inside the

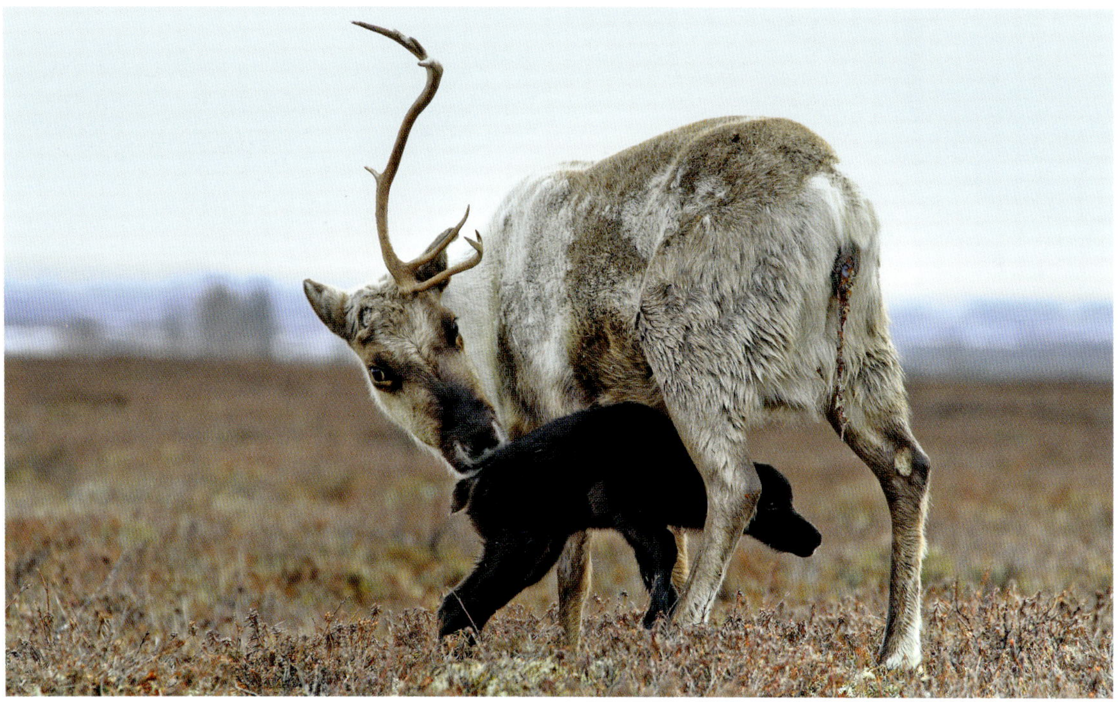

A reindeer mother with the calf she has just given birth to. Tundra near Naryan-Mar, northern Russia.

tent is lit, spreading its pleasant, cosy warmth, within less than an hour, no matter how bad the weather.

During the time of the Soviet Union, an attempt was made to settle the Nenets, as well as many other peoples (such as the Evenks), but without success; the nomadic lifestyle is part of their culture and of their way of life.

A number of very different peoples have lived in the far north of Russia for many thousands of years. At present, almost 20 different peoples live in Russia's Arctic.

The Dolgans, like the Nenets, breed reindeer. The Chukchi people inhabit the far northeast of the country, supporting themselves through fishing as well as seal and whale hunting.

The biggest country in the world can lay claim to by far the largest landmass north of the polar circle and almost half of the Arctic (together with its part of the Arctic Ocean), including the North Pole. Of the almost four million people worldwide who live north of the polar circle, the majority live in the Russian Arctic, with 300,000 of them in the world's largest Arctic town: Murmansk.

The Russian Arctic is the region from which the settlement of the Arctic north emanated. This is one of the most astonishing feats in the history of humankind, and not only because of the extreme weather conditions. The history of its inhabitants has been eventful, including – or particularly during – the time from when this area has belonged to Russia. They were attacked and killed; they were robbed of their living environment or they were forced into a way of life that did not correspond to their tradition or culture.

What they now face again threatens their existence: climate change will lead to a large proportion of their settlement areas becoming uninhabitable. Conserving the Arctic also means protecting the living space and way of life of its inhabitants.

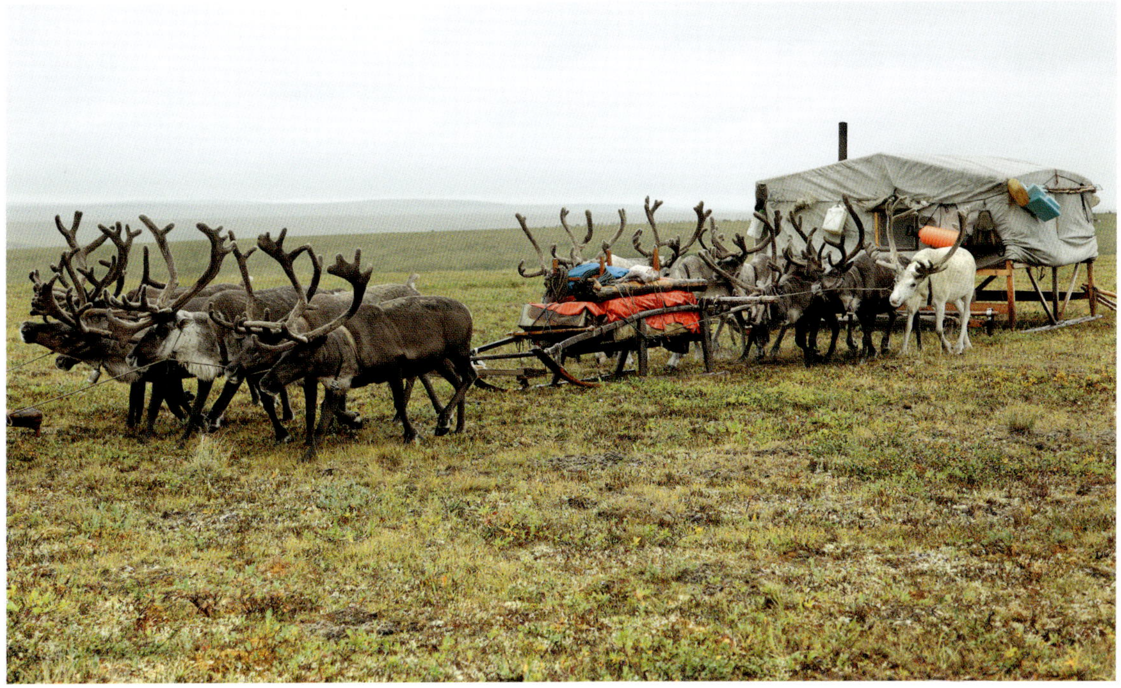

Sleds are hitched up to the reindeer, who will pull the balok (mobile homes fixed to sleds) across the tundra. Taimyr Peninsula, northern Siberia, Russia.

The Nenets are one of several indigenous peoples of Russia who live as reindeer-herding nomads in the tundra of the far north. In order to be able to cover great distances at high speed, they hitch their sleds to reindeer, who act as transport animals (bottom left). Considerable loads can be transported in this way.
Right: It is impressive how quickly the Nenets assemble their tent (known as chum), so that the entire family can take shelter from the cold in no time.

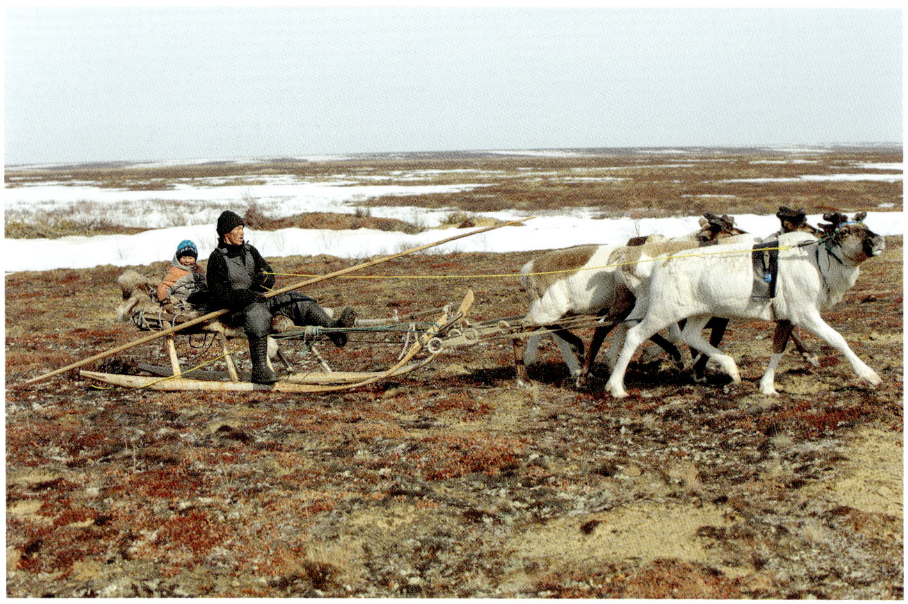

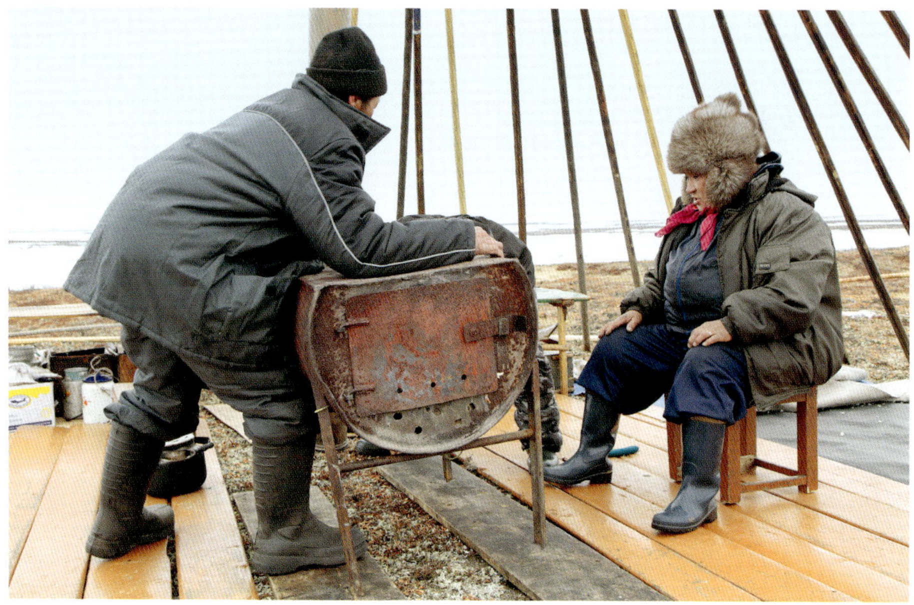

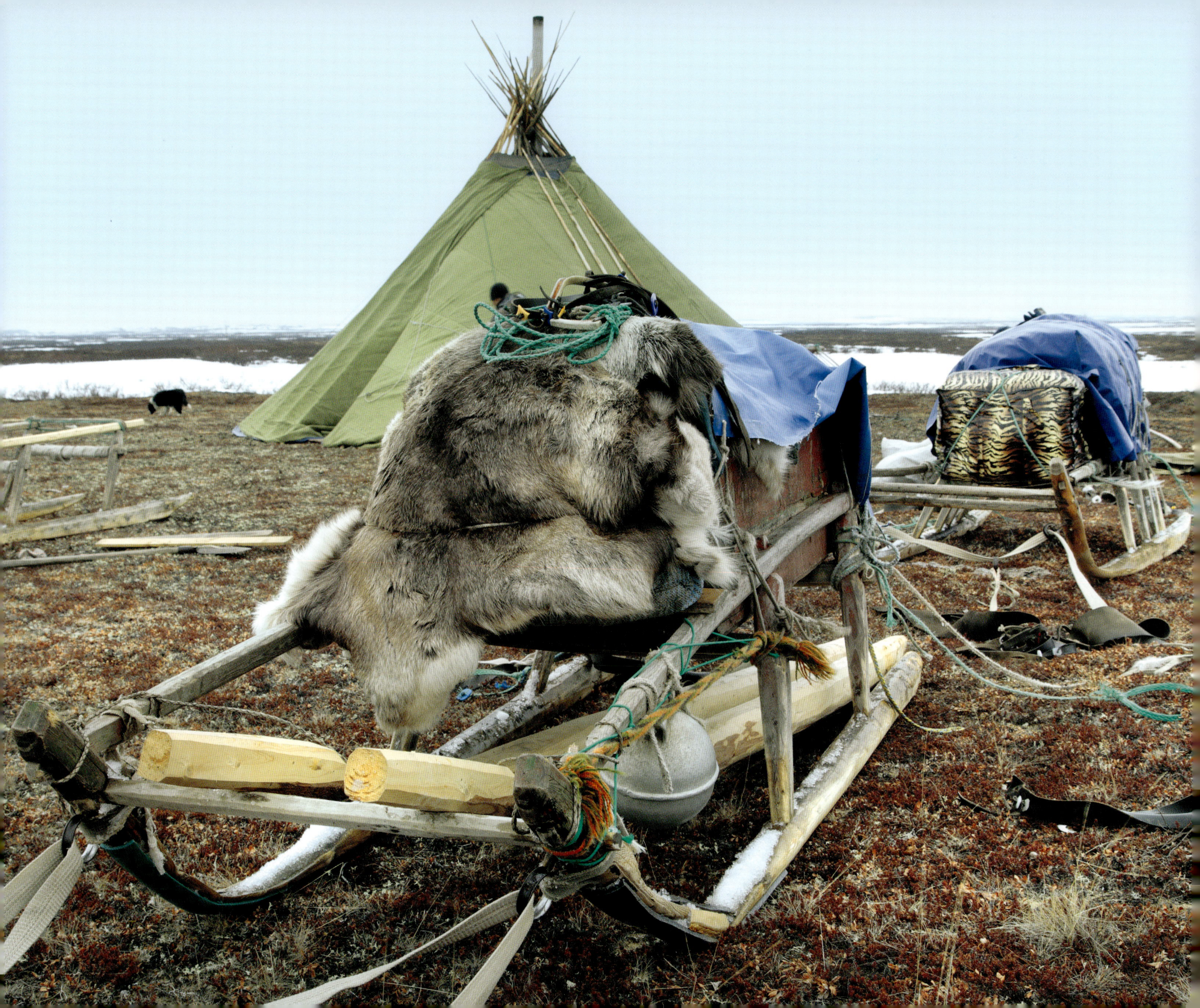

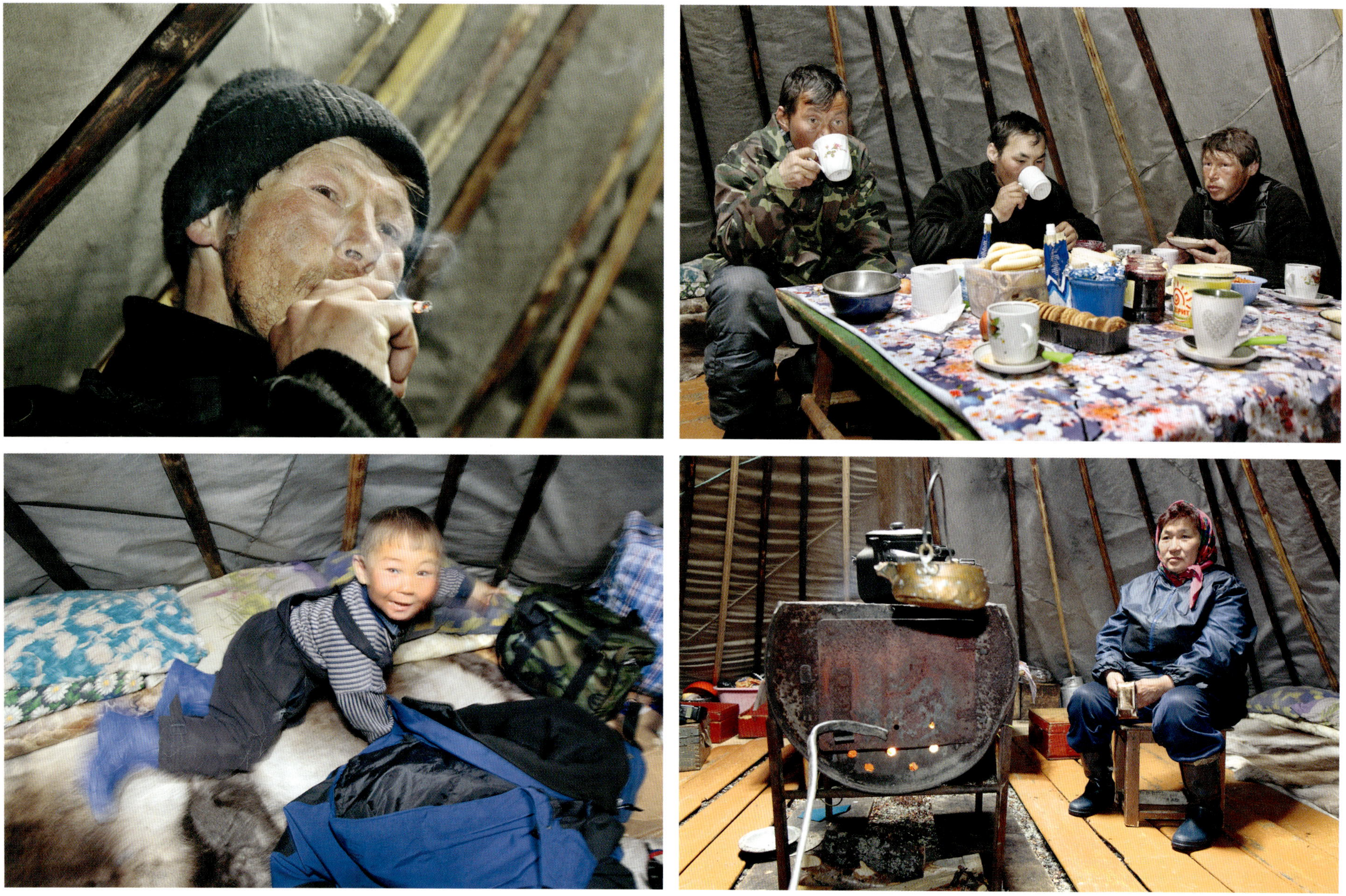

After a long, tiring day in the tundra, the entire family gets together inside the warm tent. Valentina (bottom right) has prepared tea and reindeer meat. Young Egor (bottom left and far right) plays boisterously on the reindeer skins spread out beneath him.

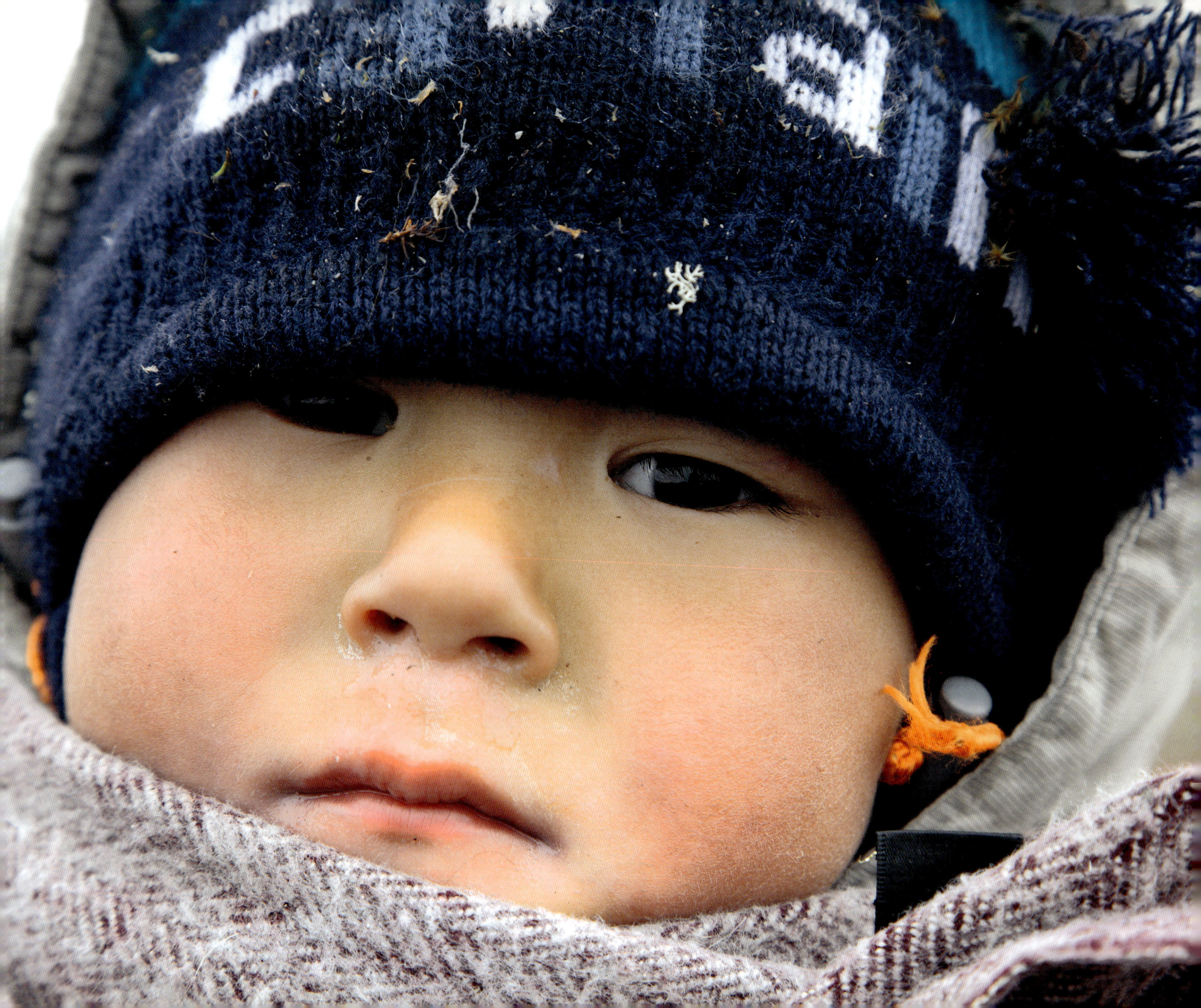

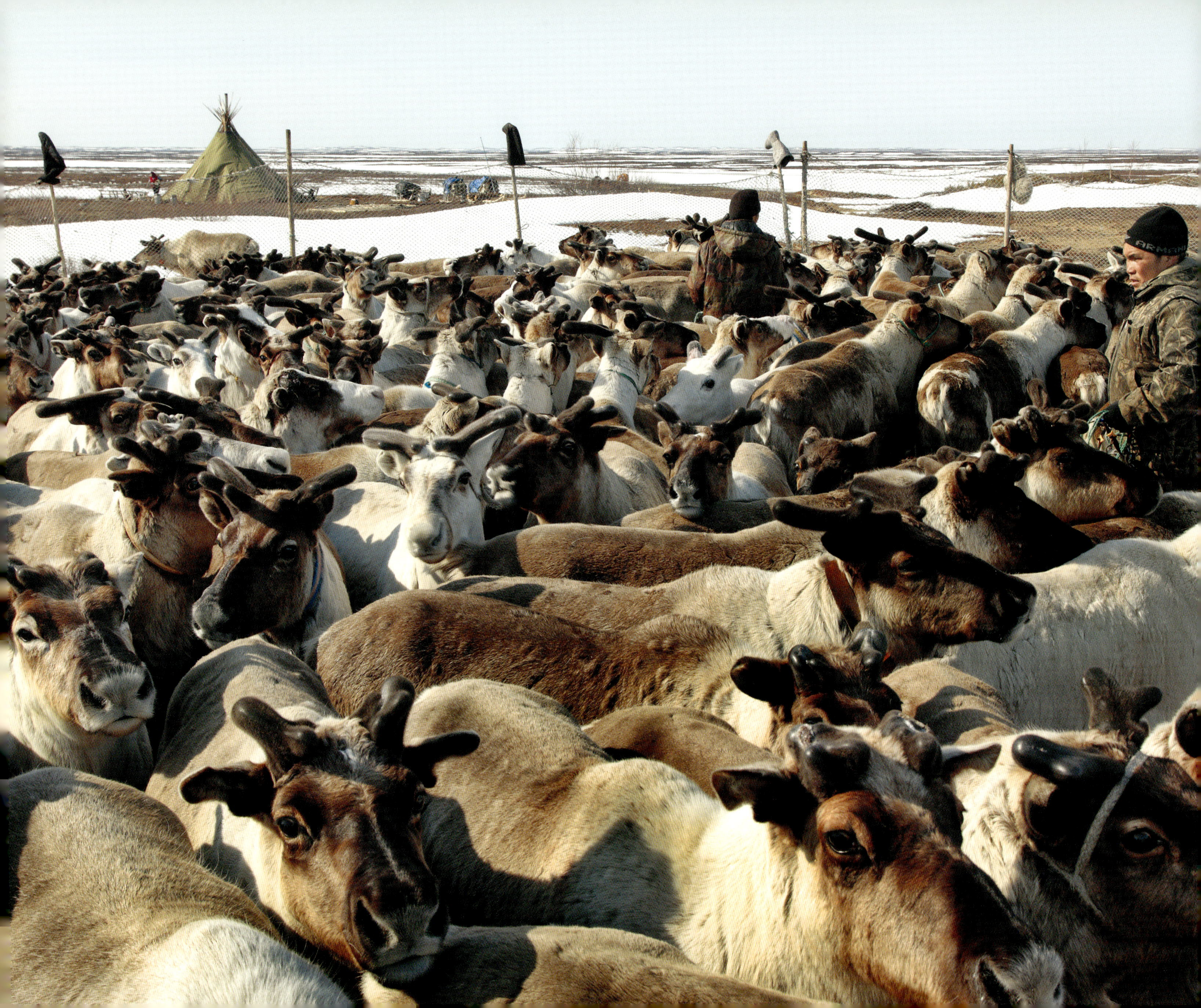

“The beckoned to us to get on. Sadly, Vasili could not accompany us. Five sleds with four reindeer each were ready and waiting to take us out into the tundra. We travelled roughly five kilometres across the tundra, which by this time was covered with just a thin layer of snow. The animals pulled the sleds across uneven ground and even snow-free areas with impressive ease. It was only when we travelled across the already heavily thawed ice covering the lakes that an uneasy feeling arose, especially when the animals fell knee deep through the broken ice. Bernd and his camera had been at the ready for some time. Then, at last, we discovered them behind a little hill: an enormous herd of reindeer with their newborn calves, who were standing on still-wobbly legs. It was an unforgettable moment in the Russian tundra.”

Thomas Henningsen

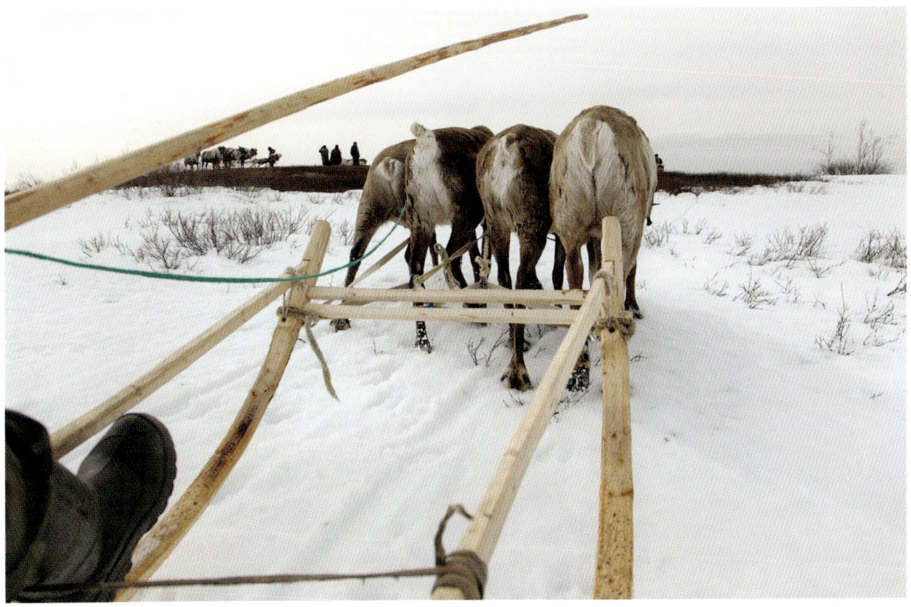

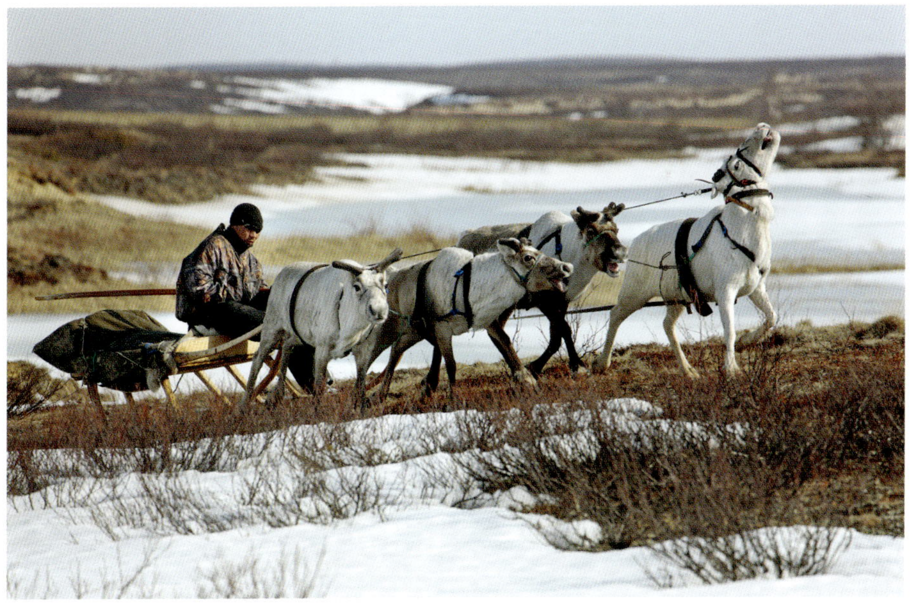

Before the herders make their way to their virtually undomesticated reindeer herds in the tundra, they select animals from among their tamer "domestic reindeer" to hitch their wooden sleds to.

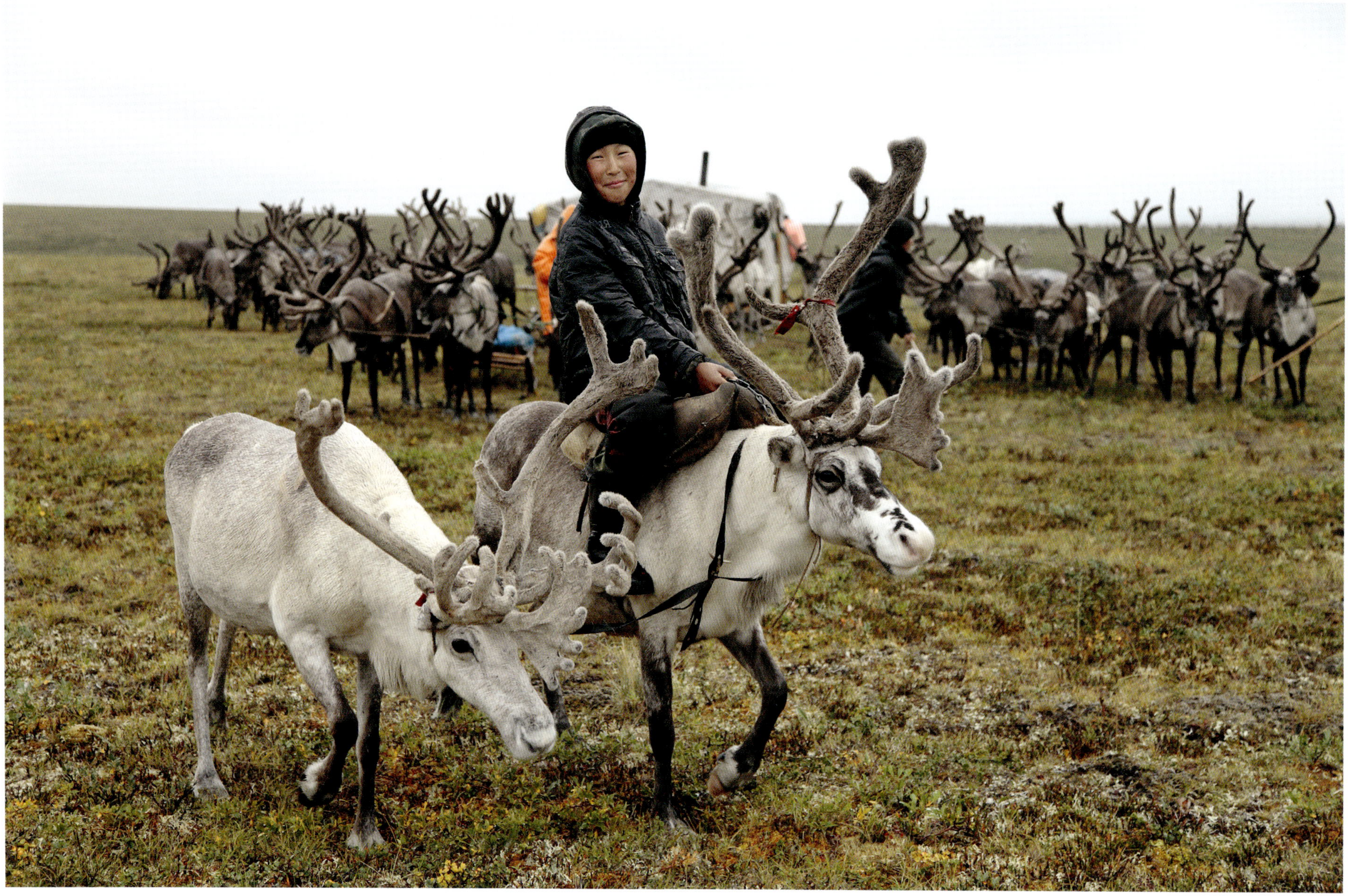

The Dolgans are a small, Turkic-speaking indigenous people of northern Russia. Of the total population of approximately 7,000 Dolgans, 5,000 live on the remote Taimyr Peninsula in the far north of Siberia. Dolgans, like the neighbouring Nenets, are reindeer nomads. Reindeer act as beasts of burden, conveying their homes across the tundra, and are also skilfully ridden by the Dolgans, as Piotr (left) and Vasili (right) show.

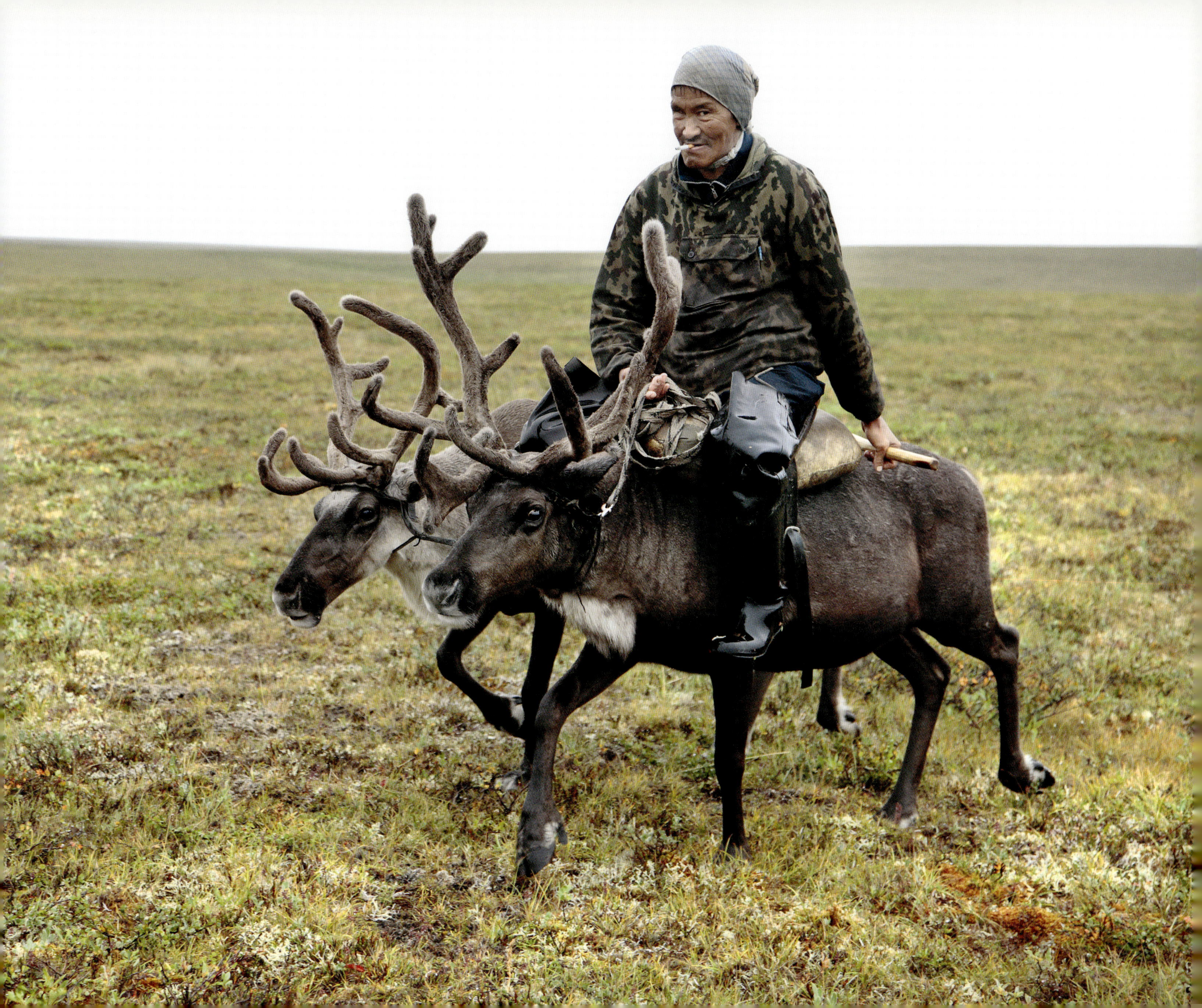

Often, three or four families form a "brigade", and jointly own a large herd of reindeer. A herd can consist of more than a thousand animals. The families stay in each place for two to three days before moving on. More than 40 reindeer are needed in order to transport the little homes. They are skilfully caught using lassos and then the sleds are hitched up.

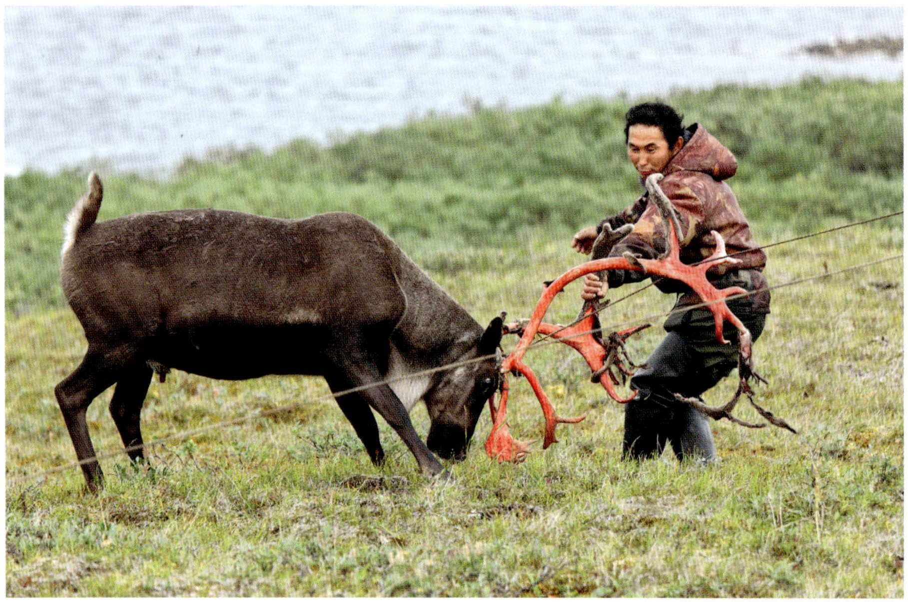

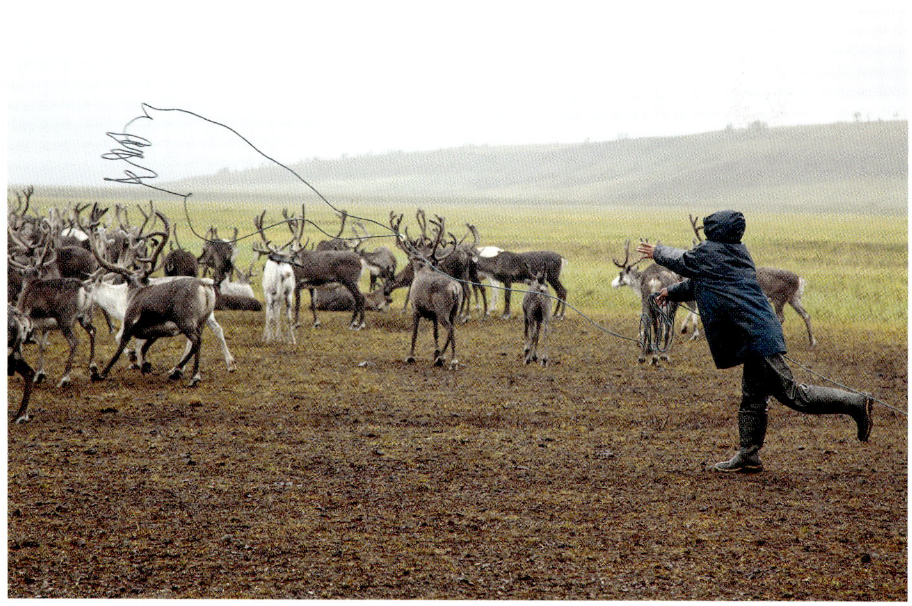

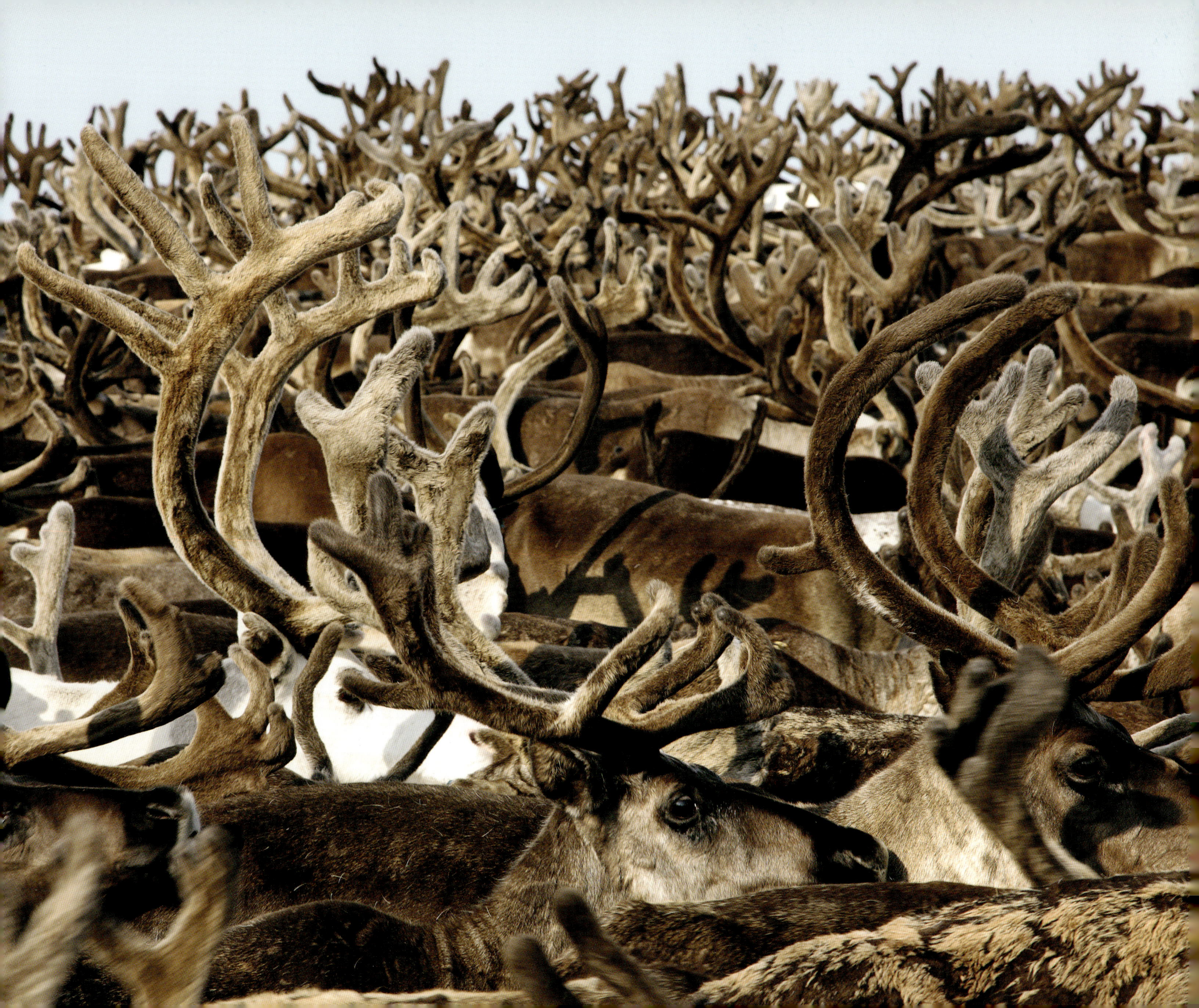

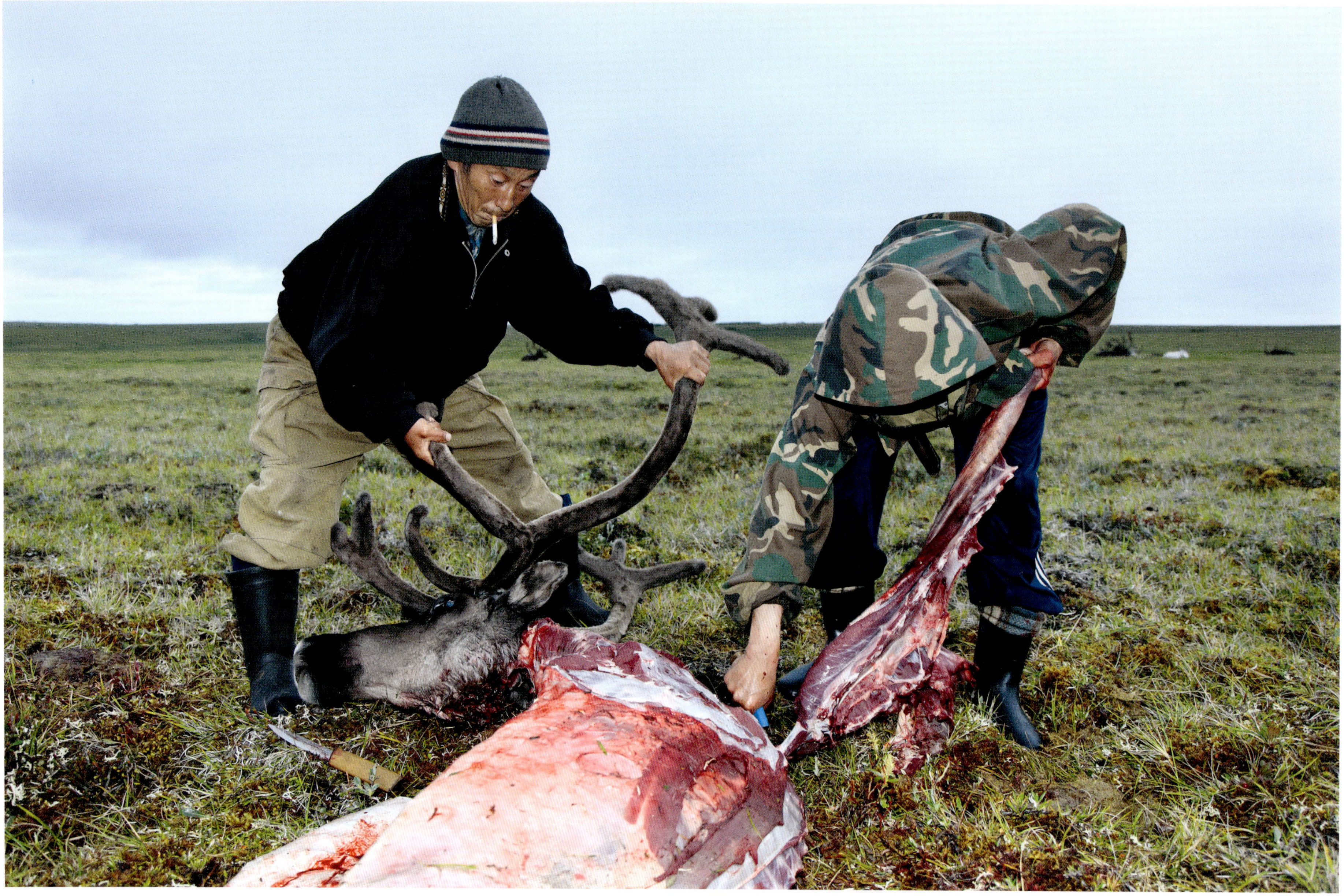

Once in a while, even reindeer are slaughtered. The meat is dried to preserve it. Only the liver is often eaten raw as it is a good source of vitamin A. The blood is turned into sausage, while the fur and skin are used to make clothing. No part of the animal is wasted.

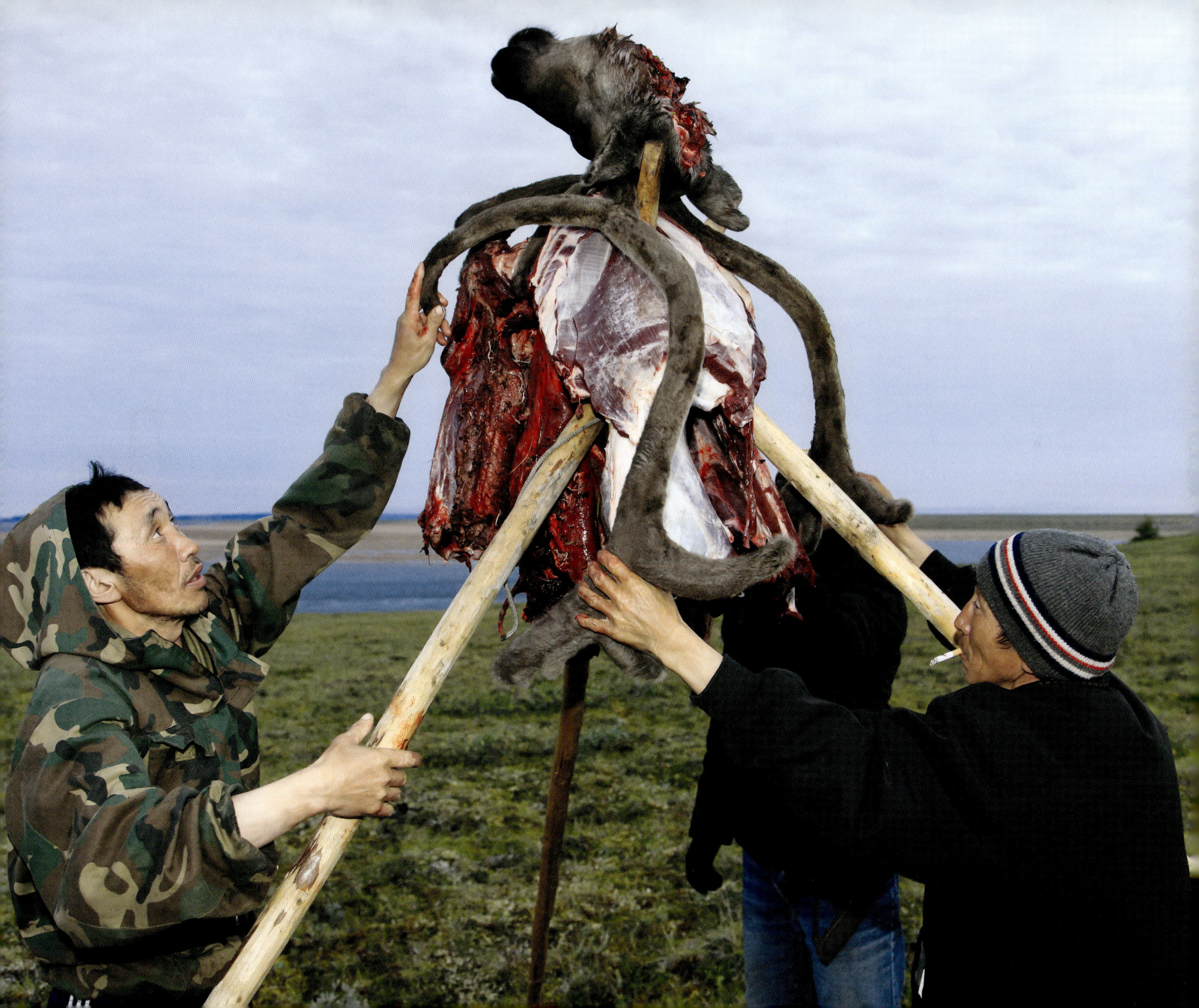

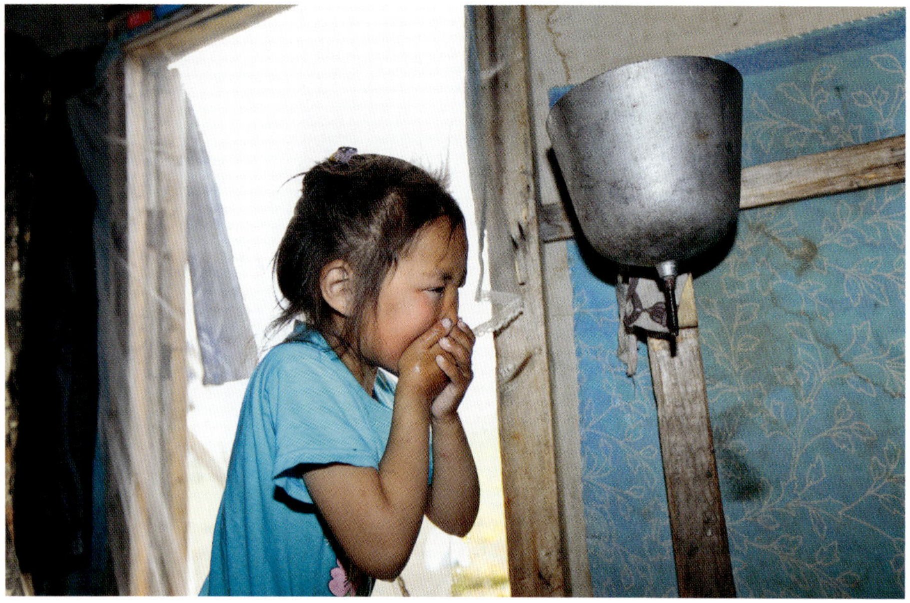

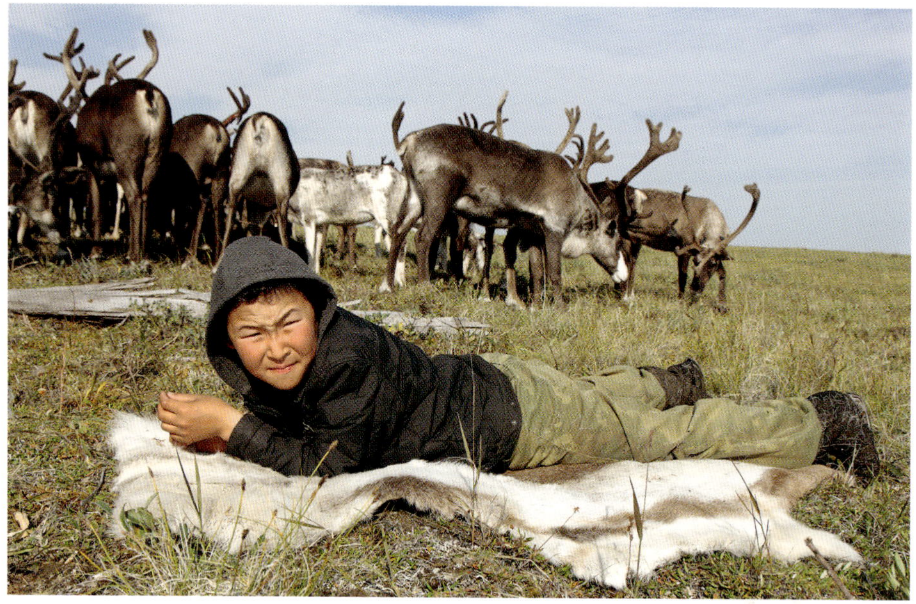

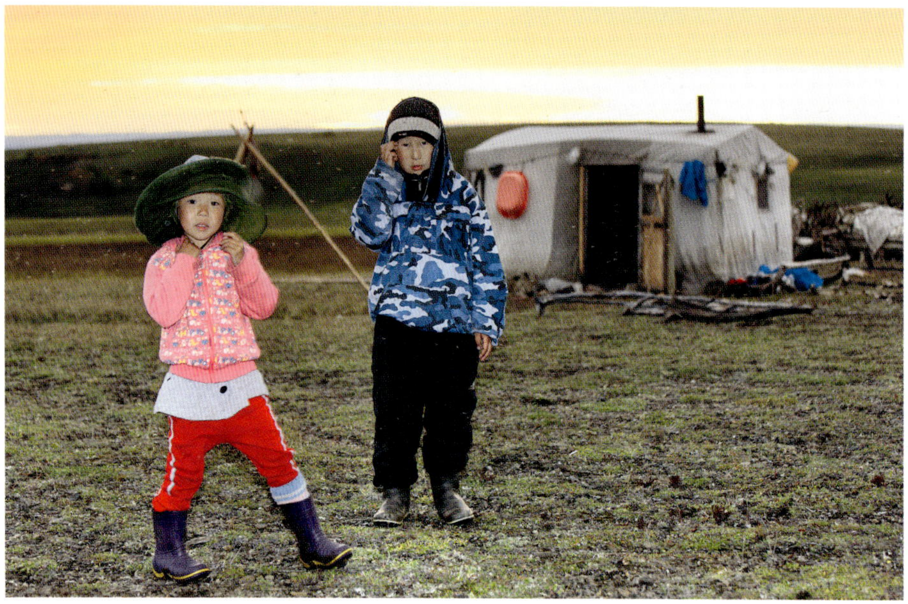

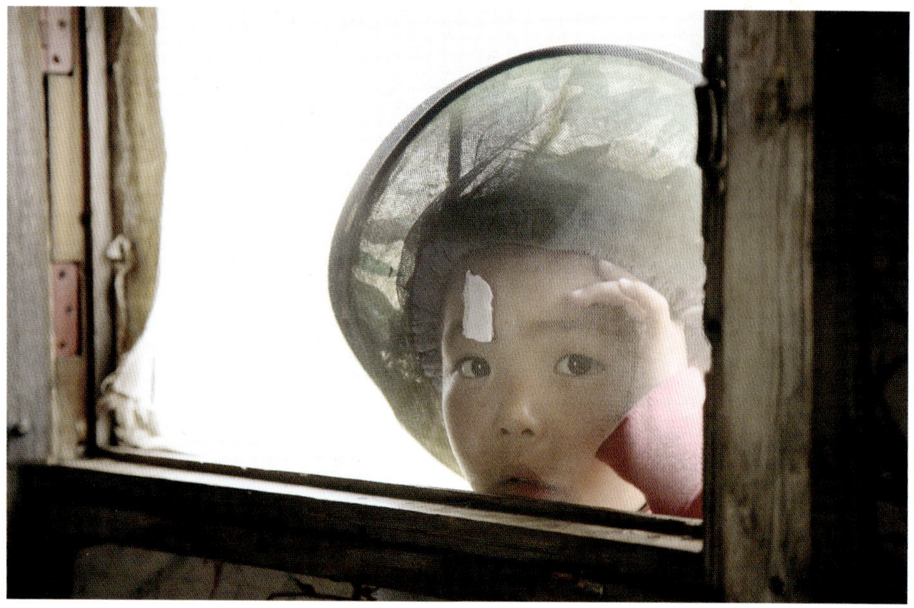

During the summer holidays, the children accompany their families in the tundra and enjoy a relatively carefree life. Clockwise from top left: Jana in the process of washing; Piotr relaxing; Jana looking to see whether the food is ready; Jana with Vadim in front of the hut.

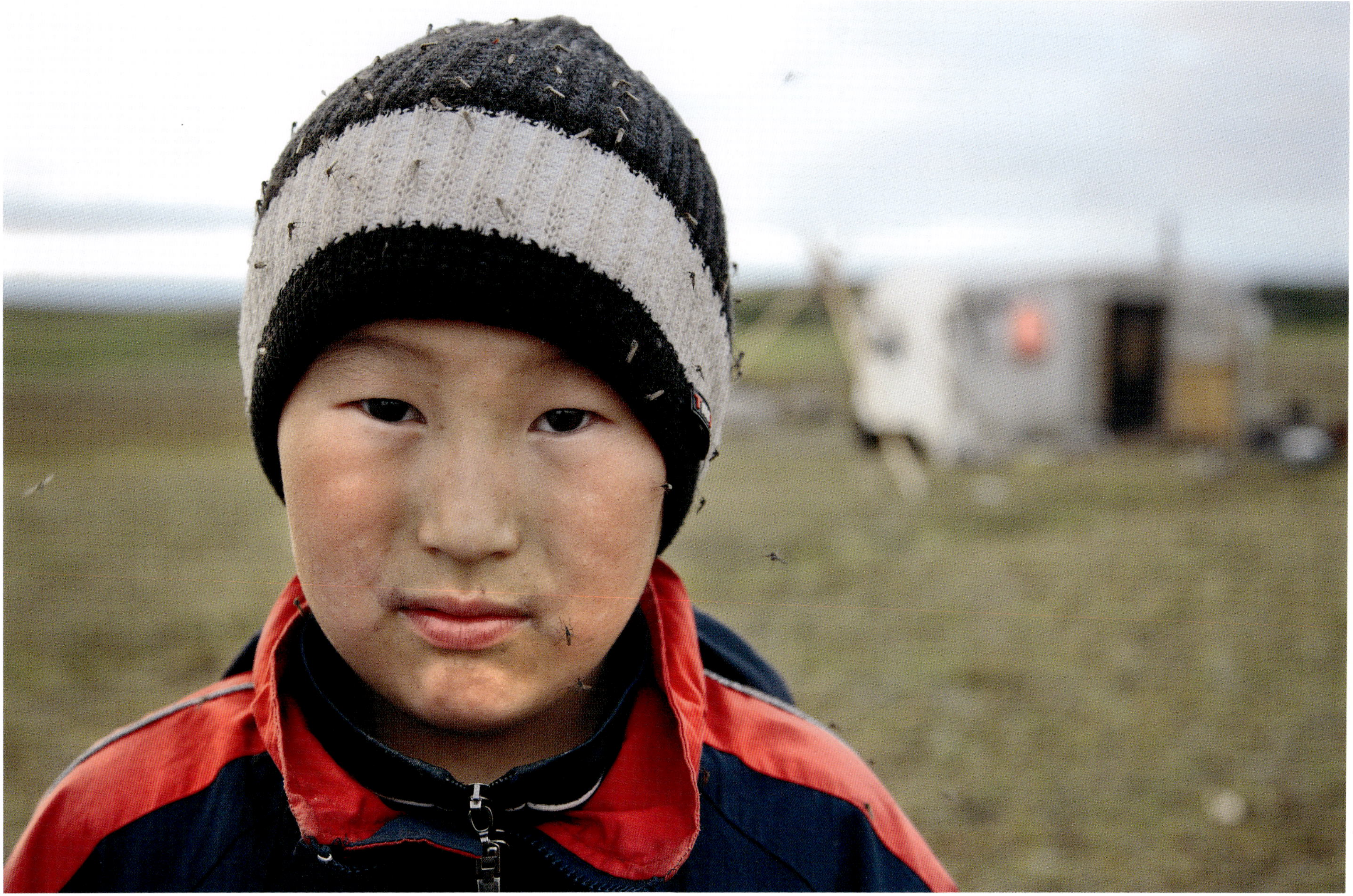

The swarms of mosquitoes seem not to bother Vadim at all.

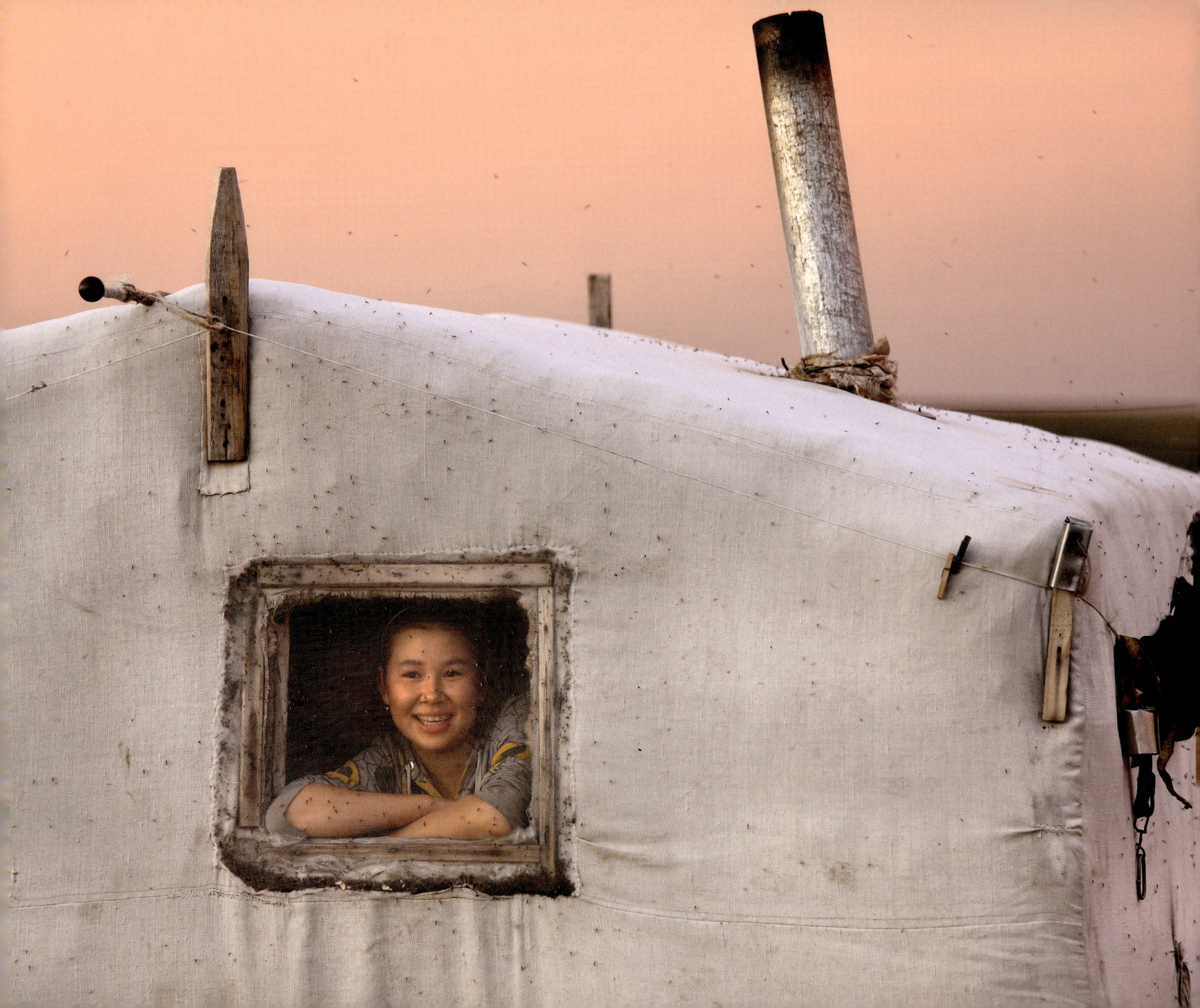

"At present, the Arctic – one of the last unique and intact places on Earth – is facing a real threat of active oil drilling. A large-scale industrial mining 'development' can irreversibly destroy the virgin purity of the Arctic region, putting at stake the physical existence and survival of indigenous peoples, who, without their traditional living patterns, without their eternal habitat, will have no future."

Rodion Sulyandziga from the Udega people and First Vice President of RAIPON (Russian Association of Indigenous Peoples of the North)

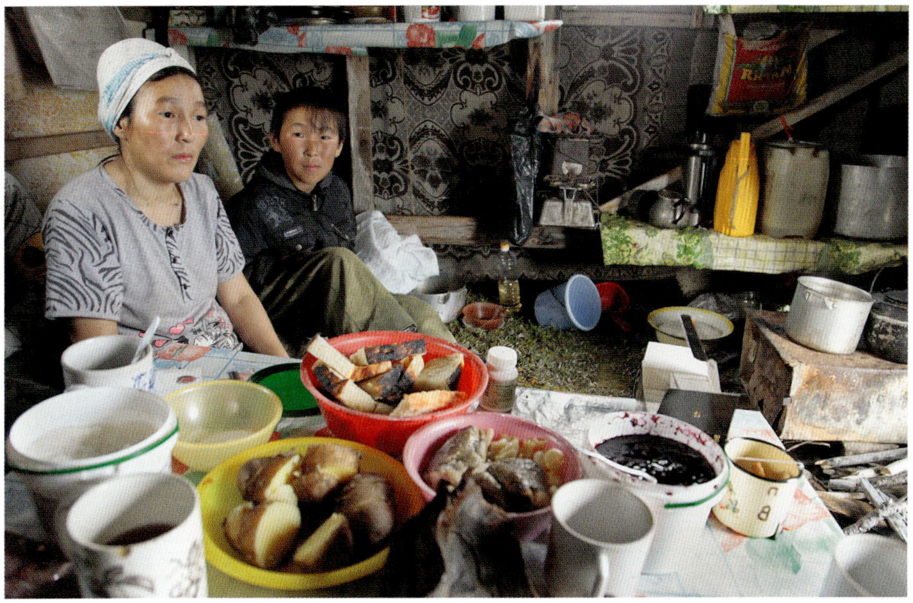

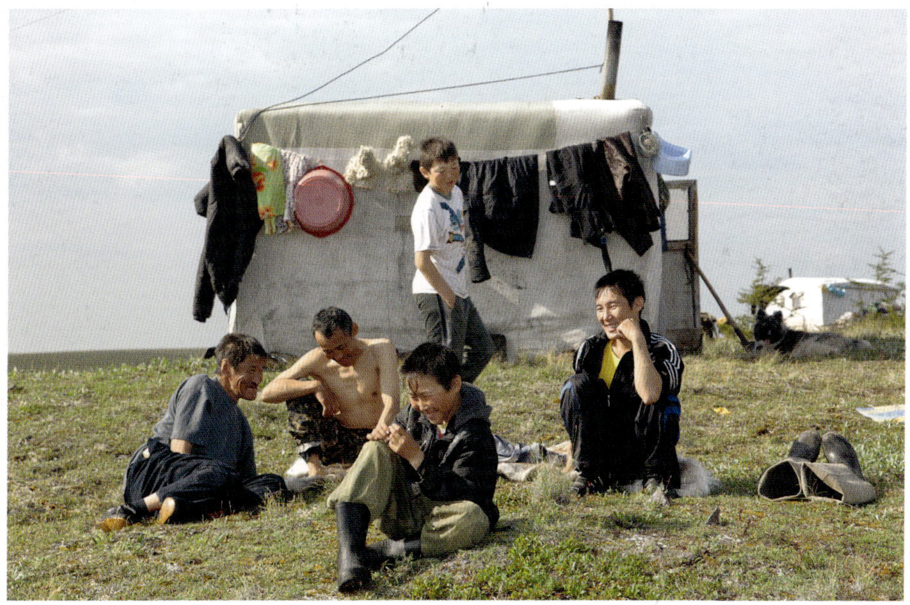

Languorously, Kristina watches the herd circling her hut (left). Svetlana and Piotr at a generously set breakfast table (centre). Vasili, (another) Vasili, Sergey, Piotr and Prokofi relax in the tundra.

CLIMATE CHANGE – THE WHITE PARADISE IS MELTING

The Arctic is to our planet what the canary was once for miners: an indicator of extreme danger. In the past, miners often took canaries underground. They knew straight away that, if the little bird appeared to be unwell, something was wrong and they were all in danger. Similarly, if the Arctic appears to be "unwell" because of the many changes that are taking place at such a rapid pace, that represents danger, too. And in this case, the danger threatens all life on Earth.

The Arctic is not simply a special environment for many animals, plants and people: the Arctic also has an influence on all life on Earth. It is like a global cooling system and a motor for the climate worldwide. It is a determinant of global sea currents and in this way influences the weather, not just of the far northern regions, but of the entire world. An intact environment in the Arctic therefore makes large parts of this planet habitable for humankind and many other forms of life.

We can no longer ignore the signs that great changes are taking place. The Arctic – as we know it – will no longer exist a couple of generations from now. If we do not begin to stop this fatal development immediately, this will entail dramatic consequences, probably for all life on earth. They would probably be the most far reaching in the history of humankind.

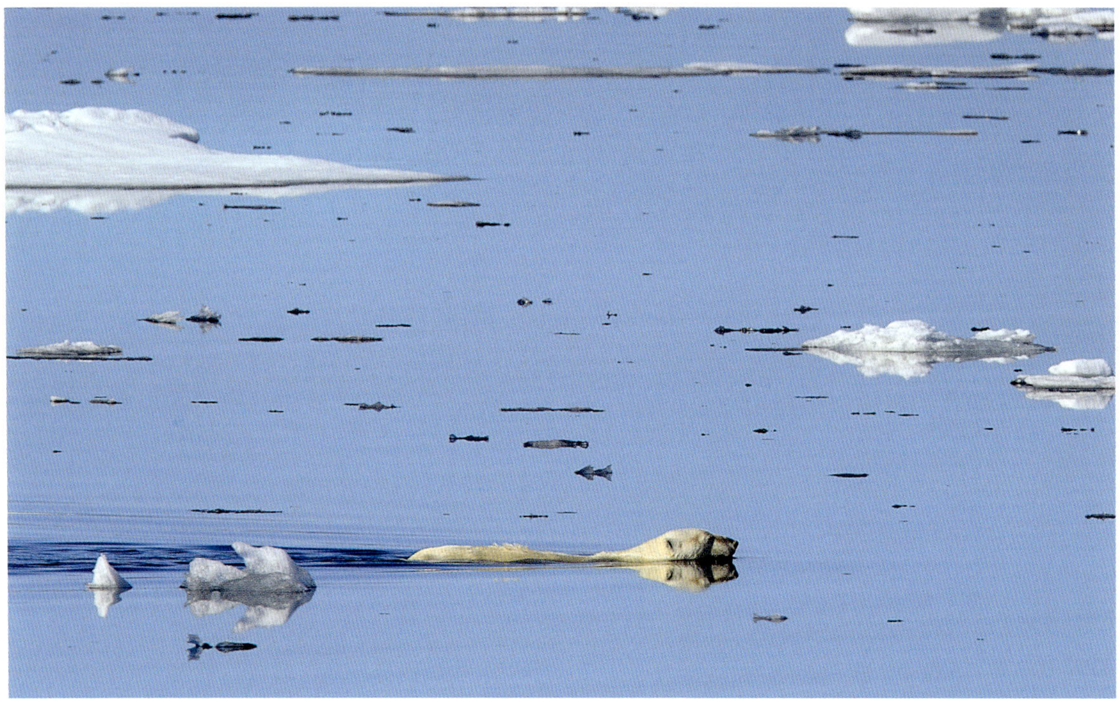

CLIMATE CHANGE – The White Paradise is Melting

The changes that threaten the Arctic and its inhabitants have one thing in common, and that is that they are all caused by humans:

Climate change already affects the Arctic more than any other region on Earth. Simultaneously, no other region on Earth aggravates this threat to itself so severely. The consequences for the Arctic and for the rest of the world are dramatic. At present, the greatest rises in temperature are measured in the Arctic, and this is expected to continue to be the case. If we were to experience global warming of two degrees Celsius worldwide, the temperature in the Arctic would probably rise by up to eight degrees Celsius. The entire Arctic as we know it would not survive this increase in temperature, and this would affect many other parts of the world, too, because a rise in temperature of this magnitude would lead to an unstoppable and self-reinforcing effect.

A series of factors is responsible for this, the most important of which is the aforementioned thawing of permafrost soils. This causes the release of the greenhouse gases carbon dioxide and methane, leading to a rise in global temperature. The Albedo effect, which concerns the reflecting power of the Arctic snow and ice expanses, is another factor. Melting ice expanses reflect less sunlight, which in turn increases the warming process, which further accelerates the melting.

These self-reinforcing effects mean that the ice that has already begun to melt will continue to melt to a much greater degree. The melting of the millennia-old ice crusts (that of Greenland in particular) will result in a worldwide rise in sea levels of between six and seven metres. This does not simply mean that hundreds of islands such as the Seychelles and the Maldives, some of which are inhabited, will be submerged; it will also apply to many coastal regions in Europe, Asia, Africa, North and South America. Even the most elaborate dyke-building measure could not prevent this from happening. Billions of people and animals would have to find new living spaces, and all of this would take place amidst heavy ecological and social conflicts.

The **thawing of permafrost** soil has taken place in more and more regions over the last few years. Almost one quarter of the entire landmass of the northern hemisphere consists of permafrost soil. This is soil that remains

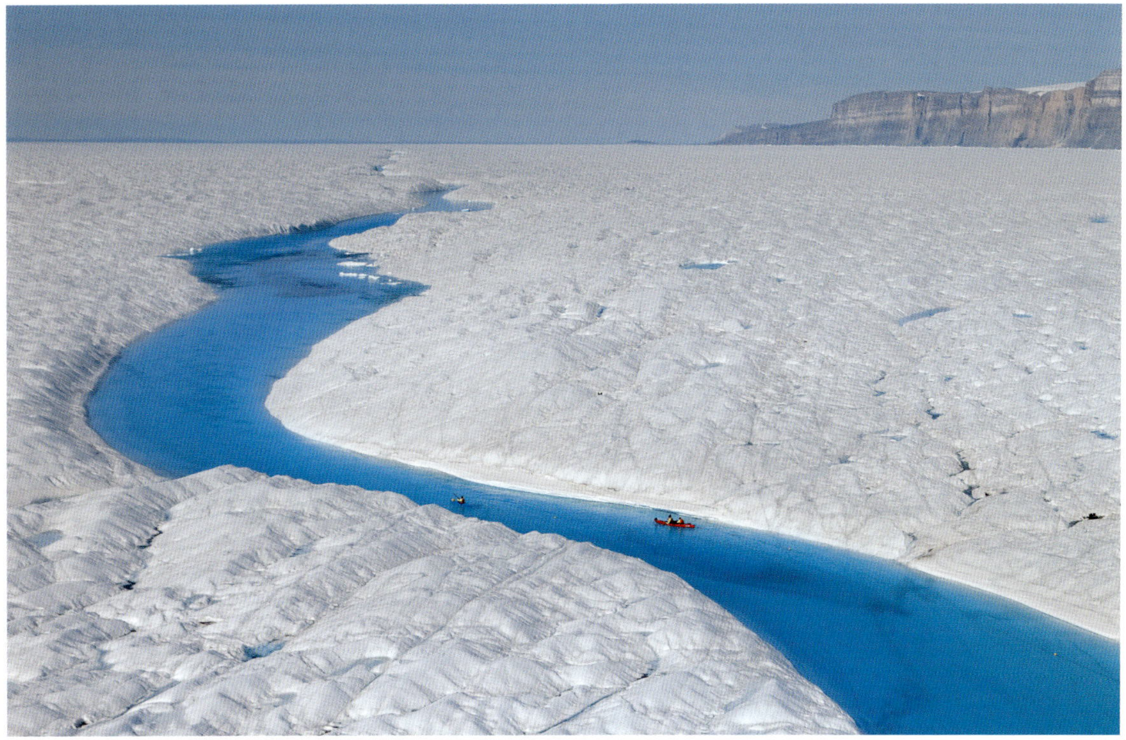

In virtually no other region on Earth is climate change as clearly in evidence and as threatening as it is in the Arctic. During the summer of 2009, a real river of meltwater arose in the Petermann Glacier in Greenland.

Left: The diminishing amount of pack ice is life-threatening even for the long-distance swimmers. The first drowned polar bears have already been found.

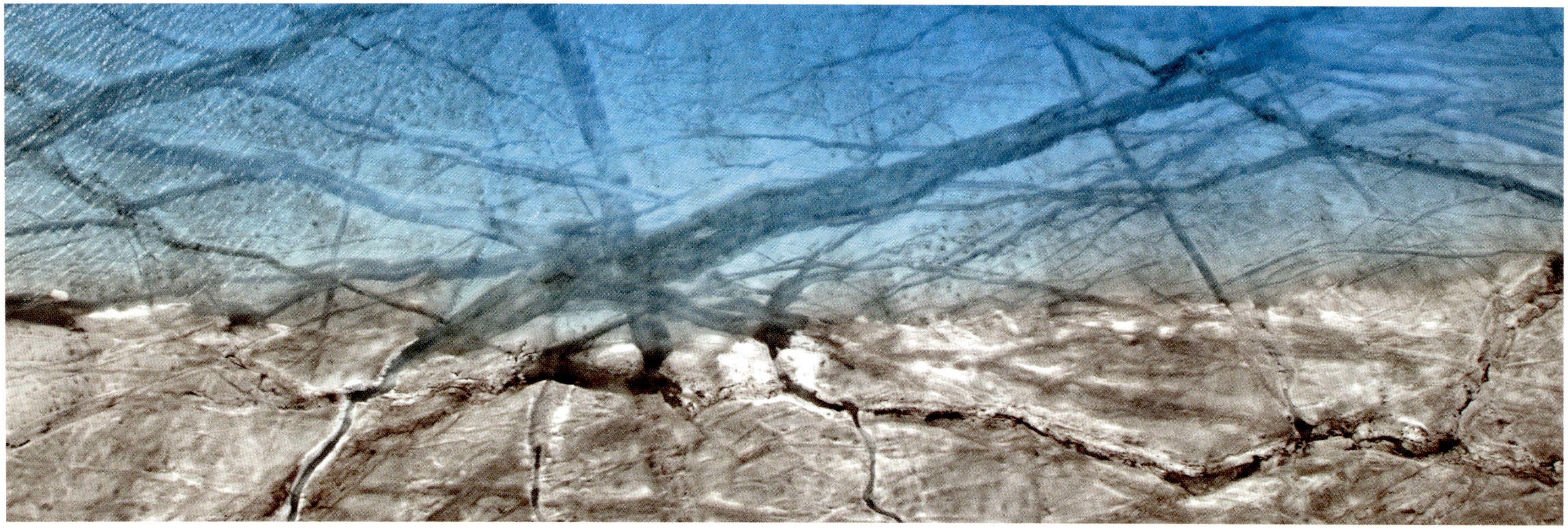

Small ponds of meltwater and lakes lie cheek by jowl in the glaciers of Greenland. The melting of the Greenland ice crust is occurring more rapidly than was hitherto estimated by climate scientists.

frozen throughout the year. This layer of frozen ground can range from a few metres to 1000 metres in depth. As a result of the increasing thaw, what is actually a firm substratum becomes unstable in many places. This leads to the sinking and slipping of roads and houses, railway lines, pipelines and settlements. In a large number of locations, tears in buildings and roads and warped railway tracks can already be observed.

The much more serious problem is the release of carbon that is linked to the thawing. It takes the shape of gases detrimental to the climate, including in particular carbon dioxide and methane. At far more than 1,000 gigatonnes, or 1,000 billion tonnes, the permafrost soils are among the biggest depots of carbon on earth. To give some idea of what this means: this is more than is produced by Germany over the course of more than a thousand years. If these enormous quantities are released as greenhouse gases as a result of the advancing thaw, this would greatly accelerate climate change and therefore also the rise in temperature, probably making these developments irreversible.

Black carbon: the soot deposits known as "black carbon" are the result of the global burning of coal and oil. They are to be found with increasing frequency in the polar regions, particularly in the Arctic. Black snow and black ice are not simply poisonous and carcinogenic; they decrease considerably the sunlight-reflecting qualities of what is usually white snow. In some parts of the Arctic, this is responsible for a rise in temperature of up to one degree.

DESTRUCTION and Plundering in the Far North

The managers of the oil and gas industries have set their sights firmly on the Arctic as one of the last vast untapped reservoirs. Large deposits of natural resources are thought to be located on land and in the seabed. The intensive search for and exploitation of these resources has already begun in all of the Arctic states. Here, too, the initial repercussions are dramatic: the sensitive earth of the tundra is traversed, and thereby destroyed, by heavy machinery. Leaky or broken pipelines allow inconceivable quantities of oil to seep into the Arctic ground and rivers; waste and even highly toxic drilling mud are simply "disposed of" there, which means they are poured into the countryside. Ever and larger industrial complexes with tens of thousands of kilometres of electricity, pipeline and roads have already been created in what used to be the polar wilderness.

That the search for oil constitutes a great threat even if it takes place far from the Arctic is exemplified by the **extraction of bituminous rocks**, or what is known as **tar sand**, in the Canadian province of Alberta. This is probably the greatest destruction of nature to take place worldwide. This particular extraction technique has already resulted in millions upon millions of tons of wastewater contaminated with oil. This is stored in enormous, open lakes, separated from the surrounding environment only by simple earth-fill dams. If a dam were to burst, these enormous amounts of contaminated wastewater would pour into the adjacent Mackenzie River, one of the most important tributaries of the Arctic Ocean. This would cause

The industrialisation of the Arctic is well under way and the oil industry is both the motor and the main threat for it all. Thousands of boreholes, pumping stations, oil tanks and many thousands of kilometres of pipeline have changed the intact nature here. What is more, thousands of tiny oil leaks, not to mention huge oil catastrophes, threaten the treasure chest of the north, as in the region around Archangelsk, in northern Russia.

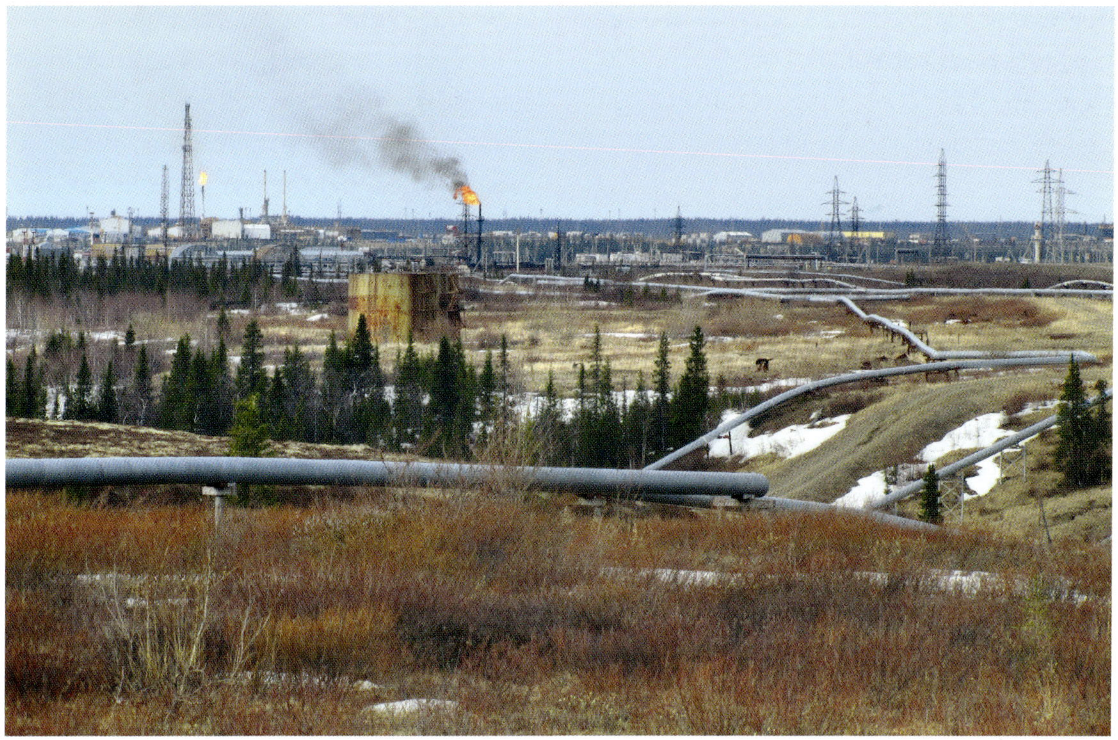

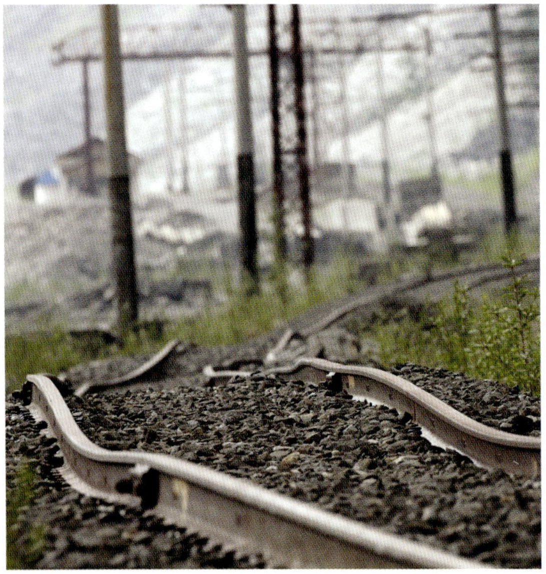

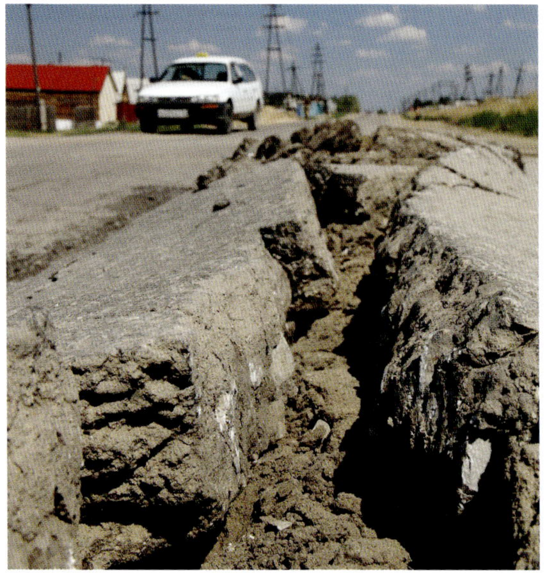

The thawing of the permafrost soil results in railway lines which can no longer be used and chaotic road connections.

irreversible damage to the sensitive Arctic environment and its inhabitants.

In the Arctic Ocean, too, the intensive search for and production of oil is taking place. No lessons have been learnt from serious accidents such as that in the Gulf of Mexico in the summer of 2010, which show that the high-risk technology of deep-sea oil production cannot actually be controlled for the environment and its inhabitants. The carefree drilling for oil continues in the north-polar region, which is considerably more sensitive to oil spills, frequently without contingency plans for possible oil disasters. And how could there be a contingency plan, given that the arrival of winter alone would make the site of the accident inaccessible for months?

Natural resources are thought to exist in large quantities in the Arctic. That applies not just to oil and gas, but also to many metals such as iron ore, nickel, gold and platinum, as well as rare soils and even sapphires and diamonds.

One place that exemplifies the total impact of this "use" is Norilsk in the Russian Arctic. It is the site of the world's largest-scale nickel production. The result is shocking: immense pollution of the air, water and environment, thoroughly contaminated land, the large-scale destruction of the countryside and a plethora of harmful effects on human health. This area is considered to be one of the most heavily contaminated regions on Earth. It would be easy to dismiss this by thinking "how typical of Russia", but the fact is that there is a virtually universal connection between the search for, extraction and processing of these natural resources and damage to, or destruction of the environment. In the Arctic, this is an even greater problem as the regeneration of nature takes place at a much slower pace than it does in the vast majority of regions of the Earth. This means that even over a period of hundreds of years, a destroyed area will not recover.

Overfishing poses the greatest threat to seas worldwide. Many marine areas are considered to have been so heavily overfished that virtually no fish are left.

Two thirds of the world's fish stocks have either already been overfished, or are on the verge of being overfished. And yet there is not a single large-scale marine conservation area in which fishing is not allowed. The Arctic, which has been covered with ice for thousands of years, is the only large – if not actually official – marine conservation area that actually protects the fish stocks and all other sea creatures that live there. Fishing fleets from many countries are already on standby and enter areas from which the sea ice recedes. In particular, demersal trawling, which destroys everything in its path and with which one can access greater and greater depths, threatens to cause a disaster for one of the last untouched marine areas on Earth.

Furthermore, it can be assumed that a large number of previously undiscovered species live underneath the protective covering of ice.

Shipping traffic: The northwest and northeast passage through the waters of the Arctic Ocean represent the possibility to reduce greatly the distance to be travelled between North America, Asia and Europe. To date, these sea routes are frozen and therefore impassable for most of the year, which is why only a small number of ships use these passages. Because the sea ice is constantly receding, these routes will be accessible to thousands of ships in the near future. These new routes are particularly attractive to big container vessels and tankers. The consequences would be

Endless pipelines, daily oil leaks and cost-saving but irresponsible working methods are threatening the Arctic.

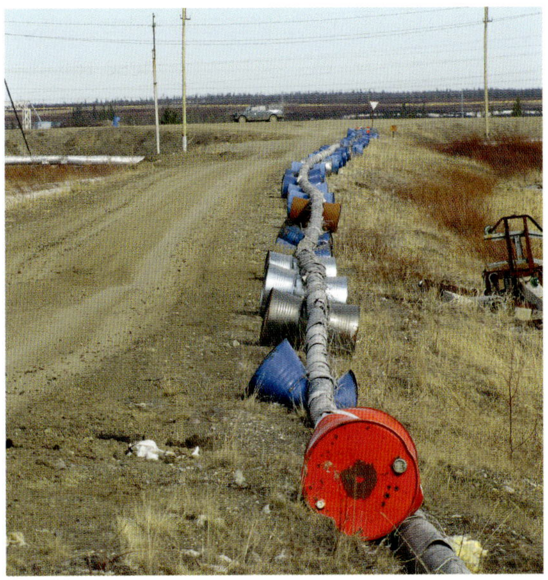

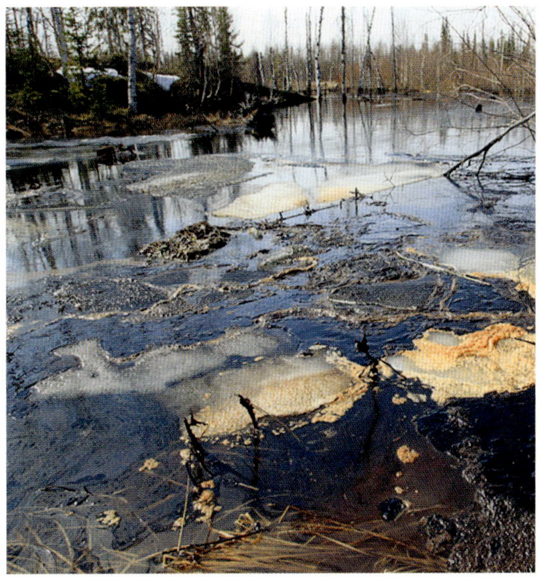

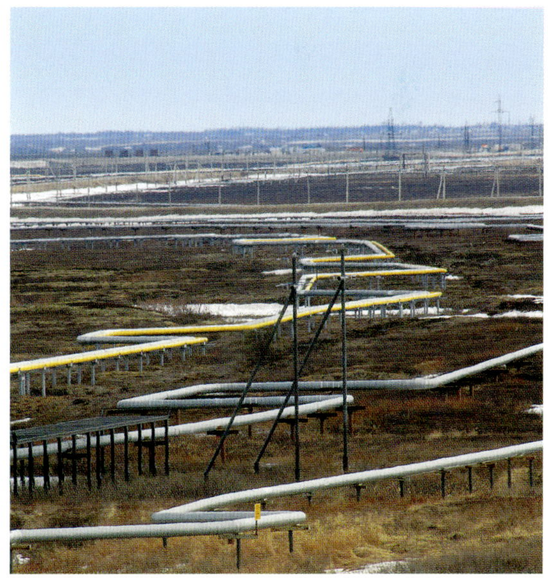

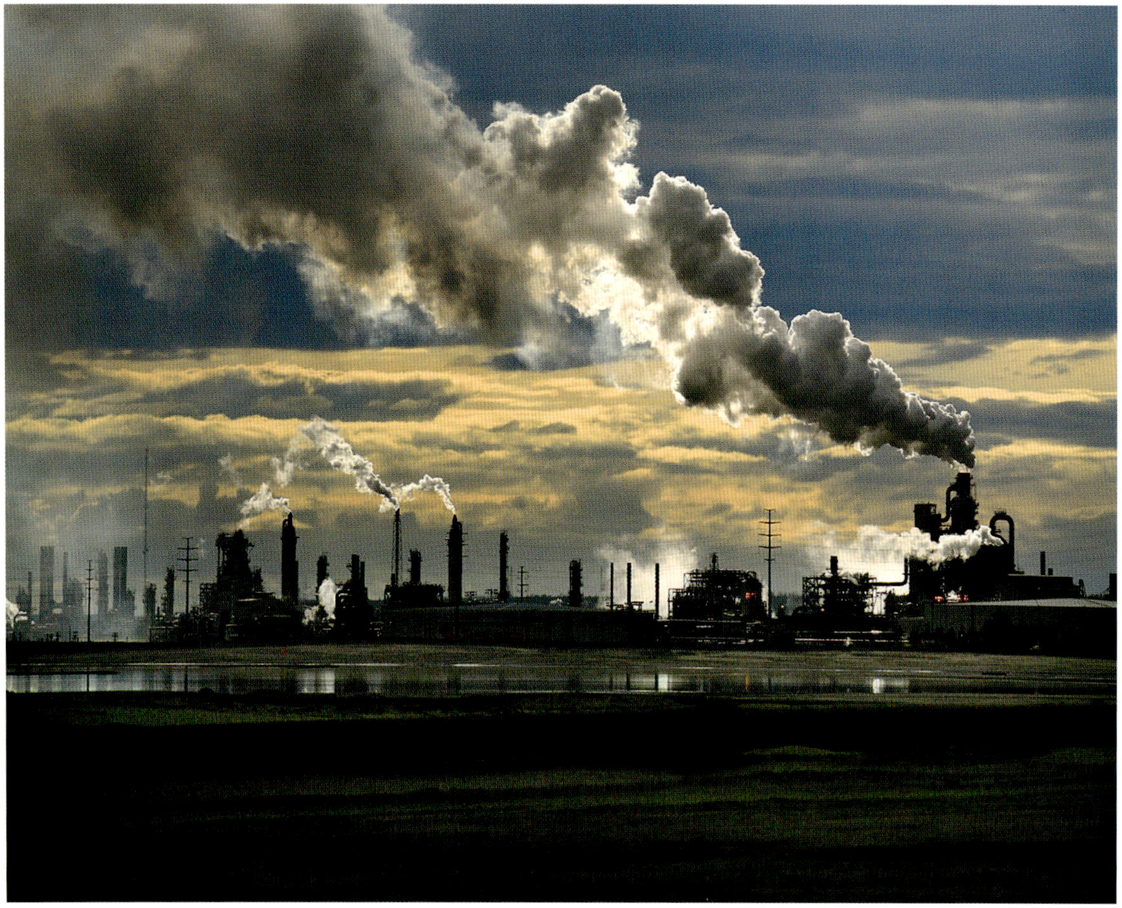

The tar sand industry in the Canadian province of Alberta not only endangers the local natural surroundings.

pollution, increasing noise and the danger of accidents which could involve large quantities of oil spilling into the sea. It is important to understand that an oil spill disaster in the Arctic would be considerably worse than elsewhere as the oil could basically never be cleaned up again. Because of the extremely low temperatures, an unimaginably large number of sea dwellers would fall victim to the oil for decades to come, or longer.

Noise exists in all seas these days, which is why people are already talking about the noise pollution of the seas. The consequences for the sea dwellers can even be more deadly than many types of chemical pollution. Sea mammals in general, and large and small whales in particular, are among those most deeply affected because they are endowed with a very powerful, and sensitive, sense of hearing. This is central to their ability to orient themselves, search for food and communicate with one another. Biologists are considering the possibility that many whale populations live in the polar regions not only because these are rich feeding grounds, but also because it is still relatively "quiet" there.

One of the last remaining refuges for these large sea mammals would be lost as a result of the major increase in shipping traffic in the Arctic that is to be expected, with the noise and the oil and gas production plants that would accompany it. It is not yet clear what exactly the consequences of the increased noise pollution would be, but the risk that it would lead to a decrease in whale populations, or to their displacement, is considerable.

Decreasing whale populations can have far-reaching consequences for the entire biological system as these marine giants play a particularly important role here.

Invasive and introduced species are animal, plant and fungal species, but also microorganisms, that are either intentionally or unintentionally introduced, or migrate into areas in which they are not indigenous.

These so-called neobiota – new life forms – are often not a problem for the area concerned. In some cases, however, there can be serious consequences: they can displace and even eradicate the naturally occurring species. Some of the most devastating examples include the introduction of rats, cats and dogs to New Zealand, and the decision by the Soviet leadership to introduce the red king crab into the waters of the Arctic. The consequences cannot yet be conclusively assessed, but in the near-absence of natural predators, the giant crab populations have increased and spread dramatically. With climate change and the rise in temperature associated with this, but also as a result of the increase in shipping traffic (ships are one of the main factors), one can assume that many new species will spread to the Arctic, thus influencing or even threatening the natural composition of indigenous species.

Mercury is considered to be one of the most dangerous poisons. A large part of the approximately 2,000 tonnes of mercury released into the environment every year, particularly through the burning of oil and coal, ends up in the Arctic as a result of wind and sea currents. The liquid metal is stored particularly in the bodies of sea mammals such as whales, polar bears and seals through various steps in the food chain. At present, a 20-fold increase in mercury levels is already to be found in polar bears. The levels of this powerful poison, which endangers health and reproductive ability, are therefore also increased in the Arctic populations who consume whale and seal meat. And quicksilver is not the only toxin to have an adverse effect on the people and animals of the north: other substances, primarily organic chlorine compounds such as dioxin (one of the most poisonous substances there is) are produced mainly in the industrial nations, but are finally accumulated in high concentrations in the fat tissue of animals and humans living in the Arctic.

The **deforestation of Nordic virgin forests** is in many respects a great danger. In Lapland, Canada, Alaska and Russia, the Nordic (so-called boreal) forests have long since become the focus of the paper and timber industry as raw-material suppliers. An increasingly mild climate will simply facilitate access to the still-intact virgin-forest areas. As these forests are among the last untouched virgin forests on Earth, the felling of this habitat of many rare and endangered

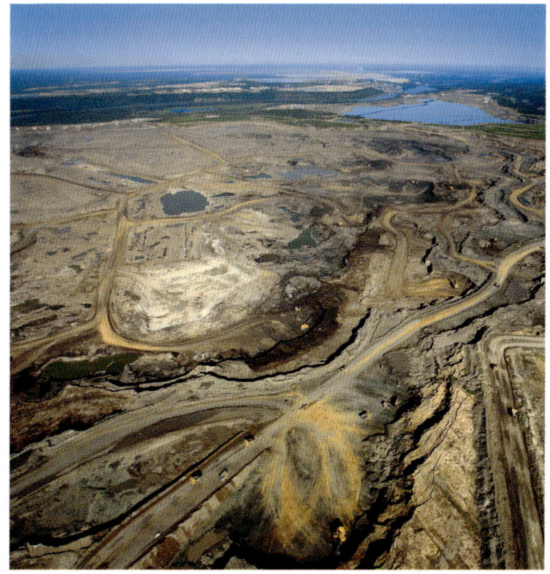

Via the river courses, the oil-polluted waters of the tar sand industry in Canada are a major danger for the distant Arctic.

The fact that the Arctic is melting can no longer be denied. Climate change is becoming a problem not only for living creatures like the walrus; it also threatens entire coastal regions with the rising water level.

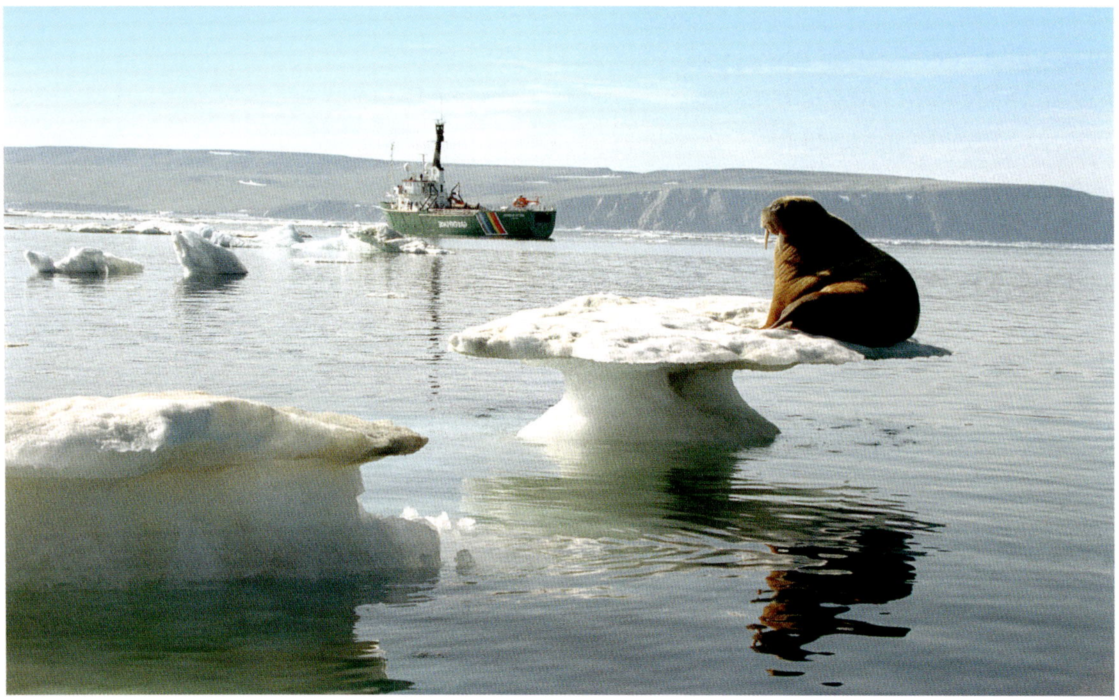

animal and plant species would be particularly tragic. In addition, these intact forests are a large and irreplaceable depot for greenhouse gases. The trees and plants in these forests absorb huge amounts of carbon dioxide, binding the carbon and even releasing oxygen. Their destruction leads to a momentous inversion of this process: destroyed forests release the carbon as carbon dioxide (and therefore as a greenhouse gas) as part of the biological decomposition processes that then take place to an even greater degree. This also occurs indirectly, when products made from trees, such as paper and construction timber, are burned after they have been used. The clearing of virgin forests thus contributes to a considerable degree to the continued rise in atmospheric temperature.

Forest fires are even part of natural regeneration in some Nordic regions. In the increasingly warm polar regions of the Arctic, however, these fires could soon appear everywhere, even in those areas in which they do not normally occur. The consequences for these areas could include the long-term and comprehensive destruction of many animal, plant and fungal species. This in turn would threaten the livelihoods of a number of polar peoples.

Mosquitoes are already omnipresent in many regions of the Arctic, but until now, this has only been the case during the few weeks that constitute the summer. The thawing permafrost soils that constantly provide new water surfaces for the development of the larvae of these blood-sucking insects combine with longer warm periods and winters that are less cold than they used to be. The result could be that some areas become totally uninhabitable for many animals, and even for people, at certain times. The disappearance of endotherms, and the resulting scarcity of "blood donors", would make survival difficult for the mosquitoes, too, but that would hardly bring back the displaced inhabitants of the Arctic.

Stopping the Plundering

The Arctic is therefore currently facing a plethora of threats.

And so the culture of the Polar peoples, their traditions and lifestyles, is also under threat. After all, if their living environment is destroyed, polluted, poisoned or exploited, the lifestyle of the original inhabitants is in danger.

Where those responsible for all big oil corporations (and, to a degree, the fishing industry) are concerned, the greatest possible degree of exploitation and the smallest possible degree of responsibility govern their actions. How else could one explain the fact that they unconcernedly adhere to their plans to exploit the last oil reserves in even the most remote regions of the world and to catch the last intact fish stocks?

And then there are the politicians of today, who could stop these developments with simple countermeasures such as the establishment of much-needed conservation areas and a ban on mining in the sensitive polar regions. They do not represent the real needs of this unique region, but instead support the plundering and exploitation. If this continues for just a few more decades, many of the natural environments, wildernesses, animals, plants and natural wonders shown in this book will not survive this onslaught of threats. The disappearance of the Arctic would lead to the disappearance of many other regions of the world. This development must – and can – be stopped by the voices of people throughout the world.

The Arctic is not simply one of the last treasure troves of the Earth; the Arctic is also the Earth's protective shield.

Thomas Henningsen

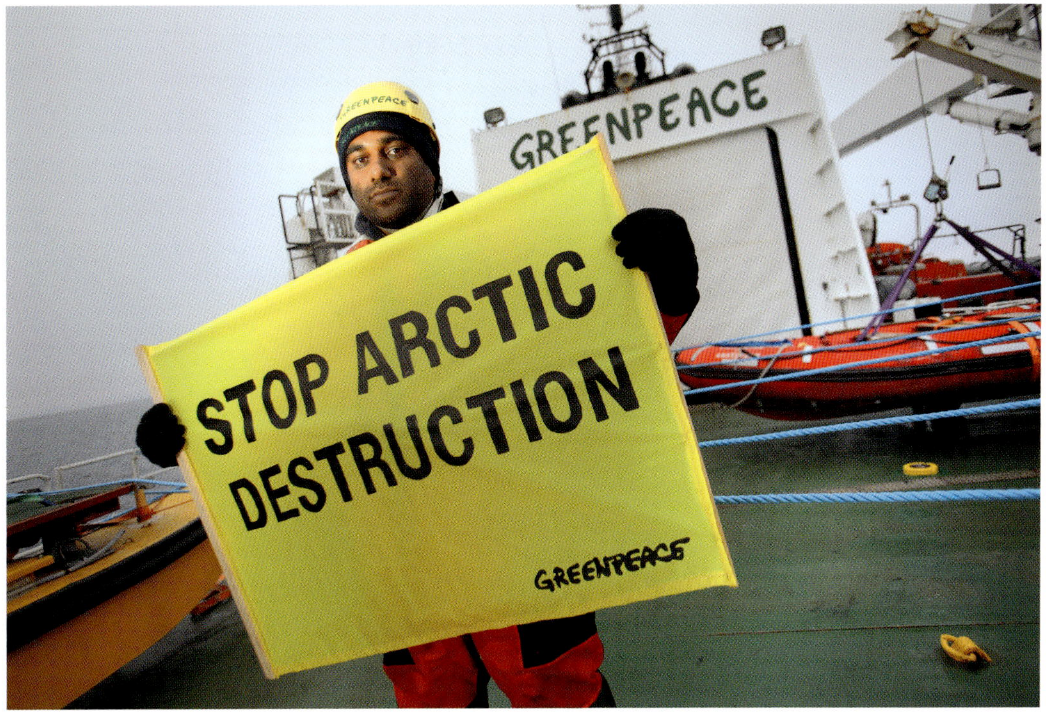

Kumi Naidoo,
Executive Director of Greenpeace International

GREENPEACE IN THE ARCTIC

With the establishment of the Greenpeace office in Alaska in 1977, the environmental organisation made a decision early on to campaign for the preservation of the Arctic. It was important to conserve this area, one of the last intact ecosystems on earth. A series of Greenpeace actions followed. A selection:

Emergency operation following tanker disaster

Black Friday **1989**: The 300-metre-long tanker *Exxon Valdez* ran aground on a reef in Prince William Sound in Alaska, and sprang a leak. Almost 40,000 tonnes of crude oil flowed into the sea. Greenpeace immediately sent a ship to the site of the accident, but little could be done. The thick oil slick killed millions of living creatures and damaged the entire food chain, from plankton to mussels, and from crabs and fish to sea birds, sea otters, sea lions, bears and whales. As herring and salmon populations collapsed, the regional fishing industry, too, was badly damaged.Today, more than 20 years later, the sound has not yet fully recovered. As oil is not easily broken down in low temperatures, thousands of tonnes are thought to remain on the Alaskan coast, covered by sand and gravel.

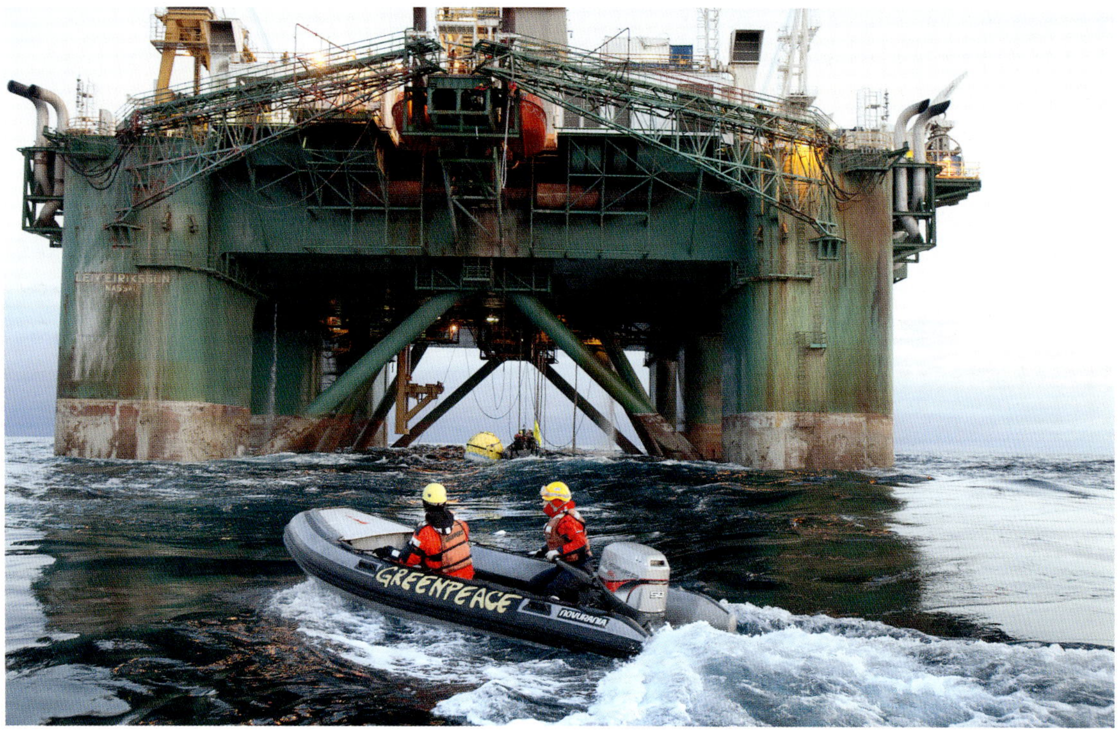

Protests against nuclear tests

In October **1990**, the *MV Greenpeace* sailed to the island of Novaya in the Arctic Ocean, where the Russian military was testing nuclear weapons. Russia justified these crimes against the environment on the grounds of the region's remote location and inhospitably cold temperatures. The Greenpeace crew measured high levels of radiation; back on board their ship they were overpowered by the Russian military. The environment activists were arrested and not released until days later.

In spite of this, another Greenpeace team ventured to the Novaya Zemlya region in **1992**. The aim of this expedition was to document the radioactive waste in the Kara Sea. The reactors of old Russian nuclear submarines, amongst other things, have been submerged in the sea there. Again, the Greenpeace ship was shot at and boarded. And yet these actions have not been without effect: Russia's president Boris Yeltsin later ordered an investigation of the radioactive contamination of the Arctic Ocean, and in 1996 the UN General Assembly adopted the Comprehensive Test Ban Treaty. This treaty has not officially come into effect to this day.

Long struggle against oil drilling

In **1997**, Greenpeace started a campaign against oil production in the Beaufort Sea, where British Petroleum (BP) planned to use the *Northstar* to build the first offshore oil-production platform in the Arctic Ocean. The oil is to be transported to the mainland through a pipeline. Over the course of the following years, Greenpeace repeatedly protested against the construction of this platform. The Greenpeace ship *Arctic Sunrise* sailed to the drilling platform four years in a row, and activists organised protests in front of BP offices and at shareholder meetings. Together with the Inupiat, who live in the North Slope region of Alaska, Greenpeace filed a petition at the US circuit court. In the year 2,000, Greenpeace established an ice camp near the platform to document BP's sins against the environment in freezing conditions of 45 degrees Celsius.

Climate research expedition no. 1

In June **2009**, Greenpeace set off for a four-month Greenland expedition aboard the *Arctic Sunrise*. The aim was to investigate the consequences of climate change in the northern polar region and to make the heads of state who were to meet in Copenhagen for a UN climate summit at the end of the year aware of this global danger, and to make them take action. Renowned climate scientists from the universities of Ohio, Maine and Cambridge, as well as from the Woods Hole Oceanographic Institute, were on board. The researchers measured temperature, salt content and the currents of the polar sea. Their conclusion: the melting of Greenland's ice shelf and the resulting rise in the sea level was progressing at a much faster pace than predicted by previous assessments published by the UN Intergovernmental Panel on Climate Change.

Climate research expedition no. 2

Greenpeace set off for a second Arctic expedition with the *Esperanza* in May **2010**. Researchers from the Leibniz Institute of Marine Sciences (IFM-GEOMAR) in Kiel, Germany were aboard, investigating the consequences of the acidification of the sea. In the Kongsfjord, near Spitsbergen, the acidification of the sea was simulated. Attention was paid to the lime skeletons of many sea creatures such as snails, mussels and crabs, which are important creatures of the marine ecosystems. The acidic water can damage their lime shells and in this way destroy them. The crew also mapped unknown deep-sea regions of the Barents Sea, filmed the underwater life and documented the activities of fish trawlers. As a result of the receding Arctic ice, the big fishing fleets go further and further north into new fishing grounds which are as yet unprotected. The fishermen may be destroying oculinidae and other natural treasures about which very little is known at present.

2010 – "Go beyond oil"

The explosion at BP's drilling platform *Deepwater Horizon* in the Gulf of Mexico in April **2010** caused one of the greatest oil catastrophes of all time. Greenpeace reacted with worldwide actions and protests against deepwater oil production and other dangerous oil-production methods.

In August **2010**, a Greenpeace team travelled to the west coast of Greenland, where the British oil company Cairn Energy was carrying out test drillings. The company threatened lasting damage to the sensitive ecosystem of the polar region. Four Greenpeace activists managed to scale the drilling rig *Stena Don*. They held out day after day, wearing survival suits, on a small platform suspended about 15 metres above the icy sea, during which time the drilling operations were stopped. It is time to stop depending on oil!

2011 – "Go beyond oil"

The British oil company Cairn Energy continued to exploit the Arctic with further exploratory drillings on the west coast of Greenland. Greenpeace reacted immediately because Cairn refused to publish an emergency plan for dealing with oil leaks. Environmental activists were able to delay the drillings by preventing the oil platform *Leiv Eiriksson* from setting out from the Bosphorus, and by boarding the rig off the coast of Greenland. Simultaneously, another team investigated the effect of oil production in the Russian Arctic, as well as that of the resulting leaks, on the environment and on the people who live there. The results were terrifying.

Greenpeace demands a moratorium on the industrial exploitation of the Arctic. The moratorium must remain in effect until a legally binding agreement by all states and all companies operating in the Arctic has been passed, guaranteeing the protection of an ecosystem of great global importance, and of its inhabitants.

Find information about Greenpeace and about the Greenpeace Arctic campaign at: www.greenpeace.org

IMPRINT

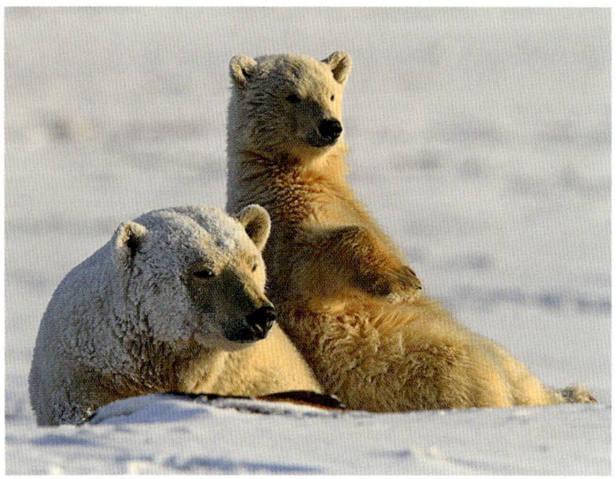

WHITE STAR PUBLISHERS

ISBN 978-88-544-0636-0
1 2 3 4 5 6 15 14 13 12 11

FSC www.fsc.org MIX Paper from responsible sources FSC® C015829

Printed in Europe
Translation: Jane Michael
Design and layout: Janette Schroeder, www.wortundart.de
Cover Design: Michela Barbonaglia

Photo credits:
All photographs by © Bernd Römmelt, except p. 9 left: Jeremy Sutton-Hibbert; p. 9 right: Markus Mauthe; pp. 197, 198: Nick Cobbing; pp. 199, 201: Dr Thomas Henningsen; p. 200 left: Kajsa Sjolander; p. 200 right: Will Rose; pp. 202, 203, 205: Jiri Rezac; p. 204: Daniel Beltra; p. 206: Steve Morgan; all photos © Greenpeace

Texts: All texts were written by Dr Thomas Henningsen except for: Foreword: Kumi Naidoo, Dr Thomas Henningsen; Captions: Bernd Römmelt, Dr Thomas Henningsen; Greenpeace in the Arctic: Nicoline Haas, Melanie Dutchin, Dr Thomas Henningsen

SPECIAL THANKS TO

Ben Ayliffe, Conny Böttger, Yossi Cadan, Nora Christensen, Melanie Duchin, Greenpeace Russia (Andrey, Sergey, Ivan, Valodia, Evgeny), Truls Gulowsen, Berni and Uta Hicker, Hans Jensen, Andrey Petrov, Dave Reid, Jochen Reinhold, Norbert Rosing, David Russell, Ari Sääski, Robert Thompson, Vicky Wyatt.